CW00960542

Renault 19 Owners Workshop Manual

A K Legg LAE MIMI

Models covered
Renault 19 models, including Chamade and special/limited editions
1390 cc, 1397 cc and 1721 cc petrol engines

Does not cover Diesel engine, 1764 cc 16-valve engine, fuel injection/catalyst models or Cabriolet

(1646 - 10T1)

ABCDE
FGHIJ
KLMNO
PQR

THE BOOK

Haynes Publishing Group
Sparkford Nr Yeovil
Somerset BA22 7JJ England

Haynes Publications, Inc
861 Lawrence Drive
Newbury Park
California 91320 USA

Acknowledgements

Thanks are due to Champion Spark Plug who supplied the illustrations showing spark plug conditions, to Holt Lloyd Limited who supplied the illustrations showing bodywork repair, and to Duckhams Oils who provided lubrication data. Certain other illustrations are the copyright of Renault (UK) Limited and are used with their permission. Thanks are also due to Sykes-Pickavant Limited, who provided some of the workshop tools, and to all those people at Sparkford who helped in the production of this manual.

© **Haynes Publishing Group 1992**

A book in the **Haynes Owners Workshop Manual Series**

Printed by J. H. Haynes & Co. Ltd., Sparkford, Nr Yeovil, Somerset BA22 7JJ, England

All rights reserved. No part of this book may be reproduced or transmitted in any form or by any means, electronic or mechanical, including photocopying, recording or by any information storage or retrieval system, without permission in writing from the copyright holder.

ISBN 1 85010 646 0

British Library Cataloguing in Publication Data
A catalogue record for this book is available from the British Library

We take great pride in the accuracy of information given in this manual, but vehicle manufacturers make alterations and design changes during the production run of a particular vehicle of which they do not inform us. No liability can be accepted by the authors or publishers for loss, damage or injury caused by any errors in, or omissions from, the information given.

Restoring and Preserving our Motoring Heritage

Few people can have had the luck to realise their dreams to quite the same extent and in such a remarkable fashion as John Haynes, Founder and Chairman of the Haynes Publishing Group.

Since 1965 his unique approach to workshop manual publishing has proved so successful that millions of Haynes Manuals are now sold every year throughout the world, covering literally thousands of different makes and models of cars, vans and motorcycles.

A continuing passion for cars and motoring led to the founding in 1985 of a Charitable Trust dedicated to the restoration and preservation of our motoring heritage. To inaugurate the new Museum, John Haynes donated virtually his entire private collection of 52 cars.

Now with an unrivalled international collection of over 210 veteran, vintage and classic cars and motorcycles, the Haynes Motor Museum in Somerset is well on the way to becoming one of the most interesting Motor Museums in the world.

A 70 seat video cinema, a cafe and an extensive motoring bookshop, together with a specially constructed one kilometre motor circuit, make a visit to the Haynes Motor Museum a truly unforgettable experience.

Every vehicle in the museum is preserved in as near as possible mint condition and each car is run every six months on the motor circuit.

Enjoy the picnic area set amongst the rolling Somerset hills. Peer through the William Morris workshop windows at cars being restored, and browse through the extensive displays of fascinating motoring memorabilia.

From the 1903 Oldsmobile through such classics as an MG Midget to the mighty 'E' Type Jaguar, Lamborghini, Ferrari Berlinetta Boxer, and Graham Hill's Lola Cosworth, there is something for everyone, young and old alike, at this Somerset Museum.

Haynes Motor Museum

Situated mid-way between London and Penzance, the Haynes Motor Museum is located just off the A303 at Sparkford, Somerset (home of the Haynes Manual) and is open to the public 7 days a week all year round, except Christmas Day and Boxing Day.

Contents

Renault 19 TXE Hatchback

Renault 19 GTS Chamade

Renault 19 TSE Hatchback

Renault 19 TXE Chamade

About this manual

Its aim

The aim of this manual is to help you get the best value from your vehicle. It can do so in several ways. It can help you decide what work must be done (even should you choose to get it done by a garage), provide information on routine maintenance and servicing, and give a logical course of action and diagnosis when random faults occur. However, it is hoped that you will use the manual by tackling the work yourself. On simpler jobs it may even be quicker than booking the car into a garage and going there twice, to leave and collect it. Perhaps most important, a lot of money can be saved by avoiding the costs a garage must charge to cover its labour and overheads.

The manual has drawings and descriptions to show the function of the various components so that their layout can be understood. Then the tasks are described and photographed in a clear step-by-step sequence.

Its arrangement

The manual is divided into Chapters, each covering a logical sub-division of the vehicle. The Chapters are each divided into Sections, numbered with single figures, eg 5; and the Sections into paragraphs (or sub-sections), with decimal numbers following on from the Section they are in, eg 5.1, 5.2, 5.3 etc.

It is freely illustrated, especially in those parts where there is a detailed sequence of operations to be carried out. There are two forms of illustration: figures and photographs. The figures are numbered in sequence with decimal numbers, according to their position in the Chapter - eg Fig. 6.4 is the fourth drawing/illustration in Chapter 6. Photographs carry the same number (either individually or in related groups) as the Section or sub-section to which they relate.

There is an alphabetical index at the back of the manual as well as a contents list at the front. Each Chapter is also preceded by its own individual contents list.

References to the 'left' or 'right' of the vehicle are in the sense of a person in the driver's seat, facing forward.

Unless otherwise stated, nuts and bolts are removed by turning anti-clockwise, and tightened by turning clockwise.

Vehicle manufacturers continually make changes to specifications and recommendations, and these, when notified, are incorporated into our manuals at the earliest opportunity.

Whilst every care is taken to ensure that the information in this manual is correct, no liability can be accepted by the authors or publishers for loss, damage or injury caused by any errors in, or omissions from, the information given.

Project vehicles

The main project vehicle used in the preparation of this manual, and appearing in many of the photographic sequences was a Renault 19 TSE Hatchback. Additional work was carried out and photographed on a Renault 19 Chamade TXE Saloon.

Introduction to the Renault 19

The Renault 19 was first introduced in France, in September 1988, in a Hatchback form, with a sloping front end and no grille or gutter rails. Its transverse engine and transmission unit is accommodated within a subframe, and the front wheels are driven by two driveshafts. The Renault 19 Hatchback became available in the UK in February 1989, and was followed by the Chamade saloon version in November 1989.

Three engine types are available - the overhead valve 1397 cc engine, and the overhead camshaft 1390 cc and 1721 cc engines. The 1390 cc engine is completely new and is called the 'Energy' engine. It has been designed for economy and will return 42.8 mpg at a steady speed of 75 mph. All three engines are fitted with carburettors.

The front suspension is of MacPherson type and the rear suspension is of either tubular or four-bar type. Automatic transmission, power-assisted steering and anti-lock braking are available according to model.

The car is quite conventional in design and the DIY home mechanic should find most work straightforward.

General dimensions and weights

Dimensions
Overall length	4155 mm
Overall width:	
TR and TS	1676 mm
All except TR and TS	1694 mm
Overall height:	
Unladen	1416 mm
Laden	1342 mm
Wheelbase	2545 mm
Front track	1418 mm
Rear track:	
GTX and TXE	1406 mm
All except GTX and TXE	1417 mm

Weights
Kerb weight:	
TR 3-door	900 kg
TR 5-door	920 kg
TS, GTS and TSE 3-door	920 kg
TS, GTS and TSE 5-door	940 kg
GTX and TXE 3-door	945 kg
GTX and TXE 5-door	965 kg
Maximum gross vehicle weight:	
TR 3-door	1350 kg
TR 5-door	1370 kg
TS, GTS and TSE 3-door	1380 kg
TS, GTS and TSE 5-door	1400 kg
GTX and TXE 3-door	1425 kg
GTX and TXE 5-door	1445 kg
Maximum roof rack load	70 kg
Maximum towing weight:	
Braked trailer:	
TR and GTR	850 kg
TS, GTS and TSE (4-speed gearbox)	800 kg
TS, GTS and TSE (5-speed gearbox)	900 kg
GTX and TXE	1000 kg
Unbraked trailer:	
TR 3-door	450 kg
TR 5-door	460 kg
TS, GTS and TSE 3-door	460 kg
TS, GTS and TSE 5-door	470 kg
GTX and TXE 3-door	470 kg
GTX and TXE 5-door	480 kg

Jacking, towing and wheel changing

To change a wheel, remove the spare wheel and jack, apply the handbrake and chock the wheel diagonally opposite the one to be changed (photos). On automatic transmission models, place the selector lever in P. Make sure that the car is located on firm level ground and then slightly loosen the wheel bolts with the brace provided (where applicable remove the trim first). Locate the jack head in the jacking point nearest to the wheel to be changed (photo) and raise the jack using the other end of the brace. When the wheel is clear of the ground remove the bolts (and trim where applicable) and lift off the wheel. Fit the spare wheel (and trim where applicable) and moderately tighten the bolts. Lower the car and then tighten the bolts securely, to the specified torque setting (see Chapter 10 specifications). Refit the trim where applicable. With the spare wheel in position, remove the chock and stow the jack and tools.

When jacking up the car to carry out repair or maintenance tasks position the jack as follows.

If the front of the car is to be raised, position the jack head under a stout wooden beam placed transversely across the underside of the car and in contact with the front subframe side rails; the beam should not touch the exhaust front pipe or the gearbox. Lower the beam onto axle stands or position axle stands beneath the front jacking points.

To raise the rear of the car, jack up each side in turn with the jack head positioned under the rear jacking points, just forward of the rear wheels. *Do not under any circumstances jack up the rear of the car under the rear axle.*

To raise the side of the car place a block of wood under the side sill and locate it centrally under the front door. Place the jack head in contact with the block and raise the car. Shape the wooden blocks as necessary to avoid damaging the sill edges and lower the car onto axle stands positioned under the jacking points. Never work under, around or near a raised car unless it is adequately supported in at least two places with axle stands or suitable sturdy blocks.

The car may be towed for breakdown recovery purposes only using the towing eyes positioned at the front and rear of the vehicle (photos). These eyes are intended for towing loads only and must not be used for lifting the car either directly or indirectly. If the car is equipped with

Using the wheelbrace to lower the spare wheel

Jack location in the luggage compartment

Jack correctly located in the jacking point

Front towing eye

Rear towing eye

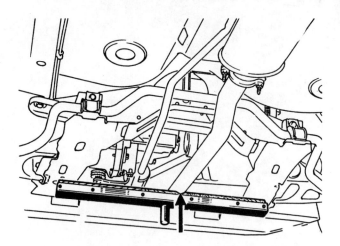

Beam for raising the front of the car – cut where shown if necessary to clear the exhaust system

Jacking up the side of the car

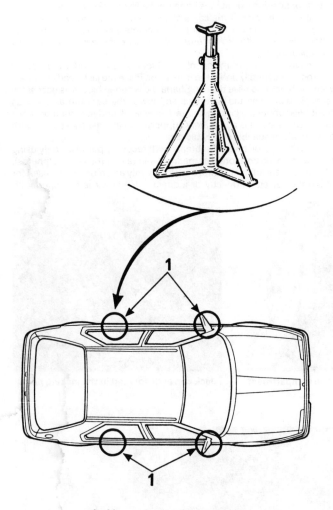

Jacking and axle stand points (1)

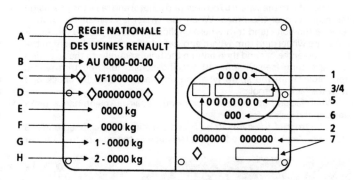

Vehicle identification plate codes

A	Manufacturer's name	1	Vehicle type
B	EEC official approval number	2	Special features of vehicle
C	Worldwide identification code and official type number	3	Equipment number and options
D	Chassis number	4	Equipment number and options
E	Gross vehicle weight	5	Factory of manufacture and fabrication number
F	Gross train weight	6	Paint identification code
G	Maximum permissible front axle weight	7	Additional marking
H	Maximum permissible rear axle weight		

automatic transmission the following precautions must be observed if the vehicle is to be towed. Preferably a front end suspended tow should be used. If this is not possible, add an extra 2 litres of the specified automatic transmission fluid to the transmission. The car may now be towed for a maximum of 30 miles (48 km) at a speed not exceeding 18 mph (30 kph). The selector lever must be in the N position during the tow. Drain off the surplus transmission fluid on completion of the tow.

Buying spare parts and vehicle identification numbers

Buying spare parts

Spare parts are available from many sources; for example, Renault garages, other garages and accessory shops, and motor factors. Our advice regarding spare part sources is as follows.

Officially appointed Renault garages – This is the best source for parts which are peculiar to your car, and are not generally available (eg complete cylinder heads, internal gearbox components, badges, interior trim etc). It is also the only place at which you should buy parts if the vehicle is still under warranty. To be sure of obtaining the correct parts, it will be necessary to give the storeman your car's vehicle identification number, and if possible, take the old parts along for positive identification. Many parts are available under a factory exchange scheme – any parts returned should always be clean. It obviously makes good sense to go straight to the specialists on your car for this type of part, as they are best equipped to supply you.

Other garages and accessory shops – These are often very good places to buy materials and components needed for the maintenance of your car (eg oil filters, spark plugs, bulbs, drivebelts, oils and greases, touch-up paint, filler paste, etc). They also sell general accessories, usually have convenient opening hours, charge lower prices and can often be found not far from home.

Motor factors – Good factors will stock all the more important components which wear out comparatively quickly (eg exhaust systems, brake pads, seals and hydraulic parts, clutch components, bearing shells, pistons, valves etc). Motor factors will often provide new or reconditioned components on a part exchange basis – this can save a considerable amount of money.

Vehicle identification numbers

Modifications are a continuing and unpublicised process in vehicle manufacture, quite apart from major model changes. Spare parts manuals and lists are compiled upon a numerical basis, the individual vehicle identification numbers being essential to correct identification of the component concerned.

When ordering spare parts, always give as much information as possible. Quote the car model, year of manufacture, body and engine numbers as appropriate.

The *vehicle identification plate* is located on one or two plates attached to the front right-hand side suspension strut turret (photo).

The *chassis number* is located in the same position and is also etched into the top of the turret (photo).

The *body number and paint code numbers* are located within the oval area of the vehicle identification plate.

The *engine number* is stamped on the front facing side of the cylinder block. On the 1397 cc (C1J) engine it is located below the distributor, on the 1390 cc (E6J) engine it is on the left-hand side of the exhaust manifold, and on the 1721 cc (F2N) engine it is on the left-hand side, below the crankcase ventilation oil separator.

Vehicle identification plate

Chassis number etched into the front right-hand side suspension strut turret

Safety first!

However enthusiastic you may be about getting on with the job in hand, do take the time to ensure that your safety is not put at risk. A moment's lack of attention can result in an accident, as can failure to observe certain elementary precautions. There will always be new ways of having accidents, and the following points do not pretend to be a comprehensive list of all dangers; they are intended rather to make you aware of the risks and to encourage a safety-conscious approach to all work you carry out on your vehicle.

Essential DOs and DON'Ts

DON'T rely on a single jack when working underneath the vehicle. Always use reliable additional means of support, such as axle stands, securely placed under a structural part of the vehicle that you know will not give way.

DON'T attempt to loosen or tighten high-torque nuts (eg wheel hub nuts) while the vehicle is on a jack; it may be pulled off.

DON'T start the engine without first ascertaining that the transmission is in neutral (or 'Park' where applicable) and the handbrake applied.

DON'T suddenly remove the filler cap from a hot cooling system – cover it with a cloth and release the pressure gradually first, or you may get scalded by escaping coolant.

DON'T attempt to drain oil, automatic transmission fluid, or coolant until you are sure it has cooled sufficiently to avoid scalding you.

DON'T grasp any part of the engine, exhaust or catalytic converter without first ascertaining that it is sufficiently cool to avoid burning you.

DON'T allow brake fluid or antifreeze to contact vehicle paintwork.

DON'T syphon toxic liquids such as fuel, brake fluid or antifreeze by mouth, or allow them to remain on your skin.

DON'T inhale dust – it may be injurious to health (see *Asbestos* below).

DON'T allow any spilt oil or grease to remain on the floor – wipe it up straight away, before someone slips on it.

DON'T use ill-fitting spanners or other tools which may slip and cause injury.

DON'T attempt to lift a heavy component which may be beyond your capability – get assistance.

DON'T rush to finish a job, or take unverified short cuts.

DON'T allow children or animals in or around an unattended vehicle.

DON'T park vehicles with catalytic converters over combustible materials such as dry grass, oily rags, etc if the engine has recently been run. As catalytic converters reach extremely high temperatures, any such materials in close proximity may ignite.

DON'T run vehicles equipped with catalytic converters without the exhaust system heat shields fitted.

DO wear eye protection when using power tools such as an electric drill, sander, bench grinder etc, and when working under the vehicle.

DO use a barrier cream on your hands prior to undertaking dirty jobs – it will protect your skin from infection as well as making the dirt easier to remove afterwards; but make sure your hands aren't left slippery. Note that long term contact with used engine oil can be a health hazard.

DO keep loose clothing (cuffs, tie etc) and long hair well out of the way of moving mechanical parts.

DO remove rings, wristwatch etc, before working on the vehicle – especially the electrical system.

DO ensure that any lifting tackle or jacking equipment used has a safe working load rating adequate for the job, and is used precisely as recommended by the manufacturer.

DO keep your work area tidy – it is only too easy to fall over articles left lying around.

DO get someone to check periodically that all is well when working alone on the vehicle.

DO carry out work in a logical sequence and check that everything is correctly assembled and tightened afterwards.

DO remember that your vehicle's safety affects that of yourself and others. If in doubt on any point, get specialist advice.

IF, in spite of following these precautions, you are unfortunate enough to injure yourself, seek medical attention as soon as possible.

Asbestos

Certain friction, insulating, sealing, and other products – such as brake linings, brake bands, clutch linings, gaskets, etc – contain asbestos. *Extreme care must be taken to avoid inhalation of dust from such products since it is hazardous to health.* If in doubt, assume that they *do* contain asbestos.

Fire

Remember at all times that petrol is highly flammable. Never smoke, or have any kind of naked flame around, when working on the vehicle. But the risk does not end there – a spark caused by an electrical short-circuit, by two metal surfaces contacting each other, by careless use of tools, or even by static electricity built up in your body under certain conditions, can ignite petrol vapour, which in a confined space is highly explosive.

Whenever possible disconnect the battery earth terminal before working on any part of the fuel or electrical system, and never risk spilling fuel on to a hot engine or exhaust. Catalytic converters run at extremely high temperatures, and consequently can be an additional fire hazard. Observe the precautions outlined elsewhere in this section.

It is recommended that a fire extinguisher of a type suitable for fuel and electrical fires is kept handy in the garage or workplace at all times. Never try to extinguish a fuel or electrical fire with water.

Note: *Any reference to a 'torch' appearing in this manual should always be taken to mean a hand-held battery-operated electric lamp or flashlight. It does NOT mean a welding/gas torch or blowlamp.*

Fumes

Certain fumes are highly toxic and can quickly cause unconsciousness and even death if inhaled to any extent, especially if inhalation takes place through a lighted cigarette or pipe. Petrol vapour comes into this category, as do the vapours from certain solvents such as trichloroethylene. Any draining or pouring of such volatile fluids should be done in a well ventilated area.

When using cleaning fluids and solvents, read the instructions carefully. Never use materials from unmarked containers – they may give off poisonous vapours.

Never run the engine of a motor vehicle in an enclosed space such as a garage. Exhaust fumes contain carbon monoxide which is extremely poisonous; if you need to run the engine, always do so in the open air or at least have the rear of the vehicle outside the workplace. Although vehicles fitted with catalytic converters have greatly reduced toxic exhaust emissions, the above precautions should still be observed.

If you are fortunate enough to have the use of an inspection pit, never drain or pour petrol, and never run the engine, while the vehicle is standing over it; the fumes, being heavier than air, will concentrate in the pit with possibly lethal results.

The battery

Batteries which are sealed for life require special precautions which are normally outlined on a label attached to the battery. Such precautions are primarily related to situations involving battery charging and jump starting from another vehicle.

With a conventional battery, never cause a spark, or allow a naked light, in close proximity to it. It will normally be giving off a certain amount of hydrogen gas, which is highly explosive.

Whenever possible disconnect the battery earth terminal before working on the fuel or electrical systems.

If possible, loosen the filler plugs or cover when charging the battery from an external source. Do not charge at an excessive rate or the battery may burst. Special care should be taken with the use of high charge-rate boost chargers to prevent the battery from overheating.

Take care when topping up and when carrying the battery. The acid electrolyte, even when diluted, is very corrosive and should not be allowed to contact clothing, eyes or skin.

Always wear eye protection when cleaning the battery to prevent the caustic deposits from entering your eyes.

Mains electricity and electrical equipment

When using an electric power tool, inspection light, diagnostic equipment etc, which works from the mains, always ensure that the appliance is correctly connected to its plug and that, where necessary, it is properly earthed. Do not use such appliances in damp conditions and, again, beware of creating a spark or applying excessive heat in the vicinity of fuel or fuel vapour. Also ensure that the appliances meet the relevant national safety standards.

Ignition HT voltage

A severe electric shock can result from touching certain parts of the ignition system, such as the HT leads, when the engine is running or being cranked, particularly if components are damp or the insulation is defective. Where an electronic ignition system is fitted, the HT voltage is much higher and could prove fatal, especially to wearers of cardiac pacemakers.

Jacking and vehicle support

The jack provided with the vehicle is designed primarily for emergency wheel changing, and its use for servicing and overhaul work on the vehicle is best avoided. Instead, a more substantial workshop jack (trolley jack or similar) should be used. Whichever type is employed, it is essential that additional safety support is provided by means of axle stands designed for this purpose. Never use makeshift means such as wooden blocks or piles of house bricks, as these can easily topple or, in the case of bricks, disintegrate under the weight of the vehicle. Further information on the correct positioning of the jack and axle stands is provided in the *Jacking, towing and wheel changing* section.

If removal of the wheels is not required, the use of drive-on ramps is recommended. Caution should be exercised to ensure that they are correctly aligned with the wheels, and that the vehicle is not driven too far along them so that it promptly falls off the other ends or tips the ramps.

General repair procedures

Whenever servicing, repair or overhaul work is carried out on the car or its components, it is necessary to observe the following procedures and instructions. This will assist in carrying out the operation efficiently and to a professional standard of workmanship.

Joint mating faces and gaskets

When separating components at their mating faces, never insert screwdrivers or similar implements into the joint between the faces in order to prise them apart. This can cause severe damage which results in oil leaks, coolant leaks, etc upon reassembly. Separation is best achieved by tapping along the joint with a soft-faced hammer in order to break the seal. However, note that this method may not be suitable where dowels are used for component location.

Where a gasket is used between the mating faces of two components, ensure that it is renewed on reassembly and fit it dry unless otherwise stated in the repair procedure. Make sure that the mating faces are clean and dry with all traces of old gasket removed. When cleaning a joint face, use a tool which is not likely to score or damage the face, and remove any burrs or nicks with an oilstone or fine file.

Make sure that tapped holes are cleaned with a pipe cleaner and keep them free of jointing compound, if this is being used, unless specifically instructed otherwise.

Ensure that all orifices, channels or pipes are clear and blow through them, preferably using compressed air.

Oil seals

Oil seals can be removed by levering them out with a wide flat-bladed screwdriver or similar implement. Alternatively, a number of self-tapping screws may be screwed into the seal and these used as a purchase for pliers or some similar device in order to pull the seal free.

Whenever an oil seal is removed from its working location, either individually or as part of an assembly, it should be renewed.

The very fine sealing lip of the seal is easily damaged and will not seal if the surface it contacts is not completely clean and free from scratches, nicks or grooves. If the original sealing surface of the component cannot be restored, and the manufacturer has not made provision for slight relocation of the seal relative to the sealing surface, the component should be renewed.

Protect the lips of the seal from any surface which may damage them in the course of fitting. Use tape or a conical sleeve where possible. Lubricate the seal lips with oil before fitting and, on dual-lipped seals, fill the space between the lips with grease.

Unless otherwise stated, oil seals must be fitted with their sealing lips toward the lubricant to be sealed.

Use a tubular drift or block of wood of the appropriate size to install the seal and, if the seal housing is shouldered, drive the seal down to the shoulder. If the seal housing is unshouldered, the seal should be fitted with its face flush with the housing top face (unless otherwise instructed).

Screw threads and fastenings

Seized nuts, bolts and screws are quite a common occurrence where corrosion has set in, and the use of penetrating oil or releasing fluid will often overcome this problem if the offending item is soaked for a while before attempting to release it. The use of an impact driver may also provide a means of releasing such stubborn fastening devices when used in conjunction with the appropriate screwdriver bit or socket. If none of these methods works, it may be necessary to resort to the careful application of heat, or the use of a hacksaw or nut splitter device.

Studs are usually removed by locking two nuts together on the threaded part and then using a spanner on the lower nut to unscrew the stud. Studs or bolts which have broken off below the surface of the component in which they are mounted can sometimes be removed using a proprietary stud extractor. Always ensure that a blind tapped hole is completely free from oil, grease, water or other fluid before installing the bolt or stud. Failure to do this could cause the housing to crack due to the hydraulic action of the bolt or stud as it is screwed in.

When tightening a castellated nut to accept a split pin, tighten the nut to the specified torque, where applicable, and then tighten further to the next split pin hole. Never slacken the nut to align the split pin hole unless stated in the repair procedure.

When checking or retightening a nut or bolt to a specified torque setting, slacken the nut or bolt by a quarter of a turn, and then retighten to the specified setting. However, this should not be attempted where angular tightening has been used.

For some screw fastenings, notably cylinder head bolts or nuts, torque wrench settings are no longer specified for the latter stages of tightening, 'angle-tightening' being specified instead. Typically, a fairly low torque wrench setting will be applied to the bolts/nuts in the correct sequence, followed by one or more stages of tightening through specified angles.

Locknuts, locktabs and washers

Any fastening which will rotate against a component or housing in the course of tightening should always have a washer between it and the relevant component or housing.

Spring or split washers should always be renewed when they are used to lock a critical component such as a big-end bearing retaining bolt or nut. Locktabs which are folded over to retain a nut or bolt should always be renewed.

Self-locking nuts can be reused in non-critical areas, providing resistance can be felt when the locking portion passes over the bolt or stud thread. However, it should be noted that self-locking stiffnuts tend to lose their effectiveness after long periods of use, and in such cases should be renewed as a matter of course.

Split pins must always be replaced with new ones of the correct size for the hole.

When thread-locking compound is found on the threads of a fastener which is to be re-used, it should be cleaned off with a wire brush and solvent, and fresh compound applied on reassembly.

Special tools

Some repair procedures in this manual entail the use of special tools such as a press, two or three-legged pullers, spring compressors etc. Wherever possible, suitable readily available alternatives to the manufacturer's special tools are described, and are shown in use. In some instances, where no alternative is possible, it has been necessary to resort to the use of a manufacturer's tool and this has been done for reasons of safety as well as the efficient completion of the repair operation. Unless you are highly skilled and have a thorough understanding of the procedures described, never attempt to bypass the use of any special tool when the procedure described specifies its use. Not only is there a very great risk of personal injury, but expensive damage could be caused to the components involved.

Environmental considerations

When disposing of used engine oil, brake fluid, antifreeze etc, give due consideration to any detrimental environmental effects. Do not, for instance, pour any of the above liquids down drains into the general sewage system or onto the ground to soak away. Many local council refuse tips provide a facility for waste oil disposal as do some garages. If none of these facilities are available, consult your local Environmental Health Department for further advice.

With the universal tightening-up of legislation regarding the emission of environmentally harmful substances from motor vehicles, most current vehicles have tamperproof devices fitted to the main adjustment points of the fuel system. These devices are primarily designed to prevent unqualified persons from adjusting the fuel/air mixture with the chance of a consequent increase in toxic emissions. If such devices are encountered during servicing or overhaul, they should, wherever possible, be renewed or refitted in accordance with the vehicle manufacturer's requirements or current legislation.

Tools and working facilities

Introduction

A selection of good tools is a fundamental requirement for anyone contemplating the maintenance and repair of a motor vehicle. For the owner who does not possess any, their purchase will prove a considerable expense, offsetting some of the savings made by doing-it-yourself. However, provided that the tools purchased meet the relevant national safety standards and are of good quality, they will last for many years and prove an extremely worthwhile investment.

To help the average owner to decide which tools are needed to carry out the various tasks detailed in this manual, we have compiled three lists of tools under the following headings: *Maintenance and minor repair*, *Repair and overhaul*, and *Special*. Newcomers to practical mechanics should start off with the *Maintenance and minor repair* tool kit and confine themselves to the simpler jobs around the vehicle. Then, as confidence and experience grow, more difficult tasks can be undertaken, with extra tools being purchased as, and when, they are needed. In this way, a *Maintenance and minor repair* tool kit can be built up into a *Repair and overhaul* tool kit over a considerable period of time without any major cash outlays. The experienced do-it-yourselfer will have a tool kit good enough for most repair and overhaul procedures and will add tools from the *Special* category when it is felt that the expense is justified by the amount of use to which these tools will be put.

Maintenance and minor repair tool kit

The tools given in this list should be considered as a minimum requirement if routine maintenance, servicing and minor repair operations are to be undertaken. We recommend the purchase of combination spanners (ring one end, open-ended the other); although more expensive than open-ended ones, they do give the advantages of both types of spanner.

Combination spanners:
   Metric – 8, 9, 10, 11, 12, 13, 14, 15, 17 & 19 mm
Adjustable spanner – 35 mm jaw (approx)
Engine sump/gearbox/rear axle drain plug key (where applicable)
Spark plug spanner (with rubber insert)
Spark plug gap adjustment tool
Set of feeler blades
Brake adjuster spanner (where applicable)

Brake bleed nipple spanner
Screwdrivers:
   Flat blade – approx 100 mm long x 6 mm dia
   Cross blade – approx 100 mm long x 6 mm dia
Combination pliers
Hacksaw (junior)
Tyre pump
Tyre pressure gauge
Grease gun (where applicable)
Oil can
Oil filter removal tool
Fine emery cloth
Wire brush (small)
Funnel (medium size)

Repair and overhaul tool kit

These tools are virtually essential for anyone undertaking any major repairs to a motor vehicle, and are additional to those given in the *Maintenance and minor repair* list. Included in this list is a comprehensive set of sockets. Although these are expensive, they will be found invaluable as they are so versatile – particularly if various drives are included in the set. We recommend the $\frac{1}{2}$ in square-drive type, as this can be used with most proprietary torque wrenches. If you cannot afford a socket set, even bought piecemeal, then inexpensive tubular box spanners are a useful alternative.

The tools in this list will occasionally need to be supplemented by tools from the *Special* list.

Sockets (or box spanners) to cover range in previous list
Reversible ratchet drive (for use with sockets) (photo)
Extension piece, 250 mm (for use with sockets)
Universal joint (for use with sockets)
Torque wrench (for use with sockets)
Self-locking grips
Ball pein hammer
Soft-faced mallet (plastic/aluminium or rubber)
Screwdrivers:
   Flat blade – long & sturdy, short (chubby), and narrow (electricians) types
   Cross blade – Long & sturdy, and short (chubby) types

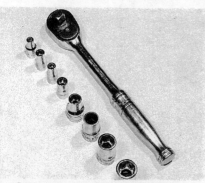
Sockets and reversible ratchet drive

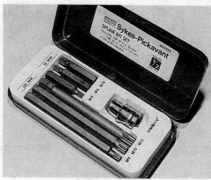
Spline bit set

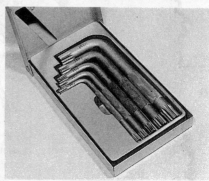
Spline key set

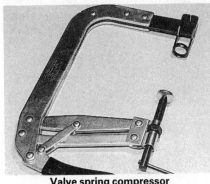

Valve spring compressor

Piston ring compressor

Piston ring removal/installation tool

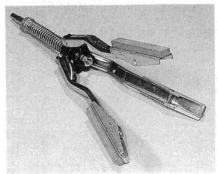

Cylinder bore hone

Three-legged hub and bearing puller

Micrometer set

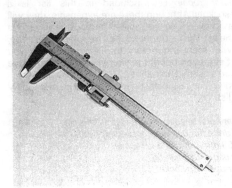

Vernier calipers

Dial test indicator and magnetic stand

Stroboscopic timing light

Compression testing gauge

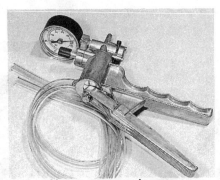

Vacuum pump and gauge

Pliers:
  Long-nosed
  Side cutters (electricians)
  Circlip (internal and external)
Cold chisel – 25 mm
Scriber
Scraper
Centre punch
Pin punch
Hacksaw
Brake hose clamp
Brake bleeding kit
Selection of twist drills
Steel rule/straight-edge
Allen keys (inc. splined/Torx type) (photos)
Selection of files
Wire brush
Axle-stands
Jack (strong trolley or hydraulic type)
Light with extension lead

Special tools

The tools in this list are those which are not used regularly, are expensive to buy, or which need to be used in accordance with their manufacturers' instructions. Unless relatively difficult mechanical jobs are undertaken frequently, it will not be economic to buy many of these tools. Where this is the case, you could consider clubbing together with friends (or joining a motorists' club) to make a joint purchase, or borrowing the tools against a deposit from a local garage or tool hire specialist. It is worth noting that many of the larger DIY superstores now carry a large range of special tools for hire at modest rates.

The following list contains only those tools and instruments freely available to the public, and not those special tools produced by the vehicle manufacturer specifically for its dealer network. You will find occasional references to these manufacturers' special tools in the text of this manual. Generally, an alternative method of doing the job without the vehicle manufacturer's special tool is given. However, sometimes there is no alternative to using them. Where this is the case and the relevant tool cannot be bought or borrowed, you will have to entrust the work to a franchised garage.

Valve spring compressor (photo)
Valve grinding tool
Piston ring compressor (photo)
Piston ring removal/installation tool (photo)
Cylinder bore hone (photo)
Balljoint separator
Coil spring compressors (where applicable)
Two/three-legged hub and bearing puller (photo)
Impact screwdriver
Micrometer and/or vernier calipers (photos)
Dial test indicator (photo)
Stroboscopic timing light (photo)
Dwell angle meter/tachometer
Universal electrical multi-meter
Cylinder compression gauge (photo)
Hand-operated vacuum pump and gauge (photo)
Clutch plate alignment set (photo)
Brake shoe steady spring cup removal tool (photo)
Bush and bearing removal/installation set (photo)
Stud extractors (photo)
Tap and die set (photo)
Lifting tackle
Trolley jack

Buying tools

For practically all tools, a tool factor is the best source since he will have a very comprehensive range compared with the average garage or

Clutch plate alignment set

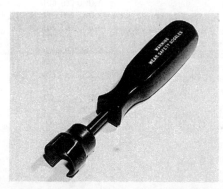

Brake shoe steady spring cup removal tool

Bush and bearing removal/installation set

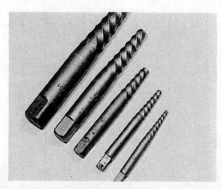

Stud extractor set

Tap and die set

accessory shop. Having said that, accessory shops often offer excellent quality tools at discount prices, so it pays to shop around.

Remember, you don't have to buy the most expensive items on the shelf but it is always advisable to steer clear of the very cheap tools. There are plenty of good tools around at reasonable prices, but always aim to purchase items which meet the relevant national safety standards. If in doubt, ask the proprietor or manager of the shop for advice before making a purchase.

Care and maintenance of tools

Having purchased a reasonable tool kit, it is necessary to keep the tools in a clean and serviceable condition. After use, always wipe off any dirt, grease and metal particles using a clean, dry cloth, before putting the tools away. Never leave them lying around after they have been used. A simple tool rack on the garage or workshop wall for items such as screwdrivers and pliers is a good idea. Store all normal spanners and sockets in a metal box. Any measuring instruments, gauges, meters, etc, must be carefully stored where they cannot be damaged or become rusty.

Take a little care when tools are used. Hammer heads inevitably become marked and screwdrivers lose the keen edge on their blades from time to time. A little timely attention with emery cloth or a file will soon restore items like this to a good serviceable finish.

Working facilities

Not to be forgotten when discussing tools is the workshop itself. If anything more than routine maintenance is to be carried out, some form of suitable working area becomes essential.

It is appreciated that many an owner mechanic is forced by circumstances to remove an engine or similar item without the benefit of a garage or workshop. Having done this, any repairs should always be done under the cover of a roof.

Wherever possible, any dismantling should be done on a clean, flat workbench or table at a suitable working height.

Any workbench needs a vice; one with a jaw opening of 100 mm (4 in) is suitable for most jobs. As mentioned previously, some clean dry storage space is also required for tools, as well as for any lubricants, cleaning fluids, touch-up paints and so on, which become necessary.

Another item which may be required, and which has a much more general usage, is an electric drill with a chuck capacity of at least 8 mm ($\frac{5}{16}$ in). This, together with a good range of twist drills, is virtually essential for fitting accessories.

Last, but not least, always keep a supply of old newspapers and clean, lint-free rags available, and try to keep any working area as clean as possible.

Spanner jaw gap and bolt size comparison table

Jaw gap – in (mm)	Spanner size	Bolt size
0.197 (5.00)	5 mm	M 2.5
0.216 (5.50)	5.5 mm	M 3
0.218 (5.53)	$\frac{7}{32}$ in AF	
0.236 (6.00)	6 mm	M 3.5
0.250 (6.35)	$\frac{1}{4}$ in AF	
0.275 (7.00)	7 mm	M 4
0.281 (7.14)	$\frac{9}{32}$ in AF	
0.312 (7.92)	$\frac{5}{16}$ in AF	
0.315 (8.00)	8 mm	M 5
0.343 (8.71)	$\frac{11}{32}$ in AF	
0.375 (9.52)	$\frac{3}{8}$ in AF	
0.394 (10.00)	10 mm	M 6
0.406 (10.32)	$\frac{13}{32}$ in AF	
0.433 (11.00)	11 mm	M 7
0.437 (11.09)	$\frac{7}{16}$ in AF	$\frac{1}{4}$ in SAE
0.468 (11.88)	$\frac{15}{32}$ in AF	
0.500 (12.70)	$\frac{1}{2}$ in AF	$\frac{5}{16}$ in SAE
0.512 (13.00)	13 mm	M8
0.562 (14.27)	$\frac{9}{16}$ in AF	$\frac{3}{8}$ in SAE
0.593 (15.06)	$\frac{19}{32}$ in AF	
0.625 (15.87)	$\frac{5}{8}$ in AF	$\frac{7}{16}$ in SAE
0.669 (17.00)	17 mm	M 10
0.687 (17.44)	$\frac{11}{16}$ in AF	
0.709 (19.00)	19 mm	M 12
0.750 (19.05)	$\frac{3}{4}$ in AF	$\frac{1}{2}$ in SAE
0.781 (19.83)	$\frac{25}{32}$ in AF	
0.812 (20.62)	$\frac{13}{16}$ in AF	
0.866 (22.00)	22 mm	M 14
0.875 (22.25)	$\frac{7}{8}$ in AF	$\frac{9}{16}$ in SAE
0.937 (23.79)	$\frac{15}{16}$ in AF	$\frac{5}{8}$ in SAE
0.945 (24.00)	24 mm	M 16
0.968 (24.58)	$\frac{31}{32}$ in AF	
1.000 (25.40)	1 in AF	$\frac{11}{16}$ in SAE
1.062 (26.97)	1 $\frac{1}{16}$ in AF	$\frac{3}{4}$ in SAE
1.063 (27.00)	27 mm	M 18
1.125 (28.57)	1 $\frac{1}{8}$ in AF	
1.182 (30.00)	30 mm	M 20
1.187 (30.14)	1 $\frac{3}{16}$ in AF	
1.250 (31.75)	1 $\frac{1}{4}$ in AF	$\frac{7}{8}$ in SAE
1.260 (32.00)	32 mm	M 22
1.312 (33.32)	1 $\frac{5}{16}$ in AF	
1.375 (34.92)	1 $\frac{3}{8}$ in AF	
1.418 (36.00)	36 mm	M 24
1.437 (36.49)	1 $\frac{7}{16}$ in AF	1 in SAE
1.500 (38.10)	1 $\frac{1}{2}$ in AF	
1.615 (41.00)	41 mm	M 27

Booster battery (jump) starting

When jump starting a car using a booster battery, observe the following precautions:

(a) *Before connecting the booster battery, make sure that the ignition is switched off*

(b) *Ensure that all electrical equipment (lights, heater, wipers etc) is switched off*

(c) *Make sure that the booster battery is the same voltage as the discharged one in the vehicle*

(d) *If the battery is being jump started from the battery in another vehicle, the two vehicles MUST NOT TOUCH each other*

(e) *Make sure that the transmission is in Neutral (manual gearbox) or Park (automatic transmission)*

Connect one jump lead between the positive (+) terminals of the two batteries. Connect the other jump lead first to the negative (–) terminal of the booster battery, and then to a good earthing point on the vehicle to be started, such as a bolt or bracket on the engine block, at least 45 cm (18 in) from the battery if possible. Make sure that the jump leads will not come into contact with the fan, drivebelts or other moving parts of the engine.

Start the engine using the booster battery, then with the engine running at idle speed, disconnect the jump leads in the reverse order of connection.

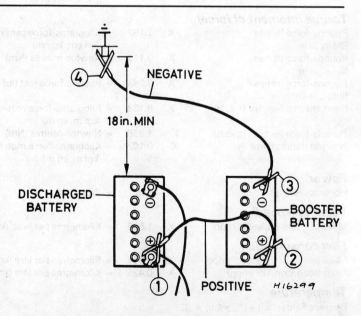

Jump start lead connections for negative earth vehicles – connect leads in order shown

Conversion factors

Length (distance)

	X		=		X		=	
Inches (in)	X	25.4	=	Millimetres (mm)	X	0.0394	=	Inches (in)
Feet (ft)	X	0.305	=	Metres (m)	X	3.281	=	Feet (ft)
Miles	X	1.609	=	Kilometres (km)	X	0.621	=	Miles

Volume (capacity)

	X		=		X		=	
Cubic inches (cu in; in^3)	X	16.387	=	Cubic centimetres (cc; cm^3)	X	0.061	=	Cubic inches (cu in; in^3)
Imperial pints (Imp pt)	X	0.568	=	Litres (l)	X	1.76	=	Imperial pints (Imp pt)
Imperial quarts (Imp qt)	X	1.137	=	Litres (l)	X	0.88	=	Imperial quarts (Imp qt)
Imperial quarts (Imp qt)	X	1.201	=	US quarts (US qt)	X	0.833	=	Imperial quarts (Imp qt)
US quarts (US qt)	X	0.946	=	Litres (l)	X	1.057	=	US quarts (US qt)
Imperial gallons (Imp gal)	X	4.546	=	Litres (l)	X	0.22	=	Imperial gallons (Imp gal)
Imperial gallons (Imp gal)	X	1.201	=	US gallons (US gal)	X	0.833	=	Imperial gallons (Imp gal)
US gallons (US gal)	X	3.785	=	Litres (l)	X	0.264	=	US gallons (US gal)

Mass (weight)

	X		=		X		=	
Ounces (oz)	X	28.35	=	Grams (g)	X	0.035	=	Ounces (oz)
Pounds (lb)	X	0.454	=	Kilograms (kg)	X	2.205	=	Pounds (lb)

Force

	X		=		X		=	
Ounces-force (ozf; oz)	X	0.278	=	Newtons (N)	X	3.6	=	Ounces-force (ozf; oz)
Pounds-force (lbf; lb)	X	4.448	=	Newtons (N)	X	0.225	=	Pounds-force (lbf; lb)
Newtons (N)	X	0.1	=	Kilograms-force (kgf; kg)	X	9.81	=	Newtons (N)

Pressure

	X		=		X		=	
Pounds-force per square inch (psi; lbf/in^2; lb/in^2)	X	0.070	=	Kilograms-force per square centimetre (kgf/cm^2; kg/cm^2)	X	14.223	=	Pounds-force per square inch (psi; lbf/in^2; lb/in^2)
Pounds-force per square inch (psi; lbf/in^2; lb/in^2)	X	0.068	=	Atmospheres (atm)	X	14.696	=	Pounds-force per square inch (psi; lbf/in^2; lb/in^2)
Pounds-force per square inch (psi; lbf/in^2; lb/in^2)	X	0.069	=	Bars	X	14.5	=	Pounds-force per square inch (psi; lbf/in^2; lb/in^2)
Pounds-force per square inch (psi; lbf/in^2; lb/in^2)	X	6.895	=	Kilopascals (kPa)	X	0.145	=	Pounds-force per square inch (psi; lbf/in^2; lb/in^2)
Kilopascals (kPa)	X	0.01	=	Kilograms-force per square centimetre (kgf/cm^2; kg/cm^2)	X	98.1	=	Kilopascals (kPa)
Millibar (mbar)	X	100	=	Pascals (Pa)	X	0.01	=	Millibar (mbar)
Millibar (mbar)	X	0.0145	=	Pounds-force per square inch (psi; lbf/in^2; lb/in^2)	X	68.947	=	Millibar (mbar)
Millibar (mbar)	X	0.75	=	Millimetres of mercury (mmHg)	X	1.333	=	Millibar (mbar)
Millibar (mbar)	X	0.401	=	Inches of water (inH$_2$O)	X	2.491	=	Millibar (mbar)
Millimetres of mercury (mmHg)	X	0.535	=	Inches of water (inH$_2$O)	X	1.868	=	Millimetres of mercury (mmHg)
Inches of water (inH$_2$O)	X	0.036	=	Pounds-force per square inch (psi; lbf/in^2; lb/in^2)	X	27.68	=	Inches of water (inH$_2$O)

Torque (moment of force)

	X		=		X		=	
Pounds-force inches (lbf in; lb in)	X	1.152	=	Kilograms-force centimetre (kgf cm; kg cm)	X	0.868	=	Pounds-force inches (lbf in; lb in)
Pounds-force inches (lbf in; lb in)	X	0.113	=	Newton metres (Nm)	X	8.85	=	Pounds-force inches (lbf in; lb in)
Pounds-force inches (lbf in; lb in)	X	0.083	=	Pounds-force feet (lbf ft; lb ft)	X	12	=	Pounds-force inches (lbf in; lb in)
Pounds-force feet (lbf ft; lb ft)	X	0.138	=	Kilograms-force metres (kgf m; kg m)	X	7.233	=	Pounds-force feet (lbf ft; lb ft)
Pounds-force feet (lbf ft; lb ft)	X	1.356	=	Newton metres (Nm)	X	0.738	=	Pounds-force feet (lbf ft; lb ft)
Newton metres (Nm)	X	0.102	=	Kilograms-force metres (kgf m; kg m)	X	9.804	=	Newton metres (Nm)

Power

	X		=		X		=	
Horsepower (hp)	X	745.7	=	Watts (W)	X	0.0013	=	Horsepower (hp)

Velocity (speed)

	X		=		X		=	
Miles per hour (miles/hr; mph)	X	1.609	=	Kilometres per hour (km/hr; kph)	X	0.621	=	Miles per hour (miles/hr; mph)

Fuel consumption

	X		=		X		=	
Miles per gallon, Imperial (mpg)	X	0.354	=	Kilometres per litre (km/l)	X	2.825	=	Miles per gallon, Imperial (mpg)
Miles per gallon, US (mpg)	X	0.425	=	Kilometres per litre (km/l)	X	2.352	=	Miles per gallon, US (mpg)

Temperature

Degrees Fahrenheit = (°C x 1.8) + 32

Degrees Celsius (Degrees Centigrade; °C) = (°F − 32) x 0.56

It is common practice to convert from miles per gallon (mpg) to litres/100 kilometres (l/100km), where mpg (Imperial) x l/100 km = 282 and mpg (US) x l/100 km = 235

Fault diagnosis

Contents

Introduction

The vehicle owner who does his or her own maintenance according to the recommended service schedules should not have to use this section of the manual very often. Modern component reliability is such that, provided those items subject to wear or deterioration are inspected or renewed at the specified intervals, sudden failure is comparatively rare. Faults do not usually just happen as a result of sudden failure, but develop over a period of time. Major mechanical failures in particular are usually preceded by characteristic symptoms over hundreds or even thousands of miles. Those components which do occasionally fail without warning are often small and easily carried in the vehicle.

With any fault finding, the first step is to decide where to begin investigations. Sometimes this is obvious, but on other occasions a little detective work will be necessary. The owner who makes half a dozen haphazard adjustments or replacements may be successful in curing a fault (or its symptoms), but will be none the wiser if the fault recurs and ultimately may have spent more time and money than was necessary. A calm and logical approach will be found to be more satisfactory in the long run. Always take into account any warning signs or abnormalities that may have been noticed in the period preceding the fault – power

loss, high or low gauge readings, unusual smells, etc – and remember that failure of components such as fuses or spark plugs may only be pointers to some underlying fault.

The pages which follow provide an easy reference guide to the more common problems which may occur during the operation of the vehicle. These problems and their possible causes are grouped under headings denoting various components or systems, such as Engine, Cooling system, etc. The Chapter and/or Section which deals with the problem is also shown in brackets. Whatever the fault, certain basic principles apply. These are as follows:

Verify the fault. This is simply a matter of being sure that you know what the symptoms are before starting work. This is particularly important if you are investigating a fault for someone else who may not have described it very accurately.

Don't overlook the obvious. For example, if the vehicle won't start, is there petrol in the tank? (Don't take anyone else's word on this particular point, and don't trust the fuel gauge either!) If an electrical fault is indicated, look for loose or broken wires before digging out the test gear.

Cure the disease, not the symptom. Substituting a flat battery with a fully charged one will get you off the hard shoulder, but if the underlying cause is not attended to, the new battery will go the same way. Similarly, changing oil-fouled spark plugs for a new set will get you moving again, but remember that the reason for the fouling (if it wasn't simply an incorrect grade of plug) will have to be established and corrected.

Don't take anything for granted. Particularly, don't forget that a 'new' component may itself be defective (especially if it's been rattling around in the boot for months), and don't leave components out of a fault diagnosis sequence just because they are new or recently fitted. When you do finally diagnose a difficult fault, you'll probably realise that all the evidence was there from the start.

1   Engine

Engine fails to rotate when attempting to start

1   Battery terminal connections loose or corroded (Chapter 12).
2   Battery discharged or faulty (Chapter 12).
3   Broken, loose or disconnected wiring in the starting circuit (Chapter 12).
4   Defective starter solenoid or switch (Chapter 12).
5   Defective starter motor (Chapter 12).
6   Starter pinion or flywheel ring gear teeth loose or broken (Chapter 12).
7   Engine earth strap broken or disconnected (Chapter 12).
8   Automatic transmission not in Park/Neutral position or starter inhibitor switch faulty (Chapter 7).

Engine rotates but will not start

1   Fuel tank empty.
2   Battery discharged (engine rotates slowly) (Chapter 12).
3   Battery terminal connections loose or corroded (Chapter 12).
4   Ignition components damp or damaged (Chapters 1 and 5).
5   Broken, loose or disconnected wiring in the ignition circuit (Chapters 1 and 5).
6   Worn, faulty or incorrectly gapped spark plugs (Chapter 1).
7   Dirty or incorrectly gapped contact points – 1397 cc (C1J) engine only (Chapter 1).
8   Faulty condenser – 1397 cc (C1J) engine (Chapter 1).
9   Choke mechanism sticking, incorrectly adjusted, or faulty (Chapter 4).
10   Major mechanical failure (eg camshaft drive) (Chapter 2).

Engine difficult to start when cold

1   Battery discharged (Chapter 12).
2   Battery terminal connections loose or corroded (Chapter 12).
3   Worn, faulty or incorrectly gapped spark plugs (Chapter 1).
4   Choke mechanism sticking, incorrectly adjusted, or faulty (Chapter 4).
5   Other ignition system fault (Chapters 1 and 5).
6   Low cylinder compressions (Chapter 2).

Engine difficult to start when hot

1   Air filter element dirty or clogged (Chapter 4).
2   Choke mechanism sticking, incorrectly adjusted, or faulty (Chapter 4).
3   Carburettor float chamber flooding or fuel percolation (Chapter 4).
4   Low cylinder compressions (Chapter 2).

Starter motor noisy or excessively rough in engagement

1   Starter pinion or flywheel ring gear teeth loose or broken (Chapter 12).
2   Starter motor mounting bolts loose or missing (Chapter 12).
3   Starter motor internal components worn or damaged (Chapter 12).

Engine starts but stops immediately

1   Insufficient fuel reaching carburettor (Chapter 4).
2   Loose or faulty electrical connections in the ignition circuit (Chapters 1 and 5).
3   Vacuum leak at the carburettor or inlet manifold (Chapter 4).
4   Blocked carburettor jet(s) or internal passages (Chapter 4).

Engine idles erratically

1   Incorrectly adjusted idle speed and/or mixture settings (Chapter 1).
2   Air filter element clogged (Chapter 4).
3   Vacuum leak at the carburettor, inlet manifold or associated hoses (Chapter 4).
4   Worn, faulty or incorrectly gapped spark plugs (Chapter 1).
5   Dirty or incorrectly gapped contact points – 1397 cc (C1J) engine only (Chapter 1).
6   Incorrectly adjusted valve clearances (Chapter 2).
7   Uneven or low cylinder compressions (Chapter 2).
8   Camshaft lobes worn (Chapter 2).
9   Timing belt/chain incorrectly tensioned (Chapter 2).

Engine misfires at idle speed

1   Worn, faulty or incorrectly gapped spark plugs (Chapter 1).
2   Dirty or incorrectly gapped contact points – 1397 cc (C1J) engine only (Chapter 1).
3   Faulty spark plug HT leads (Chapter 1).
4   Incorrectly adjusted idle mixture settings (Chapter 1).
5   Incorrect ignition timing (Chapter 1).
6   Vacuum leak at the carburettor, inlet manifold or associated hoses (Chapter 4).
7   Distributor cap cracked or tracking internally (Chapter 1).
8   Incorrectly adjusted valve clearances (Chapter 2).
9   Uneven or low cylinder compressions (Chapter 2).
10   Disconnected, leaking or perished crankcase ventilation hoses (Chapter 4).

Engine misfires throughout the driving speed range

1   Blocked carburettor jet(s) or internal passages (Chapter 4).
2   Carburettor worn or incorrectly adjusted (Chapters 1 and 4).
3   Fuel filter choked (Chapter 1).
4   Fuel pump faulty or delivery pressure low (Chapter 4).
5   Fuel tank vent blocked or fuel pipes restricted (Chapter 4).
6   Vacuum leak at the carburettor, inlet manifold or associated hoses (Chapter 4).
7   Worn, faulty or incorrectly gapped spark plugs (Chapter 1).
8   Faulty spark plug HT leads (Chapter 1).
9   Dirty or incorrectly gapped contact points – 1397 cc (C1J) engine only (Chapter 1).
10   Distributor cap cracked or tracking internally (Chapter 1).
11   Faulty ignition coil or condenser (Chapter 5).
12   Uneven or low cylinder compressions (Chapter 2).

Engine hesitates on acceleration

1   Worn, faulty or incorrectly gapped spark plugs (Chapter 1).
2   Carburettor accelerator pump faulty or diaphragm punctured (Chapter 4).
3   Blocked carburettor jets or internal passages (Chapter 4).
4   Vacuum leak at the carburettor, inlet manifold or associated hoses (Chapter 4).
5   Carburettor worn or incorrectly adjusted (Chapters 1 and 4).

Engine stalls

1   Incorrectly adjusted idle speed and/or mixture settings (Chapter 1).
2   Blocked carburettor jet(s) or internal passages (Chapter 4).
3   Vacuum leak at the carburettor, inlet manifold or associated hoses (Chapter 4).
4   Fuel filter choked (Chapter 1).
5   Fuel pump faulty or delivery pressure low (Chapter 4).
6   Fuel tank vent blocked or fuel pipes restricted (Chapter 4).

Engine lacks power

1   Incorrect ignition timing (Chapter 1).
2   Carburettor worn or incorrectly adjusted (Chapter 1).
3   Timing belt/chain incorrectly fitted or tensioned (Chapter 2).
4   Fuel filter choked (Chapter 1).
5   Fuel pump faulty or delivery pressure low (Chapter 4).
6   Uneven or low cylinder compressions (Chapter 2).
7   Worn, faulty or incorrectly gapped spark plugs (Chapter 1).
8   Dirty or incorrectly gapped contact points – 1397 cc (C1J) engine only (Chapter 1).
9   Vacuum leak at the carburettor, inlet manifold or associated hoses (Chapter 4).

10 Brakes binding (Chapter 1).
11 Clutch slipping (Chapter 6).
12 Automatic transmission fluid level incorrect (Chapter 1).

Engine backfires

1 Ignition timing incorrect (Chapter 1).
2 Timing belt/chain incorrectly fitted or tensioned (Chapter 2).
3 Carburettor worn or incorrectly adjusted (Chapter 1).
4 Vacuum leak at the carburettor, inlet manifold or associated hoses (Chapter 4).

Oil pressure warning light illuminated with engine running

1 Low oil level or incorrect grade (Chapter 1).
2 Faulty oil pressure transmitter (sender) unit (Chapter 2).
3 Worn engine bearings and/or oil pump (Chapter 2).
4 High engine operating temperature (Chapter 2).
5 Oil pressure relief valve defective (Chapter 2).
6 Oil pick-up strainer clogged (Chapter 2).

Engine runs-on after switching off

1 Idle speed excessively high (Chapter 1).
2 Faulty anti run-on solenoid (Chapter 4).
3 Excessive carbon build-up in engine (Chapter 2).
4 High engine operating temperature (Chapters 2 and 3).

Engine noises

Pre-ignition (pinking) or knocking during acceleration or under load
1 Ignition timing incorrect (Chapter 1).
2 Incorrect grade of fuel (Chapter 4).
3 Vacuum leak at the carburettor, inlet manifold or associated hoses (Chapter 4).
4 Excessive carbon build-up in engine (Chapter 2).
5 Worn or damaged distributor or other ignition system component (Chapter 5).
6 Carburettor worn or incorrectly adjusted (Chapter 4).

Whistling or wheezing noises
7 Leaking inlet manifold or carburettor gasket (Chapter 4).
8 Leaking exhaust manifold gasket or pipe to manifold joint (Chapter 4).
9 Leaking vacuum hose (Chapters 4, 5 and 9).
10 Blowing cylinder head gasket (Chapter 2).

Tapping or rattling noises
11 Incorrect valve clearances (Chapter 2).
12 Worn valve gear or camshaft (Chapter 2).
13 Worn timing chain or tensioner – 1397 cc (C1J) engine only (Chapter 2).
14 Ancillary component fault (water pump, alternator etc) (Chapters 3 and 12).

Knocking or thumping noises
15 Worn big-end bearings (regular heavy knocking, perhaps less under load) (Chapter 2).
16 Worn main bearings (rumbling and knocking, perhaps worsening under load) (Chapter 2).
17 Piston slap (most noticeable when cold) (Chapter 2).
18 Ancillary component fault (alternator, water pump etc) (Chapters 3 and 12).

2 Cooling system

Overheating

1 Insufficient coolant in system (Chapter 3).
2 Thermostat faulty (Chapter 3).
3 Radiator core blocked or grille restricted (Chapter 3).
4 Electric cooling fan or thermoswitch faulty (Chapter 3).
5 Pressure cap faulty (Chapter 3).

6 Water pump drivebelt worn, or incorrectly adjusted (Chapter 1).
7 Ignition timing incorrect (Chapter 1).
8 Inaccurate temperature gauge sender unit (Chapter 3).
9 Air lock in cooling system (Chapter 3).

Overcooling

1 Thermostat faulty (Chapter 3).
2 Inaccurate temperature gauge sender unit (Chapter 3).

External coolant leakage

1 Deteriorated or damaged hoses or hose clips (Chapter 1).
2 Radiator core or heater matrix leaking (Chapter 3).
3 Pressure cap faulty (Chapter 3).
4 Water pump seal leaking (Chapter 3).
5 Boiling due to overheating (Chapter 3).
6 Core plug leaking (Chapter 2).

Internal coolant leakage

1 Leaking cylinder head gasket (Chapter 2).
2 Cracked cylinder head or cylinder bore (Chapter 2).
3 Leaking cylinder liner base seals (Chapter 2).

Corrosion

1 Infrequent draining and flushing (Chapter 1).
2 Incorrect antifreeze mixture or inappropriate type (Chapter 1).

3 Fuel and exhaust system

Excessive fuel consumption

1 Air filter element dirty or clogged (Chapter 1).
2 Carburettor worn or incorrectly adjusted (Chapter 4).
3 Choke cable incorrectly adjusted or choke sticking (Chapter 4).
4 Ignition timing incorrect (Chapter 1).
5 Tyres underinflated (Chapter 1).

Fuel leakage and/or fuel odour

1 Damaged or corroded fuel tank, pipes or connections (Chapter 1).
2 Carburettor float chamber flooding (Chapter 4).

Excessive noise or fumes from exhaust system

1 Leaking exhaust system or manifold joints (Chapter 1).
2 Leaking, corroded or damaged silencers or pipe (Chapter 1).
3 Broken mountings causing body or suspension contact (Chapter 1).

4 Clutch

Pedal travels to floor – no pressure or very little resistance

1 Broken clutch cable (Chapter 6).
2 Incorrect clutch adjustment (Chapter 6).
3 Faulty clutch pedal self-adjust mechanism (Chapter 6).
4 Broken clutch release bearing or fork (Chapter 6).
5 Broken diaphragm spring in clutch pressure plate (Chapter 6).

Clutch fails to disengage (unable to select gears)

1 Incorrect clutch adjustment (Chapter 6).
2 Faulty clutch pedal self-adjust mechanism (Chapter 6).
3 Clutch disc sticking on gearbox input shaft splines (Chapter 6).
4 Clutch disc sticking to flywheel or pressure plate (Chapter 6).
5 Faulty pressure plate assembly (Chapter 6).
6 Gearbox input shaft seized in crankshaft spigot bearing (Chapter 2).
7 Clutch release mechanism worn or incorrectly assembled (Chapter 6).

Clutch slips (engine speed increases with no increase in vehicle speed)

1 Incorrect clutch adjustment (Chapter 6).

2   Faulty clutch pedal self-adjust mechanism (Chapter 6).
3   Clutch disc linings excessively worn (Chapter 6).
4   Clutch disc linings contaminated with oil or grease (Chapter 6).
5   Faulty pressure plate or weak diaphragm spring (Chapter 6).

Judder as clutch is engaged
1   Clutch disc linings contaminated with oil or grease (Chapter 6).
2   Clutch disc linings excessively worn (Chapter 6).
3   Clutch cable sticking or frayed (Chapter 6).
4   Faulty or distorted pressure plate or diaphragm spring (Chapter 6).
5   Worn or loose engine or gearbox mountings (Chapter 2).
6   Clutch disc hub or gearbox input shaft splines worn (Chapter 6).

Noise when depressing or releasing clutch pedal
1   Worn clutch release bearing (Chapter 6).
2   Worn or dry clutch pedal bushes (Chapter 6).
3   Faulty pressure plate assembly (Chapter 6).
4   Pressure plate diaphragm spring broken (Chapter 6).
5   Broken clutch disc cushioning springs (Chapter 6).

5   Manual gearbox

Noisy in neutral with engine running
1   Input shaft bearings worn (noise apparent with clutch pedal released but not when depressed) (Chapter 7).*
2   Clutch release bearing worn (noise apparent with clutch pedal depressed, possibly less when released) (Chapter 6).

Noisy in one particular gear
1   Worn, damaged or chipped gear teeth (Chapter 7).*

Difficulty engaging gears
1   Clutch fault (Chapter 6).
2   Worn or damaged gear linkage (Chapter 7).
3   Incorrectly adjusted gear linkage (Chapter 7).
4   Worn synchroniser units (Chapter 7).*

Jumps out of gear
1   Worn or damaged gear linkage (Chapter 6).
2   Incorrectly adjusted gear linkage (Chapter 6).
3   Worn synchroniser units (Chapter 7).*
4   Worn selector forks (Chapter 7).*

Vibration
1   Lack of oil (Chapter 1).
2   Worn bearings (Chapter 7).*

Lubricant leaks
1   Leaking differential output oil seal (Chapter 7).
2   Leaking housing joint (Chapter 7).*
3   Leaking input shaft oil seal (Chapter 7).*

*Although the corrective action necessary to remedy the symptoms described is beyond the scope of the home mechanic, the above information should be helpful in isolating the cause of the condition so that the owner can communicate clearly with a professional mechanic

6   Automatic transmission

Note: Due to the complexity of the automatic transmission, it is difficult for the home mechanic to properly diagnose and service this unit. For problems other than the following, the vehicle should be taken to a dealer service department or automatic transmission specialist

Fluid leakage
1   Automatic transmission fluid is usually deep red in colour. Fluid leaks should not be confused with engine oil which can easily be blown onto the transmission by airflow.
2   To determine the source of a leak, first remove all built-up dirt and grime from the transmission housing and surrounding areas using a

degreasing agent or by steam cleaning. Drive the vehicle at low speed so airflow will not blow the leak far from its source. Raise and support the vehicle and determine where the leak is coming from. Common areas of leakage are:

(a) Oil pan (Chapters 1 and 7)
(b) Dipstick tube (Chapters 1 and 7)
(c) Transmission to oil cooler fluid pipes/unions (Chapter 7)

Transmission fluid brown or has burned smell
1   Transmission fluid level low or fluid in need of renewal (Chapter 1).

General gear selection problems
1   Chapter 7, Part B, deals with checking and adjusting the selector linkage on automatic transmissions. Common problems which may be attributed to a poorly adjusted linkage are:

(a) Engine starting in gears other than Park or Neutral
(b) Indicator on gear selector lever pointing to a gear other than the one actually being used
(c) Vehicle moves when in Park or Neutral
(d) Poor gearshift quality or erratic gear changes

2   Refer to Chapter 7, Part B for the selector linkage adjustment procedure.

Transmission will not downshift (kickdown) with accelerator fully depressed
1   Low transmission fluid level (Chapter 1).
2   Incorrect selector mechanism adjustment (Chapter 7, Part B).

Engine will not start in any gear, or starts in gears other than Park or Neutral
1   Incorrect starter/inhibitor switch adjustment (Chapter 7, Part B).
2   Incorrect selector mechanism adjustment (Chapter 7, Part B).

Transmission slips, shifts roughly, is noisy or has no drive in forward or reverse gears
1   There are many probable causes for the above problems, but the home mechanic should be concerned with only one possibility – fluid level. Before taking the vehicle to a dealer or transmission specialist, check the fluid level and condition of the fluid as described in Chapter 1. Correct the fluid level as necessary or change the fluid and filter if needed. If the problem persists, professional help will be necessary.

7   Driveshafts

Clicking or knocking noise on turns (at slow speed on full lock)
1   Lack of constant velocity joint lubricant (Chapter 8).
2   Worn outer constant velocity joint (Chapter 8).

Vibration when accelerating or decelerating
1   Worn inner constant velocity joint (Chapter 8).
2   Bent or distorted driveshaft (Chapter 8).

8   Braking system

Note: Before assuming that a brake problem exists, make sure that the tyres are in good condition and correctly inflated, the front wheel alignment is correct and the vehicle is not loaded with weight in an unequal manner. Apart from checking the condition of all pipe and hose connections, any faults occurring on the Anti-lock braking system should be referred to a Renault dealer for diagnosis

Vehicle pulls to one side under braking
1   Worn, defective, damaged or contaminated front or rear brake pads/shoes on one side (Chapter 1).
2   Seized or partially seized front or rear brake caliper/wheel cylinder piston (Chapter 9).

3   A mixture of brake pad/shoe lining materials fitted between sides (Chapter 1).
4   Brake caliper mounting bolts loose (Chapter 9).
5   Rear brake backplate mounting bolts loose (Chapter 9).
6   Worn or damaged steering or suspension components (Chapter 10).

Noise (grinding or high-pitched squeal) when brakes applied

1   Brake pad or shoe friction lining material worn down to metal backing (Chapter 1).
2   Excessive corrosion of brake disc or drum (especially if the vehicle has been standing for some time) (Chapter 1).
3   Foreign object (stone chipping etc) trapped between brake disc and splash shield (Chapter 1).

Excessive brake pedal travel

1   Inoperative rear brake self-adjust mechanism (Chapter 1).
2   Faulty master cylinder (Chapter 9).
3   Air in hydraulic system (Chapter 9).

Brake pedal feels spongy when depressed

1   Air in hydraulic system (Chapter 9).
2   Deteriorated flexible rubber brake hoses (Chapter 9).
3   Master cylinder mounting nuts loose (Chapter 9).
4   Faulty master cylinder (Chapter 9).

Excessive brake pedal effort required to stop vehicle

1   Faulty vacuum servo unit (Chapter 9).
2   Disconnected, damaged or insecure brake servo vacuum hose (Chapter 9).
3   Primary or secondary hydraulic circuit failure (Chapter 9).
4   Seized brake caliper or wheel cylinder piston(s) (Chapter 9).
5   Brake pads or brake shoes incorrectly fitted (Chapter 1).
6   Incorrect grade of brake pads or brake shoes fitted (Chapter 1).
7   Brake pads or brake shoe linings contaminated (Chapter 1).

Judder felt through brake pedal or steering wheel when braking

1   Excessive run-out or distortion of front discs or rear drums (Chapter 9).
2   Brake pad or brake shoe linings worn (Chapter 1).
3   Brake caliper or rear brake backplate mounting bolts loose (Chapter 9).
4   Wear in suspension, steering components or mountings (Chapter 10).

Brakes binding

1   Seized brake caliper or wheel cylinder piston(s) (Chapter 9).
2   Incorrectly adjusted handbrake mechanism or linkage (Chapter 1).
3   Faulty master cylinder (Chapter 9).

Rear wheels locking under normal braking

1   Rear brake shoe linings contaminated (Chapter 1).
2   Faulty brake pressure compensators in the rear wheel cylinders (Chapter 9).

9   Suspension and steering systems

Note: *Before diagnosing suspension or steering faults, be sure that the trouble is not due to incorrect tyre pressures, mixtures of tyre types or binding brakes*

Vehicle pulls to one side

1   Defective tyre (Chapter 1).
2   Excessive wear in suspension or steering components (Chapter 10).
3   Incorrect front wheel alignment (Chapter 10).
4   Accident damage to steering or suspension components (Chapter 10).

Wheel wobble and vibration

1   Front roadwheels out of balance (vibration felt mainly through the steering wheel) (Chapter 10).

2   Rear roadwheels out of balance (vibration felt throughout the vehicle) (Chapter 10).
3   Roadwheels damaged or distorted (Chapter 10).
4   Faulty or damaged tyre (Chapter 10).
5   Worn steering or suspension joints, bushes or components (Chapter 10).
6   Wheel bolts loose (Chapter 10).

Excessive pitching and/or rolling around corners or during braking

1   Defective shock absorbers (Chapter 10).
2   Broken or weak coil spring and/or suspension component (Chapter 10).
3   Worn or damaged anti-roll bar or mountings (Chapter 10).

Wandering or general instability

1   Incorrect front wheel alignment (Chapter 10).
2   Worn steering or suspension joints, bushes or components (Chapter 10).
3   Roadwheels out of balance (Chapter 10).
4   Faulty or damaged tyre (Chapter 10).
5   Wheel bolts loose (Chapter 10).
6   Defective shock absorbers (Chapter 10).

Excessively stiff steering

1   Lack of steering gear lubricant (Chapter 10).
2   Seized tie-rod end balljoint or suspension balljoint (Chapter 10).
3   Broken or incorrectly adjusted power-assisted steering pump drivebelt (Chapter 1).
4   Incorrect front wheel alignment (Chapter 10).
5   Steering rack or column bent or damaged (Chapter 10).

Excessive play in steering

1   Worn steering column universal joint(s) or intermediate coupling (Chapter 10).
2   Worn steering track-rod end balljoints (Chapter 10).
3   Worn rack and pinion steering gear (Chapter 10).
4   Worn steering or suspension joints, bushes or components (Chapter 10).

Lack of power assistance

1   Broken or incorrectly adjusted power-assisted steering pump drivebelt (Chapter 1).
2   Incorrect power-assisted steering fluid level (Chapter 1).
3   Restriction in power-assisted steering fluid hoses (Chapter 10).
4   Faulty power-assisted steering pump (Chapter 10).
5   Faulty rack and pinion steering gear (Chapter 10).

Tyre wear excessive

Tyres worn on inside or outside edges

1   Tyres underinflated (wear on both edges) (Chapter 1).
2   Incorrect camber or castor angles (wear on one edge only) (Chapter 10).
3   Worn steering or suspension joints, bushes or components (Chapter 10).
4   Excessively hard cornering.
5   Accident damage.

Tyre treads exhibit feathered edges

6   Incorrect toe setting (Chapter 10).

Tyres worn in centre of tread

7   Tyres overinflated (Chapter 1).

Tyres worn on inside and outside edges

8   Tyres underinflated (Chapter 1).

Tyres worn unevenly

9   Tyres out of balance (Chapter 1).
10   Excessive wheel or tyre run-out (Chapter 1).
11   Worn shock absorbers (Chapter 10).
12   Faulty tyre (Chapter 1).

10   Electrical system

Note: *For problems associated with the starting system, refer to the faults listed under the 'Engine' heading earlier in this Section*

Battery will not hold a charge for more than a few days

1   Battery defective internally (Chapter 12).
2   Battery electrolyte level low (Chapter 1).
3   Battery terminal connections loose or corroded (Chapter 12).
4   Alternator drivebelt worn or incorrectly adjusted (Chapter 1).
5   Alternator not charging at correct output (Chapter 12).
6   Alternator or voltage regulator faulty (Chapter 12).
7   Short-circuit causing continual battery drain (Chapter 12).

Ignition warning light remains illuminated with engine running

1   Alternator drivebelt broken, worn, or incorrectly adjusted (Chapter 1).
2   Alternator brushes worn, sticking, or dirty (Chapter 12).
3   Alternator brush springs weak or broken (Chapter 12).
4   Internal fault in alternator or voltage regulator (Chapter 12).
5   Broken, disconnected, or loose wiring in charging circuit (Chapter 12).

Ignition warning light fails to come on

1   Warning light bulb blown (Chapter 12).
2   Broken, disconnected, or loose wiring in warning light circuit (Chapter 12) .
3   Alternator faulty (Chapter 12).

Lights inoperative

1   Bulb blown (Chapter 12).
2   Corrosion of bulb or bulbholder contacts (Chapter 12).
3   Blown fuse (Chapter 12).
4   Faulty relay (Chapter 12).
5   Broken, loose, or disconnected wiring (Chapter 12).
6   Faulty switch (Chapter 12).

Instrument readings inaccurate or erratic

Instrument readings increase with engine speed
1   Faulty voltage regulator (Chapter 12).

Fuel or temperature gauge give no reading
2   Faulty gauge sender unit (Chapters 3 or 4).
3   Wiring open circuit (Chapter 12).
4   Faulty gauge (Chapter 12).

Fuel or temperature gauges give continuous maximum reading
5   Faulty gauge sender unit (Chapters 3 or 4).
6   Wiring short-circuit (Chapter 12).
7   Faulty gauge (Chapter 12).

Horn inoperative or unsatisfactory in operation

Horn operates all the time
1   Horn push either earthed or stuck down (Chapter 12).
2   Horn cable to horn push earthed (Chapter 12).

Horn fails to operate
3   Blown fuse (Chapter 12).
4   Cable or cable connections loose, broken or disconnected (Chapter 12).
5   Faulty horn (Chapter 12).

Horn emits intermittent or unsatisfactory sound
6   Cable connections loose (Chapter 12).
7   Horn mountings loose (Chapter 12).
8   Faulty horn (Chapter 12).

Windscreen/tailgate wipers inoperative or unsatisfactory in operation

Wipers fail to operate or operate very slowly
1   Wiper blades stuck to screen, or linkage seized or binding (Chapter 12).

2   Blown fuse (Chapter 12).
3   Cable or cable connections loose, broken or disconnected (Chapter 12).
4   Faulty relay (Chapter 12).
5   Faulty wiper motor (Chapter 12).

Wiper blades sweep over too large or too small an area of the glass

6   Wiper arms incorrectly positioned on spindles (Chapter 1).
7   Excessive wear of wiper linkage (Chapter 1)
8   Wiper motor or linkage mountings loose or insecure (Chapter 12).

Wiper blades fail to clean the glass effectively

9   Wiper blade rubbers worn or perished (Chapter 1).
10   Wiper arm tension springs broken or arm pivots seized (Chapter 1).
11   Insufficient windscreen washer additive to adequately remove road dirt film (Chapter 1).

Windscreen/tailgate washers inoperative or unsatisfactory in operation

One or more washer jets inoperative
1   Blocked washer jet (Chapter 12).
2   Disconnected, kinked or restricted fluid hose (Chapter 12).
3   Insufficient fluid in washer reservoir (Chapter 1).

Washer pump fails to operate
4   Broken or disconnected wiring or connections (Chapter 12).
5   Blown fuse (Chapter 12).
6   Faulty washer switch (Chapter 12).
7   Faulty washer pump (Chapter 12).

Washer pump runs for some time before fluid is emitted from jets
8   Faulty one-way valve in fluid supply hose (Chapter 12).

Electric windows inoperative or unsatisfactory in operation

Window glass will only move in one direction
1   Faulty switch (Chapter 11).

Window glass slow to move
2   Incorrectly adjusted door glass guide channels (Chapter 11).
3   Regulator seized or damaged, or in need of lubrication (Chapter 11).
4   Door internal components or trim fouling regulator (Chapter 11).
5   Faulty motor (Chapter 11).

Window glass fails to move
6   Incorrectly adjusted door glass guide channels (Chapter 11).
7   Blown fuse (Chapter 12).
8   Faulty relay (Chapter 12).
9   Broken or disconnected wiring or connections (Chapter 12).
10   Faulty motor (Chapter 12).

Central locking system inoperative or unsatisfactory in operation

Complete system failure
1   Blown fuse (Chapter 12).
2   Faulty relay (Chapter 12).
3   Broken or disconnected wiring or connections (Chapter 12).

Latch locks but will not unlock, or unlocks but will not lock
4   Faulty master switch (Chapter 12).
5   Broken or disconnected latch operating rods or levers (Chapter 12).
6   Faulty relay (Chapter 12).

One solenoid/motor fails to operate
7   Broken or disconnected wiring or connections (Chapter 12).
8   Faulty solenoid/motor (Chapter 12).
9   Broken, binding or disconnected latch operating rods or levers (Chapter 12) .
10   Fault in door latch (Chapter 12).

MOT test checks

Introduction

Motor vehicle testing has been compulsory in Great Britain since 1960 when the Motor Vehicle (Tests) Regulations were first introduced. At that time testing was only applicable to vehicles ten years old or older, and the test itself only covered lighting equipment, braking systems and steering gear. Current vehicle testing is far more extensive and, in the case of private cars, is now an annual inspection commencing three years after the date of first registration.

This section is intended as a guide to getting your car through the MOT test. It lists all the relevant testable items, how to check them yourself, and what is likely to cause the vehicle to fail. Obviously it will not be possible to examine the vehicle to the same standard as the professional MOT tester who will be highly experienced in this work and will have all the necessary equipment available. However, working through the following checks will provide a good indication as to the condition of the vehicle and will enable you to identify any problem areas before submitting the vehicle for the test. Where a component is found to need repair or renewal, a cross reference is given to the relevant Chapter in the manual where further information and the appropriate repair procedures will be found.

The following checks have been sub-divided into three categories as follows:

(a) Checks carried out from the driver's seat
(b) Checks carried out with the car on the ground
(c) Checks carried out with the car raised and with the wheels free to rotate

In most cases the help of an assistant will be necessary to carry out these checks thoroughly.

Checks carried out from the driver's seat

Handbrake (Chapter 9)

Test the operation of the handbrake by pulling on the lever until the handbrake is in the normal fully-applied position. Ensure that the travel of the lever (the number of clicks of the ratchet) is not excessive before full resistance of the braking mechanism is felt. If so this would indicate incorrect adjustment of the rear brakes or incorrectly adjusted handbrake cables. With the handbrake fully applied, tap the lever sideways and make sure that it does not release, indicating wear in the ratchet and pawl. Release the handbrake and move the lever from side to side to check for excessive wear in the pivot bearing. Check the security of the lever mountings and make sure that there is no corrosion of any part of the body structure within 30 cm (12 in) of the lever mounting. If the lever mountings cannot be readily seen from inside the vehicle, carry out this check later when working underneath.

Footbrake (Chapter 9)

Check that the brake pedal is sound without visible defects such as excessive wear of the pivot bushes or a broken or damaged pedal pad. Check also for signs of fluid leaks on the pedal, floor or carpets, indicating failed seals in the brake master cylinder. Depress the brake pedal slowly at first, then rapidly until sustained pressure can be held. Maintain this pressure and check that the pedal does not creep down to the floor, indicating problems with the master cylinder. Release the pedal, wait a few seconds then depress it once until firm resistance is felt. Check that this resistance occurs near the top of the pedal travel. If the pedal travels nearly to the floor before firm resistance is felt, this indicates incorrect brake adjustment resulting in 'insufficient reserve travel' of the footbrake. If firm resistance cannot be felt, ie the pedal feels spongy, this indicates the presence of air in the hydraulic system, which will necessitate complete bleeding of the system. Check that the servo unit is operating correctly by depressing the brake pedal several times to exhaust the vacuum. Keep the pedal depressed and start the engine. As soon as the engine starts, the brake pedal resistance will be felt to alter. If this is not the case, there may be a leak from the brake servo vacuum hose, or the servo unit itself may be faulty.

Steering wheel and column (Chapter 10)

Examine the steering wheel for fractures or looseness of the hub, spokes or rim. Move the steering wheel from side to side and then up and down, in relation to the steering column. Check that the steering wheel is not loose on the column, indicating wear in the column splines or a loose steering wheel retaining nut. Continue moving the steering wheel as before, but also turn it slightly from left to right. Check that there is no abnormal movement of the steering wheel, indicating excessive wear in the column upper support bearing, universal joint(s) or flexible coupling.

Electrical equipment (Chapter 12)

Switch on the ignition and operate the horn. The horn must operate and produce a clear sound audible to other road users. Note that a gong, siren or two-tone horn fitted as an alternative to the manufacturer's original equipment is not acceptable.

Check the operation of the windscreen washers and wipers. The washers must operate with adequate flow and pressure and with the jets adjusted so that the liquid strikes the windscreen near the top of the glass.

Operate the windscreen wipers in conjunction with the washers and check that the blades cover their designed sweep of the windscreen without smearing. The blades must effectively clean the glass so that the driver has an adequate view of the road ahead and to the front nearside and offside of the vehicle. If the screen smears or does not clean adequately, it is advisable to renew the wiper blades before the MOT test.

Depress the footbrake with the ignition switched on and have your assistant check that both rear stop lights operate, and are extinguished when the footbrake is released. If one stop light fails to operate it is likely that a bulb has blown or there is a poor electrical contact at, or near the bulbholder. If both stop lights fail to operate, check for a blown fuse, faulty stop light switch or possibly two blown bulbs. If the lights stay on when the brake pedal is released, it is possible that the switch is at fault.

Seat belts (Chapter 11)

Note: *The following checks are applicable to the seat belts provided for the driver's seat and front passenger's seat. Both seat belts must be of a type that will restrain the upper part of the body; lap belts are not acceptable*

Check the security of all seat belt mountings

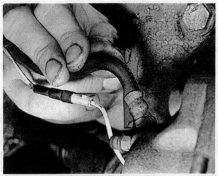
Check the flexible brake hoses for cracks or deterioration

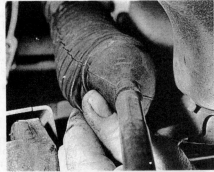
Examine the steering rack rubber gaiters for condition and security

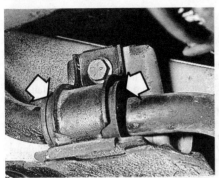

Check all rubber suspension mounting bushes (arrowed) for damage or deterioration

Shake the roadwheel vigorously to check for excess play in the wheel bearings and suspension components

Check the condition of the shock absorber mountings and bushes (arrowed)

Carefully examine the seat belt webbing for cuts or any signs of serious fraying or deterioration. If the seat belt is of the retractable type, pull the belt all the way out and examine the full extent of the webbing.

Fasten and unfasten the belt ensuring that the locking mechanism holds securely and releases properly when intended. If the belt is of the retractable type, check also that the retracting mechanism operates correctly when the belt is released.

Check the security of all seat belt mountings and attachments which are accessible, without removing any trim or other components, from inside the car (photo). Any serious corrosion, fracture or distortion of the body structure within 30 cm (12 in) of any mounting point will cause the vehicle to fail. Certain anchorages will not be accessible, or even visible from inside the car and in this instance further checks should be carried out later, when working underneath. If any part of the seat belt mechanism is attached to the front seat, then the seat mountings are treated as anchorages and must also comply as above.

Checks carried out with the car on the ground

Electrical equipment (Chapter 12)

Switch on the side lights and check that both front and rear side lights are illuminated and that the lenses and reflectors are secure and undamaged. This is particularly important at the rear where a cracked or damaged lens would allow a white light to show to the rear, which is unacceptable. It is also worth noting that any lens that is excessively dirty, either inside or out, such that the light intensity is reduced, could also constitute a fail.

Switch on the headlamps and check that both dipped beam and main beam units are operating correctly and at the same light intensity. If either headlamp shows signs of dimness, this is usually attributable to a poor earth connection or severely corroded internal reflector. Inspect the headlamp lenses for cracks or stone damage. Any damage to the headlamp lens will normally constitute a fail, but this is very much down to the tester's discretion. Bear in mind that with all light units they must operate correctly when first switched on – it is not acceptable to tap a light unit to make it operate.

The headlamps must be aligned so as not to dazzle other road users when switched to dipped beam. This can only be accurately checked using optical beam setting equipment so if you have any doubts about the headlamp alignment, it is advisable to have this professionally checked and if necessary reset, before the MOT test.

With the ignition switched on, operate the direction indicators and check that they show a white or amber light to the front and red or amber light to the rear, that they flash at the rate of between one and two flashes per second and that the 'tell-tale' on the instrument panel also functions. Examine the lenses for cracks or damage as described previously.

Footbrake (Chapter 9)

From within the engine compartment examine the brake pipes for signs of leaks, corrosion, insecurity, chafing or other damage and check the master cylinder and servo unit for leaks, security of their mountings or excessive corrosion in the vicinity of the mountings.

Turn the steering as necessary so that the right-hand front brake

flexible hose can be examined. Inspect the hose carefully for any sign of cracks or deterioration of the rubber. This will be most noticeable if the hose is bent in half and is particularly common where the rubber portion enters the metal end fitting (photo). Turn the steering onto full left then full right lock and ensure that the hose does not contact the wheel, tyre, or any part of the steering or suspension mechanism. While your assistant depresses the brake pedal firmly, check the hose for any bulges or fluid leaks under pressure. Now repeat these checks on the left-hand front hose. Should any damage or deterioration be noticed, renew the hose.

Steering mechanism and suspension (Chapter 10)

Have your assistant turn the steering wheel from side to side slightly, up to the point where the steering gear just begins to transmit this movement to the roadwheels. Check for excessive free play between the steering wheel and the steering gear which would indicate wear in the steering column joints, wear or insecurity of the steering column to steering gear coupling, or insecurity, incorrect adjustment, or wear in the steering gear itself. Generally speaking, free play greater than 1.3 cm (0.5 in) for vehicles with rack and pinion type steering or 7.6 cm (3.0 in) for vehicles with steering box mechanisms should be considered excessive.

Have your assistant turn the steering wheel more vigorously in each direction up to the point where the roadwheels just begin to turn. As this is done, carry out a complete examination of all steering joints, linkages, fittings and attachments. Any component that shows signs of wear, damage, distortion, or insecurity should be renewed or attended to accordingly. On vehicles equipped with power-assisted steering also check that the power steering pump is secure, that the pump drivebelt is in satisfactory condition and correctly adjusted, that there are no fluid leaks or damaged hoses, and that the system operates correctly. Additional checks can be carried out later with the vehicle raised, when there will be greater working clearance underneath.

Check that the vehicle is standing level and at approximately the correct ride height. Ensure that there is sufficient clearance between the suspension components and the bump stops to allow full suspension travel over bumps.

Shock absorbers (Chapter 10)

Depress each corner of the car in turn and then release it. If the shock absorbers are in good condition the corner of the car will rise and then settle in its normal position. If there is no noticeable damping effect from the shock absorber, and the car continues to rise and fall, then the shock absorber is defective.

Exhaust system (Chapter 4)

Start the engine and with your assistant holding a rag over the tailpipe, check the entire system for leaks which will appear as a rhythmic fluffing or hissing sound at the source of the leak. Check the effectiveness of the silencer by ensuring that the noise produced is of a level to be expected from a vehicle of similar type. Providing that the system is structurally sound, it is acceptable to cure a leak using a proprietary exhaust system repair kit or similar method.

Inspect the constant velocity joint gaiters for splits or damage

Check the handbrake mechanism for signs of frayed or broken cables or insecurity of the linkage

Check the condition of the exhaust system paying particular attention to the mountings

Checks carried out with the car raised and with the wheels free to rotate.

Jack up the front and rear of the car and securely support it on axle stands positioned at suitable load bearing points under the vehicle structure. Position the stands clear of the suspension assemblies and ensure that the wheels are clear of the ground and that the steering can be turned onto full right and left lock.

Steering mechanism (Chapter 10)

Examine the steering rack rubber gaiters for signs of splits, lubricant leakage or insecurity of their retaining clips (photo). If power-assisted steering is fitted, check for signs of deterioration, damage, chafing of or leakage from the fluid hoses, pipes or connections. Also check for excessive stiffness or binding of the steering, a missing split pin or locking device or any severe corrosion of the body structure within 30 cm (12 in) of any steering component attachment point.

Have your assistant turn the steering onto full left then full right lock. Check that the steering turns smoothly without undue tightness or roughness and that no part of the steering mechanism, including a wheel or tyre, fouls any brake flexible or rigid hose or pipe, or any part of the body structure.

Front and rear suspension and wheel bearings (Chapter 10)

Starting at the front right-hand side of the vehicle, grasp the roadwheel at the 3 o'clock and 9 o'clock positions and shake it vigorously. Check for any free play at the wheel bearings, suspension ball joints, or suspension mountings, pivots and attachments. Check also for any serious deterioration of the rubber or metal casing of any mounting bushes, or any distortion, deformation or severe corrosion of any components (photo). Look for missing split pins, tab washers or other locking devices on any mounting or attachment, or any severe corrosion of the vehicle structure within 30 cm (12 in) of any suspension component attachment point. If any excess free play is suspected at a component pivot point, this can be confirmed by using a large screwdriver or similar tool and levering between the mounting and the component attachment. This will confirm whether the wear is in the pivot bush, its retaining bolt or in the mounting itself (note that the bolt holes can often become elongated). Now grasp the wheel at the 12 o'clock and 6 o'clock positions, shake it vigorously and repeat the previous inspection (photo). Rotate the wheel and check for roughness or tightness of the front wheel bearing such that imminent failure of the bearing is indicated. Carry out all the above checks at the other front wheel and then at both rear wheels. Note, however, that the condition of the rear wheel bearings is not actually part of the MOT test, but if they are at all suspect, it is likely that this will be brought to the owner's attention at the time of the test.

Roadsprings and shock absorbers (Chapter 10)

On vehicles with strut type suspension units, examine the strut assembly for signs of fluid leakage, corrosion or severe pitting of the piston rod or damage to the casing. Check also for security of the mounting points.

If coil springs are fitted check that the spring ends locate correctly in their spring seats, that there is no severe corrosion of the spring and that it is not cracked, broken or in any way damaged.

If the vehicle is fitted with leaf springs, check that all leaves are intact, that the axle is securely attached to each spring and that there is no wear or deterioration of the spring eye mountings, bushes, and shackles.

The same general checks apply to vehicles fitted with other suspension types, such as torsion bars, hydraulic displacer units etc. In all cases ensure that all mountings and attachments are secure, that there are no signs of excessive wear, corrosion, cracking, deformation or damage to any component or bush, and that there are no fluid leaks or damaged hoses or pipes (hydraulic types).

Inspect the shock absorbers for signs of fluid leakage, excessive wear of the mounting bushes or attachments or damage to the body of the unit (photo).

Driveshafts (Chapter 8)

With the steering turned onto full lock, rotate each front wheel in turn and inspect the constant velocity joint gaiters for splits or damage (photo). Also check the gaiter is securely attached to its respective housings by clips or other methods of retention.

Continue turning the wheel and check that each driveshaft is straight with no sign of damage.

Braking system (Chapter 9)

If possible, without dismantling, check for wear of the brake pads and the condition of the discs. Ensure that the friction lining material has not worn excessively and that the discs are not fractured, pitted, scored or worn excessively.

Carefully examine all the rigid brake pipes underneath the car and the flexible hoses at the rear. Look for signs of excessive corrosion, chafing or insecurity of the pipes and for signs of bulging under pressure, chafing, splits or deterioration of the flexible hoses.

Look for signs of hydraulic fluid leaks at the brake calipers or on the brake backplates, indicating failed hydraulic seals in the components concerned.

Slowly spin each wheel while your assistant depresses the footbrake then releases it. Ensure that each brake is operating and that the wheel is free to rotate when the pedal is released.

Examine the handbrake mechanism and check for signs of frayed or broken cables, excessive corrosion or wear or insecurity of the linkage (photo). Have your assistant operate the handbrake while you check that the mechanism works on each relevant wheel and releases fully without binding.

Exhaust system (Chapter 4)

Starting at the front, examine the exhaust system over its entire length checking for any damaged, broken or missing mountings, security of the pipe retaining clamps and condition of the system with regard to rust and corrosion (photo).

Wheels and tyres (Chapter 10)

Carefully examine each tyre in turn on both the inner and outer walls and over the whole of the tread area, checking for signs of cuts, tears, lumps, bulges, separation of the tread and exposure of the ply or cord due to wear or other damage. Check also that the tyre bead is correctly seated on the wheel rim and that the tyre valve is sound and properly seated. Spin the wheel and check that it is not excessively distorted or damaged particularly at the bead rim. Check that the tyres are of the correct size for the car and that they are of the same size and type on each axle. They should also be inflated to the specified pressures.

Using a suitable gauge check the tyre tread depth. The current legal requirement states that the tread pattern must be visible over the whole tread area and must be of a minimum depth of 1.6 mm over at least three-quarters of the tread width. It is acceptable for some wear of the inside or outside edges of the tyre to be apparent but this wear must be in one even circumferential band and the tread must be visible. Any excessive wear of this nature may indicate incorrect front wheel alignment which should be checked before the tyre becomes excessively worn. See Chapters 1 and 10 for further information on tyre wear patterns and front wheel alignment.

Body corrosion

Check the condition of the entire vehicle structure for signs of corrosion in any load bearing areas. For the purpose of the MOT test all chassis box sections, side sills, subframes, crossmembers, pillars, suspension, steering, braking system and seat belt mountings and anchorages should all be considered as load bearing areas. As a general guide, any corrosion which has seriously reduced the metal thickness of a load bearing area to weaken it, is likely to cause the vehicle to fail. Should corrosion of this nature be encountered, professional repairs are likely to be needed.

Chapter 1 Routine maintenance and servicing

Contents

Specifications

Engine
Oil filter type:
1390 cc (E6J) engine	Champion F101
1397 cc (C1J) engine	Champion F101
1721 cc (F2N) engine	Champion F102

Cooling system
Expansion tank pressure cap release pressure .... 1.2 bar (17.4 lbf/in^2)

Antifreeze mixtures:

	Antifreeze	Water
Protection to −23°C (−9°F)	35%	65%
Protection to −40°C (−40°F)	50%	50%

Fuel and exhaust system
Air filter element type:
1390 cc (E6J) engine	Champion W145
1397 cc (C1J) engine	Champion W115
1721 cc (F2N) engine	Champion W190

Idle speed:
1390 cc (E6J) engine	750 ± 50 rpm
1397 cc (C1J) engine	700 ± 50 rpm
1721 cc (F2N) engine	800 ± 50 rpm
Idle mixture CO content	1.5 ± 0.5 %
Fuel octane requirement	95 RON unleaded or 97 RON leaded

Ignition system – general
Firing order	1–3–4–2
Location of No 1 cylinder	Flywheel end

Transistor-assisted contact breaker ignition system – 1397 cc (C1J) engine
Contact breaker points gap	0.4 mm
Dwell angle	57° ± 3°

Ignition timing:
Static	5° ± 2° BTDC

Dynamic at idling speed:
Vacuum hose disconnected	5° ± 2° BTDC
Vacuum hose connected	10° ± 1° BTDC

Spark plugs:
Type	Champion N9YCC or N281YC
Electrode gap	0.8 mm

Electronic ignition system – 1390 cc (E6J) and 1721 cc (F2N) engines

Ignition timing .... Non-adjustable, computer controlled
Spark plugs:
    Type:
        1390 cc (E6J) engine .... Champion C9YCC or C9YC
        1721 cc (F2N) engine .... Champion N7YCC or N279YC
    Electrode gap .... 0.8 mm

Braking system

Minimum front brake disc pad thickness (including backplate) .... 6.0 mm
Minimum rear brake disc pad thickness (including backplate) .... 6.0 mm
Minimum rear brake shoe lining thickness (including shoe)..................... 2.5 mm

Suspension and steering

Power-assisted steering pump drivebelt deflection .... See alternator drivebelt deflection
Tyre pressures (cold):   **Front**   **Rear**
    Manual transmission models.................................... 2.0 bar (29 lbf/in^2)   2.2 bar (32 lbf/in^2)
    Automatic transmission models .... 2.1 bar (31 lbf/in^2)   2.2 bar (32 lbf/in^2)

Electrical system

Alternator drivebelt deflection (see text – Section 10):
    1390 cc (E6J) engine .... 3 mm
    1397 cc (C1J) engine .... 4 mm
    1721 cc (F2N) engine.. 3.5 mm
Wiper blade type:
    Windscreen .... Champion X-5103
    Tailgate... Champion X-4503

Torque wrench settings

	Nm	lbf ft
Spark plugs	24 to 30	18 to 22
Automatic transmission sump........................	6	4
Automatic transmission gauze filter...............	9	7

Lubricants, fluids and capacities

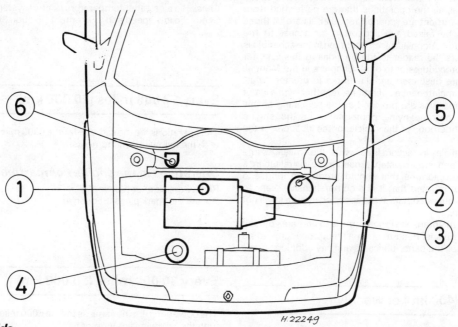

H.22249

Lubricants and fluids

Component or system	Lubricant type/specification	Duckhams recommendation
1 Engine	Multigrade engine oil, viscosity 15W/40 to 20W/40, or 15W/50 to 20W/50	Duckhams QXR or Hypergrade
2 Manual gearbox	TRANSELF TRX 80W	–
3 Automatic transmission	Dexron type ATF	Duckhams Uni-Matic or D-Matic
4 Power steering reservoir	Dexron type ATF	Duckhams Uni-Matic or D-Matic
5 Cooling system	Ethylene-glycol based antifreeze	Duckhams Universal Antifreeze and Summer Coolant
6 Brake fluid reservoir	Hydraulic fluid to SAE J1703, DOT 3, or DOT 4	Duckhams Universal Brake and Clutch Fluid

Capacities

Engine oil
Capacity (excluding filter):

1390 cc (E6J) engine	3.5 litres
1397 cc (C1J) engine	3.0 litres
1721 cc (F2N) engine..........	4.7 litres

Difference between MAX and MIN dipstick marks:

1390 cc (E6J) engine	1.5 litres
1397 cc (C1J) engine	1.0 litre
1721 cc (F2N) engine..........	2.0 litres

Cooling system

1390 cc (E6J) engine.................	5.2 litres
1397 cc (C1J) engine.................	5.4 litres
1721 cc (F2N) engine	6.0 litres

Fuel tank .... 55.0 litres

Manual gearbox
Four-speed:

JB0 and JB2	3.25 litres
JB4....................................	2.75 litres

Five-speed:

JB1 and JB3	3.40 litres
JB5....................................	2.90 litres

Automatic transmission

Total capacity	4.5 litres
Drain and refill	2.0 litres

Power-assisted steering reservoir .... 1.1 litres

Maintenance schedule

Introduction

This Chapter is designed to help the DIY owner maintain the Renault 19 with the goals of maximum economy, safety, reliability and performance in mind.

On the following pages is a master maintenance schedule, listing the servicing requirements, and the intervals at which they should be carried out as recommended by the manufacturers. The operations are listed in the order in which the work can be most conveniently undertaken. For example, all the operations that are performed from within the engine compartment are grouped together, as are all those that require the car to be raised and supported for access to the suspension and underbody. Alongside each operation in the schedule is a reference which directs the reader to the Sections in this Chapter covering maintenance procedures or to other Chapters in the Manual, where the operations are described and illustrated in greater detail. Specifications for all the maintenance operations, together with a list of lubricants, fluids and capacities are provided at the beginning of this Chapter. Refer to the accompanying photographs of the engine compartment and the underbody of the vehicle for the locations of the various components.

Servicing your vehicle in accordance with the mileage/time maintenance schedule and step-by-step procedures will result in a planned maintenance programme that should produce a long and reliable service life. Bear in mind that it is a comprehensive plan, so maintaining some items but not others at the specified intervals will not produce the same results.

The first step in this maintenance programme is to prepare yourself before the actual work begins. Read through all the procedures to be undertaken then obtain all the parts, lubricants and any additional tools needed.

Every 250 miles (400 km) or weekly

Operations internal and external

Visually examine the tyres for tread depth, and wear or damage (Section 8)
Check, and if necessary adjust, the tyre pressures (Section 8)

Operations in the engine compartment

Check the engine oil level (Section 1)
Check the engine coolant level (Section 2)
Check the screen washer fluid level (Section 10)
Check the battery electrolyte level (Section 10)

Every 6000 miles (10 000 km)

In addition to all the items listed above, carry out the following:

Operations internal and external

Check the operation of all lights, indicators, instruments and windscreen washer system(s) (Section 10)
Check the operation of the heating/air conditioning system (Section 2)
Check and adjust the headlight beam alignment (Section 10)

Operations with the car raised and supported

Renew the engine oil (Section 1)
Renew the oil filter* (Section 1)
Check the manual gearbox oil level (Section 5)
Check the front brake disc pads for wear (Section 7)
Visually examine the underbody, wheelarches and body panels for damage (Section 9)
Check the exhaust system for condition, leakage and security (Section 3)
Check the driveshafts and rubber gaiters for damage and leakage (Section 6)

*At first 6000 miles 10 000 km) then at every 12 000 miles (20 000 km) thereafter

Operations in the engine compartment

Check for oil and coolant leaks (Sections 1 and 2)
Check the brake fluid level (Section 7)
Check the power-assisted steering fluid level (Section 8)
Check the condition and tension of all drivebelts (Section 10)
Check the automatic transmission fluid level (Section 5)
Check, and if necessary renew, the spark plugs (Section 4)
Check the ignition timing – 1397 cc (C1J) engine (Section 4)
Check the air cleaner temperature control system (Section 3)
Check the idle speed and CO content (Section 3)

Every 12 000 miles (20 000 km)

The operations are the same as for the 6000 mile (10 000 km) service but with the following amendments:

Operations in the engine compartment

Renew the air filter (Section 3)
Renew the spark plugs (Section 4)

Every 30 000 miles (50 000 km)

The operations are the same as for the 6000 mile (10 000 km) service but with the following amendments:

Operations internal and external

Check and if necessary adjust the front wheel alignment (Chapter 10)

Operations with the car raised and supported

Renew the automatic transmission fluid and the gauze filter (Section 5)
Check the rear brake shoe linings or disc pads for wear (Section 7)
Renew the brake hydraulic fluid (Section 7)
Adjust the handbrake (Section 7)

Operations in the engine compartment

Renew the fuel filter (Section 3)

Every 72 000 miles (120 000 km)

Operations in the engine compartment

Renew the timing belt (Chapter 2)

Every 24 months

Operations in the engine compartment

Drain, flush and refill the cooling system, and renew the antifreeze (Section 5)

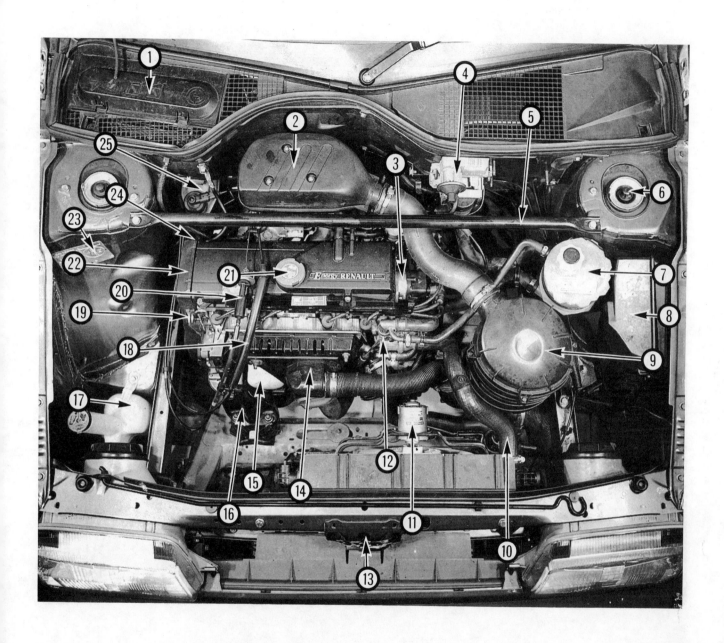

View of the engine compartment (Renault 19 TSE Hatchback – 1390 cc) (Sec 1)

1 Battery compartment
2 Air inlet duct on carburettor
3 Distributor and cap
4 Electronic ignition computer control unit
5 Strengthening bar
6 Front suspension strut upper mounting
7 Cooling system expansion tank
8 Cover for main engine wiring connectors, electric fan relay, and inlet manifold heating relay

9 Air cleaner assembly
10 Radiator top hose
11 Electric cooling fan
12 Engine oil level dipstick
13 Bonnet lock
14 Hot air shroud on exhaust manifold
15 Oil filter
16 Right-hand front engine mounting
17 Windscreen washer fluid reservoir

18 Choke cable
19 Engine lifting eye
20 Accelerator cable
21 Engine oil filler cap
22 Alternator (hidden from view)
23 Vehicle identification plate
24 Timing belt cover
25 Brake fluid reservoir

View of the front underside (Renault 19 TSE Hatchback – 1390 cc) (Sec 1)

1 Front towing eyes	7 Transmission/gearbox	13 Exhaust intermediate pipe and
2 Subframe	8 Front suspension lower arm	expansion chamber
3 Driveshaft	9 Steering track rod	14 Steering gear
4 Engine oil drain plug	10 Front anti-roll bar	15 Fuel supply and return pipes
5 Exhaust front downpipe	11 Hydraulic brake lines	16 Front subframe mounting
6 Transmission drain plug	12 Gearshift rod	

View of the rear underside (Renault 19 TSE Hatchback – 1390 cc) (Sec 1)

1 Exhaust tailpipe and silencer
2 Spare wheel
3 Fuel tank
4 Filler neck

5 Rear shock absorber
6 Rear anti-roll bar
7 Rear axle
8 Fuel supply and return pipes

9 Exhaust intermediate pipe and
   expansion chamber
10 Handbrake cables

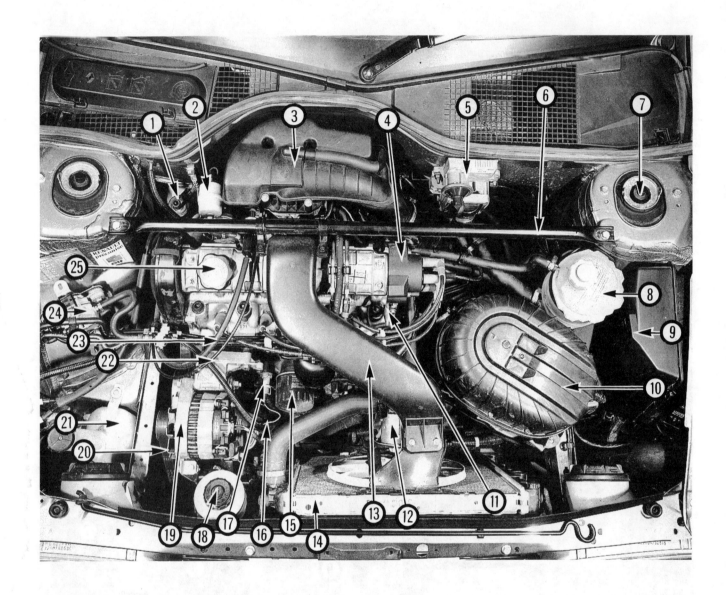

View of the engine compartment (Renault 19 Chamade TXE – 1721 cc) (Sec 1)

1   Brake fluid reservoir
2   Fuel filter
3   Air inlet duct on the carburettor
4   Distributor
5   Electronic ignition computer control unit
6   Strengthening bar
7   Front suspension strut upper mounting
8   Cooling system expansion tank
9   Cover for main engine wiring connectors, electric fan relay, and inlet manifold heating relay
10 Air cleaner assembly
11 Engine lifting eye
12 Electric cooling fan
13 Carburettor cooling air duct
14 Radiator
15 Oil filter
16 Engine oil level dipstick
17 Oil pressure switch
18 Power-assisted steering hydraulic fluid reservoir
19 Alternator
20 Alternator/water pump drivebelt
21 Windscreen washer fluid reservoir
22 Choke cable
23 Accelerator cable
24 Fuel flowmeter
25 Engine oil filler cap
26 Battery compartment

View of the front underside (Renault 19 Chamade TXE – 1721 cc) (Sec 1)

1 Front suspension lower arm	5 Hydraulic brake lines	9 Driveshaft
2 Gearshift rod	6 Exhaust intermediate pipe	10 Engine oil drain plug
3 Steering track rod	7 Exhaust front downpipe	11 Transmission drain plug
4 Front subframe mounting	8 Front anti-roll bar	12 Power-assisted steering cooling pipes

View of the rear underside (Renault 19 Chamade TXE – 1721 cc) (Sec 1)

1 Fuel filler neck	5 Handbrake cables	9 Rear shock absorber
2 Fuel tank	6 Exhaust intermediate pipe and silencer	10 Exhaust tailpipe and silencer
3 Brake hydraulic pipes	7 Rear axle side bearing bracket	11 Spare wheel
4 Fuel supply and return hoses	8 Rear axle	

Maintenance procedures

1 Engine

Engine oil level check

1 The engine oil level is checked with a dipstick that extends through a tube and into the sump at the bottom of the engine. The dipstick is located towards the rear left-hand side of the engine (photo). On models equipped with an oil level gauge, the check can be made by switching on the ignition – the upper and lower limits on the gauge correspond to the upper and lower marks on the dipstick.

2 The oil level should be checked with the vehicle standing on level ground and before it is driven, or at least 5 minutes after the engine has been switched off. If the oil is checked immediately after driving the vehicle, some of the oil will remain in the upper engine components and oil galleries, resulting in an inaccurate reading on the dipstick.

3 Withdraw the dipstick from the tube and wipe all the oil from the end with a clean rag or paper towel. Insert the clean dipstick back into the tube as far as it will go, then withdraw it once more. Check that the oil level is between the upper (MAX) and lower (MIN) marks/notches on the dipstick. If the level is towards the lower (MIN) mark/notch, unscrew the oil filler cap on the front of the valve cover and add fresh oil until the level is on the upper (MAX) mark/notch (photos). Note that the difference between the minimum and maximum marks/notches on the dipstick corresponds to 1 litre on C-type engines, 1.5 litres on E-type engines, and 2 litres on F-type engines.

4 Always maintain the level between the two dipstick marks/notches. If the level is allowed to fall below the lower mark/notch, oil starvation may result which could lead to severe engine damage. If the engine is overfilled by adding too much oil, this may result in oil fouled spark plugs, oil leaks or oil seal failures.

5 An oil can spout or funnel may help to reduce spillage when adding oil to the engine. Always use the correct grade and type of oil as shown in 'Lubricants, fluids and capacities'.

Engine oil and filter renewal

6 Frequent oil and filter changes are the most important preventative maintenance procedures that can be undertaken by the DIY owner. As engine oil ages, it becomes diluted and contaminated, which leads to premature engine wear.

7 Before starting this procedure, gather together all the necessary tools and materials (photo). Also make sure that you have plenty of clean rags and newspapers handy to mop up any spills. Ideally, the engine oil should be warm as it will drain better and more built-up sludge will be removed with it. Take care, however, not to touch the exhaust or any other hot parts of the engine when working under the vehicle. To avoid any possibility of scalding, and to protect yourself from possible skin irritants and other harmful contaminants in used engine oils, it is advisable to wear rubber gloves when carrying out this work. Access to the underside of the vehicle will be greatly improved if it can be raised on a lift, driven onto ramps or jacked up and supported on axle stands. Whichever method is chosen, the sump drain plug should be at the lowest point to enable the oil to drain fully. This requires the car to be as level as possible since the drain plug is located in the centre of the sump. Access to the drain plug is gained by removing a cover in the engine splash shield, so this should also be considered when raising the car to make sure that the oil will not pour onto the splash shield.

8 Remove the access cover then position a suitable container beneath the hole. Clean the drain plug and the area around it, then slacken it half a turn using a special drain plug key (photo). If possible, try to keep the plug pressed into the sump while unscrewing it by hand the last couple of turns. As the plug releases from the threads, move it away sharply so the stream of oil issuing from the sump runs into the container, not up your sleeve!

9 Allow some time for the old oil to drain, noting that it may be necessary to reposition the container as the oil flow slows to a trickle.

10 After all the oil has drained, wipe off the drain plug with a clean rag and renew its sealing washer. Clean the area around the drain plug

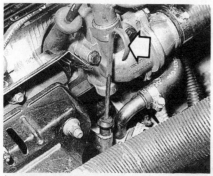

1.1 Engine oil level dipstick (arrowed) on the 1390 cc (E6J) engine

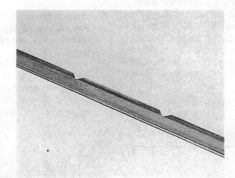

1.3A Engine oil level dipstick MIN and MAX level notches

1.3B Oil is added through the filler on the front of the valve cover

1.7 Tools necessary for the engine oil change and filter renewal

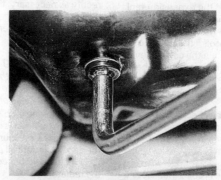

1.8 Using the special drain plug key to unscrew the sump drain plug on the 1390 cc (E6J) engine

1.14 Applying a light coating of clean oil to the sealing ring before fitting the new oil filter

opening then refit and tighten the plug to the specified torque setting (where available).

11   If applicable at this service, move the container into position under the oil filter, located on the left-hand side of the cylinder block.

12   Using an oil filter removal tool, slacken the filter initially. Loosely wrap some rags around the oil filter, then unscrew it and immediately position it with its open end uppermost to prevent further spillage of oil. Remove the oil filter from the engine compartment and empty the oil into the container.

13   Use a clean rag to remove all oil, dirt and sludge from the filter sealing area on the engine. Check the old filter to make sure that the rubber sealing ring hasn't stuck to the engine. If it has, carefully remove it.

14   Apply a light coating of clean oil to the sealing ring on the new filter then screw it into position on the engine (photo). Tighten the filter firmly by hand only, do not use any tools. Wipe clean the exterior of the oil filter.

15   Remove the old oil and all tools from under the car then if applicable, lower the car to the ground.

16   Unscrew the oil filler cap on the valve cover and fill the engine with the specified quantity and grade of oil, as described earlier in this Section. Pour the oil in slowly otherwise it may overflow from the top of the valve cover. Check that the oil level is up to the maximum mark on the dipstick.

17   Start the engine and run it for a few minutes while checking for leaks around the oil filter seal and the sump drain plug.

18   Switch off the engine and wait a few minutes for the oil to settle in the sump once more. With the new oil circulated and the filter now completely full, recheck the level on the dipstick and add more oil if necessary.

19   Dispose of the used engine oil safely with reference to *'General repair procedures'* in the preliminary Sections of this Manual.

General engine checks

20   Visually inspect the engine joint faces, gaskets and seals for any signs of water or oil leaks. Pay particular attention to the areas around the cylinder head gasket joint, valve cover joint, sump joint, and oil filter. Bear in mind that over a period of time some very slight seepage from these areas is to be expected but what you are really looking for is any indication of a serious leak. Should a leak be found, renew the offending gasket or oil seal by referring to the appropriate Chapters in this Manual.

21   Also check the security and condition of all the engine related pipes and hoses. Ensure that all cable ties or securing clips are in place and in good condition. Clips which are broken or missing can lead to chafing of the hoses, pipes or wiring which could cause more serious problems in the future.

2   Cooling, heating and ventilation systems

Coolant level check

Warning: *DO NOT attempt to remove the expansion tank pressure cap when the engine is hot, as there is a very great risk of scalding*

1   All vehicles covered by this manual are equipped with a pressurised cooling system. An expansion tank is located on the left-hand side of the engine compartment. On the C1J (1397 cc) engine the expansion tank has only one hose which is connected directly to the radiator. As engine temperature increases, the coolant expands and travels through the hose to the expansion tank. As the engine cools, the coolant is automatically drawn back into the system to maintain the correct level. On the E6J (1390 cc) and F2N (1721 cc) engines the expansion tank has a continual flow of coolant in order to purge air from the cooling system. Hoses are connected to the tank from the top of the cylinder head and from the tank to the water pump inlet.

2   The coolant level in the expansion tank should be checked regularly. The level in the tank varies with the temperature of the engine. When the engine is cold, the coolant level should be up to the maximum (MAX) level mark on the side of the tank. When the engine is hot, the level will be slightly above the mark.

3   If topping up is necessary, wait until the engine is cold, then slowly unscrew the pressure cap on the expansion tank. Allow any remaining pressure to escape then fully unscrew the cap.

4   Add a mixture of water and antifreeze (see below) through the

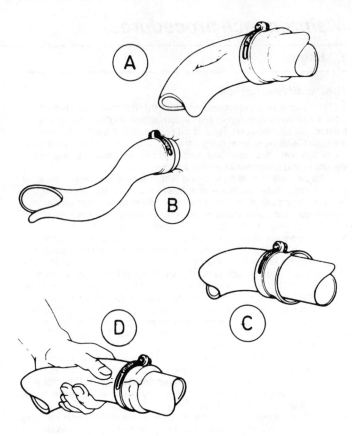

Fig. 1.1 Coolant hose inspection (Sec 2)

A   Check hose for chafed or burned areas; these may lead to sudden and costly failure

B   A soft hose indicates inside deterioration, leading to contamination of the cooling system and clogging of the radiator

C   A hardened hose can fail at any time; tightening the clamps will not seal the joint or prevent leaks

D   A swollen hose or one with oil-soaked ends indicates contamination from oil or grease. Cracks and breaks can be easily seen by squeezing the hose

expansion tank filler neck until the coolant is up to the maximum (MAX) level mark. Refit and tighten the pressure cap.

5   With a sealed type cooling system, the addition of coolant should only be necessary at very infrequent intervals. If frequent topping up is required, it is likely there is a leak in the system. Check the radiator, all hoses and joint faces for any sign of staining or actual wetness, and rectify as necessary. If no leaks can be found, it is advisable to have the pressure cap and the entire system pressure tested by a dealer or suitably equipped garage as this will often show up a small leak not previously visible.

Coolant draining

Warning: *Wait until the engine is cold before starting this procedure. Do not allow antifreeze to come in contact with your skin or painted surfaces of the vehicle. Rinse off spills immediately with plenty of water*

6   If the engine is cold, unscrew and remove the pressure cap from the expansion tank. If it is not possible to wait until the engine is cold, place a cloth over the pressure cap of the expansion tank and slowly unscrew the cap. Wait until all pressure has escaped, then remove the cap.

7   Place a suitable container beneath the bottom hose connection to the radiator.

8   Loosen the clip, then disconnect the bottom hose and allow the coolant to drain into the container.

9   Move the container beneath the cylinder block drain plug. On the

2.18A Open the coolant bleed screw located in the top hose on the 1390 cc (E6J) engine

2.18B Coolant bleed screw (arrowed) located in the top right-hand side of the radiator on the 1390 cc (E6J) engine

2.26 Adding antifreeze to the cooling system

C1J (1397 cc) engine the drain plug is located on the front right-hand side of the cylinder block. On the E6J (1390 cc) and F2N (1721 cc) engines it is located on the rear right-hand side of the cylinder block.

10 Unscrew the plug and drain the coolant into the container.

11 If the system needs to be flushed after draining, refer to the following paragraphs, otherwise refit the drain plug and secure the bottom hose to the radiator. Use a new hose clip if necessary.

System flushing

12 With time the cooling system may gradually lose its efficiency if the radiator matrix becomes choked with rust and scale deposits. If this is the case, the system must be flushed as follows. First drain the coolant as already described.

13 Loosen the clip and disconnect the top hose from the radiator. Insert a garden hose in the radiator top hose connection stub and allow the water to circulate through the radiator until it runs clear from the bottom outlet.

14 To flush the engine and the remainder of the system, disconnect the top hose at the water pump on the 1397 cc engine, or remove the thermostat as described in Chapter 3 on the 1390 cc and 1721 cc engines. Insert the garden hose and allow the water to circulate through the engine until it runs clear from the bottom hose.

15 In severe cases of contamination the radiator should be reverse-flushed. To do this, first remove it from the car, as described in Chapter 3, invert it and insert a hose in the bottom outlet. Continue flushing until clear water runs from the top hose outlet.

16 If, after a reasonable period, the water still does not run clear, the radiator should be flushed with a good proprietary cleaning system such as Holts Radflush or Holts Speedflush. The regular renewal of corrosion inhibiting antifreeze should prevent severe contamination of the system. Note that as the radiator is of aluminium it is important not to use caustic soda or alkaline compounds to clean it.

Coolant filling

17 Refit the cylinder block drain plug, radiator bottom hose and any other hoses removed if the system has just been flushed.

18 Open the coolant bleed screws. On the 1397 cc engine there are two on the heater supply and return hoses and one in the top hose next to the thermostat. On the 1390 cc engine there is one in the top hose, and one on the top right-hand side of the radiator (photos). On the 1721 cc engine there is only one, situated on the top left-hand side of the radiator.

19 Pour the appropriate mixture of water and antifreeze into the expansion tank, and close each bleed screw in turn as soon as a continuous flow of bubble-free coolant can be seen flowing from it. Continue to fill the expansion tank until the coolant is at the maximum level.

20 Start the engine and run it at 1500 rpm (ie a fast idle speed) for approximately 4 minutes. Keep the expansion tank topped up to the maximum level during this period.

21 Refit the pressure cap to the expansion tank and run the engine at 1500 rpm for approximately 10 minutes until the electric cooling fan cuts in. During this period the coolant will circulate around the engine and any remaining air will be purged to the expansion tank.

22 Switch off the engine and allow it to cool, then check the coolant level as described earlier and top up if necessary.

Antifreeze mixture

23 The antifreeze should always be renewed at the specified intervals. This is necessary not only to maintain the antifreeze properties, but also to prevent corrosion which would otherwise occur as the corrosion inhibitors become progressively less effective.

24 Always use an ethylene-glycol based antifreeze which is suitable for use in mixed metal cooling systems. The percentage quantity of antifreeze and levels of protection afforded are indicated in the Specifications.

25 Before adding antifreeze the cooling system should be completely drained, preferably flushed, and all hoses checked for condition and security.

26 After filling with the correct water/antifreeze mixture, a label should be attached to the radiator or expansion tank stating the type and concentration of antifreeze used and the date installed. Any subsequent topping up should be made with the same type and concentration of antifreeze (photo).

27 Do not use engine antifreeze in the screen washer system, as it will cause damage to the vehicle paintwork. A screen wash such as Turtle Wax High Tech Screen Wash should be added to the washer system in the recommended quantities.

General cooling system checks

28 The engine should be cold for the cooling system checks, so perform the following procedure before driving the vehicle or after the engine has been switched off for at least three hours.

29 Remove the expansion tank filler cap (see above) and clean it thoroughly inside and out with a rag. Also clean the filler neck on the expansion tank. The presence of rust or corrosion in the filler neck indicates that the coolant should be changed. The coolant inside the expansion tank should be relatively clean and transparent. If it is rust coloured, drain and flush the system and refill with a fresh coolant mixture.

30 Carefully check the radiator hoses and heater hoses along their entire length. Renew any hose which is cracked, swollen or deteriorated. Cracks will show up better if the hose is squeezed. Pay close attention to the hose clips that secure the hoses to the cooling system components. Hose clips can pinch and puncture hoses, resulting in cooling system leaks. If wire type hose clips are used, it may be a good idea to replace them with screw-type clips.

31 Inspect all the cooling system components (hoses, joint faces etc) for leaks. A leak in the cooling system will usually show up as white or rust-coloured deposits on the area adjoining the leak. Where any problems of this nature are found on system components, renew the component or gasket with reference to Chapter 3.

32 Clean the front of the radiator with a soft brush to remove all insects, leaves etc imbedded in the radiator fins. Be extremely careful not to damage the radiator fins or cut your fingers on them.

Heating/air conditioning system check

33 Check that the heating system and, where fitted, the air conditioning system operates correctly.

34 During the winter period it is advisable to run the air conditioning system occasionally in order to ensure correct functioning of the compressor.

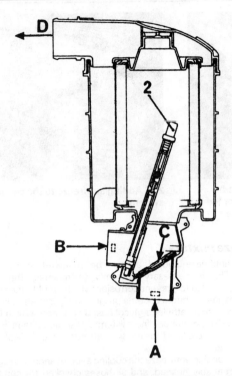

Fig. 1.2 Air cleaner temperature control system fitted to the 1390 cc (E6J) engine (Sec 3)

A   Cold air intake

B   Hot air intake

C   Flap

D   Air to the carburettor

2   Wax-controlled thermostatic valve

3   Fuel and exhaust systems

Warning: *Certain procedures in this Section require the removal of fuel lines and connections which may result in some fuel spillage. Before carrying out any operation on the fuel system refer to the precautions given in Safety first! at the beginning of this Manual and follow them implicitly. Petrol is a highly dangerous and volatile liquid and the precautions necessary when handling it cannot be overstressed*

Air cleaner filter element renewal

1   On the 1390 cc (E6J) engine remove the four screws and lift the cover from the air cleaner (photo).

2   On the 1397 cc (C1J) engine unscrew the central wing nut, then release the spring clips and lift the cover from the air cleaner.

3   On the 1721 cc (F2N) engine remove the nine screws, including the central one, and lift the cover from the air cleaner (photos).

4   Remove the filter element from inside the air cleaner body (photos).

5   Clean the inside of the air cleaner body and fit a new filter element.

6   Refit the top cover and secure with the screws or wing nut and spring clips.

Air cleaner temperature control system check

7   In order for the engine to operate efficiently, the temperature of the air entering the inlet system must be controlled within certain limits.

8   The air cleaner has two sources of air, one direct from the outside of the engine compartment, and the other from a shroud on the exhaust manifold. A wax-controlled thermostatic valve controls a flap inside the air cleaner inlet (photos). When the ambient air temperature is below the predetermined level the flap directs air from the exhaust manifold shroud, and as the temperature of the incoming air rises the flap opens to admit more air from outside the car until eventually it is fully open.

9   The temperature control system fitted to each type of engine is shown in Figs. 1.2, 1.3 and 1.4.

10   To test the system, remove the air cleaner body as described in

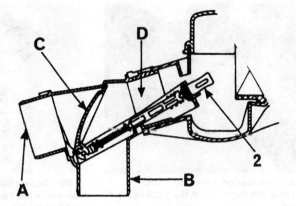

Fig. 1.3 Air cleaner temperature control system fitted to the 1397 cc (C1J) engine (Sec 3)

A   Cold air intake

B   Hot air intake

C   Flap

D   Air to the carburettor

2   Wax-controlled thermostatic valve

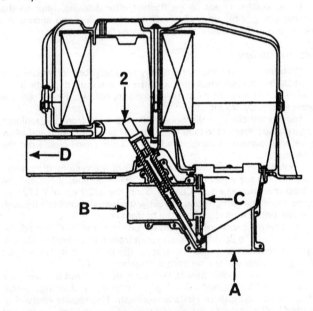

Fig. 1.4 Air cleaner temperature control system fitted to the 1721 cc (F2N) engine (Sec 3)

A   Cold air intake

B   Hot air intake

C   Flap

D   Air to the carburettor

2   Wax-controlled thermostatic valve

Chapter 4, detach the temperature control unit (photo) and immerse it in water at a temperature of 26°C. After a maximum of 5 minutes the flap should shut off the cold air inlet. Now increase the temperature of the water to 36°C and check that the flap shuts off the hot air inlet. If the flap does not operate correctly check that it is not seized. Apart from this there is no adjustment possible and the unit should be renewed if faulty.

Fuel filter renewal

11   An in-line fuel filter is provided in the fuel pump outlet line (photo). To remove it, release the clips (if fitted) and pull the filter from the hoses.

12   Fit the new filter making sure that the fuel direction arrow is pointing away from the fuel pump side. If crimped type clips were used to secure the hoses, these should be replaced with worm-drive alternatives.

Idle speed and CO content adjustment

13   The procedure for idle speed and CO content adjustment is the

3.1 Removing the air cleaner cover on the 1390 cc (E6J) engine

3.3A Remove the screws ...

3.3B ... and lift the cover from the air cleaner on the 1721 cc (F2N) engine

3.4A Removing the air cleaner filter element on the 1390 cc (E6J) engine

3.4B Removing the air cleaner filter element on the 1721 cc (F2N) engine

3.8A 1721 cc (F2N) engine air cleaner temperature control flap ...

3.8B ... and wax thermostat

3.10 Air cleaner temperature control unit on the 1390 cc (E6J) engine

same on each of the three carburettor types that may be fitted. Refer to the accompanying illustrations and identify the carburettor type fitted and the adjustment screw locations.

14 Before carrying out the following adjustments, ensure that the spark plugs are in good condition and correctly gapped. On the 1397 cc (C1J) engine, also ensure that the contact breaker points and ignition timing settings are correct.

15 Make sure that all electrical components are switched off during the following procedure. If the electric cooling fan operates, wait until it has stopped before continuing.

16 Connect a tachometer to the engine in accordance with the manufacturer's instructions. The use of an exhaust gas analyser (CO meter) is also recommended to obtain an accurate setting.

17 Remove the tamperproof cap (where fitted) from the mixture adjustment screw by hooking it out with a scriber or small screwdriver.

18 Run the engine at a fast idling speed until it reaches normal operating temperature. Increase the engine speed to 2000 rpm for 30 seconds and repeat this at three minute intervals during the adjustment procedure. This will ensure that any excess fuel is cleared from the inlet manifold.

19 With the engine idling, turn the idle speed screw until the engine is idling at the specified speed (photos).

20 Turn the mixture adjustment screw clockwise to weaken the mixture or anti-clockwise to richen it until the CO reading is as given in the Specifications. If a CO meter is not being used, weaken the mixture as described, then richen it until the maximum engine speed is obtained, consistent with even running.

21 If necessary, re-adjust the idling speed then check the CO reading again. Repeat as necessary until both the idling speed and CO reading are correct.

22 Where required by law, fit a new tamperproof cap to the mixture adjustment screw.

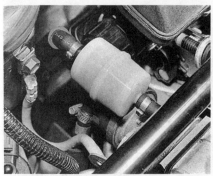

3.11 In-line fuel filter on the 1721 cc (F2N) engine

3.19A Adjusting the idle speed on the 1390 cc (E6J) engine

3.19B Idle speed adjustment screw (arrowed) on the 1721 cc (F2N) engine

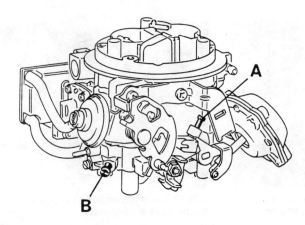

Fig. 1.5 Idle speed (A) and mixture (B) adjustment screw locations on the 1390 cc (E6J) engine (Sec 3)

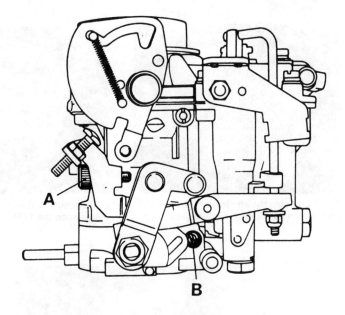

Fig. 1.6 Idle speed (A) and mixture (B) adjustment screw locations on the 1397 cc (C1J) engine (Sec 3)

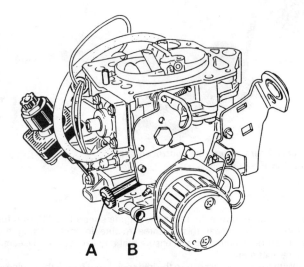

Fig. 1.7 Idle speed (A) and mixture (B) adjustment screw locations on the 1721 cc (F2N) engine (Sec 3)

General fuel system checks

23   The fuel system is most easily checked with the vehicle raised on a hoist or suitably supported on axle stands so the components underneath are readily visible and accessible.

24   If the smell of petrol is noticed while driving or after the vehicle has been parked in the sun, the system should be thoroughly inspected immediately.

25   Remove the petrol tank filler cap and check for damage, corrosion and an unbroken sealing imprint on the gasket. Renew the cap if necessary.

26   With the vehicle raised, inspect the petrol tank and filler neck for punctures, cracks and other damage. The connection between the filler neck and tank is especially critical. Sometimes a rubber filler neck or connecting hose will leak due to loose retaining clamps or deteriorated rubber.

27   Carefully check all rubber hoses and metal fuel lines leading away from the petrol tank. Check for loose connections, deteriorated hoses, crimped lines and other damage. Pay particular attention the vent pipes and hoses which often loop up around the filler neck and can become blocked or crimped. Follow the lines to the front of the vehicle, carefully inspecting them all the way. Renew damaged sections as necessary.

28   From within the engine compartment, check the security of all fuel hose attachments and inspect the fuel hoses and vacuum hoses for kinks, chafing and deterioration.

29   Check the operation of the throttle linkage and lubricate the linkage components with a few drops of light oil.

Exhaust system check

30   With the engine cold (at least an hour after the vehicle has been driven), check the complete exhaust system from the engine to the end of the tailpipe. Ideally the inspection should be carried out with the

4.1 Removing the rotor arm

4.4 Contact breaker points adjusting nut (A) and baseplate retaining screws (B)

4.5 Disengage the adjustment rod from the fixed contact and withdraw the rod and spring

vehicle on a hoist to permit unrestricted access, but if a hoist is not available raise and support the vehicle safely on axle stands.

31   Check the exhaust pipes and connections for evidence of leaks, severe corrosion and damage. Make sure that all brackets and mountings are in good condition and tight. Leakage at any of the joints or in other parts of the system will usually show up as a black sooty stain in the vicinity of the leak. Holts Flexiwrap and Holts Gun Gum exhaust repair systems can be used for effective repairs to exhaust pipes and silencer boxes, including ends and bends. Holts Flexiwrap is an MOT approved permanent exhaust repair. Holts Firegum is suitable for the assembly of all exhaust system joints.

32   Rattles and other noises can often be traced to the exhaust system, especially the brackets and mountings. Try to move the pipes and silencers. If the components can come into contact with the body or suspension parts, secure the system with new mountings or if possible, separate the joints and twist the pipes as necessary to provide additional clearance.

33   Run the engine at idling speed then temporarily place a cloth rag over the rear end of the exhaust pipe and listen for any escape of exhaust gases that would indicate a leak.

34   On completion lower the car to the ground.

35   The inside of the exhaust tailpipe can be an indication of the running condition of the engine. The exhaust deposits here are an indication of the engine's state-of-tune. If the pipe is black and sooty, the engine is in need of a tune-up, including a thorough fuel system inspection and adjustment.

4   Ignition system

Warning: *Voltages produced by an electronic ignition system are considerably higher than those produced by conventional systems. Extreme care must be taken when working on the system with the ignition switched on. Persons with surgically-implanted cardiac pacemaker devices should keep well clear of the ignition circuits, components and test equipment*

Contact breaker points and condenser check, adjustment and renewal –   1397 cc (C1J) engine

1   Release the two spring clips and lift off the distributor cap. Pull the rotor arm off the shaft and remove the plastic shield (photo).

2   With the ignition switched off, use a screwdriver to open the contact breaker points then visually check the points surfaces for pitting, roughness and discoloration. If the points have been arcing, there will be a build-up of metal on the moving contact and a corresponding hole in the fixed contact; if this is the case, the points should be renewed.

3   Another method of checking the contact breaker points is by using a test meter available from most car accessory shops. If necessary, rotate the engine until the points are fully shut then connect the meter between the distributor LT wiring terminal and earth, and read off the condition of the points.

4   To remove the points, first unscrew the adjusting nut on the side of the distributor body and then unscrew the two baseplate retaining screws. Lift off the support bracket (photo).

5   Disengage the end of the adjustment rod from the fixed contact and slide the rod and spring out of the distributor body (photo).

6   Prise out the small plug and then remove the retaining clip, noting that the hole in the clip is uppermost (photos).

7   Slacken the LT terminal nut and detach the lead (photo).

8   Remove the spring retaining clip from the top of the moving contact pivot post and take off the fibre insulating washer (photo).

9   Ease the spring blade away from its nylon support and lift the moving contact upwards and off the pivot post (photo).

10   Unscrew the retaining screw and remove the fixed contact from the baseplate (photo).

11   The purpose of the condenser, located externally on the side of the distributor body, is to ensure that when the contact breaker points open, there is no sparking across them, which would cause wear of their faces and prevent the rapid collapse of the magnetic field in the coil. Failure of the condenser would cause a reduction in coil HT voltage and ultimately lead to engine misfire.

12   If the engine becomes very difficult to start, or begins to miss after several miles of running, and the contact breaker points show signs of

4.6A Prise out the small plastic plug ...

4.6B ... to gain access to the retaining clip (arrowed) ...

4.6C ... which can then be removed using pliers. Note the fitted position of the clip

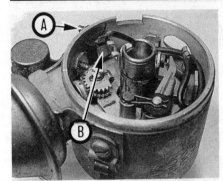

4.7 Slacken the LT terminal nut (A) and detach the lead (B) from the connector

4.8 Remove the spring retaining clip and fibre washer from the pivot post

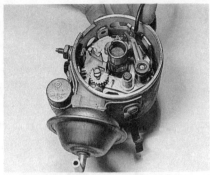

4.9 Ease the spring blade off its support and withdraw the moving contact from the pivot post

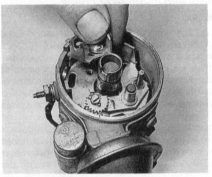

4.10 Unscrew the retaining screw and remove the fixed contact

4.18 Measure the points gap with a feeler blade and adjust if necessary by turning nut (A)

4.44 Checking the ignition timing with a stroboscopic timing light

excessive burning, the condition of the condenser must be suspect. A further test can be made by separating the points by hand with the ignition switched on. If this is accompanied by a strong bright flash, it is indicative that the condenser has failed.

13   Without special test equipment, the only sure way to diagnose condenser trouble is to substitute a suspect unit with a new one and note if there is any improvement.

14   To remove the condenser, unscrew the nut at the LT terminal post and slip off the lead. Unscrew the condenser retaining screw and remove the unit from the side of the distributor body.

15   Refitting of the condenser is a reversal of the removal procedure.

16   To fit the new contact breaker points, first check if there is any greasy deposit on them and if necessary clean them using methylated spirit.

17   Fit the points using a reversal of the removal procedure, then adjust them as follows. Turn the engine over using a socket or spanner on the crankshaft pulley bolt, until the heel of the contact breaker arm is on the peak of one of the four cam lobes.

18   With the points fully open, a feeler blade equal to the contact breaker points gap, as given in the Specifications, should now just fit between the contact faces (photo).

19   If the gap is too large or too small, turn the adjusting nut on the side of the distributor body using a small spanner until the specified gap is obtained.

20   With the points correctly adjusted, refit the plastic shield, rotor arm and distributor cap.

21   If a dwell meter is available, a far more accurate method of setting the contact breaker points is by measuring and setting the distributor dwell angle.

22   The dwell angle is the number of degrees of distributor shaft rotation during which the contact breaker points are closed (ie the period from when the points close after being opened by one cam lobe until they are opened again by the next cam lobe). The advantages of setting the points by this method are that any wear of the distributor shaft or cam lobes is taken into account, and also the inaccuracies of using a feeler gauge are eliminated.

23   To check and adjust the dwell angle, connect one lead of the meter to the ignition coil + terminal and the other lead to the coil – terminal, or in accordance with the maker's instructions.

24   Start the engine, allow it to idle and observe the reading on the dwell meter scale. If the dwell angle is not as specified, turn the adjusting nut on the side of the distributor body as necessary to obtain the correct setting. **Note:** *Owing to machining tolerances, or wear in the distributor shaft or bushes, it is not uncommon for a contact breaker points gap correctly set with feeler gauges, to give a dwell angle outside the specified tolerances. If this is the case the dwell angle should be regarded as the preferred setting.*

25   After completing the adjustment, switch off the engine and disconnect the dwell meter.

Ignition timing check and adjustment –   1397 cc (C1J) engine

26   In order that the engine can run efficiently, it is necessary for a spark to occur at the spark plug and ignite the fuel/air mixture at the instant just before the piston on the compression stroke reaches the top of its travel. The precise instant at which the spark occurs is determined by the ignition timing, and this is quoted in degrees before top-dead centre (BTDC).

27   The timing may be checked and adjusted in one of two ways, either by using a test bulb to obtain a static setting with the engine stationary or by using a stroboscopic timing light to obtain a dynamic setting with the engine running.

28   Before checking or adjusting the ignition timing, make sure that the contact breaker points are in good condition and correctly adjusted, as described previously.

Static setting

29   Refer to the Specifications at the beginning of this Chapter and note the specified setting for static ignition timing. This value will also be found stamped on a clip fastened to one of the HT leads.

30   Pull off the HT lead and remove No 1 spark plug (nearest the flywheel end of the engine).

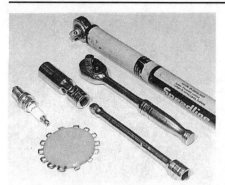

4.53 Tools required for removing, refitting and adjusting the spark plugs

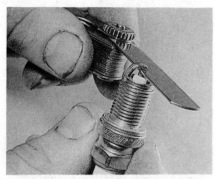

4.59 Measuring the spark plug gap with a feeler blade

4.60A Measuring the spark plug gap with a wire blade

31   Place a finger over the plug hole and turn the engine in the normal direction of rotation (clockwise from the crankshaft pulley end) until pressure is felt in No 1 cylinder. This indicates that the piston is commencing its compression stroke. The engine can be turned using a socket or spanner on the crankshaft pulley bolt.
32   Continue turning the engine until the mark on the flywheel is aligned with the appropriate notch on the clutch bellhousing.
33   Remove the distributor cap and check that the rotor arm is pointing towards the No 1 spark plug HT lead segment in the cap.
34   Connect a 12 volt test lamp and leads between a good earth point and the LT terminal nut on the side of the distributor body.
35   Slacken the distributor clamp retaining nut and then switch on the ignition.
36   If the test lamp is on, turn the distributor slightly clockwise until the lamp goes out.
37   Now turn the distributor anti-clockwise until the test lamp just lights up, hold the distributor in this position and tighten the clamp retaining nut.
38   Test the setting by turning the engine two complete revolutions and observing when the lamp lights up in relation to the timing marks.
39   Switch off the ignition and remove the test lamp. Refit No 1 spark plug, the distributor cap and HT lead.

Dynamic setting

40   Refer to the Specifications at the beginning of this Chapter and note the specified setting for stroboscopic ignition timing. This initial value will also be found stamped on a clip fastened to one of the HT leads. To make subsequent operations easier it is advisable to highlight the mark on the flywheel and the appropriate notch on the clutch bellhousing with white paint or chalk.
41   Connect the timing light in accordance with the manufacturer's instructions (usually interposed between the end of No 1 spark plug HT lead and No 1 spark plug terminal).
42   Disconnect the vacuum advance pipe from the distributor vacuum unit and plug its end.
43   Start the engine and leave it idling at the specified idling speed (refer to the Specifications).
44   Point the timing light at the timing marks. They should appear to be stationary with the mark on the flywheel aligned with the appropriate notch on the clutch bellhousing (photo).
45   If adjustment is necessary (ie the flywheel mark does not line up with the appropriate notch) slacken the distributor clamp retaining nut and turn the distributor body either anti-clockwise to advance the timing, or clockwise to retard it. Tighten the clamp nut when the setting is correct.
46   Gradually increase the engine speed while still pointing the timing light at the marks. The mark on the flywheel should appear to advance further, indicating that the distributor centrifugal advance mechanism is functioning. If the mark remains stationary or moves in a jerky, erratic fashion, the advance mechanism must be suspect.
47   Reconnect the vacuum pipe to the distributor and check that the advance alters when the pipe is connected. If not, the vacuum unit on the distributor may be faulty.
48   After completing the checks and adjustments, switch off the engine and disconnect the timing light.

Ignition timing check and adjustment – 1390 cc (E6J) and 1721 cc (F2N) engines
49   It is not possible to either check or adjust the ignition timing on the E6J or F2N engines. The timing is controlled automatically by the computer control unit and no value is specified by Renault.

Spark plug check and renewal
50   The correct functioning of the spark plugs is vital for the correct running and efficiency of the engine. It is essential that the plugs fitted are appropriate for the engine, the suitable type being specified at the beginning of this Chapter. If the correct type of plug is used and the engine is in good condition, the spark plugs should not need attention between scheduled renewal intervals, except for adjustment of their gaps. Spark plug cleaning is rarely necessary and should not be attempted unless specialised equipment is available as damage can easily be caused to the firing ends.
51   To remove the plugs, first open the bonnet and mark the HT leads one to four to correspond to the appropriate cylinder number (number one cylinder is at the flywheel end of the engine). Pull the HT leads from the plugs by gripping the end fitting, not the lead, otherwise the lead connection may be fractured.
52   It is advisable to remove any dirt from the spark plug recesses using a clean brush, vacuum cleaner or compressed air before removing the plugs, to prevent the dirt dropping into the cylinders.
53   Unscrew the plugs using a spark plug spanner, suitable box spanner or a deep socket and extension bar (photo). Keep the socket in alignment with the spark plug, otherwise if it is forcibly moved to either side, the ceramic top of the spark plug may be broken off. As each plug is removed, examine it as follows.
54   Examination of the spark plugs will give a good indication of the condition of the engine. If the insulator nose of the spark plug is clean and white, with no deposits, this is indicative of a weak mixture or too hot a plug (a hot plug transfers heat away from the electrode slowly, a cold plug transfers heat away quickly).
55   If the tip and insulator nose are covered with hard black-looking deposits, then this is indicative that the mixture is too rich. Should the plug be black and oily, then it is likely that the engine is fairly worn, as well as the mixture being too rich.
56   If the insulator nose is covered with light tan to greyish brown deposits, then the mixture is correct and it is likely that the engine is in good condition.
57   If the spark plug has only completed 6000 miles (10 000 km) in accordance with the routine maintenance schedule, it should still be serviceable until the 12 000 mile (20 000 km) service when it is renewed. However, it is recommended that it is re-gapped in order to maintain peak engine efficiency and to allow for the 0.025 mm (0.001 in) normal increase in gap which occurs approximately every 1000 miles. If, due to engine condition, the spark plug is not serviceable, it should be renewed.
58   The spark plug gap is of considerable importance as, if it is too large or too small, the size of the spark and its efficiency will be seriously impaired. For the best results the spark plug gap should be set in accordance with the Specifications at the beginning of this Chapter.
59   To set it, measure the gap with a feeler blade, and then bend open, or close, the outer plug electrode until the correct gap is achieved

4.60B Adjusting the spark plug gap using a special adjusting tool

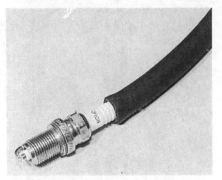

4.62 Using a short length of rubber hose to facilitate inserting the spark plugs

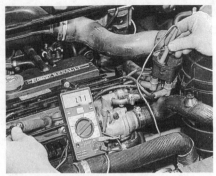

4.68 Checking the resistance of the HT leads with a digital ohmmeter

(photo). The centre electrode should never be bent, as this may crack the insulation and cause plug failure, if nothing worse.

60   Special spark plug electrode gap adjusting tools are available from most motor accessory shops (photos).

61   Before fitting the spark plugs check that the threaded connector sleeves are tight and that the plug exterior surfaces and threads are clean.

62   It is very often difficult to insert spark plugs into their holes without cross-threading them. To avoid this possibility, fit a short length of $\frac{5}{16}$ inch internal diameter rubber hose over the end of the spark plug (photo). The flexible hose acts as a universal joint to help align the plug with the plug hole. Should the plug begin to cross-thread, the hose will slip on the spark plug, preventing thread damage to the aluminium cylinder head. Remove the rubber hose and tighten the plug to the specified torque using the spark plug socket and a torque wrench. Refit the remaining spark plugs in the same manner.

63   Wipe clean the HT leads, then reconnect them in their correct order.

HT leads, distributor cap and rotor arm check and renewal

64   The spark plug HT leads should be checked whenever new spark plugs are installed in the engine.

65   Ensure that the leads are numbered before removing them to avoid confusion when refitting. Pull one HT lead from its plug by gripping the end fitting, not the lead, otherwise the lead connection may be fractured.

66   Check inside the end fitting for signs of corrosion, which will look like a white crusty powder. Push the end fitting back onto the spark plug ensuring that it is a tight fit on the plug. If it isn't, remove the lead again and use pliers to carefully crimp the metal connector inside the end fitting until it fits securely on the end of the spark plug.

67   Using a clean rag, wipe the entire length of the lead to remove any built-up dirt and grease. Once the lead is clean, check for burns, cracks and other damage. Do not bend the lead excessively or pull the lead lengthwise – the conductor inside might break.

68   Disconnect the other end of the lead from the distributor cap. Again, pull only on the end fitting. Check for corrosion and a tight fit in the same manner as the spark plug end. If an ohmmeter is available, check the continuity of the HT lead by connecting the meter between the spark plug end of the lead and the segment inside the distributor cap (photo). Refit the lead securely on completion.

69   Check the remaining HT leads one at a time, in the same way.

70   If new HT leads are required, purchase a set suitable for your specific vehicle and engine.

71   Remove the distributor cap, wipe it clean and carefully inspect it inside and out for signs of cracks, carbon tracks (tracking) and worn, burned or loose contacts. Similarly inspect the rotor arm. Renew these components if any defects are found. It is common practice to renew the cap and rotor arm whenever new HT leads are fitted. When fitting a new cap, remove the HT leads from the old cap one at a time and fit them to the new cap in the exact same location – do not simultaneously remove all the leads from the old cap or firing order confusion may occur.

72   Even with the ignition system in first class condition, some engines

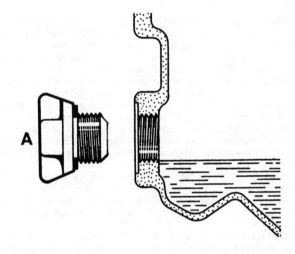

Fig. 1.8 Manual gearbox steel filler plug (A) (Sec 5)

may still occasionally experience poor starting attributable to damp ignition components. To disperse moisture Holts Wet Start can be very effective. Holts Damp Start should be used for providing a sealing coat to exclude moisture from the ignition system, and in extreme difficulty, Holts Cold Start will help to start a car when only a very poor spark occurs.

---

5   Manual gearbox and automatic transmission

Manual gearbox oil level check

1   Position the car over an inspection pit, on car ramps, or jack it up, but make sure that it is level. Where applicable remove the engine splash shield.

2   Unscrew the filler plug from the front-facing side of the gearbox (photo).

3   Where a steel filler plug is fitted, the oil level should be up to the lower edge of the filler hole. Insert a finger to check the level.

4   Where a plastic filler plug is fitted, wipe clean the dipstick part of the plug then check the level by inserting the shouldered end of the plug through the hole without engaging the threads. Position the plug so that the outer arrow is pointing upwards and the inner dipstick is pointing downwards. On removal of the plug the level should be at the top of the collar on the dipstick. The bottom of the collar indicates the minimum level.

5   Where necessary top up the level using the correct grade of oil then refit and tighten the filler plug (photo).

6   If the gearbox requires frequent topping up, check it for leakage especially around the driveshaft oil seals and repair as necessary.

Are your plugs trying to tell you something?

Normal.
Grey-brown deposits, lightly coated core nose. Plugs ideally suited to engine, and engine in good condition.

Heavy Deposits.
A build up of crusty deposits, light-grey sandy colour in appearance.
Fault: Often caused by worn valve guides, excessive use of upper cylinder lubricant, or idling for long periods.

Lead Glazing.
Plug insulator firing tip appears yellow or green/yellow and shiny in appearance.
Fault: Often caused by incorrect carburation, excessive idling followed by sharp acceleration. Also check ignition timing.

Carbon fouling.
Dry, black, sooty deposits.
Fault: over-rich fuel mixture.
Check: carburettor mixture settings, float level, choke operation, air filter.

Oil fouling.
Wet, oily deposits. Fault: worn bores/piston rings or valve guides; sometimes occurs (temporarily) during running-in period.

Overheating.
Electrodes have glazed appearance, core nose very white – few deposits. Fault: plug overheating. Check: plug value, ignition timing, fuel octane rating (too low) and fuel mixture (too weak).

Electrode damage.
Electrodes burned away; core nose has burned, glazed appearance. Fault: pre-ignition. Check: for correct heat range and as for 'overheating'.

Split core nose.
(May appear initially as a crack). Fault: detonation or wrong gap-setting technique. Check: ignition timing, cooling system, fuel mixture (too weak).

WHY DOUBLE COPPER IS BETTER FOR YOUR ENGINE.

Unique Trapezoidal Copper Cored Earth Electrode

50% Larger Spark Area

Copper Cored Centre Electrode

Champion Double Copper plugs are the first in the world to have copper core in both centre _and_ earth electrode. This innovative design means that they run cooler by up to 100°C – giving greater efficiency and longer life. These double copper cores transfer heat away from the tip of the plug faster and more efficiently. Therefore, Double Copper runs at cooler temperatures than conventional plugs giving improved acceleration response and high speed performance with no fear of pre-ignition.

TRAPEZOIDAL COPPER CORED EARTH ELECTRODE

NEW TRAPEZOIDAL COPPER CORED EARTH ELECTRODE / CONVENTIONAL SOLID NICKEL ALLOY EARTH ELECTRODE

50% INCREASE IN SPARK AREA

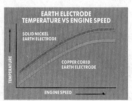

EARTH ELECTRODE TEMPERATURE VS ENGINE SPEED

SOLID NICKEL EARTH ELECTRODE

COPPER CORED EARTH ELECTRODE

TEMPERATURE / ENGINE SPEED

Champion Double Copper plugs also feature a unique trapezoidal earth electrode giving a 50% increase in spark area. This, together with the double copper cores, offers greatly reduced electrode wear, so the spark stays stronger for longer.

 FASTER COLD STARTING

 FOR UNLEADED OR LEADED FUEL

 ELECTRODES UP TO 100°C COOLER

 BETTER ACCELERATION RESPONSE

 LOWER EMISSIONS

 50% BIGGER SPARK AREA

 THE LONGER LIFE PLUG

Plug Tips/Hot and Cold.
Spark plugs must operate within well-defined temperature limits to avoid cold fouling at one extreme and overheating at the other.
Champion and the car manufacturers work out the best plugs for an engine to give optimum performance under all conditions, from freezing cold starts to sustained high speed motorway cruising.
Plugs are often referred to as hot or cold. With Champion, the higher the number on its body, the hotter the plug, and the lower the number the cooler the plug. For the correct plug for your car refer to the specifications at the beginning of this chapter.

Plug Cleaning
Modern plug design and materials mean that Champion no longer recommends periodic plug cleaning. Certainly don't clean your plugs with a wire brush as this can cause metal conductive paths across the nose of the insulator so impairing its performance and resulting in loss of acceleration and reduced m.p.g.
However, if plugs are removed, always carefully clean the area where the plug seats in the cylinder head as grit and dirt can sometimes cause gas leakage.
Also wipe any traces of oil or grease from plug leads as this may lead to arcing.

CHAMPION

DOUBLE COPPER

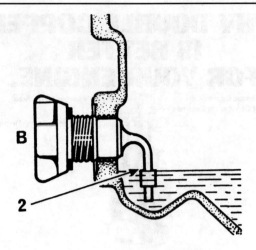

Fig. 1.9 Manual gearbox plastic filler plug (B) and oil level shoulder (2) (Sec 5)

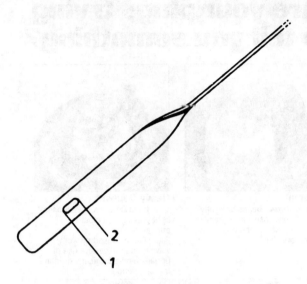

Fig. 1.10 Automatic transmission fluid level dipstick markings (Sec 5)

1   *Minimum cold*   2   *Maximum cold*

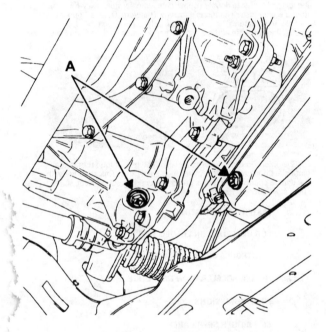

Fig. 1.11 Automatic transmission fluid drain plug locations (A) (Sec 5)

7   Where applicable refit the engine splash shield and lower the car to the ground.

Automatic transmission fluid level check

8   Check the fluid level when the car has been standing for some time and the fluid is cold.
9   Position the car on level ground then apply the handbrake and select P with the selector lever. Start the engine and allow it to run for a few minutes.
10   With the engine still idling withdraw the dipstick from the front of the transmission housing, wipe it on a clean cloth, insert it again then withdraw it once more and read off the level. Ideally the level should be in the centre of the mark on the dipstick. The fluid must never be allowed to fall below the bottom of the mark otherwise there is a risk of damaging the transmission. The transmission must never be overfilled so that the level is above the top of the mark otherwise there is a risk of overheating.
11   If topping-up is necessary, add a quantity of the specified fluid to the transmission through the dipstick tube. Use a funnel with a fine mesh screen to avoid spillage and to ensure that any foreign matter is trapped.
12   After topping-up recheck the level again, as described above, refit the dipstick and switch off the engine.

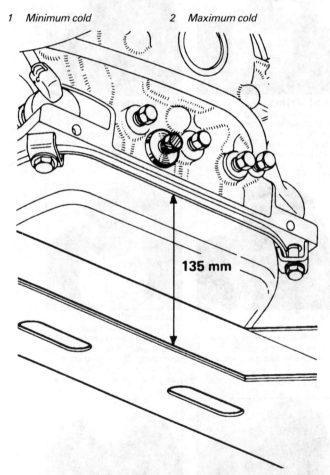

135 mm

Fig. 1.12 Raise the automatic transmission as shown before removing the sump pan (Sec 5)

Automatic transmission fluid and gauze filter renewal

13   The automatic transmission fluid should only be changed when cold.
14   Position the car over an inspection pit, on car ramps, or jack it up, but make sure that it is level. Where applicable remove the engine splash shield.

5.2 Filler plug on the front-facing side of the gearbox

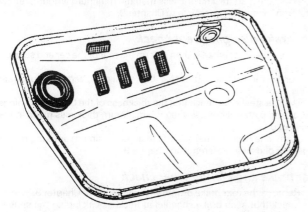

Fig. 1.13 Filter magnet location in the automatic transmission sump (Sec 5)

15 Place a suitable container beneath the drain plug on the transmission sump pan and at the base of the transmission housing.
16 Remove the dipstick to speed up the draining operation, unscrew the two drain plugs and allow the fluid to drain.

6.1 Checking the condition of the driveshaft outer constant velocity (CV) joint rubber gaiters

5.5 Topping up the manual gearbox with oil

17 When all the fluid has drained (this may take quite some time) clean the drain plugs then refit them together with new seals and tighten them securely.
18 Unbolt and remove the sump pan and gasket.
19 Unscrew the filter retaining bolts and remove the filter and sealing ring. Note which way round the filter is fitted.
20 Fit the new filter into position ensuring it is the correct way round. Tighten the bolts to the specified torque.
21 Clean the sump pan and check that the filter magnets are located as shown in Fig. 1.13, with their ribbed sides against the plate, then refit the sump pan ensuring that the new gasket is correctly located. Tighten the bolts to the specified torque.
22 Place a funnel with fine mesh screen in the dipstick tube and fill the transmission with the specified type of fluid. Depending on the extent to which the fluid was allowed to drain, refilling will only require approximately 2 litre (3.5 Imp pint). Add about half this amount and then check the level on the dipstick. When the level approaches the mark, place the selector lever in P, start the engine and allow it to run for approximately 2 minutes. Now check the level and complete the final topping up as described previously.

6 Driveshafts

Driveshaft rubber gaiter and CV joint check

1 With the vehicle raised and securely supported on stands, turn the steering onto full lock then slowly rotate the roadwheel. Inspect the condition of the outer constant velocity (CV) joint rubber gaiters while squeezing the gaiters to open out the folds (photo). Check for signs of cracking, splits or deterioration of the rubber which may allow the escape of grease and lead to the ingress of water and grit into the joint. Also check the security and condition of the retaining clips. Repeat these checks on the inner CV joints. If any damage or deterioration is found, the gaiters should be renewed as described in Chapter 8.
2 At the same time check the general condition of the outer CV joints themselves by first holding the driveshaft and attempting to rotate the wheels. Repeat this check on the right-hand inner joint by holding the inner joint yoke and attempting to rotate the driveshaft. The left-hand inner joint is concealed by a rubber gaiter which is bolted to the transmission casing, and it is not possible to hold the joint since the yoke is an integral part of the differential sun wheel. However, one way to get round this problem is to have an assistant hold the right-hand wheel stationary with 4th gear selected, and then to attempt to rotate the left-hand driveshaft. If this method is used, beware of confusing wear in the left-hand CV joint with general wear in the transmission.
3 Any appreciable movement in the CV joint indicates wear in the joint, wear in the driveshaft splines or a loose driveshaft retaining nut.

7.4 Topping up the brake hydraulic fluid reservoir

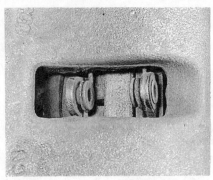

7.11 Brake pad thickness viewing aperture on Girling caliper

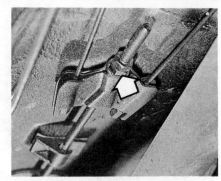

7.23 Handbrake lever primary rod locknut and adjustment nut (arrowed)

7   Braking system

Hydraulic fluid level check

1   On models without ABS the brake fluid reservoir is located on the top of the brake master cylinder which is attached to the front of the vacuum servo unit. On models with ABS the brake fluid reservoir is located on top of the ABS hydraulic unit attached to the bulkhead. The maximum and minimum marks are indicated on the side of the reservoir and the fluid level should be maintained between these marks at all times.

2   *Only on models with ABS*, first switch on the ignition, then depress the brake pedal several times in order to activate the electric hydraulic pump on the ABS unit. Leave the ignition switched on during the check.

3   The brake fluid inside the reservoir is readily visible. With the car on level ground the level should be above the minimum (Danger) mark and preferably on or near the maximum mark. Note that wear of the brake pads or brake shoe linings causes the level of the brake fluid to gradually fall, so that when the brake pads are renewed, the original level of the fluid is restored. It is not therefore necessary to top up the level to compensate for this minimal drop, however the level must never be allowed to fall below the minimum mark.

4   If topping-up is necessary, first wipe the area around the filler cap with a clean rag before removing the cap. When adding fluid, pour it carefully into the reservoir to avoid spilling it on surrounding painted surfaces. Be sure to use only the specified brake hydraulic fluid since mixing different types of fluid can cause damage to the system (photo). See *'Lubricants, fluids and capacities'* at the beginning of this Chapter.
Warning: *Brake hydraulic fluid can harm your eyes and damage painted surfaces, so use extreme caution when handling and pouring it. Do not use fluid that has been standing open for some time as it absorbs moisture from the air. Excess moisture can cause a dangerous loss of braking effectiveness.*

5   When adding fluid it is a good idea to inspect the reservoir for contamination. The system should be drained and refilled if deposits, dirt particles or contamination are seen in the fluid.

6   After filling the reservoir to the proper level, make sure that the cap is refitted securely to avoid leaks and the entry of foreign matter. On models with ABS switch off the ignition.

7   If the reservoir requires repeated replenishing to maintain the proper level, this is an indication of a hydraulic leak somewhere in the system which should be investigated immediately.

Hydraulic fluid renewal

8   The procedure is similar to that for the bleeding of the hydraulic system as described in Chapter 9, except that the brake fluid reservoir should be emptied by syphoning, using a clean poultry baster or similar before starting, and allowance should be made for the old fluid to be removed from the circuit when bleeding a section of the circuit.

Front brake disc pad wear check

9   Apply the handbrake, then jack up the front of the car and support on axle stands.

10   For better access to the front brake calipers, remove both front wheels.

11   Using a steel rule, check that the thickness of the brake pad linings and backing plates is not less than the minimum thickness given in the Specifications. On the Girling caliper it will only be possible to view the centre area of the pads through the small aperture (photo), but on the Bendix type all of the pad area is visible.

12   If any one pad thickness is less than the minimum amount, renew all the front pads with reference to Chapter 9.

Rear brake disc pad wear check

13   Chock the front wheels, then jack up the rear of the car and support on axle stands.

14   For better access to the rear brake calipers, remove both rear wheels.

15   Using a steel rule, check that the thickness of the brake pad linings and backing plates is not less than the minimum thickness given in the Specifications.

16   If any one pad thickness is less than the minimum amount, renew all the rear pads with reference to Chapter 9.

Rear brake shoe lining wear check

17   Remove the rear brake drums with reference to Chapter 9.

18   Check that each brake shoe lining thickness including the shoe is not less than the thickness given in the Specifications.

19   If any one lining thickness is less than the minimum amount, renew all the rear brake shoes, also as described in Chapter 9.

Handbrake check and adjustment

20   The handbrake lever must be adjusted correctly, otherwise the self-adjusting rear brakes will not function correctly and the brake pedal travel may be excessive. Under no circumstances should the cables be tightened to rectify excessive brake pedal travel.

21   Chock the front wheels, then jack up the rear of the car and support on axle stands.

22   From its off position, pull the handbrake lever up approximately 120 mm and release the ratchet button. Check that both rear wheels are locked by attempting to turn them by hand. If the wheels are not locked, adjust the handbrake as follows.

23   Fully release the handbrake, then working under the car slacken the locknut and adjustment nut on the end of the handbrake lever primary rod until it is clear of the compensator (photo). Now proceed as follows according to braking system type.

Rear drum brakes

24   Remove both rear wheels and drums with reference to Chapter 9.

25   Check that the automatic adjustment wheel on the adjuster strut will rotate in both directions. If it is seized, the shoes must be removed and the wheel freed.

26   Back off the adjuster wheel by about 5 to 6 teeth to slightly reduce the diameter of the shoes.

27   Check that the handbrake cables slide freely by pulling on their front ends. Also check that the operating levers on the trailing shoes return to their correct positions with the stop pegs in contact with the shoe webs.

28   Tighten the adjustment nut on the handbrake lever primary rod until the operating levers on the trailing shoes commence to lift

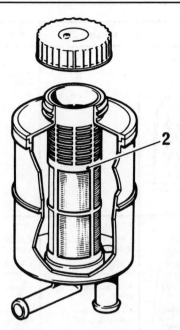

Fig. 1.14 Early type power-assisted steering fluid reservoir showing level shoulder (2) on filler neck (Sec 8)

Fig. 1.15 Later type power-assisted steering fluid reservoir (Sec 8)

between the first and second notches on the handbrake lever, and remain lifted on the second notch.

29   Refit the rear wheels and drums with reference to Chapter 9. With the car on the ground, depress the footbrake several times and at the same time have as assistant listen at each rear wheel for the automatic adjustment mechanism to operate.

Rear disc brakes

30   Adjust the nut on the handbrake lever primary rod until the rear ends of the handbrake cables can be pulled approximately 5.0 mm clear of the levers on the rear calipers.

31   Depress the footbrake pedal several times.

32   Operate the levers on the calipers several times and check that they return fully by themselves. If not, the caliper(s) will need to be overhauled or renewed as described in Chapter 9.

33   Tighten the nut on the handbrake lever primary rod until the cable end stops just touch the levers.

34   Check that from the fully released position, the handbrake lever moves at least 11 or 12 notches to the fully applied position. If necessary make final adjustments at the adjusting nut.

35   Lower the car to the ground.

8   Suspension and steering

Front suspension and steering check

1   Raise the front of the vehicle and securely support it on axle stands.

2   Visually inspect the balljoint dust covers and the steering rack and pinion gaiters for splits, chafing or deterioration (photo). Any wear of these components will cause loss of lubricant together with dirt and water entry, resulting in rapid deterioration of the balljoints or steering gear.

3   On vehicles equipped with power-assisted steering, check the fluid hoses for chafing or deterioration and the pipe and hose unions for fluid leaks. Also check for signs of fluid leakage under pressure from the steering gear rubber gaiters which would indicate failed fluid seals within the steering gear.

4   Grasp the roadwheel at the 12 o'clock and 6 o'clock positions and try to rock it (photo). Very slight free play may be felt, but if the movement is appreciable further investigation is necessary to determine the source. Continue rocking the wheel while an assistant depresses the footbrake. If the movement is now eliminated or significantly reduced, it is likely that the hub bearings are at fault. If the

free play is still evident with the footbrake depressed, then there is wear in the suspension joints or mountings.

5   Now grasp the wheel at the 9 o'clock and 3 o'clock positions and try to rock it as before. Any movement felt now may again be caused by wear in the hub bearings or the steering track-rod balljoints. If the outer balljoint is worn the visual movement will be obvious. If the inner joint is suspect it can be felt by placing a hand over the rack and pinion rubber gaiter and gripping the track-rod. If the wheel is now rocked, movement will be felt at the inner joint if wear has taken place.

6   Using a large screwdriver or flat bar check for wear in the suspension mounting bushes by levering between the relevant suspension component and its attachment point. Some movement is to be expected as the mountings are made of rubber, but excessive wear should be obvious. Also check the condition of any visible rubber bushes, looking for splits, cracks or contamination of the rubber.

7   With the car standing on its wheels, have an assistant turn the steering wheel back and forth about an eighth of a turn each way. There should be very little, if any, lost movement between the steering wheel and roadwheels. If this is not the case, closely observe the joints and mountings previously described, but in addition check the steering column universal joints for wear and also check the rack and pinion steering gear itself.

Power-assisted steering fluid level check

8   The power steering fluid reservoir is located on the front right-hand side of the engine compartment (photo).

9   For the check, the front wheels should be pointing straight ahead and the engine should be stopped. The car should be positioned on level ground.

10   Refer to Fig. 1.14 or 1.15 and check that the fluid is on the maximum level mark. There are two types of reservoir fitted. On the first type the fluid should be on the shoulder of the filter screen, on the later type the fluid should be on the MAX level mark.

11   Before removing the filler cap use a clean rag to wipe the cap and the surrounding area to prevent any foreign matter from entering the reservoir. Unscrew and remove the filler cap.

12   Top up if necessary with the specified grade of automatic transmission fluid (photo). Be careful not to introduce dirt into the system, and do not overfill. Frequent topping up indicates a leak which should be investigated.

Power-assisted steering drivebelt check, adjustment and renewal

13   Refer to Section 10 of this Chapter; the procedure is included in the alternator drivebelt section.

Condition	Probable cause	Corrective action	Condition	Probable cause	Corrective action
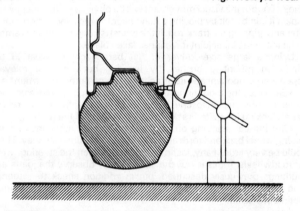 Shoulder wear	• Underinflation (wear on both sides) • Incorrect wheel camber (wear on one side) • Hard cornering	• Check and adjust pressure • Repair or renew suspension parts • Reduce speed	Feathered edge Toe wear	• Incorrect toe setting	• Adjust front wheel alignment
Centre wear	• Overinflation	• Measure and adjust pressure	Uneven wear	• Incorrect camber or castor • Malfunctioning suspension • Unbalanced wheel • Out-of-round brake disc/drum	• Repair or renew suspension parts • Repair or renew suspension parts • Balance tyres • Machine or renew disc/drum

Fig. 1.16 Tyre wear patterns and causes (Sec 8)

Fig. 1.17 Checking wheel run-out with a dial gauge and stand (Sec 8)

Wheel and tyre maintenance and tyre pressure checks

14　The original tyres on this car are equipped with tread wear safety bands which will appear when the tread depth reaches approximately 1.6 mm (0.063 in). Tread wear can be monitored with a simple, inexpensive device known as a tread depth indicator gauge (photo).

15　Wheels and tyres should give no real problems in use provided that a close eye is kept on them with regard to excessive wear or damage. To this end, the following points should be noted.

16　Ensure that tyre pressures are checked regularly and maintained correctly. Checking should be carried out with the tyres cold and not immediately after the vehicle has been in use (photo). If the pressures are checked with the tyres hot, an apparently high reading will be obtained owing to heat expansion. Under no circumstances should an attempt be made to reduce the pressures to the quoted cold reading in this instance, or effective underinflation will result.

17　Note any abnormal tread wear with reference to Fig. 1.16. Tread pattern irregularities such as feathering, flat spots and more wear on one side than the other are indications of front wheel alignment and/or balance problems. If any of these conditions are noted, they should be rectified as soon as possible.

18　Underinflation will cause overheating of the tyre owing to excessive flexing of the casing, and the tread will not sit correctly on the road surface. This will cause a consequent loss of adhesion and

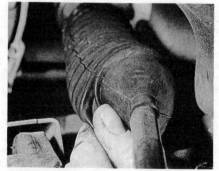

8.2 Checking the condition of the steering rack rubber gaiter

8.4 Checking for wear in the front suspension and hub bearings

8.8 Power-assisted steering fluid reservoir showing level markings

8.12 Topping up the power-assisted steering fluid reservoir

8.14 Checking the tyre tread depth with an indicator gauge

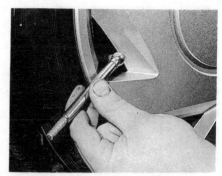

8.16 Checking the tyre pressures with a tyre pressure gauge

excessive wear, not to mention the danger of sudden tyre failure due to heat build-up.

19   Overinflation will cause rapid wear of the centre part of the tyre tread coupled with reduced adhesion, harsher ride, and the danger of shock damage occurring in the tyre casing.

20   Regularly check the tyres for damage in the form of cuts or bulges, especially in the sidewalls. Remove any nails or stones embedded in the tread before they penetrate the tyre to cause deflation. If removal of a nail reveals that the tyre has been punctured, refit the nail so that its point of penetration is marked. Then immediately change the wheel and have the tyre repaired by a tyre dealer. Do not drive on a tyre in such a condition. In many cases a puncture can be simply repaired by the use of an inner tube of the correct size and type, although make sure that the item which caused the puncture is removed first. If in any doubt as to the possible consequences of any damage found, consult your local tyre dealer for advice.

21   Periodically remove the wheels and clean any dirt or mud from the inside and outside surfaces. Examine the wheel rims for signs of rusting, corrosion or other damage. Light alloy wheels are easily damaged by 'kerbing' whilst parking, and similarly steel wheels may become dented or buckled. Renewal of the wheel is very often the only course of remedial action possible.

22   The balance of each wheel and tyre assembly should be maintained to avoid excessive wear, not only to the tyres but also to the steering and suspension components. Wheel imbalance is normally signified by vibration through the vehicle's bodyshell, although in many cases it is particularly noticeable through the steering wheel. Conversely, it should be noted that wear or damage in suspension or steering components may cause excessive tyre wear. Out-of-round or out-of-true tyres, damaged wheels and wheel bearing wear/maladjustment also fall into this category. Balancing will not usually cure vibration caused by such wear.

23   Wheel balancing may be carried out with the wheel either on or off the vehicle. If balanced on the vehicle, ensure that the wheel-to-hub relationship is marked in some way prior to subsequent wheel removal

so that it may be refitted in its original position.

24   General tyre wear is influenced to a large degree by driving style – harsh braking and acceleration or fast cornering will all produce more rapid tyre wear. Interchanging of tyres may result in more even wear, however it is worth bearing in mind that if this is completely effective, the added expense is incurred of replacing simultaneously a complete set of tyres, which may prove financially restrictive for many owners.

25   Front tyres may wear unevenly as a result of wheel misalignment. The front wheels should always be correctly aligned according to the settings specified by the vehicle manufacturer.

26   Legal restrictions apply to many aspects of tyre fitting and usage and in the UK this information is contained in the Motor Vehicle Construction and Use Regulations. It is suggested that a copy of these regulations is obtained from your local police if in doubt as to current legal requirements with regard to tyre type and condition, minimum tread depth, etc.

9   Bodywork

Underbody and general body check

1   With the car raised and supported on axle stands or over an inspection pit, thoroughly inspect the underbody and wheelarches for signs of damage and corrosion. In particular examine the bottom of the side sills and concealed areas where mud can collect. Where corrosion and rust is evident, press firmly on the panel by hand and check for possible repairs. If the panel is not seriously corroded, clean away the rust and apply a new coating of underseal. Refer to Chapter 11 for more details of body repairs.

2   Check all external body panels for damage and rectify where necessary.

10   Electrical system

Battery check and maintenance

Caution: *Before carrying out any work on the vehicle battery, read through the precautions given in Safety first! at the beginning of this manual*

1   The battery is located on the right-hand side of the engine compartment, on the bulkhead.

2   Prise up the plastic battery cover for access to the top of the battery, then pull out the two cell covers.

3   Check that the level of the electrolyte is approximately 15 mm (0.6 in) above the tops of the cell plates. Due to the angle of the bonnet it may be necessary to use a mirror and torch to view into the cells.

4   If necessary, top up the level using only distilled or demineralised water (photo).

5   Refit the two cell covers, then refit the plastic cover.

6   The exterior of the battery should be inspected periodically for damage such as a cracked case or cover.

Fig. 1.18 Checking for drivebelt wear – multi-ribbed type shown as fitted to the 1721 cc (F2N) engine (Sec 10)

10.4 Topping up the battery electrolyte level

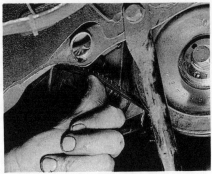

10.17 Checking the alternator drivebelt tension

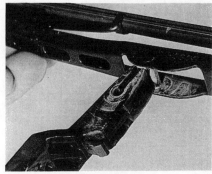

10.23 Removing a wiper blade from the arm fork

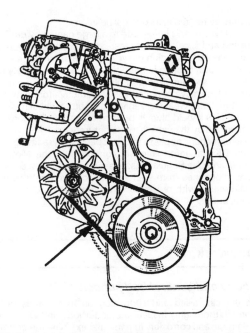

Fig. 1.19 Drivebelt tension checking point (arrowed) on the 1390 cc (E6J) engine (Sec 10)

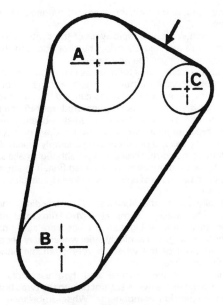

Fig. 1.20 Drivebelt tension checking point (arrowed) on the 1397 cc (C1J) engine (Sec 10)

A   Water pump pulley   C   Alternator pulley
B   Crankshaft pulley

7   Check the tightness of the battery cable clamps to ensure good electrical connections and check the entire length of each cable for cracks and frayed conductors.
8   If corrosion (visible as white, fluffy deposits) is evident, remove the cables from the battery terminals, clean them with a small wire brush then refit them. Corrosion can be kept to a minimum by applying a layer of petroleum jelly to the clamps and terminals after they are reconnected.
9   Make sure that the battery tray is in good condition and the retaining clamp is tight.
10   Corrosion on the tray, retaining clamp and the battery itself can be removed with a solution of water and baking soda. Thoroughly rinse all cleaned areas with plain water.
11   Any metal parts of the vehicle damaged by corrosion should be covered with a zinc-based primer, then painted.
12   Further information on the battery, charging and jump starting can be found in Chapter 12 and in the preliminary sections of this manual.

Alternator drivebelt check, adjustment and renewal

13   The alternator drivebelt is located on the front right-hand side of the engine. Due to its function and material makeup, the belt is prone to failure after a period of time and should therefore be inspected and adjusted periodically.
14   The belt configuration depends on the engine fitted and on whether the model is equipped with power-assisted steering or air conditioning.

15   Since the drivebelt is located very close to the right-hand side of the engine compartment, it is possible to gain better access by raising the front of the car and removing the right-hand wheel, then removing the cover plate from inside the wheelarch.
16   With the engine switched off, inspect the full length of the alternator drivebelt for cracks and separation of the belt plies. It will be necessary to turn the engine in order to move the belt from the pulleys so that the belt can be inspected thoroughly. Twist the belt between the pulleys so that both sides can be viewed. Also check for fraying, and glazing which gives the belt a shiny appearance. Check the pulleys for nicks, cracks, distortion and corrosion.
17   The tension of the belt is checked by pushing on it midway between the pulleys at the point indicated on the accompanying illustrations (photo). Renault technicians use a special spring-tensioned tool which applies a force of 30N (6.75 lbf) to the belt and then measures the deflection. An alternative arrangement can be made by using a straight-edge, steel rule and spring balance. Hold the straight-edge across the two pulleys, then position the steel rule on the belt, apply the force with the spring balance, and measure the deflection. The same arrangement is shown in Chapter 2 for the adjustment of the timing belt.
18   If adjustment is necessary, loosen the alternator pivot bolt first, then loosen the adjustment bolt (if applicable). On the F2N engine turn the nut on the adjustment rod as required, however on other engines insert a lever between the pulley end of the alternator and the cylinder

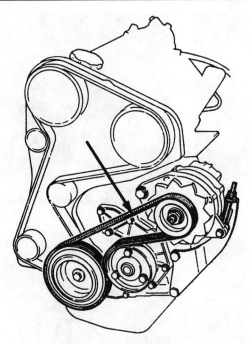

Fig. 1.21 Drivebelt tension checking point (arrowed) on the 1721 cc (F2N) engine (Sec 10)

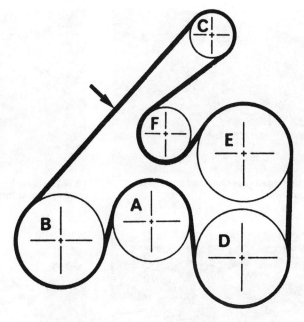

Fig. 1.22 Drivebelt configuration and tension checking point (arrowed) on the 1721 cc (F2N) engine with power-assisted steering and air conditioning (Sec 10)

A   Water pump pulley
B   Crankshaft pulley
C   Alternator pulley

D   Power-assisted steering
    pulley
E   Air conditioning
    compressor pulley
F   Tension adjustment pulley

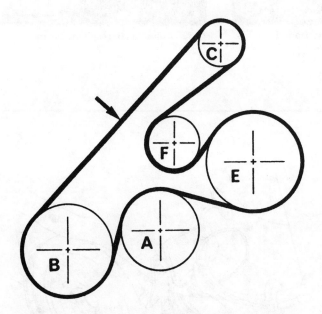

Fig. 1.23 Drivebelt configuration and tension checking point (arrowed) on the 1721 cc (F2N) engine with air conditioning but not power steering (Sec 10)

A   Water pump pulley
B   Crankshaft pulley
C   Alternator pulley

E   Air conditioning
    compressor pulley
F   Tension adjustment pulley

block and pull out the alternator to tension the belt. Tighten the adjustment bolt and the pivot bolt. On models with air conditioning refer to the accompanying illustrations and reposition the adjustment pulley as required to achieve the correct belt tension.
19   Run the engine for about five minutes, then recheck the tension.
20   To renew the belt, slacken the belt tension fully as described above, according to engine type. Slip the belt off the pulleys then fit the new belt ensuring that it is routed correctly. With the belt in position, adjust the tension as previously described.

Windscreen/tailgate wiper blades and arms check and renewal

Wiper blades

21   The wiper blades should be renewed when they are deteriorated, cracked, or no longer clean the windscreen or tailgate glass effectively.
22   Lift the wiper arm away from the glass.
23   Release the catch on the arm, turn the blade through 90° and withdraw the blade from the arm fork (photo).
24   Insert the new blade into the arm, making sure that it locates securely.

Wiper arms

25   Check the wiper arms for worn hinges and weak springs, and renew as necessary.
26   If working on the tailgate wiper, lift the hinged cover for access to the retaining nut (photo).
27   Make sure that the wiper is in its rest position, and note this position for correct refitting. If necessary, switch the wipers on and off in order to allow them to return to the 'park' position.
28   Unscrew the retaining nut and pull the arm from the spindle (photo). If necessary use a screwdriver to prise off the arm, being careful not to damage the paintwork. On the tailgate wiper it will help if the arm is moved to its fully raised position before removing it from the spindle.
29   Fit the new arm using a reversal of the removal procedure.

Windscreen/headlamp washer system check and adjustment

30   The windscreen/headlamp washer fluid reservoir is located on the right-hand front corner of the engine compartment.
31   Check that the fluid level is at least up to the bottom of the filler neck and top up if necessary (photo). When topping up the reservoir, a screen wash such as Turtle Wax High Tech Screen Wash should be added in the recommended quantities.
32   Check that the washer jets direct the fluid onto the upper part of the windscreen/tailgate/headlamp and if necessary adjust the small sphere on the jet with a pin.

10.26 Hinged cover lifted on the tailgate wiper arm

10.28 Unscrewing the wiper arm retaining nut from the spindle

10.31 Topping up the windscreen/headlamp washer fluid reservoir

10.33A Headlamp beam vertical (height) adjustment screw (arrowed)

10.33B Headlamp beam horizontal adjustment screw (arrowed)

10.33C Adjusting the foglamp beam

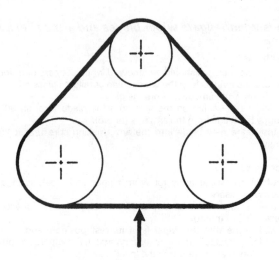

Fig. 1.24 Drivebelt configuration and tension checking point (arrowed) on the 1390 cc (E6J) engine without power-assisted steering (Sec 10)

Headlamp beam alignment check

33   Accurate adjustment of the headlamp beam is only possible using optical beam setting equipment, and this work should therefore be carried out by a Renault dealer or service station with the necessary facilities. For reference, the location of the beam adjusting screws are as shown (photos).

34   On all models it is possible to adjust the headlamp beam to compensate for the load being carried. An adjustment knob is located on the rear of each headlamp on some models, whereas on other models a five-position knob is located on the facia panel inside the car. In the latter case, position 0 should be selected for an unladen vehicle, and position 5 should be selected for maximum load.

Fig. 1.25 Renault tool for checking the drivebelt tension (Sec 10)

Chapter 2 Engine

Contents

Specifications

1390 cc engine

General

Type	Four-cylinder, in-line, overhead camshaft
Designation	E6J
Bore	75.8 mm
Stroke	77.0 mm
Capacity	1390 cc
Firing order	1–3–4–2 (No 1 cylinder at flywheel end)
Direction of crankshaft rotation	Clockwise
Compression ratio	9.5 : 1
Maximum power output – kW (bhp)	57.5 (80) at 5750 rpm
Maximum torque – Nm (lbf ft)	106 (78) at 3000 rpm

Cylinder block
Material .... Cast iron
Liner bore diameter .... 75.8 mm + 0.03 − 0.00 mm
Liner height:
    Total .... 130.0 mm
    From shoulder to top .... 91.5 mm + 0.035 − 0.005 mm
Cylinder block depth (from top to liner locating shoulder) .... 91.5 mm − 0.015 − 0.055 mm
Liner protrusion without O-ring .... 0.02 mm − 0.09 mm
Maximum difference between adjacent liners .... 0.06 mm

Crankshaft
Number of main bearings 5
Main bearing journal diameter:
    Standard .... 54.795 mm ± 0.01 mm
    1st undersize .... 54.550 mm ± 0.005 mm
Main bearing running clearance .... 0.020 to 0.058 mm
Crankpin (big-end) journal diameter:
    Standard .... 43.98 mm + 0 − 0.02 mm
    1st undersize .... 43.73 mm + 0 − 0.02 mm
Big-end bearing running clearance .... 0.014 to 0.053 mm
Crankshaft endfloat .... 0.045 mm − 0.230 mm

Pistons and piston rings
Piston ring end gaps .... Pre-adjusted
Piston ring thickness:
    Top compression ring .... 1.5 mm
    Second compression ring .... 1.75 mm
    Oil control ring .... 3.0 mm

Gudgeon pins
Length .... 60.0 mm
Outside diameter .... 19.0 mm
Bore .... 11.0 mm

Connecting rods
Small-end side play .... 0.310 to 0.572 mm

Cylinder head
Material .... Aluminium
Height .... 113.0 mm ± 0.05 mm
Maximum acceptable gasket face distortion ...... 0.05 mm
Valve seat angle:
    Inlet .... 120°
    Exhaust .... 90°
Valve seat width .... 1.7 mm

Camshaft
Drive .... Toothed belt
Number of bearings 5
Camshaft endfloat .... 0.06 mm ± 0.15 mm

Valves
Head diameter:
    Inlet .... 37.5 mm
    Exhaust .... 33.5 mm
Stem diameter .... 7.0 mm
Valve clearance (cold):
    Inlet .... 0.10 mm
    Exhaust .... 0.25 mm

Lubrication system
System pressure:
    At idle .... 1.0 bar
    At 4000 rpm .... 3.0 bar
Oil pump type .... Two gear
Oil pump clearances:
    Gear-to-body (minimum) .... 0.110 mm
    Gear-to-body (maximum) .... 0.249 mm
    Gear endfloat (minimum) .... 0.020 mm
    Gear endfloat (maximum) .... 0.086 mm

Torque wrench settings

	Nm	lbf ft
Camshaft sprocket bolt	50 to 60	37 to 44
Crankshaft pulley bolt	80 to 90	59 to 66
Rocker shaft bolt	21 to 25	16 to 19
Flywheel bolt	50 to 55	37 to 41
Exhaust manifold	22.5 to 27.5	17 to 21
Inlet manifold	22.5 to 27.5	17 to 21
Main bearing cap	60 to 67	44 to 50
Connecting rod cap (oiled)	40 to 45	30 to 33
Sump	7 to 9	5 to 7
Oil drain plug	15 to 25	11 to 19
Cylinder head bolts:		
Stage 1	30	22
Stage 2	60	44
Stage 3	Wait for at least 3 minutes	
Stage 4	Slacken bolts 1 and 2 fully	
Stage 5	Tighten bolts 1 and 2 to:	
	20	15
Stage 6	Angle-tighten bolts 1 and 2 by 97° ± 2°	
Stage 7	Slacken bolts 3, 4, 5 and 6 fully	
Stage 8	Tighten bolts 3, 4, 5 and 6 to:	
	20	15
Stage 9	Angle-tighten bolts 3, 4, 5 and 6 by 97° ± 2°	
Stage 10	Slacken bolts 7, 8, 9 and 10 fully	
Stage 11	Tighten bolts 7, 8, 9 and 10 to:	
	20	15
Stage 12	Angle-tighten bolts 7,8,9 and 10 by 97° ± 2°	

1397 cc engine

General

Type	Four-cylinder, in-line, overhead valve
Designation	C1J
Bore	76.0 mm
Stroke	77.0 mm
Capacity	1397 cc
Firing order	1–3–4–2 (No 1 cylinder at flywheel end)
Direction of crankshaft rotation	Clockwise
Compression ratio	9.0 : 1
Maximum power output – kW (bhp)	43 (60) at 5250 rpm
Maximum torque – Nm (lbf ft)	105 (74) at 2750 rpm

Cylinder block

Material	Cast iron
Liner bore diameter	76.0 mm
Liner height (shoulder to top)	95.005 to 95.035 mm
Cylinder block depth (from top to liner locating shoulder)	94.945 to 94.985 mm
Liner protrusion without O-ring	0.02 to 0.09 mm
Maximum difference between adjacent liners	0.04 mm

Crankshaft

Number of main bearings	5
Main bearing journal diameter:	
Standard	54.795 mm
1st undersize	54.545 mm ± 0.010 mm
Main bearing running clearance	0.020 to 0.058 mm
Crankpin (big-end) journal diameter:	
Standard	43.98 mm
1st undersize	43.73 mm –0.02 mm
Big-end bearing running clearance	0.014 to 0.053 mm
Crankshaft endfloat	0.05 to 0.23 mm

Pistons and piston rings

Piston ring end gaps	Pre-adjusted
Piston ring thickness:	
Top compression ring	1.75 mm
Second compression ring	2.00 mm
Oil control ring	4.0 mm

Gudgeon pins

Length	60.4 mm
Outside diameter	20.0 mm
Bore	12.0 mm

Connecting rods
Small-end side play .... 0.310 to 0.572 mm

Cylinder head
Material .... Aluminium
Height .... 73.5 mm
Maximum acceptable gasket face distortion .... 0.05 mm
Valve seat angle:
    Inlet and exhaust .... 90°
Valve seat width .... 1.1 to 1.5 mm

Camshaft
Drive .... Chain
Number of bearings 4
Camshaft endfloat .... 0.05 to 0.12 mm

Valves
Head diameter:
    Inlet .... 34.2 mm
    Exhaust .... 28.9 mm
Stem diameter .... 7.0 mm
Valve clearance (cold):
    Inlet .... 0.15 mm
    Exhaust .... 0.20 mm
Valve clearance (hot):
    Inlet .... 0.18 mm
    Exhaust .... 0.25 mm
Valve spring free length .... 46.9 mm

Pushrods
Length .... 173.5 mm

Tappets
External diameter:
    Standard .... 19.0 mm
    Oversize .... 19.2 mm

Lubrication system
System pressure:
    At idle .... 0.7 bar
    At 4000 rpm .... 3.5 bar
Oil pump type .... Two gear, or bi-rotor
Oil pump clearances:
    Two gear:
        Gear-to-body (maximum) .... 0.20 mm
    Bi-rotor:
        Inner to outer rotors (at centre of peaks) .... 0.04 mm (minimum), 0.29 mm (maximum)

Torque wrench settings

	Nm	lbf ft
Rocker shaft	15 to 20	11 to 15
Camshaft sprocket	30	22
Crankshaft sprocket:		
40 mm bolt	80	59
45 mm bolt	110	81
Connecting rod caps	45	33
Main bearing caps	55 to 65	41 to 48
Flywheel	50	37
Cylinder head bolts:		
Stage 1	60 to 65	44 to 48
Stage 2	Run engine for 20 minutes then allow to cool for 2½ hours	
Stage 3	Loosen bolt 1 fully, then tighten to:	
	60 to 65	44 to 48
Stage 4	Loosen and tighten remaining bolts to Stage 3 setting	

1721 cc engine

General
Type .... Four-cylinder, in-line, overhead camshaft
Designation F2N
Bore .... 81.0 mm
Stroke .... 83.5 mm
Capacity .... 1721 cc

General (continued)
Firing order .... 1–3–4–2 (No 1 cylinder at flywheel end)
Direction of crankshaft rotation .... Clockwise
Compression ratio .... 9.5 : 1
Maximum power output – kW (bhp) .... 66.5 (92) at 5750 rpm
Maximum torque – Nm (lbf ft).. 141 (99) at 3000 rpm

Cylinder block
Material .... Cast iron

Crankshaft
Number of main bearings... 5
Main bearing journal diameter:
    Standard .... 54.794 mm
    1st undersize .... 54.545 mm ± 0.01 mm
Main bearing running clearance .... 0.020 to 0.058 mm
Crankpin (big-end) journal diameter:
    Standard.. 48.0 mm
    1st undersize .... 47.75 mm + 0.02 + 0 mm
Big-end bearing running clearance .... 0.014 to 0.053 mm
Crankshaft endfloat.. 0.07 to 0.23 mm

Pistons and piston rings
Piston ring end gaps .... Pre-adjusted
Piston ring thickness:
    Top compression ring... 1.75 mm
    Second compression ring .... 2.0 mm
    Oil control ring .... 3.0 mm
Piston clearance in bore .... 0.023 to 0.047 mm

Gudgeon pins
Length .... 65.0 mm + 0 –0.3 mm
Outside diameter .... 21.0 mm
Bore .... 13.5 mm

Connecting rods
Small-end side play... 0.22 to 0.40 mm

Cylinder head
Material .... Aluminium
Height .... 169.5 mm ± 0.2 mm
Maximum acceptable gasket face distortion .... 0.05 mm
Valve seat angle:
    Inlet .... 120°
    Exhaust .... 90°
Valve seat width .... 1.7 mm

Camshaft
Drive.. Toothed belt
Number of bearings 5
Camshaft endfloat.. 0.048 to 0.133 mm

Auxiliary shaft
Endfloat .... 0.07 to 0.15 mm

Valves
Head diameter:
    Inlet .... 38.1 mm
    Exhaust .... 32.5 mm
Stem diameter... 8.0 mm
Valve clearance (cold):
    Inlet .... 0.20 mm
    Exhaust .... 0.40 mm
Valve spring free length .... 44.9 mm

Lubrication system
System pressure:
    At 1000 rpm .... 2.0 bar
    At 3000 rpm .... 3.5 bar
Oil pump type... Two gear

Lubrication system (continued)
Oil pump clearances:
    Gear-to-body (minimum) .... 0.110 mm
    Gear-to-body (maximum) .... 0.249 mm
    Gear endfloat (minimum) .... 0.020 mm
    Gear endfloat (maximum) .... 0.086 mm

Torque wrench settings

	Nm	lbf ft
Camshaft sprocket	50	37
Camshaft bearing caps:		
8 mm diameter	20	15
6 mm diameter	10	7
Tensioner idler	20	15
Tensioner wheel	40	30
Auxiliary shaft sprocket	50	37
Crankshaft pulley	90 to 100	66 to 74
Oil pump cover:		
6 mm diameter	10	7
8 mm diameter	20 to 25	15 to 19
Connecting rod caps	45 to 50	33 to 37
Sump	12 to 15	9 to 11
Flywheel	50 to 55	37 to 41
Valve cover	3 to 6	2 to 4
Main bearing caps	60 to 65	44 to 48
Cylinder head bolts:		
Stage 1	30	22
Stage 2	70	52
Stage 3	Wait for 3 minutes minimum	
Stage 4	Loosen all the bolts completely	
Stage 5	20	15
Stage 6	Angle tighten by 123° ± 2°	

Part A: 1390 cc engine – in-car engine repair procedures

1 General information

How to use this Chapter

This Part of Chapter 2 is devoted to in-car repair procedures for the 1390 cc engine. Similar information covering the 1397 cc and 1721 cc engines will be found in Parts B and C respectively. All procedures concerning engine removal and refitting, and engine block/cylinder head overhaul for all engine types can be found in Part D of this Chapter.

Most of the operations included in this Part are based on the assumption that the engine is still installed in the car. Therefore, if this information is being used during a complete engine overhaul, with the engine already removed, many of the steps included here will not apply.

Engine description

The engine is of four-cylinder, in-line, overhead valve type, mounted transversely in the front of the car and inclined 12° rearwards.

The cast iron cylinder block is of the replaceable wet liner type. The crankshaft is supported within the cylinder block on five shell type main bearings. Thrust washers are fitted at the centre main bearing to control crankshaft endfloat.

The connecting rods are attached to the crankshaft by horizontally split shell type big-end bearings, and to the pistons by interference fit gudgeon pins. The aluminium alloy pistons are of the slipper type and are fitted with three piston rings, comprising two compression rings and a scraper type oil control ring.

The overhead camshaft is mounted directly in the cylinder head and is driven by the crankshaft via a toothed rubber timing belt which also drives the water pump. The camshaft operates the valves via rocker arms located on a rocker shaft bolted to the top of the cylinder head.

A semi-enclosed crankcase ventilation system is employed.

Lubrication is by pressure feed from a gear-type oil pump which is chain-driven direct from the crankshaft.

The distributor rotor is driven direct from the rear end of the camshaft, and the fuel pump is also operated by the camshaft via an eccentric and lever.

Repair operations possible with the engine in the vehicle

The following operations can be carried out without having to remove the engine from the car:

(a) Removal and refitting of the cylinder head
(b) Removal and refitting of the timing belt and sprockets
(c) Removal and refitting of the camshaft
(d) Removal and refitting of the sump
(e) Removal and refitting of the connecting rods, pistons and liners*
(f) Removal and refitting of the oil pump
(g) Renewal of the engine mountings
(h) Removal and refitting of the flywheel/driveplate

*Although the operation marked with an asterisk can be carried out

Fig. 2.1 Cutaway view of the 1390 cc (E6J) engine (Sec 1)

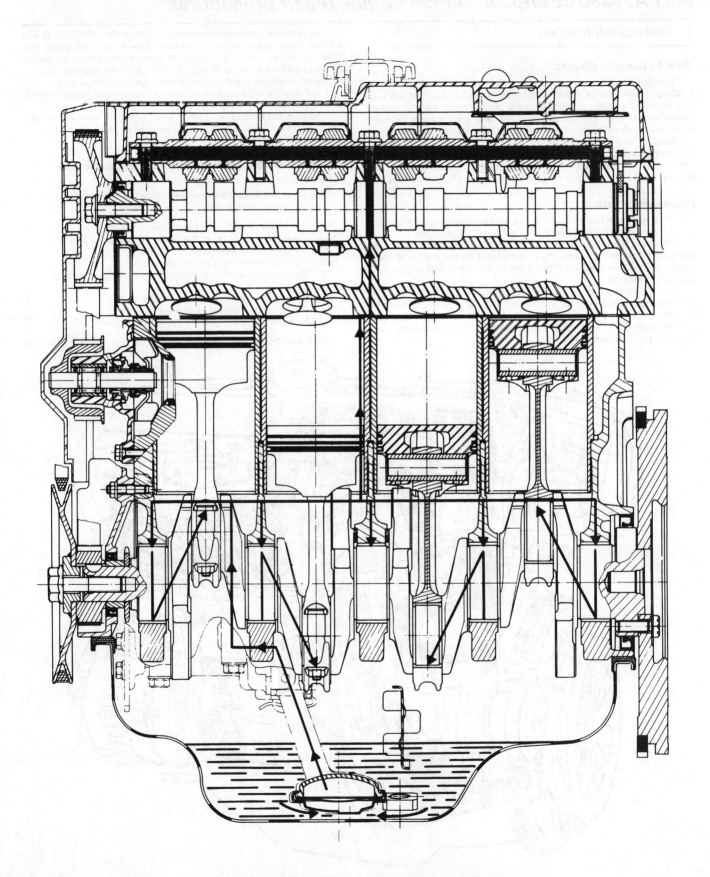

Fig. 2.2 Lubrication circuit of the 1390 cc (E6J) engine (Sec 1)

2.5 Compression gauge in use

with the engine in the car after removal of the sump, it is better for the engine to be removed in the interests of cleanliness and improved access. For this reason the procedure is described in Part D of this Chapter.

2   Compression test – description and interpretation

1   A compression check will tell you what mechanical condition the upper end (pistons, rings, valves, head gaskets) of the engine is in. Specifically, it can tell you if the compression is down due to leakage caused by worn piston rings, defective valves and seats or a blown head gasket. **Note:** *The engine must be at normal operating temperature and the battery must be fully charged for this check.*
2   Begin by cleaning the area around the spark plugs before you remove them (compressed air should be used, if available, otherwise a small brush or even a bicycle tyre pump will work). The idea is to prevent dirt from getting into the cylinders as the compression check is being done.
3   Remove all of the spark plugs from the engine (see Chapter 1).
4   Disconnect the coil HT lead from the centre of the distributor cap, and earth it on the cylinder block. Use a jumper lead or similar wire to make a good connection.
5   Fit the compression gauge into the No 1 spark plug hole (photo).
6   Have your assistant hold the accelerator pedal fully depressed to the floor while at the same time cranking the engine over several times on the starter motor. Observe the compression gauge noting that the compression should build up quickly in a healthy engine. Low compression on the first stroke, followed by gradually increasing pressure on successive strokes, indicates worn piston rings. A low compression reading on the first stroke, which does not build up during successive strokes, indicates leaking valves or a blown head gasket (a cracked head could also be the cause). Deposits on the undersides of the valve heads can also cause low compression. Record the highest gauge reading obtained, then repeat the procedure for the remaining cylinders.
7   Add some engine oil (about three squirts from a plunger-type oil can) to each cylinder, through the spark plug hole, and repeat the test.
8   If the compression increases after the oil is added, the piston rings are definitely worn. If the compression does not increase significantly, the leakage is occurring at the valves or head gasket. Leakage past the valves may be caused by burned valve seats and/or faces or warped, cracked or bent valves.
9   If two adjacent cylinders have equally low compression, there is a strong possibility that the head gasket between them is blown. The appearance of coolant in the combustion chambers or the crankcase would verify this condition.
10   If one cylinder is about 20 percent lower than the other, and the engine has a slightly rough idle, a worn lobe on the camshaft could be the cause.

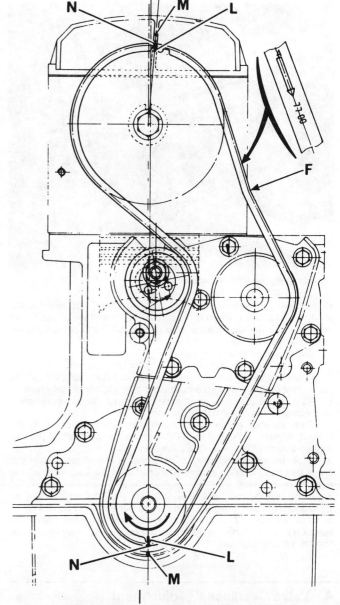

Fig. 2.3 Timing belt and timing marks (Sec 3)

F   Belt tension checking
      point
L   Timing marks on the
      camshaft and crankshaft
      sprockets

M   Fixed timing marks
N   Timing bands on the belt

11   If the compression is unusually high, the combustion chambers are probably coated with carbon deposits. If this is the case, the cylinder head should be removed and decarbonised.
12   Actual compression pressures for the engines covered by this manual are not specified by the manufacturer. However, bearing in mind the information given in the preceding paragraphs the results obtained should give a good indication of engine condition and what, if any, course of action to take.

3   Top dead centre (TDC) for number one piston – locating

1   Top dead centre (TDC) is the highest point in the cylinder that each piston reaches as the crankshaft turns. Each piston reaches TDC at the end of the compression stroke and again at the end of the exhaust

4.6 Adjusting the valve clearances

stroke, however for the purpose of timing the engine, TDC refers to the position of number 1 piston at the end of its compression stroke. On all engines in this manual, number 1 piston and cylinder is at the flywheel end of the engine.
2   Disconnect both battery leads.
3   Unscrew the bolts and remove the upper timing cover.
4   Apply the handbrake, then jack up the front right-hand side of the car and support it on axle stands. Remove the right-hand roadwheel.
5   Remove the plastic cover from within the right-hand wheelarch to give access to the crankshaft pulley bolt.
6   Turn the engine in a clockwise direction, using a socket on the crankshaft pulley bolt, until the TDC mark on the camshaft sprocket is aligned with the TDC tab on the valve cover.
7   Look through the aperture at the flywheel end of the engine and check that the TDC timing mark is aligned with the TDC mark on the gearbox bellhousing.
8   If the distributor cap is now removed, the rotor arm should be positioned so that it is aligned with the number 1 HT lead segment.
9   It is not possible to check the timing marks on the crankshaft sprocket without removing the crankshaft pulley first. The pulley is not marked with timing marks.

4   Valve clearances – adjustment

1   Remove the air cleaner and disconnect the choke cable, as described in Chapter 4.
2   Unscrew the bolts and remove the valve cover and gasket. Disconnect the crankcase ventilation hoses from the cover.
3   Remove the spark plugs (Chapter 1) in order to make turning the engine easier.
4   Draw the valve positions on a piece of paper numbering them 1 to 4 inlet and exhaust according to their cylinders, from the flywheel (left-hand) end of the engine (ie 1E, 1I, 2E, 2I et seq). As the valve clearances are adjusted cross them off.
5   Using a socket or spanner on the crankshaft pulley bolt, turn the engine in a clockwise direction until No 1 exhaust valve is completely open (ie the valve spring is completely compressed).
6   Insert a feeler blade of the correct thickness between the No 3 cylinder inlet valve stem and the end of the rocker arm. It should be a firm sliding fit. If adjustment is necessary, loosen the locknut on the rocker arm using a ring spanner and turn the adjustment screw with a BA spanner until the fit is correct (photo). Tighten the locknut and recheck the adjustment, then repeat the adjustment procedure on No 4 cylinder exhaust valve.
7   Turn the engine in a clockwise direction until No 3 exhaust valve is completely open and adjust the valve clearances on No 4 inlet, and No 2 exhaust valves. Continue to adjust the valve clearances in the following sequence:

Exhaust valve fully open	Adjust inlet valve	Adjust exhaust valve
1E	3I	4E
3E	4I	2E
4E	2I	1E
2E	1I	3E

8   Remove the socket or spanner from the crankshaft pulley bolt.
9   Refit the spark plugs, then refit the valve cover together with a new gasket where necessary. Reconnect the crankcase ventilation hoses. Refit the air cleaner and re-connect the choke cable.

5   Cylinder head – removal and refitting

Removal
1   Disconnect both battery leads.
2   Drain the cooling system, including the cylinder block, with reference to Chapter 1. The block drain plug is located on the right-hand rear face of the engine, beneath the inlet manifold. It is important to drain the block as, if the wet cylinder liners are disturbed, the coolant will drain into the sump.
3   Drain the engine oil with reference to Chapter 1.
4   Remove the timing belt with reference to Section 6 of this Chapter.
5   Remove the complete air cleaner and carburettor inlet duct with reference to Chapter 4.
6   Unbolt and remove the strengthening bar from between the front suspension turrets and place it to one side (photo).
7   Disconnect the following wires. Identify them with adhesive tags if necessary to ensure correct refitting:

(a)   Temperature sender
(b)   Fuel cut-off solenoid
(c)   Ignition AEI unit

8   Disconnect the accelerator cable and choke cable from the carburettor and valve cover brackets and position them to one side.
9   Remove the inlet and exhaust manifolds with reference to Chapter 4.

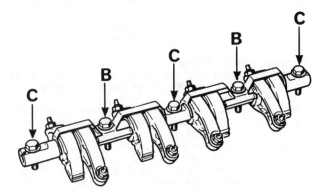

Fig. 2.4 Rocker shaft bolt identification (Sec 5)

B   Solid bolts coloured yellow

C   Hollow bolts coloured black

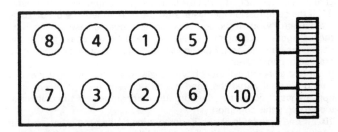

Fig. 2.5 Cylinder head bolt tightening sequence (Sec 5)

5.6 Removing the strengthening bar from the front suspension turrets

5.12A Removing the valve cover ...

5.12B ... and gasket

5.13 Rocker shaft mounting bolts (arrowed)

5.16A Lifting the cylinder head from the block

5.16B Removing the cylinder head gasket

5.16C Cylinder head locating dowel (arrowed)

5.17 Clamps (arrowed) holding the liners in place

10   Loosen the clips and disconnect the following hoses:

(a) Expansion tank purge hose from the cylinder head outlet
(b) Radiator top hose from the thermostat housing
(c) Crankcase ventilation hoses from the valve cover

11   Disconnect the HT leads from the spark plugs and pull them carefully from the HT lead holder on the valve cover. Unbolt and remove the holder.
12   Unbolt the valve cover from the cylinder head and remove the gasket (photos).
13   Progressively unscrew the bolts holding the rocker shaft and retaining plate to the cylinder head and withdraw the shaft (photo). Note that the bolts are different and should be identified for position before removal. Numbers 2 and 4 bolts have solid shanks whereas the other bolts have hollow shanks. Their heads are coloured as shown in Fig. 2.4.
14   Progressively unscrew the cylinder head bolts in the reverse order to that shown in Fig. 2.5, then remove them all except the bolt positioned on the front right-hand corner, which should be unscrewed by only three or four threads.

15   The joint between the cylinder head, gasket and cylinder block must now be broken without disturbing the wet liners. To do this, pull the distributor end of the cylinder head forward so as to swivel it around the single bolt still fitted, then locate the head back in its original position. If this procedure is not followed, there is a possibility of the wet liners moving and their bottom seals being disturbed causing leakage after refitting the head.
16   Remove the bolt and lift the head from the cylinder block followed by the gasket. Note the location dowel on the front right-hand corner of the block (photos).
17   Note that the crankshaft must not be rotated with the cylinder head removed, otherwise the wet liners will be displaced. If it is necessary to turn the engine (eg to clean the piston crowns), either use bolts with washers or make up some retaining clamps out of flat metal bar held in place with bolts screwed into the block (photo).

Refitting

18   The mating faces of the cylinder head and block must be perfectly clean before refitting the head. Use a scraper to remove all traces of

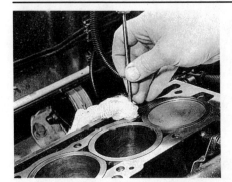

5.21 Cleaning the cylinder head bolt holes in the cylinder block

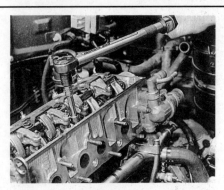

5.27A Torque tightening the cylinder head bolts

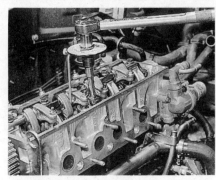

5.27B Angle-tightening the cylinder head bolts

gasket and carbon, and also clean the tops of the pistons. Take particular care with the aluminium cylinder head as the soft metal is damaged easily. Also, make sure that the carbon is not allowed to enter the oil and water channels – this is particularly important for the oil circuit, as carbon could block the oil supply to the camshaft and rocker arms or crankshaft main and big-end bearings. Using adhesive tape and paper, seal the water, oil and bolt holes in the cylinder block. To prevent carbon entering the gap between the pistons and bores, smear a little grease in the gap. After cleaning the piston, rotate the crankshaft so that the piston moves down the bore then wipe out the grease and carbon with a cloth rag. Clean the piston crowns in the same way.

19   Check the block and head for nicks, deep scratches and other damage. If slight, they may be removed carefully with a file, however, if excessive, machining may be the only alternative.

20   If warpage of the cylinder head is suspected, use a straight-edge to check it for distortion. Refer to Part D of this Chapter if necessary.

21   Clean out all the bolt holes in the block using a cloth rag and screwdriver (photo). Make sure that all oil is removed, otherwise there is a possibility of the block being cracked by hydraulic pressure when the bolts are tightened.

22   Examine the bolt threads and the threads in the cylinder block for damage. If necessary, use the correct size tap to chase out the threads in the block and use a die to clean the threads on the bolts.

23   Position number one piston at TDC, then remove the cylinder liner clamps or washers as applicable and wipe clean the faces of the head and block.

24   Check that the location dowel is in position on the front right-hand corner of the block.

25   Position the new gasket on the block and over the dowel. It can only be fitted one way round.

26   Lower the cylinder head onto the block, then insert the bolts and initially screw them in finger-tight.

27   Tighten the cylinder head bolts to the specified torques in the sequence shown in Fig. 2.5, and in the stages given in the Specifications at the beginning of this Chapter. The first two stages precompress the gasket, and the remaining stages are the main tightening procedure (photos).

28   Refit the rocker shaft and retaining plate, then insert the bolts in their original positions and tighten them to the specified torque.

29   If the cylinder head has been overhauled, it is worthwhile checking the valve clearances at this stage to prevent any possibility of the valves touching the pistons when the timing belt is being fitted. Use a socket on the camshaft sprocket to turn the camshaft, but before doing this, turn the crankshaft so that the pistons in numbers one and four cylinders are not at TDC.

30   Refit the timing belt with reference to Section 6 of this Chapter.

31   Adjust the valve clearances as described in Section 4 of this Chapter.

32   Refit the valve cover together with a new gasket and tighten the bolts progressively.

33   Refit the spark plugs if removed.

34   Refit the HT lead holder, then connect the HT leads to the spark plugs and insert the leads in the holder.

35   Reconnect the crankshaft ventilation and coolant hoses.

36   Refit the inlet and exhaust manifolds with reference to Chapter 4.

37   Refit the accelerator and choke cables and if necessary adjust them with reference to Chapter 4.

38   Reconnect all wires in their correct positions.

39   Refit the strengthening bar between the front suspension turrets and tighten the bolts.

40   Refit the air cleaner and carburettor inlet duct with reference to Chapter 4.

41   Refill the engine with oil with reference to Chapter 1.

42   Reconnect both battery leads.

43   Refill and bleed the cooling system with reference to Chapter 1.

6   Timing belt – removal, inspection and refitting

Removal

1   Disconnect both the battery leads.

2   Remove the alternator/power-assisted steering pump/air conditioning pump drive belts, as applicable.

3   Unscrew the bolts and remove the upper timing cover (photo).

4   Apply the handbrake, then jack up the front right-hand side of the car and support on axle stands. Remove the roadwheel.

5   Remove the plastic cover from within the right-hand wheelarch to give access to the crankshaft pulley.

6   Turn the engine in a clockwise direction, using a socket on the crankshaft pulley bolt, until the TDC mark on the camshaft sprocket is aligned with the TDC tab on the valve cover.

7   Unscrew the crankshaft pulley bolt while holding the crankshaft stationary (photo). To do this, have an assistant insert a screwdriver in the starter ring gear teeth through the access hole in the top of the gearbox bellhousing. Take care not to damage the ignition timing sensor.

8   Remove the crankshaft pulley from the nose of the crankshaft. If it is tight, use a puller.

9   Note that the timing mark on the crankshaft sprocket is aligned with the mark on the front oil seal cover (photo).

10   Loosen the nut securing the timing belt tensioner, then move the tensioner outwards to release the tension from the belt and re-tighten the nut again.

11   Check if the belt is marked with arrows to indicate its running direction, and if necessary, mark it. Release the belt from the camshaft sprocket, water pump sprocket, and crankshaft sprocket and remove it from the engine.

12   Clean the sprockets and tensioner and wipe them dry. Also clean the front of the cylinder head and block.

Inspection

13   Examine the timing belt carefully for any signs of cracking, fraying or general wear, particularly at the roots of the teeth. Renew the belt if there is any sign of deterioration of this nature, or if there is any oil or grease contamination. The belt must, of course, be renewed if it has completed the maximum mileage given in Chapter 1.

Refitting

14   Check the directional mark and timing bands on the back of the timing belt, then locate the belt on the crankshaft sprocket so that one of

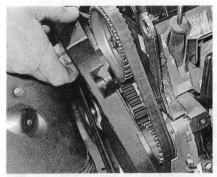

6.3 Removing the upper timing cover

6.7 Unscrewing the crankshaft pulley bolt

6.9 Timing marks (arrowed) on the crankshaft sprocket and front oil seal cover

6.14A Fitting the timing belt over the camshaft sprocket ...

6.14B ... and tensioner

6.14C Timing band on the belt aligned with the mark on the sprocket (arrowed)

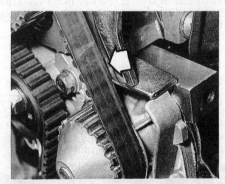

6.16A Timing belt deflection mark made on the front engine lifting bracket (arrowed)

6.16B Checking the timing belt tension using a spring balance and steel rule

the timing bands is aligned with the marks on the sprocket and cover. The other timing band should be positioned so that it will locate on the camshaft sprocket in alignment with the other timing mark. After engaging the belt with the crankshaft sprocket, pull it taught over the water pump sprocket and onto the camshaft sprocket, then position it over the tensioner wheel (photos).

15   With the belt fully engaged with the sprockets, unscrew the tensioner nut and allow the wheel to tension the belt, then tighten the nut.

16   The belt deflection must now be checked. To do this, first make a mark on the front engine lifting bracket in line with the timing belt, mid-way between the camshaft and water pump sprockets. A force of 30 N (7 lbf) must now be applied to the timing belt and its deflection checked to be 6 ± 0.5 mm (0.236 ± 0.02 in). Renault technicians use a special tool to do this, however an alternative arrangement can be made by using a spring balance and steel rule. Apply the force with the spring balance and read off the deflection on the steel rule (photos).

17   If the adjustment is incorrect, the tensioner hub will have to be repositioned.

18   Refit the crankshaft pulley to the nose of the crankshaft, then screw in the bolt. Tighten the bolt while holding the crankshaft stationary using the same method as described in paragraph 7.

19   Using a socket on the crankshaft pulley, turn the engine through two complete revolutions then recheck the timing belt tension and make sure that the timing marks are still in alignment.

20   The tensioner nut must be tightened securely, since if it was to come loose considerable engine damage would result.

21   Refit the plastic cover inside the right-hand wheelarch.

22   Refit the road wheel and lower the car to the ground.

23   Refit the upper timing belt cover.

24   Refit and tension the alternator/power-assisted steering pump/air conditioning pump drive belts (as applicable) with reference to Chapter 1.

25   Reconnect the battery leads.

7.4 Using a home-made puller to remove the crankshaft sprocket

7   Timing belt sprockets and tensioner – removal, inspection and refitting

Removal

1   Remove the timing belt as described in Section 6.
2   To remove the camshaft sprocket, hold the sprocket stationary using a metal bar with two bolts tightened onto it inserted into the holes in the sprocket, then unscrew the bolt. The Renault tool is shown in Fig. 2.6.
3   Remove the sprocket from the end of the camshaft. Note that it has a tab on its inner face which locates in a slot in the end of the camshaft.
4   A puller may be necessary to remove the crankshaft sprocket, however it is a simple matter to make up a puller using two bolts, a metal bar and the existing crankshaft pulley bolt (photo). By unscrewing the crankshaft pulley bolt, the sprocket is pulled from the end of the crankshaft.
5   If necessary, remove the Woodruff key from the slot in the crankshaft.
6   Unscrew the nut and withdraw the tensioner from the stud on the front cover (photo).

Inspection

7   Inspect the teeth of the sprockets for signs of nicks and damage. Also examine the water pump teeth. The teeth are not prone to wear

7.6 Removing the timing belt tensioner

and should normally last the life of the engine.
8   Spin the tensioner by hand and check it for any roughness or tightness. Do not attempt to clean it with solvent as this may enter the bearing. If wear is evident, renew the tensioner.

Refitting

9   Locate the tensioner on the stud on the front cover, then refit the nut and tighten it finger-tight at this stage.
10   Fit the Woodruff key in its slot in the crankshaft, making sure that it is level to ensure engagement with the sprocket.
11   Slide the sprocket fully onto the crankshaft; use a metal tube if necessary to tap it into position.
12   Locate the sprocket on the end of the camshaft making sure that the tab locates in the special slot, then screw in the bolt. Tighten the bolt to the specified torque while holding the sprocket stationary using the method described in paragraph 2.
13   Refit the timing belt as described in Section 6.

8   Camshaft oil seal – renewal

1   Remove the camshaft sprocket as described in Section 7.
2   Using a small screwdriver, prise out the oil seal from the cylinder head. To ensure correct fitting, note the fitted position of the old oil seal.
3   Wipe clean the seating in the cylinder head.

8.4 Installing a new camshaft oil seal

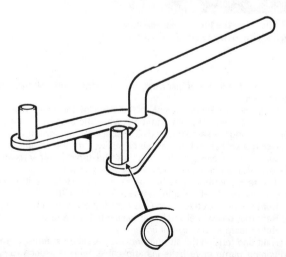

Fig. 2.6 Renault tool for holding the camshaft sprocket stationary (Sec 7)

9.2 Removing the camshaft sprocket retaining bolt

9.4 Checking the camshaft endfloat with a dial test gauge

9.5 Removing the camshaft thrust plate

9.6 Removing the camshaft

9.13 Tightening the camshaft retaining bolt

4   Smear a little oil on the outer surface of the new oil seal, then locate it squarely in the cylinder head and drive it into position using a metal tube which has an external diameter slightly less than that of the cylinder head (photo). Make sure that the oil seal is the correct way round with its sealed face outwards.

5   Refit the camshaft sprocket as described in Section 7.

9   Camshaft – removal, inspection and refitting

Removal

1   Remove the cylinder head as described in Section 5 and place it on the workbench.

2   Hold the camshaft stationary using a spanner on the special flats provided on the camshaft, then unscrew the bolt and withdraw the sprocket (photo).

3   Using a Torx key, unscrew the two bolts holding the distributor on the cylinder head and remove the distributor. There is no need to mark the distributor as it is not possible to adjust its position. Although there is an elongated slot for one of the bolts, the other bolt locates in a single hole.

4   Using a dial gauge, measure the endfloat of the camshaft and compare with that given in the Specifications (photo). This will give an indication of the amount of wear in the thrust plate.

5   Unscrew the two bolts and lift the thrust plate out from the slot in the camshaft (photo).

6   Carefully withdraw the camshaft from the sprocket end of the cylinder head, taking care not to damage the bearing surfaces (photo).

Inspection

7   Examine the camshaft bearing surfaces, cam lobes and fuel pump eccentric for wear ridges and scoring. Renew the camshaft if any of these conditions are apparent.

8   Examine the condition of the bearing surfaces both on the camshaft and in the cylinder head. If the head bearing surfaces are worn excessively, the cylinder head will need to be renewed.

Refitting

9   Lubricate the bearing surfaces in the cylinder head and the camshaft journals, then insert the camshaft into the head.

10   Refit the thrust plate, then insert and tighten the bolts.

11   Measure the endfloat as described in paragraph 4 and make sure that it is within the limits given in the Specifications.

12   Refit the distributor and tighten the two bolts using a Torx key.

13   Refit the camshaft sprocket making sure that the tab engages with the cut-out in the end of the camshaft. Hold the camshaft stationary with a spanner on the special flats, then insert the bolt and tighten it to the specified torque (photo).

14   Refit the cylinder head as described in Section 5.

10   Sump – removal and refitting

Note: *An engine lifting hoist is required during this procedure*

Removal

1   Disconnect the battery leads.

2   Drain the engine oil as described in Chapter 1, then refit and tighten the drain plug to the specified torque setting.

3   Jack up the front right-hand side of the car and support on axle stands. Remove the roadwheel.

4   Remove the plastic cover from inside the wheelarch for access to the engine.

5   Unscrew the nuts securing the exhaust front pipe to the exhaust manifold and remove the springs.

6   Working under the car disconnect the front exhaust pipe from the

10.7A Unscrew the bolts ...

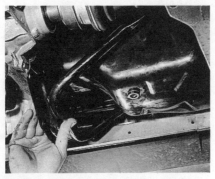
10.7B ... and remove the tie-bar and cover assembly

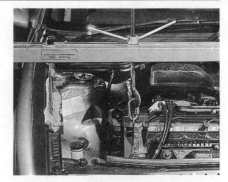
10.8A Using a lifting bar to raise the right-hand side of the engine

10.8B Right-hand engine mounting nut

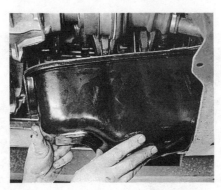
10.10 Lowering the sump from the engine

10.12 Fitting the gasket to the sump

rear system by unscrewing the clamp bolts. Remove the front pipe.

7   Unscrew the bolts securing the tie-bar and cover assembly to the gearbox bellhousing and engine block, and lower it from the sump (photos).

8   The engine must now be raised by approximately 75 to 100 mm (3 to 4 in) before the sump can be removed. To do this, first unscrew the right-hand engine mounting nut from under the car and remove the bracket plate. Attach a hoist to the engine lifting eye next to the timing cover, and raise the engine (photos).

9   Unscrew the bolts securing the sump to the cylinder block.

10   Break the joint by striking the sump with the palm of the hand, then lower the sump over the oil pump and withdraw it (photo).

Refitting

11   Clean all traces of gasket from the cylinder block and sump, and wipe them dry.

12   Locate a new gasket on the sump making sure that it is correctly positioned on the curved sections (photo).

13   Offer the sump to the cylinder block and insert the bolts. Progressively tighten the bolts in diagonal sequence to the specified torque.

14   Lower the engine and refit the right-hand engine mounting plate and nut. Remove the hoist.

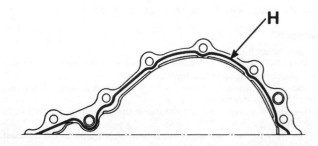
Fig. 2.7 Sealant bead application (H) around the front cover (Sec 11)

15   Refit the tie-bar and cover assembly to the gearbox bellhousing and engine block.

16   Refit the front exhaust pipe and tighten the bolts. Refer to Chapter 4 if necessary.

17   Refit the plastic cover to the inside of the wheelarch.

18   Refit the roadwheel and lower the car to the ground.

19   Refill the engine with oil with reference to Chapter 1.

20   Reconnect the battery leads.

11   Oil pump and sprockets – removal, inspection and refitting

Removal

1   Remove the timing belt and crankshaft sprocket with reference to Sections 6 and 7.

2   Remove the sump as described in Section 10.

3   Remove the Woodruff key from its slot in the crankshaft (photo).

4   Unbolt the front cover from the cylinder block (photo).

5   Slide off the oil seal spacer.

6   Unscrew the bolts securing the sprocket to the oil pump hub. Use a screwdriver through one of the holes in the sprocket to hold it stationary (photo).

7   Remove the oil pump sprocket and release the chain from the crankshaft sprocket.

8   Slide the sprocket from the crankshaft.

9   Unscrew the two mounting bolts and withdraw the oil pump from the crankcase (photo). If the two locating dowels are displaced, refit them in the crankcase.

Inspection

10   Unscrew the four retaining bolts and lift off the pump cover and pick-up tube.

11   Using a feeler gauge, check the clearance between each of the

11.3 Removing the Woodruff key (arrowed) from the front of the crankshaft

11.4 Removing the front cover from the cylinder block

11.6 Unscrewing the oil pump sprocket bolts

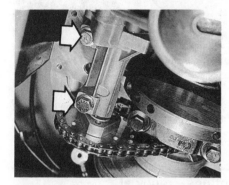

11.9 Oil pump mounting bolts (arrowed)

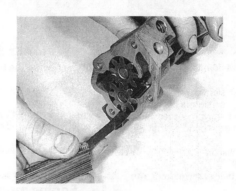

11.11A Checking the clearance between the oil pump gears and body

11.11B Checking the clearance between the oil pump gears and cover

11.12 Oil pump relief valve components

11.21A Removing the oil seal from the front cover

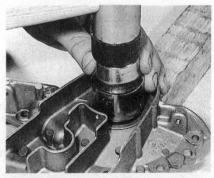

11.21B Driving a new oil seal into the front cover

gears and the oil pump body. Also check the clearance between the gears and the cover joint face (photos). If any clearance is outside the tolerances given in the Specifications, the oil pump must be renewed.

12   Mount the cover in a vice, then depress the relief valve end stop and extract the spring clip. Release the end stop and remove the spring and piston (photo).

13   Examine the relief valve piston and seat for signs of wear and damage. If evident, renew the oil pump complete.

14   If the components are serviceable, clean them and reassemble in the reverse order to dismantling. Before refitting the cover, fill the pump with fresh engine oil to assist circulation when the engine is first started.

15   Examine the chain for excessive wear and renew it if necessary. Similarly check the sprockets.

Refitting

16   Wipe clean the oil pump and crankcase mating surfaces.

17   Check that the two locating dowels are fitted in the crankcase, then position the oil pump on them and insert the two mounting bolts.

Tighten the bolts securely.

18   Slide the sprocket onto the crankshaft.

19   Engage the oil pump sprocket with the chain, then engage the chain with the crankshaft sprocket and locate the sprocket on the oil pump hub.

20   Align the holes then insert the sprocket bolts and tighten them securely while holding the sprocket stationary with a screwdriver.

21   The oil seal in the front cover should be renewed whenever the cover is removed. Note the fitted position of the old seal, then prise it out with a screwdriver and wipe clean the seating. Smear the outer perimeter of the new seal with fresh engine oil and locate it squarely on the cover with its closed side facing outwards. Place the cover on a block of wood, then use a socket or metal tube to drive in the oil seal (photos).

22   Clean all traces of sealant from the front cover and block mating faces. Apply a 0.6 to 1.0 mm diameter bead of sealant around the perimeter of the front cover, then refit it to the cylinder block and tighten the bolts securely.

11.23 Sliding the spacer onto the front of the crankshaft

23   Smear the oil seal with a little engine oil, then slide the spacer onto the front of the crankshaft (photo). Turn it slightly as it enters the oil seal to prevent damage to the seal lip. If the spacer is worn excessively where the old oil seal contacted it, it may be turned around so that the new oil seal contacts the unworn area.
24   Refit the Woodruff key to its slot in the crankshaft.
25   Refit the sump with reference to Section 10.
26   Refit the crankshaft sprocket and timing belt with reference to Sections 7 and 6.

12   Crankshaft oil seals – renewal

Front/right-hand oil seal

1   Remove the timing belt and crankshaft sprocket with reference to Sections 6 and 7.
2   Remove the sump as described in Section 10.
3   Remove the Woodruff key from its slot in the crankshaft.
4   Unbolt the front cover from the cylinder block.
5   Slide off the oil seal spacer.
6   Note the fitted position of the old seal in the cover, then prise it out with a screwdriver and wipe clean the seating. Smear the outer perimeter of the new seal with fresh engine oil and locate it squarely on the cover with its closed side facing outwards. Place the cover on a block of wood, then use a socket or metal tube to drive in the oil seal (see photos 11.21A and 11.21B).
7   Clean all traces of sealant from the front cover and block mating faces. Apply a 0.6 to 1.0 mm diameter bead of sealant around the perimeter of the front cover, then refit it to the cylinder block and tighten the bolts securely.
8   Smear the oil seal with a little fresh engine oil, then slide the spacer onto the front of the crankshaft. Turn it slightly as it enters the oil seal to prevent damage to the seal lip. If the spacer is worn excessively where the old oil seal contacted it, it may be turned around so that the new oil seal contacts the unworn area.
9   Refit the Woodruff key to its slot in the crankshaft.
10   Refit the sump with reference to Section 10.
11   Refit the crankshaft sprocket and timing belt with reference to Sections 7 and 6.

Rear/left-hand oil seal

12   Remove the flywheel/driveplate as described in Section 14.
13   Prise out the old oil seal using a small screwdriver, taking care not to damage the surface on the crankshaft. Alternatively, the oil seal can be removed by drilling two small holes diagonally opposite each other and inserting self-tapping screws in them. A pair of grips can then be used to pull out the oil seal, by pulling on each side in turn.
14   Wipe clean the oil seal seating, then dip the new seal in fresh engine oil and locate it over the crankshaft with its closed side facing

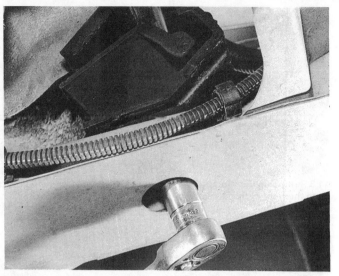

13.7 Unscrewing the front engine left-hand mounting lower nut

outwards. Make sure that the oil seal lip is not damaged as it is located on the crankshaft.
15   Using a metal tube, drive the oil seal squarely into the bore until flush. A block of wood cut to pass over the end of the crankshaft may be used instead.
16   Refit the flywheel/driveplate with reference to Section 14.

13   Engine mountings – renewal

1   Apply the handbrake, then jack up the front of the car and support it on axle stands.

Front right-hand mounting

2   Unscrew the nut and remove the plate from under the front subframe.
3   Using a hoist, raise the right-hand side of the engine 2 or 3 in (50 to 75 mm).
4   Unscrew the nuts and remove the mounting from the bracket.
5   If necessary, unbolt the bracket from the cylinder block.
6   Fit the new mounting using a reversal of the removal procedure.

Front left-hand mounting

7   Using a socket through the hole in the subframe, unscrew the lower mounting nut (photo).

13.12 Unscrewing the rear mounting through-bolt

8   Take the weight of the transmission with a trolley jack, then unscrew the upper nut and withdraw the mounting from the engine compartment. If necessary, the mounting bracket can be unbolted from the cylinder block.
9   Fit the new mounting using a reversal of the removal procedure.

Rear mounting

10   Apply the handbrake, then jack up the front of the car and support it on axle stands.
11   Support the weight of the engine/transmission using a hoist or trolley jack.
12   Unscrew and remove the through-bolt (photo).
13   Fit the new mounting using a reversal of the removal procedure.

Gearbox mounting

14   Apply the handbrake, then jack up the front of the car and support it on axle stands.
15   Take the weight of the transmission with a trolley jack, then unscrew the nuts/bolts and withdraw the mounting from the transmission.

14   Flywheel/driveplate – removal, inspection and refitting

Removal

1   Remove the transmission as described in Chapter 7.
2   On manual gearbox models, remove the clutch.
3   Mark the flywheel or driveplate in relation to the crankshaft.
4   The flywheel/driveplate must now be held stationary while the bolts are loosened. To do this, locate a long bolt in one of the transmission mounting bolt holes and either insert a wide-bladed screwdriver in the starter ring gear or use a piece of bent metal bar engaged with the ring gear.
5   Unscrew the mounting bolts and withdraw the flywheel/driveplate from the crankshaft (photo).

Inspection

6   Examine the flywheel for scoring of the clutch face and for wear or

14.5 Flywheel mounting bolts

chipping of the ring gear teeth. If the clutch face is scored, the flywheel may be machined until flat, but renewal is preferable. If the ring gear is worn or damaged it may be possible to renew it separately, but this job is best left to a Renault dealer or engineering works. The temperature to which the new ring gear must be heated for installation is critical and, if not done accurately, the hardness of the teeth will be destroyed.
7   Check the torque converter driveplate carefully for signs of distortion or any hairline cracks around the bolt holes or radiating outwards from the centre.

Refitting

8   Clean the flywheel/driveplate and crankshaft faces, then locate the unit on the crankshaft making sure that any previously made marks are aligned.
9   Apply a few drops of thread-locking fluid to the mounting bolt threads, fit the bolts and tighten them in a diagonal sequence to the specified torque.
10   On manual gearbox models, refit the clutch.
11   Refit the transmission as described in Chapter 7.

Part B: 1397 cc engine – in-car engine repair procedures

15 General information

How to use this Chapter

This Part of Chapter 2 is devoted to in-car repair procedures for the 1397 cc engine. Similar information covering the 1390 cc and 1721 cc engines will be found in Parts A and C respectively. All procedures concerning engine removal and refitting, and engine block/cylinder head overhaul for all engine types can be found in Part D of this Chapter.

Most of the operations included in this Part are based on the assumption that the engine is still installed in the car. Therefore, if this information is being used during a complete engine overhaul, with the engine already removed, many of the steps included here will not apply.

Engine description

The engine is of four-cylinder, in-line, overhead valve type, mounted transversely in the front of the car.

The cast iron cylinder block is of the replaceable wet liner type. The crankshaft is supported within the cylinder block on five shell type main bearings. Thrust washers are fitted at the centre main bearing to control crankshaft endfloat.

The connecting rods are attached to the crankshaft by horizontally split shell type big-end bearings, and to the pistons by interference fit gudgeon pins. The aluminium alloy pistons are of the slipper type and are fitted with three piston rings, comprising two compression rings and a scraper type oil control ring.

The camshaft is chain driven from the crankshaft and operates the rocker arms via pushrods. The inlet and exhaust valves are each closed by a single valve spring and operate in guides pressed into the cylinder head. The valves are actuated directly by the rocker arms.

A semi-closed crankcase ventilation system is employed, and crankcase gases are drawn from the rocker cover via a hose to the air cleaner and inlet manifold.

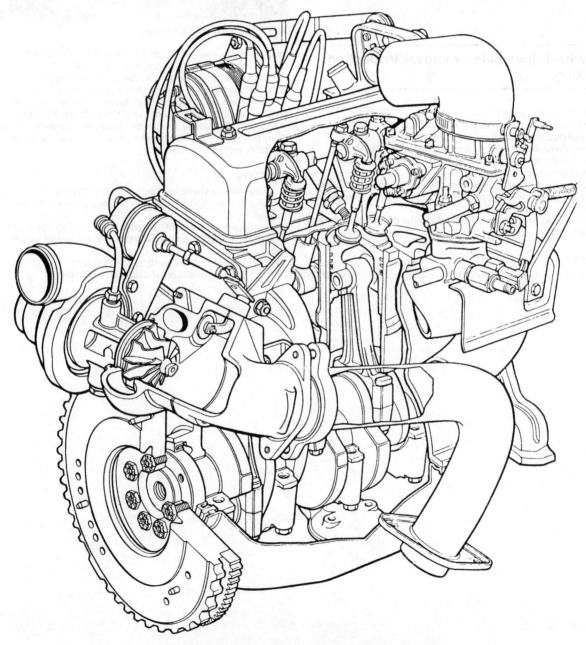

Fig. 2.8 Cutaway view of the 1397 cc (C1J) engine (Sec 15)

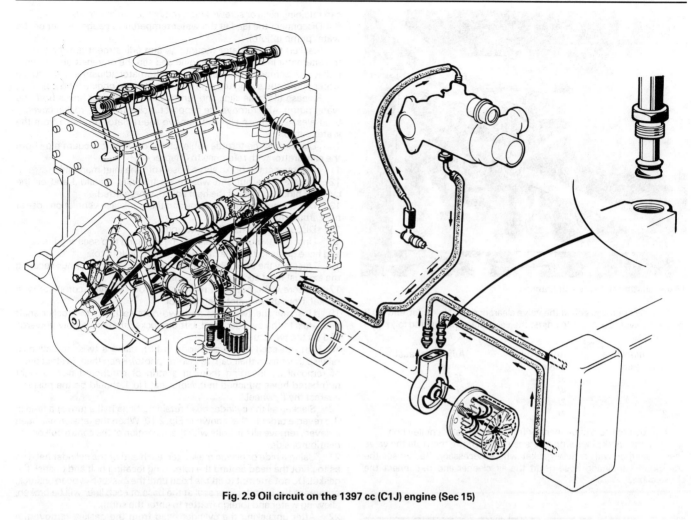

Fig. 2.9 Oil circuit on the 1397 cc (C1J) engine (Sec 15)

Lubrication is provided by a gear type oil pump, driven from the camshaft and located in the crankcase. Engine oil is fed through an externally mounted full-flow filter to the engine oil gallery, and then to the crankshaft, camshaft and rocker shaft bearings. A pressure relief valve is incorporated in the oil pump.

Repair operations possible with the engine in the vehicle

The following operations can be carried out without having to remove the engine from the car:

(a) *Removal and refitting of the cylinder head*
(b) *Removal and refitting of the timing cover, chain and gears*
(c) *Removal and refitting of the sump*
(d) *Removal and refitting of the connecting rods, pistons and liners**
(e) *Removal, overhaul and refitting of the oil pump*
(f) *Renewal of the engine mountings*
(g) *Removal and refitting of the flywheel*

*Although the pistons and liners can be removed and refitted with the engine in the car, it is better to carry this work out with the engine removed in the interests of cleanliness and improved access. Refer to Part D for details.

16 Compression test – description and interpretation

Refer to Part A: Section 2.

17 Top dead centre (TDC) for number one piston – locating

Refer to Part A: Section 3.

18 Valve clearances – adjustment

1   Remove the air cleaner and disconnect the choke cable, as described in Chapter 4.
2   Unscrew the nuts and remove the valve cover and gasket. Disconnect the crankcase ventilation hose from the cover.
3   Remove the spark plugs (Chapter 1) in order to make turning the engine easier.
4   Draw the valve positions on a piece of paper numbering them 1 to 4 inlet and exhaust according to their cylinders, from the flywheel (left-hand) end of the engine (ie 1E, 1I, 2E, 2I et seq). As the valve clearances are adjusted cross them off.
5   Using a socket or spanner on the crankshaft pulley bolt, turn the engine in a clockwise direction until No 1 exhaust valve is completely open (ie the valve spring is completely compressed).
6   Insert a feeler blade of the correct thickness between the No 3 cylinder inlet valve stem and the end of the rocker arm. It should be a firm sliding fit. If adjustment is necessary, loosen the locknut on the rocker arm using a ring spanner and turn the adjustment screw with a screwdriver until the fit is correct (photo). Tighten the locknut and recheck the adjustment, then repeat the adjustment procedure on No 4 cylinder exhaust valve.
7   Turn the engine in a clockwise direction until No 3 exhaust valve is

18.6 Adjusting the valve clearances

completely open and adjust the valve clearances on No 4 inlet, and No 2 exhaust valves. Continue to adjust the valve clearances in the following sequence:

Exhaust valve fully open	Adjust inlet valve	Adjust exhaust valve
1E	3I	4E
3E	4I	2E
4E	2I	1E
2E	1I	3E

8   Remove the socket or spanner from the crankshaft pulley bolt.
9   Refit the spark plugs with reference to Chapter 1, then refit the valve cover together with a new gasket where necessary. Reconnect the crankshaft ventilation hose. Refit the air cleaner and re-connect the choke cable.

19   Cylinder head – removal and refitting

Removal

1   Disconnect both battery leads, referring to Chapter 12 if necessary.
2   Drain the cooling system, including the cylinder block, with reference to Chapter 1. The block drain plug is located on the right-hand rear face of the engine, beneath the inlet manifold. It is important to drain the block as, if the wet cylinder liners are disturbed, the coolant will drain into the sump.
3   Drain the engine oil with reference to Chapter 1.
4   Remove the air cleaner with reference to Chapter 4.
5   Disconnect the HT leads at the spark plugs, release the distributor

cap retaining clips or screws and remove the cap and leads.
6   Disconnect the lead at the water temperature gauge sender on the water pump (photo).
7   Slacken the alternator mountings and adjustment arm bolt, push the alternator in towards the engine and slip the drivebelt off the three pulleys. Unscrew the bolt securing the alternator adjustment arm to the water pump and swing the alternator clear of the engine (photos).
8   Release the hose clips and remove the two heater hoses from the water pump. Also remove the support bracket from the rocker cover.
9   Release the hose clip and remove the radiator top hose from the water pump.
10   Disconnect the throttle cable, choke cable and vacuum pipe from the carburettor with reference to Chapter 4.
11   Disconnect the brake servo hose from the inlet manifold.
12   Unscrew the nut and washer on the inlet manifold and on the cylinder block and lift off the heat shield, where fitted.
13   Disconnect the fuel inlet pipe and the crankcase ventilation hose at the carburettor.
14   Disconnect the distributor wiring.
15   Unscrew the bolt and release the retaining clip securing the cable and hose guide to the side of the cylinder head (photo).
16   Unscrew the two bolts and withdraw the tension springs securing the exhaust front section to the manifold.
17   Unscrew the nuts and remove the rocker cover, complete with gasket, from the cylinder head (photo).
18   Unscrew the two bolts and two nuts securing the rocker shaft pedestals to the cylinder head. Lift the rocker shaft assembly upwards and off the two studs (photo).
19   Lift out each of the pushrods in turn using a twisting action to release them from their cam followers (photo). Keep them in strict order of removal by inserting them in a strip of cardboard having eight numbered holes punched in it. Note that No 1 should be the pushrod nearest the flywheel.
20   Slacken all the cylinder head retaining bolts half a turn at a time in the reverse order to that shown in Fig. 2.10. When the tension has been relieved, remove all the bolts with the exception of the centre bolt on the distributor side.
21   Using a hide or plastic mallet, tap each end of the cylinder head so as to pivot the head around the remaining locating bolt and unstick the gasket. Do not attempt to lift the head until the gasket has been unstuck, otherwise the cylinder liner seal at the base of each liner will be broken, allowing water and foreign matter to enter the sump.
22   After unsticking the cylinder head from the gasket, remove the remaining bolt and lift the head, complete with water pump, manifolds and carburettor, off the engine (photo). **Note:** *The crankshaft must not be rotated with the head removed, otherwise the liners will be displaced.* If it is necessary to turn the engine (eg to clean the piston crowns), use liner clamps or bolts with suitable washers screwed into the top of the block to retain the liners. If the sealing of the liner seals is in any doubt, they must be renewed with reference to Part D of this Chapter.

Refitting

23   The mating faces of the cylinder head and block must be perfectly clean before refitting the head. Use a scraper to remove all traces of gasket and carbon, and also clean the tops of the pistons. Take particular care with the aluminium cylinder head as the soft metal is damaged

19.6 Disconnecting the water temperature sender lead

19.7A Slacken the alternator mountings and slip the drivebelt off the pulleys

19.7B Unscrew the bolt (A) and remove the alternator adjustment arm from the pump at (B)

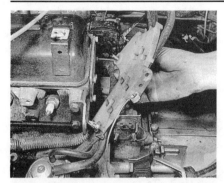

19.15 Remove the cable and hose guide

19.17 Unscrew the three nuts and lift off the rocker cover

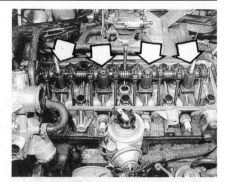

19.18 Unscrew the two nuts and two bolts (arrowed) and withdraw the rocker shaft

19.19 Take out the pushrods and keep them in order

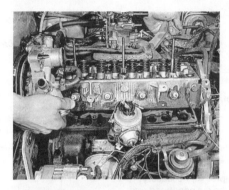

19.22 Free the cylinder head from the gasket then lift the head, complete with manifolds and water pump, off the engine

19.28 Place the cylinder head gasket in position

19.29A Lower the cylinder head onto the gasket and ...

19.29B ... fit the retaining bolts; tighten in the correct sequence to the specified torque

19.31 Refit the rocker shaft assembly

easily. Also, make sure that the carbon is not allowed to enter the oil and water channels – this is particularly important for the oil circuit, as carbon could block the oil supply to the camshaft, rocker shaft, rocker arms or crankshaft main and big-end bearings. Using adhesive tape and paper, seal the water, oil and bolt holes in the cylinder block. To prevent carbon entering the gap between the pistons and bores, smear a little grease in the gap. After cleaning the piston, rotate the crankshaft so that the piston moves down the bore then wipe out the grease and carbon with a cloth rag. Clean the piston crowns in the same way.

24   Check the block and head for nicks, deep scratches and other damage. If slight, they may be removed carefully with a file, however, if excessive, machining may be the only alternative.

25   If warpage of the cylinder head is suspected, use a straight-edge to check it for distortion. Refer to Part D of this Chapter if necessary.

26   Clean out all the bolt holes in the block using a cloth rag and screwdriver. Make sure that all oil is removed, otherwise there is a possibility of the block being cracked by hydraulic pressure when the bolts are tightened.

27   Examine the bolt threads and the threads in the cylinder block for

damage. If necessary, use the correct size tap to chase out the threads in the block and use a die to clean the threads on the bolts.

28   Remove the cylinder liner clamps or washers, and make sure that the faces of the cylinder head and the cylinder block are perfectly clean. Lay a new gasket on the cylinder block with the words 'Haut-Top' uppermost. Do not use any kind of jointing compound (photo).

29   Lower the cylinder head into position, insert the cylinder head bolts, and tighten them to the specified torque in the sequence shown in Fig. 2.5 (photos).

30   Install the pushrods in their original locations.

31   Lower the rocker shaft assembly onto the cylinder head, making sure that the adjusting ball-ends locate in the pushrods (photo). Install the spring washer (convex side uppermost), nuts and bolts, and tighten them to the specified torque.

32   Adjust the valve clearances as described in Section 18 to the cold setting.

33   Refit the rocker cover together with a new gasket, and tighten the nuts.

34   Connect the exhaust front section to the manifold, then refit the

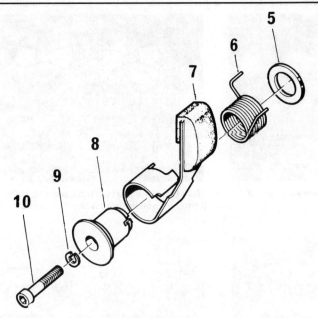

Fig. 2.10 Mechanical timing chain tensioner components (Sec 20)

5	Washer	8	Collar
6	Spring	9	Washer
7	Slipper arm	10	Retaining bolt

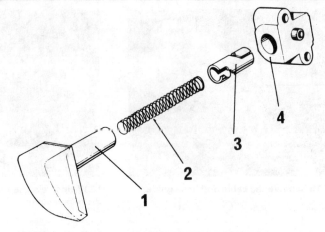

Fig. 2.11 Hydraulic timing chain tensioner components (Sec 20)

1	Piston with tensioner	3	Sleeve
	slipper	4	Tensioner body
2	Spring		

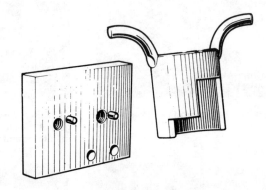

Fig. 2.12 Renault tool for holding the mechanical tensioner together (Sec 20)

tension springs and tighten the bolts. Refer to Chapter 4 if necessary.

35   Refit the cable and hose guide to the side of the cylinder head and retain with the clip and bolt.

36   Reconnect the distributor wiring.

37   Reconnect the crankcase ventilation hose and fuel inlet pipe at the carburettor.

38   Refit the heat shield (where fitted) and tighten the nut.

39   Reconnect the brake servo hose to the inlet manifold.

40   Reconnect the throttle cable, choke cable and vacuum pipe to the carburettor with reference to Chapter 4.

41   Reconnect the radiator top hose to the water pump and tighten the clip.

42   Fit the support bracket to the rocker cover, then reconnect the two heater hoses to the water pump and tighten the clips.

43   Refit the alternator and drivebelt and adjust with reference to Chapter 1.

44   Reconnect the lead to the water temperature gauge sender on the water pump.

45   Refit the distributor cap and leads, and connect the HT leads to the spark plugs.

46   Refit the air cleaner with reference to Chapter 4.

47   Refill the engine with oil with reference to Chapter 1.

48   Refit the cylinder block drain plug, if removed. Refill the cooling system with reference to Chapter 1.

49   Reconnect the battery leads.

20 Timing cover, chain and gears – removal, inspection and refitting

Removal

1   Remove the alternator drivebelt with reference to Chapter 1.

2   Remove the sump with reference to Section 21.

3   Using a socket on the crankshaft pulley bolt, turn the engine until the notch in the flywheel is aligned with the TDC mark on the bellhousing timing scale, and the distributor rotor is pointing towards the No 1 cylinder HT lead segment in the cap.

4   Lock the starter ring gear to prevent the engine turning by using a wide-bladed screwdriver inserted between the ring gear teeth and the crankcase, or alternatively apply the handbrake and engage top gear. With the engine locked, use a socket or spanner to unscrew the crankshaft pulley retaining bolt.

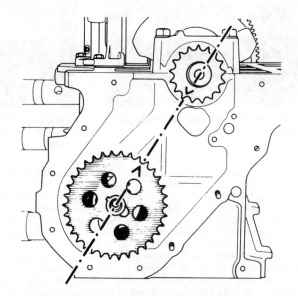

Fig. 2.13 Correct alignment of crankshaft and camshaft sprocket timing marks (Sec 20)

5   With the bolt removed, lift off the pulley and withdraw the pulley hub. If the hub is tight, carefully lever it off using two screwdrivers or use a two or three-legged puller (photo).

6   Unscrew the nuts and bolts securing the timing cover to the cylinder block and carefully prise the timing cover off using a screwdriver to

20.5 A puller may be needed to remove the crankshaft pulley hub

20.10 Removing the timing chain and sprockets

20.16 Use a socket or tube to renew the timing cover oil seal

release it. Remove the gasket where fitted.

7   Observe the components of the timing chain tensioner, noting that one of two types may be fitted. The mechanical tensioner is identified by its coil tensioning spring and single mounting bolt, and the automatic hydraulic tensioner by its piston plunger and two mounting bolts.

8   To remove the mechanical type tensioner, Renault technicians use a special tubular tool which locates over the tensioner and spring and holds all the components together until the assembly is refitted. The tool is shown in Fig. 2.13, however it is not essential to use this. If the tool is not available, simply unscrew the retaining bolt using an Allen key, hold the tensioner slipper and spring end together and withdraw the assembly from the cylinder block.

9   If a hydraulic tensioner is fitted, lock the plunger with locking wire tied around the body, then unscrew the mounting bolts and withdraw it from the block. Extract the special filter from the hole in the cylinder block.

10   To remove the chain, first bend back the locktab then unscrew and remove the camshaft sprocket retaining bolt. Remove the washer. Withdraw the camshaft and chain from the camshaft, then release the chain from the crankshaft sprocket (photo). Use two screwdrivers or a puller to remove the sprocket from the crankshaft.

11   With the sprockets and chain removed, check that the Woodruff key in the nose of the crankshaft is a tight fit in its slot. If not, remove it now and store it safely to avoid the risk of it dropping out and getting lost.

Inspection

12   Examine all the teeth on the camshaft and crankshaft sprockets. If these are 'hooked' in appearance, renew the sprockets.

13   If a mechanical type chain tensioner is fitted, examine the chain contact pad and renew the tensioner assembly if the pad is heavily scored.

14   If a hydraulic type chain tensioner is fitted, dismantle it by releasing the slipper piston with a 3 mm Allen key. Examine the piston, spring, sleeve and tensioner body bore for signs of scoring and renew if evident. Also renew the tensioner if the chain contact pad is heavily scored.

15   If the hydraulic tensioner is serviceable, lubricate the components and reassemble. Lock the sleeve in the slipper piston first by turning it clockwise with an Allen key, then slide this assembly into the tensioner body. Avoid pressing the slipper now or the sleeve will be released and the whole assembly will fly apart. New hydraulic tensioners are supplied with a 2 mm thick safety spacer inserted between the pad and the tensioner body to prevent the assembly flying apart.

16   Renew the oil seal in the timing cover by driving out the old seal using a suitable drift and then install the new seal using a large socket or block of wood (photo).

Refitting

17   Refit the Woodruff key to the crankshaft slot and then tap the crankshaft sprocket into position. Ensure that the timing mark on the sprocket is on the side facing away from the engine.

18   Turn the crankshaft until the timing notch on the flywheel or torque converter is in line with the TDC mark on the bellhousing timing scale.

19   Temporarily place the camshaft sprocket in position and turn the

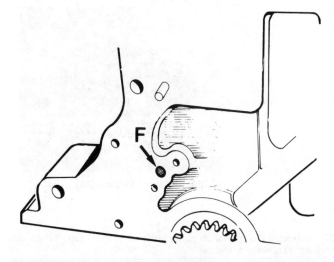

Fig. 2.14 Location (F) of filter in the cylinder block for the hydraulic tensioner (Sec 20)

camshaft so that the timing marks on the sprocket faces are facing each other, and coincide with an imaginary line joining the crankshaft and camshaft centres, then remove the camshaft sprocket (photo).

20   Fit the timing chain to the camshaft sprocket, position the sprocket in its approximate fitted position and locate the chain over the crankshaft sprocket. Position the camshaft sprocket on the camshaft and check that the marks are still aligned when there is an equal amount of slack on both sides of the chain.

21   Refit the camshaft sprocket retaining bolt using a new locktab and tighten the bolt to the specified torque. Bend up the locktabs to retain the bolt.

22   If a mechanical tensioner is fitted, place it in position and locate the spring ends in the block and over the slipper arm. Refit the retaining bolt and tighten it securely with an Allen key.

23   If a hydraulic type tensioner is fitted, first insert the special filter in the cylinder block. Remove the 2 mm thick safety spacer (if fitting a new tensioner), and locate the tensioner on the cylinder block. Insert the bolts and tighten to the specified torque. Push the slipper fully inwards, then release it. The piston should spring out automatically under spring pressure.

24   Ensure that the mating faces of the timing cover are clean and dry with all traces of old sealant removed and a new oil seal in place in the timing cover.

25   If there are no locating dowels for the timing cover, a gasket must be fitted. Locate the gasket on the cylinder block then fit the timing cover, inserting the bolts loosely. Oil the pulley hub and temporarily fit it on the end of the crankshaft so that the timing cover is positioned correctly, then tighten the cover bolts.

26   Where locating dowels are fitted, apply a bead of CAF 4/60 THIXO paste to the timing cover joint face then position the cover over the dowels and the two studs (photo). Refit the nuts and retaining bolts then progressively tighten them in a diagonal sequence.

20.19 Correct alignment of crankshaft and camshaft sprocket timing marks (arrowed)

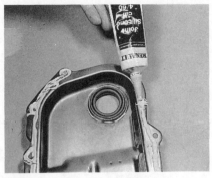

20.26 Apply a bead of sealant to the timing cover face

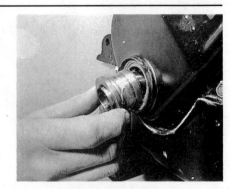

20.27 Refit the crankshaft pulley hub ...

20.28A ... followed by the pulley ...

20.28B ... and retaining bolt

27   Lubricate the crankshaft pulley hub and carefully slide it onto the end of the crankshaft (photo).

28   Place the pulley in position, refit the retaining bolt and washer and tighten the bolt to the specified torque (photos). Hold the crankshaft stationary using the method described in paragraph 4.
29   Refit the sump with reference to Section 21.
30   Refit and tension the alternator drivebelt with reference to Chapter 1.

21 Sump – removal and refitting

Removal
1   Disconnect the battery negative and positive leads.

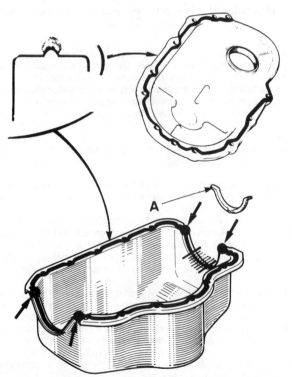

Fig. 2.15 Sealing paste application diagram for the sump and timing cover (Sec 21)

A   Alternative rubber seal

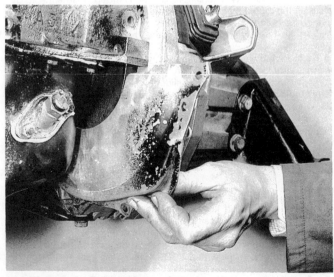

21.5 Remove the flywheel cover plate

21.7 Unscrew the retaining bolts and remove the sump

2   Jack up the front of the car and support it on axle stands.
3   Where fitted, remove the splash shield then unscrew the two bolts, noting the position of the spacer, and remove the engine steady rod.
4   Drain the engine oil as described in Chapter 1, then refit and tighten the drain plug.
5   Unscrew the bolts and remove the flywheel or torque converter cover plate from the bellhousing (photo).
6   Where fitted, disconnect the two wires at the oil level sensor on the front face of the sump.
7   Unscrew and remove the bolts securing the sump to the crankcase (photo).
8   Tap the sump with a hide or plastic mallet to break the seal between the sump flange, crankcase and timing cover. Lower the sump and remove the gaskets and rubber seals where fitted. Note that on some models a gasket is not used, only a sealing compound.

Refitting

9   Check that the mating faces of the sump, timing cover and cylinder block are perfectly clean and dry.
10   Where gaskets are fitted, first locate the rubber seals in the curved sections of the sump. These seals locate on the front timing cover and rear main bearing cap. Apply a little CAF 4/60 THIXO paste to the ends of the side gaskets, then locate them on the sump so that their ends are over the rubber seals.
11   Where gaskets are not used, apply a 3 mm diameter bead of CAF 4/60 THIXO paste on the sump as shown in Fig. 2.15, adding an extra amount at each of the four corners. Where a rubber seal is fitted instead of the previous cork type, do not apply the paste in the hatched area. Do not apply excessive paste otherwise it may find its way into the lubrication circuit and cause damage to the engine.
12   If no gaskets are fitted, it is important that the sump is positioned correctly and not moved around after the paste has touched the crankcase. Temporary long bolts or dowel rods may be used to help achieve this.
13   To prevent oil dripping from the oil pump and crankcase, wipe these areas clean before refitting the sump.
14   Lift the sump into position then insert the bolts and tighten them progressively until they are secure.
15   Reconnect the two wires at the oil level sensor on the front face of the sump.
16   Refit the flywheel or torque converter cover plate to the bellhousing and tighten the bolts.
17   Fill the engine with oil with reference to Chapter 1.
18   Refit the engine steady rod and splash shield and tighten the bolts.
19   Lower the car to the ground.
20   Reconnect the battery.

22 Oil pump – removal, inspection and refitting

Removal

1   Remove the sump as described in Section 21.
2   Unscrew the mounting bolts and withdraw the oil pump from the crankcase and drivegear (photo).

22.2 Unscrew the retaining bolts and withdraw the oil pump

22.4 Lift off the oil pump cover

22.5A Remove the pressure relief valve ball seat and ball ...

22.5B ... followed by the spring and spring seat

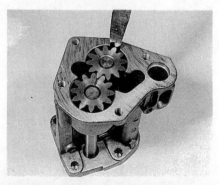

22.8 Check the gear-to-body clearance using feeler blades

22.10 Refitting the oil pump

Inspection

3   Clean the exterior of the oil pump.
4   Unscrew the four retaining bolts and lift off the pump cover taking care not to lose the oil pressure relief valve components which may be ejected under the action of the spring (photo).
5   Remove the pressure relief valve ball seat, ball, spring and spring seat from the pump body (photos).
6   Lift out the idler gear, and the drivegear and shaft.
7   Clean the components and carefully examine the gears, pump body and relief valve ball and seat for any signs of scoring or wear. Renew the pump if these conditions are apparent.
8   If the components appear serviceable, measure the clearance between the pump body and the gears using a feeler blade (photo). If the clearance exceeds the specified amount, the pump must be renewed.
9   If the pump is satisfactory, reassemble the components in the order of removal, fill the pump with oil and refit the cover.

Refitting

10   Enter the oil pump shaft into its location in the cylinder block and engage the shaft with the distributor drivegear (photo).
11   Push the pump up into contact with the block, then refit and tighten the three mounting bolts. Note that a gasket is not used.
12   Refit the sump with reference to Section 21.

23   Crankshaft oil seals – renewal

Front/right-hand oil seal

1   Remove the alternator drivebelt with reference to Chapter 1.
2   Remove the sump with reference to Section 21.
3   Lock the starter ring gear to prevent the engine turning by using a wide-bladed screwdriver inserted between the ring gear teeth and the crankcase, or alternatively apply the handbrake and engage top gear. With the engine locked, use a socket or spanner to unscrew the crankshaft pulley retaining bolt.
4   With the bolt removed, lift off the pulley and withdraw the pulley hub. If the hub is tight, carefully lever it off using two screwdrivers or use a two or three-legged puller.
5   Unscrew the nuts and bolts securing the timing cover to the cylinder block and carefully prise the timing cover off using a screwdriver to release it. Remove the gasket.
6   Renew the oil seal in the timing cover by driving out the old seal using a suitable drift and install the new seal using a large socket or block of wood.
7   Ensure that the mating faces of the timing cover are clean and dry

with all traces of old sealant removed and a new oil seal in place in the timing cover.
8   If there are no locating dowels for the timing cover, a gasket must be fitted. Locate the gasket on the cylinder block then fit the timing cover inserting the bolts loosely. Oil the pulley hub and temporarily fit it on the end of the crankshaft so that the timing cover is positioned correctly then tighten the cover bolts.
9   Where locating dowels are fitted, apply a bead of CAF 4/60 THIXO paste to the timing cover joint face then position the cover over the dowels and the two studs. Refit the nuts and retaining bolts then progressively tighten them in a diagonal sequence.
10   Lubricate the crankshaft pulley hub and carefully slide it onto the end of the crankshaft.
11   Place the pulley in position, refit the retaining bolt and washer and tighten the bolt to the specified torque. Hold the crankshaft stationary using the method described in paragraph 3.
12   Refit the sump with reference to Section 21.
13   Refit and tension the alternator drivebelt with reference to Chapter 1.

Rear/left-hand oil seal

14   Remove the flywheel as described in Section 25.
15   Prise out the old oil seal using a small screwdriver, taking care not to damage the surface of the crankshaft. Alternatively, the oil seal can be removed by drilling two small holes diagonally opposite each other and inserting self-tapping screws in them. A pair of grips can then be used to pull out the oil seal, by pulling on each side in turn.
16   Wipe clean the oil seal seating, then dip the new seal in fresh engine oil and locate it over the crankshaft with its closed side facing outwards. Make sure that the oil seal lip is not damaged as it is located on the crankshaft.
17   Using a metal tube, drive the oil seal squarely into the bore until flush. A block of wood cut to pass over the end of the crankshaft may be used instead.
18   Refit the flywheel with reference to Section 25.

24   Engine mountings – renewal

Refer to Part A: Section 13.

25   Flywheel – removal, inspection and refitting

Refer to Part A: Section 14.

Part C: 1721 cc engine – in-car engine repair procedures

26 General information

How to use this Chapter

This Part of Chapter 2 is devoted to in-car repair procedures for the 1721 cc engine. Similar information covering the 1390 cc and 1397 cc engines will be found in Parts A and B respectively. All procedures concerning engine removal and refitting, and engine block/cylinder head overhaul for all engine types can be found in Part D of this Chapter.

Most of the operations included in this Part are based on the assumption that the engine is still installed in the car. Therefore, if this information is being used during a complete engine overhaul, with the engine already removed, many of the steps included here will not apply.

Engine description

The engine is of four-cylinder, in-line, overhead camshaft type, mounted transversely at the front of the car.

The crankshaft is supported in five shell type main bearings. Thrust washers are fitted to No 2 main bearing to control crankshaft endfloat.

The connecting rods are attached to the crankshaft by horizontally split shell type big-end bearings, and to the pistons by interference fit gudgeon pins. The aluminium alloy pistons are of the slipper type and are fitted with three piston rings, comprising two compression rings and a scraper type oil control ring.

The overhead camshaft is mounted directly in the cylinder head and is driven by the crankshaft via a toothed rubber timing belt. The camshaft operates the valves via inverted bucket type tappets which operate in bores machined directly in the cylinder head. Valve clearance adjustment is by selected shims located externally between the tappet bucket and the cam lobe. The inlet and exhaust valves are mounted vertically in the cylinder head and are each closed by a single valve spring.

An auxiliary shaft located alongside the crankshaft is also driven by the toothed timing belt and actuates the oil pump via a skew gear.

A semi-closed crankcase ventilation system is employed, and crankcase fumes are drawn from an oil separator on the cylinder block and passed via a hose to the inlet manifold.

Engine lubrication is by pressure feed from a gear type oil pump located beneath the crankshaft. Engine oil is fed through an externally-mounted oil filter to the main oil gallery feeding the crankshaft, auxiliary shaft and camshaft.

Fig. 2.16 Cutaway view of the 1721 cc (F2N) engine (Sec 26)

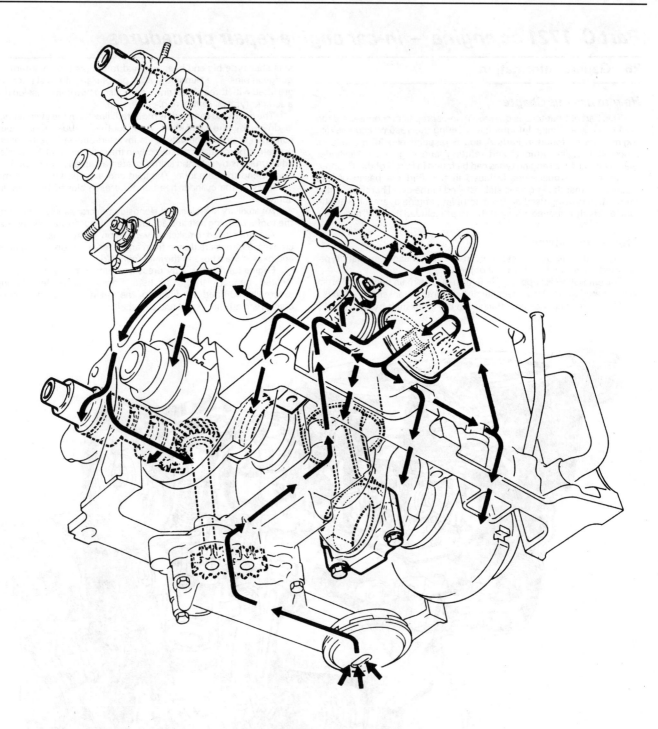

Fig. 2.17 Lubrication circuit of the 1721 cc (F2N) engine (Sec 26)

The distributor rotor and the fuel pump are driven by the camshaft; the rotor being driven directly, and the fuel pump via and eccentric and plunger.

Repair operations possible with the engine in the vehicle

The following operations can be carried out without having to remove the engine from the car:

(a)　*Removal and refitting of the cylinder head*
(b)　*Removal and refitting of the timing belt and sprockets*
(c)　*Renewal of the camshaft oil seal*
(d)　*Removal and refitting of the camshaft*

(e)　*Removal and refitting of the auxiliary shaft*
(f)　*Removal and refitting of the sump*
(g)　*Removal and refitting of the connecting rods and pistons* *
(h)　*Removal and refitting of the oil pump*
(i)　*Renewal of the crankshaft oil seals*
(j)　*Renewal of the engine mountings*
(k)　*Removal and refitting of the flywheel/driveplate*

*Although the operation marked with an asterisk can be carried out with the engine in the car after removal of the sump, it is better for the engine to be removed in the interests of cleanliness and improved access. For this reason the procedure is described in Part D of this Chapter.

27   Compression test – description and interpretation

Refer to Part A: Section 2.

28   Top dead centre (TDC) for number one piston – locating

1   Top dead centre (TDC) is the highest point in the cylinder that each piston reaches as the crankshaft turns. Each piston reaches TDC at the end of the compression stroke and again at the end of the exhaust stroke, however for the purpose of timing the engine, TDC refers to the position of number 1 piston at the end of its compression stroke. On all engines in this manual, number 1 piston and cylinder is at the flywheel end of the engine.
2   Disconnect both battery leads.
3   Remove the alternator/power-assisted steering pump/air conditioning pump drive belts, as applicable (Chapter 1).
4   Release the spring clip where fitted, then unscrew the bolts and lift off the timing belt cover (photos).
5   Apply the handbrake, then jack up the front right-hand side of the car and support it on axle stands. Remove the roadwheel.
6   Remove the plastic cover from within the right-hand wheelarch to give access to the crankshaft pulley.
7   Turn the engine in a clockwise direction, using a socket on the crankshaft pulley bolt, until the TDC mark on the camshaft sprocket is uppermost and in line with the corresponding mark or notch on the metal plate behind the sprocket. On some models it may be possible to align the sprocket mark with a pointer on the timing cover (photo).
8   If the distributor cap is now removed, the rotor arm should be in alignment with the number 1 HT lead segment.
9   Remove the plug on the lower front facing side of the engine, at the flywheel end, and obtain a metal rod which is a snug fit in the plug hole. Turn the crankshaft slightly as necessary to the TDC position, then push the rod through the hole to locate in the slot in the crankshaft web. Make sure that the crankshaft is exactly at TDC for No 1 piston (flywheel end) by aligning the timing notch on the flywheel with the corresponding mark on the transmission bellhousing. If the crankshaft is not positioned accurately it is possible to engage the rod with a balance hole in the crankshaft web which is not the TDC slot.
10   After locating the TDC position, remove the metal rod and refit the plug.
11   Refit the distributor cap.
12   Remove the socket from the crankshaft pulley bolt.
13   Refit the plastic cover to the right-hand wheelarch.
14   Refit the roadwheel and lower the car to the ground.
15   Refit the timing belt cover.
16   Refit and adjust the drivebelt(s).
17   Reconnect the battery leads.

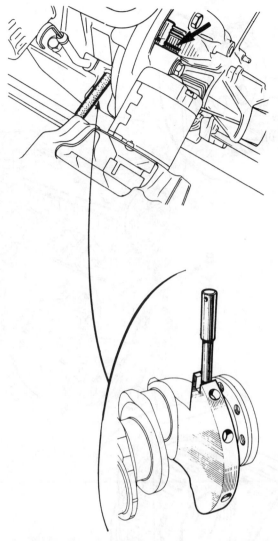

Fig. 2.18 Showing how the metal rod engages with the TDC slot in the crankshaft web (Sec 28)

29   Valve clearances – adjustment

1   Remove the air cleaner as described in Chapter 4.
2   Unbolt the fuel vapour separator from the front of the engine, but do not disconnect the hoses from it.
3   Unscrew the nuts, lift the fuel pipe cluster slightly, and remove the

28.4A Releasing the timing cover clip

28.4B Removing the timing cover

28.7 Camshaft sprocket mark aligned with pointer

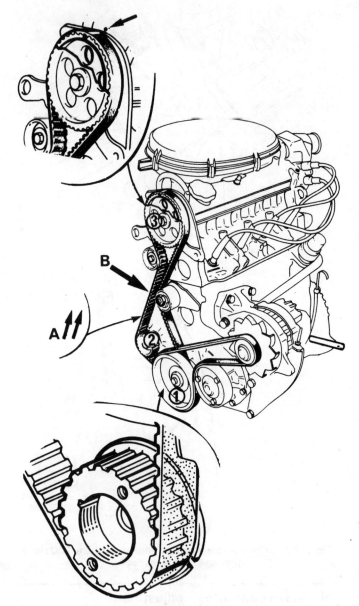

Fig. 2.19 Timing belt run, showing alignment of lines on belt with
camshaft and crankshaft sprocket backplate marks (Sec 28)

1	Crankshaft pulley	3	Camshaft sprocket
2	Auxiliary shaft sprocket	A	Arrows showing belt running direction

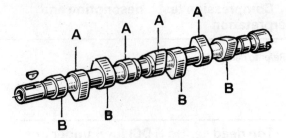

Fig. 2.20 Cam lobe identification (Sec 29)

A   Inlet   B   Exhaust

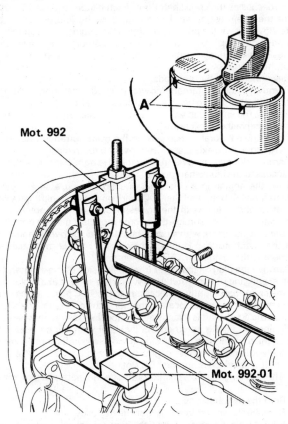

Fig. 2.21 Renault tool for compressing tappet buckets to change
tappet shims (Sec 29)

Fit slots (A) at right-angles to the camshaft

valve cover and gasket (photo). Where applicable disconnect the
crankcase ventilation hose from the cover.
4   Remove the spark plugs with reference to Chapter 1 in order to
make turning the engine easier.
5   Draw the valve positions on a piece of paper numbering them 1 to 8
from the flywheel end of the engine. Identify them as inlet or exhaust (ie
1E, 2I, 3E et seq).
6   Using a socket or spanner on the crankshaft pulley bolt, turn the
engine until the valves of No 1 cylinder (flywheel end) are 'rocking'. The
exhaust valve will be closing and the inlet valve will be opening. The
piston of No 4 cylinder will be at the top of its compression stroke, both
valves will be fully closed, and the valve clearances for both valves of No
4 cylinder may be checked at the same time.
7   Insert a feeler blade of the correct thickness between the cam lobe
and the shim on the top of the tappet bucket, and check that it is a firm
sliding fit (photo). If it is not, use the feeler blades to ascertain the exact
clearance and record this in order to calculate the new shim thickness
required. Note that the inlet and exhaust valve clearances are different –

see the Specifications.
8   With No 4 cylinder valve clearances checked, turn the engine
through half a turn so that No 3 valves are 'rocking', then check the valve
clearances of No 2 cylinder in the same way. Similarly check the
remaining valve clearances in the following sequence:

Valves rocking in cylinder	Check valve clearances in cylinder
1	4
3	2
4	1
2	3

9   Where a valve clearance differs from the specified value then the
shim for that valve must be replaced with a thinner or thicker shim
accordingly. The size of shim required can be calculated as follows. If
the measured clearance is less than specified, subtract the measured
clearance from the specified clearance and deduct the result from the
thickness of the existing shim. If the measured clearance is more than
specified, subtract the specified clearance from the measured clearance

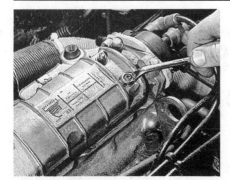

29.3 Removing the valve cover

29.7 Measuring a valve clearance

29.9 Shim thickness engraved on the underside

and add the result to the thickness of the existing shim. The shim size is stamped on the bottom face of the shim (photo).

10   The shims can be removed from their locations on top of the tappet buckets without removing the camshaft if the Renault tool shown in the accompanying illustration can be borrowed, or a suitable alternative fabricated. The fuel pump must also be removed if the tool is being used. To remove the shim, the tappet bucket has to be pressed down against valve spring pressure just far enough to allow the shim to be slid out. Theoretically this could be done by levering against the camshaft between the cam lobes with a suitable pad to push the bucket down, but this is not recommended by the manufacturers. Alternatively an arrangement similar to the Renault tool can be made by bolting a bar to the camshaft bearing studs and levering down against this with a stout screwdriver. The contact pad should be a triangular-shaped metal block with a lip filed along each side to contact the edge of the buckets. Levering down against this will open the valve and allow the shim to be withdrawn. Make sure that the cam lobe peaks are uppermost when doing this and rotate the buckets so that the notches are at right angles to the camshaft centreline. When refitting the shims ensure that the size markings face the tappet buckets (ie downwards).

11   If the Renault tool cannot be borrowed or a suitable alternative made up, then it will be necessary to remove the camshaft to gain access to the shims, as described in Section 34.

12   Remove the socket or spanner from the crankshaft pulley bolt.

13   Refit the spark plugs with reference to Chapter 1, then refit the valve cover together with a new gasket where necessary. Reconnect the crankcase ventilation hose and fuel pipe cluster. Refit the fuel vapour separator and air cleaner.

30   Cylinder head – removal, inspection and refitting

Removal

1   Disconnect both battery leads.

2   Drain the cooling system with reference to Chapter 1. Also drain the cylinder block by unscrewing the drain plug located on the right-hand rear face of the engine. Refit the plug after draining.

3   Drain the engine oil with reference to Chapter 1. Refit the plug after draining.

4   Remove the timing belt with reference to Section 31 of this Chapter.

5   Disconnect the ignition HT lead at the centre of the distributor cap.

6   Disconnect the lead at the water temperature gauge sender on the cylinder head.

7   Disconnect the fuel feed and return pipes at the fuel pump and plug their ends.

8   Disconnect the accelerator and choke cables with reference to Chapter 4.

9   Disconnect the brake servo vacuum hose from the inlet manifold.

10   Disconnect the heater hoses, crankcase ventilation hoses and the two nuts securing the support plate to the rear facing side of the cylinder head.

11   Disconnect the radiator top hose from the thermostat housing.

12   Unscrew the two bolts and withdraw the tension springs securing

the exhaust front section to the manifold.

13   Unscrew the domed nuts, lift off the washers and withdraw the valve cover from the cylinder head. Recover the gasket.

14   Unbolt the timing belt backplate from behind the camshaft sprocket.

15   Using a suitable hexagon-headed socket bit, slacken the cylinder head retaining bolts half a turn at a time in the reverse order to that shown in Fig. 2.25. When the tension has been relieved, remove all the bolts.

16   Lift the cylinder head, complete with manifolds and carburettor upwards and off the engine. If it is stuck, tap it upwards using a hammer and block of wood. Do no try to turn it as it is located by two dowels, and make no attempt whatsoever to prise it free using a screwdriver inserted between the block and head faces.

17   If necessary, remove and clean the inlet and exhaust manifolds with reference to Chapter 4 in order to fit new gaskets.

Inspection

18   The mating faces of the cylinder head and block must be perfectly clean before refitting the head. Use a scraper to remove all traces of gasket and carbon, and also clean the tops of the pistons. Take particular care with the aluminium cylinder head as the soft metal is damaged easily. Also, make sure that the carbon is not allowed to enter the oil and water channels – this is particularly important for the oil circuit, as carbon could block the oil supply to the camshaft and rocker arms or crankshaft main and big-end bearings. Using adhesive tape and paper, seal the water, oil and bolt holes in the cylinder block. To prevent carbon entering the gap between the pistons and bores, smear a little grease in the gap. After cleaning the piston, rotate the crankshaft so that the piston moves down the bore then wipe out the grease and carbon with a cloth rag. Clean the piston crowns in the same way.

19   Check the block and head for nicks, deep scratches and other damage. If slight, they may be removed carefully with a file, however, if excessive, machining may be the only alternative.

20   If warpage of the cylinder head is suspected, use a straight-edge to check it for distortion. Refer to Part D of this Chapter if necessary.

21   Clean out all the bolt holes in the block using a cloth rag and screwdriver. Make sure that all oil is removed, otherwise there is a possibility of the block being cracked by hydraulic pressure when the bolts are tightened.

22   Examine the bolt threads and the threads in the cylinder block for damage. If necessary, use the correct size tap to chase out the threads in the block and use a die to clean the threads on the bolts.

Refitting

23   Ensure that the mating faces of the cylinder block and head are spotlessly clean, that the retaining bolt threads are also clean and dry and that they screw easily in and out of their locations.

24   Check that No 1 piston is at TDC, and that the timing mark on the camshaft sprocket is aligned with the mark on the backplate.

25   Fit a new cylinder head gasket to the block, locating it over the dowels. Make sure it is the right way up.

26   Where removed, refit the inlet and exhaust manifolds together with new gaskets with reference to Chapter 4.

27   Lower the cylinder head onto the block, engaging it over the dowels.

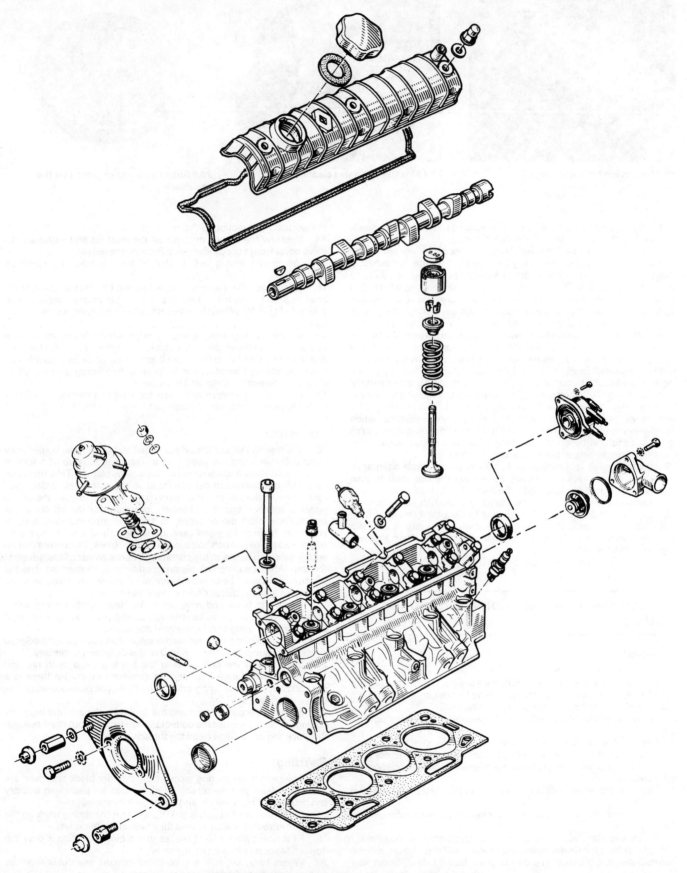

Fig. 2.22 Exploded view of the cylinder head (Sec 30)

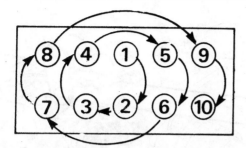

Fig. 2.23 Cylinder head bolt tightening sequence (Sec 30)

28   Lightly oil the cylinder head bolts, both on their threads and under their heads. Insert the bolts and tighten them finger-tight.
29   Following the sequence in Fig. 2.23 tighten the bolts to the torque specified for Stage 1. Repeat the sequence by tightening to the torque specified for Stage 2.
30   Wait three minutes, then progressively slacken all the bolts in the reverse of the tightening sequence until completely loose. This is Stage 3.
31   Again following the tightening sequence, tighten the bolts to the torque specified for Stage 4.
32   Final tightening is carried out by turning each bolt through the angle specified for Stage 5. Measure the angle using a commercially available gauge, or make up a cardboard template cut to the angle required (photo).
33   Refit the timing belt backplate behind the camshaft sprocket, followed by the valve cover, together with a new gasket.
34   Reconnect the exhaust front section to the manifold, and tighten the two bolts together with the tension springs.
35   Reconnect the radiator top hose to the thermostat housing.
36   Reconnect the heater hoses and crankcase ventilation hoses, also refit the support plate to the rear facing side of the cylinder head.
37   Reconnect the brake servo vacuum hose to the inlet manifold.
38   Reconnect the accelerator and choke cables with reference to Chapter 4.
39   Reconnect the fuel feed and return pipes at the fuel pump.
40   Reconnect the water temperature gauge sender lead on the cylinder head.
41   Reconnect the ignition HT lead at the centre of the distributor cap.
42   Refit the timing belt with reference to Section 31 of this Chapter.
43   Refill the engine with oil with reference to Chapter 1.
44   Refill the cooling system with reference to Chapter 1.
45   Reconnect the battery leads, with reference to Chapter 12 if necessary.

30.32 Angle-tightening the cylinder head bolts

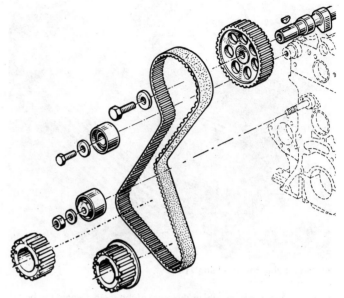

Fig. 2.24 Timing belt and sprockets (Secs 31 and 32)

31   Timing belt – removal and refitting

Removal

1   Disconnect both battery leads.
2   Remove the alternator/power-assisted steering pump/air condition pump drive belts, as applicable (Chapter 1).
3   Release the spring clip where fitted, then unscrew the bolts and lift off the timing belt cover.
4   Apply the handbrake, then jack up the front right-hand side of the car and support it on axle stands. Remove the roadwheel.
5   Remove the plastic cover from within the right-hand wheelarch to give access to the crankshaft pulley.
6   Turn the engine in a clockwise direction, using a socket on the crankshaft pulley bolt, until the TDC mark on the camshaft sprocket is uppermost and in line with the corresponding mark or notch on the metal plate behind the sprocket.
7   Unscrew the crankshaft pulley bolt while holding the crankshaft stationary. To do this, have an assistant insert a screwdriver in the starter ring gear teeth through the access hole in the top of the gearbox bellhousing. Take care not to damage the ignition timing sensor.
8   Remove the crankshaft pulley from the nose of the crankshaft (photo). If it is tight, use a puller.
9   Remove the plug on the lower front facing side of the engine, at the flywheel end, and obtain a metal rod which is a snug fit in the plug hole. Turn the crankshaft slightly as necessary to the TDC position, then push the rod through the hole to locate in the slot in the crankshaft web. Make sure that the crankshaft is exactly at TDC for No 1 piston (flywheel end) by aligning the timing notch on the flywheel with the corresponding mark on the transmission bellhousing. If the crankshaft is not positioned accurately it is possible to engage the rod with a balance hole in the crankshaft web which is not the TDC slot.
10   Double check that the camshaft sprocket timing mark is aligned with the corresponding mark on the metal plate.
11   Check if the belt is marked with arrows to indicate its running direction, and if necessary, mark it.
12   Loosen the nut then turn the timing belt tensioner clockwise to release the tension from the belt and re-tighten it again.
13   Release the belt from the camshaft sprocket, idler wheel, auxiliary shaft sprocket and crankshaft sprocket, and remove it from the engine.
14   Clean the sprockets and tensioners and wipe them dry, although do not apply excessive amounts of solvent to the tensioner wheels otherwise the bearing lubricant may be contaminated. Also clean the front of the cylinder head and block.

Inspection

15   Examine the timing belt carefully for any signs of cracking, fraying

31.8 Removing the crankshaft pulley

or general wear, particularly at the roots of the teeth. Renew the belt if there is any sign of deterioration of this nature, or if there is any oil or grease contamination. The belt must, of course, be renewed if it has completed the maximum mileage given in Chapter 1.

Refitting

16   Check that the crankshaft is at the TDC position for No 1 cylinder and that the crankshaft is locked in this position using the metal rod through the hole in the crankcase.
17   Check that the timing mark on the camshaft sprocket is in line with the corresponding mark on the metal backing plate.
18   Align the timing mark bands on the belt with those on the sprockets noting that the running direction arrows on the belt should be positioned between the auxiliary shaft sprocket and the idler pulley. The crankshaft sprocket mark is in the form of a notch in its rear guide perimeter. The auxiliary shaft sprocket has no timing mark. Fit the timing belt over the crankshaft sprocket first, then the auxiliary shaft sprocket followed by the camshaft sprocket.
19   Check that all the timing marks are still aligned then temporarily tension the belt by turning the tensioner pulley anti-clockwise and tightening the retaining nut. As a rough guide to the correct tension, it should just be possible to turn the belt through 90° using a finger and thumb placed approximately midway between the auxiliary shaft sprocket and the idler wheel.
20   Remove the TDC locating rod.
21   Refit the crankshaft pulley and retaining bolt. Prevent the crankshaft turning using the method given in paragraph 7, and tighten the bolt to the specified torque.
22   Using a socket or spanner on the crankshaft pulley bolt, turn the crankshaft two complete turns in the normal direction of rotation then return it to the TDC position with No 1 cylinder on compression and insert the TDC locating rod again.
23   Check that the timing marks are still aligned.
24   The belt deflection must now be checked. To do this, first make a mark on the front of the engine in line with the outer surface of the timing belt, midway between the auxiliary shaft sprocket and idler wheel. A force of 30 N (7 lbf) must now be applied to the timing belt and its deflection checked to be 7.5 mm (0.3 in) with the engine cold. Should the deflection be checked with the engine hot, the deflection should be 5.5 mm (0.22 in). Renault technicians use a special tool to do this, however an alternative arrangement can be made by using a spring balance and steel rule. Apply the force with the spring balance and read off the deflection on the steel rule. Refer to Part A of this Chapter if necessary.
25   If the tension is incorrect, adjust the tensioner as necessary then re-tighten the nut to the specified torque. This torque is critical, since if the nut were to come loose considerable engine damage would result.
26   Remove the TDC locating rod and refit the plug.
27   Refit the plastic cover to the right-hand wheelarch.
28   Refit the roadwheel and lower the car to the ground.

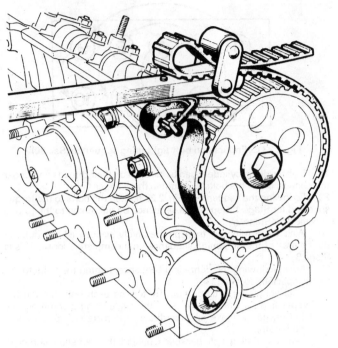

Fig. 2.25 Hold the camshaft sprocket with an old timing belt, then unscrew the bolt (Sec 32)

29   Refit the timing belt cover and tighten the bolts. Refit the spring clip where fitted.
30   Refit and tension the alternator/power-assisted steering pump/air condition pump drive belts (as applicable) with reference to Chapter 1.
31   Reconnect both battery leads.

32   Timing belt sprockets and tensioners – removal, inspection and refitting

Removal

1   Remove the timing belt as described in Section 31.
2   To remove the camshaft sprocket, hold the sprocket stationary using a metal bar with two bolts tightened onto it, inserted into the holes in the sprocket, then unscrew the bolt. Alternatively, an old timing belt may be wrapped around the sprocket and held firm with a pair of grips to hold the sprocket stationary.
3   Pull the sprocket from the end of the camshaft, if necessary using two levers or screwdrivers. Check whether the locating Woodruff key is likely to drop out of its camshaft slot, if so, remove it and store it safely.
4   The sprocket can be removed from the auxiliary shaft in the same manner. Again check that the Woodruff key is firmly in the slot in the shaft.
5   A puller may be necessary to remove the crankshaft sprocket. It is a simple matter to make up a puller using two bolts, a metal bar and the existing crankshaft pulley bolt. By unscrewing the crankshaft pulley bolt, the sprocket is pulled from the end of the crankshaft. If necessary, remove the Woodruff key from the slot in the crankshaft.
6   Unscrew the nut or bolt and remove the timing belt idler wheel. Similarly remove the timing belt tensioner.

Inspection

7   Inspect the teeth of the sprockets for signs of nicks and damage. The teeth are not prone to wear and should normally last the life of the engine.
8   Spin the tensioner and idler wheel by hand and check it for any roughness or tightness. Do not attempt to clean them with solvent as this may enter the bearings. If wear is evident, renew the tensioner and/or idler wheel.

Refitting

9 Refit the timing belt idler wheel and tighten the nut or bolt to the specified torque.
10 Refit the tensioner, although do not tighten the nut at this stage.
11 Check that the Woodruff key is in the crankshaft slot, then slide on the crankshaft pulley. Use a piece of metal tube to tap it fully home.
12 Check that the Woodruff key is in the auxiliary shaft slot, then slide on the sprocket. Use a metal tube to tap it home, if necessary. Fit the bolt and washer and tighten the bolt to the specified torque while holding it stationary using one of the methods described in paragraph 2.
13 Fit the camshaft sprocket in the same way and tighten the bolt to the specified torque.
14 Refit the timing belt with reference to Section 31.

33 Camshaft oil seal – renewal

1 Remove the camshaft sprocket with reference to Section 32.
2 Unscrew the bolts securing the metal backing plate to the cylinder head and remove the plate (photo).
3 Note the fitted depth of the oil seal, then prise it out using a small screwdriver.
4 Wipe clean the seating in the cylinder head.
5 Smear a little fresh oil on the outer surface of the new oil seal, then locate it squarely in the cylinder head and drive it into position using a metal tube of diameter slightly less than that of the cylinder head. Make sure that the oil seal is the correct way round with its sealed face outwards.
6 Refit the cylinder head backing plate.
7 Refit the camshaft sprocket with reference to Section 32.

34 Camshaft – removal, inspection and refitting

Removal

1 Remove the timing belt as described in Section 31.
2 Disconnect the HT leads and remove the distributor cap and rotor arm (Chapter 5). Remove the rotor arm shield.
3 Remove the air cleaner (Chapter 4).
4 Unbolt the fuel vapour separator from the front of the engine, but do not disconnect the hoses from it.
5 Remove the nuts which secure the valve cover. Lift the fuel pipe cluster slightly and remove the cover and gasket.
6 Remove the fuel pump (Chapter 4).
7 Remove the camshaft sprocket with reference to Section 32.
8 Unbolt and remove the cylinder head backing plate.
9 Using a dial gauge, measure the endfloat of the camshaft and compare with that given in the Specifications. This will give an indication of the amount of wear present on the thrust surfaces.
10 Make identifying marks on the camshaft bearing caps so that they can be refitted in the same positions and the same way round.
11 Progressively slacken the bearing cap bolts until valve spring

33.2 Metal backing plate located behind the camshaft sprocket

pressure is released. Remove the bolts, and the bearing caps themselves (photos).
12 Lift out the camshaft together with the oil seals (photo).
13 Remove the tappets, each with its shim (photo). Place them in a compartmented box, or on a sheet of card marked into eight sections, so that they may be refitted to their original locations. Write down the shim thicknesses – they will be needed later if any of the valve clearances are incorrect.

Inspection

14 Examine the camshaft bearing surfaces, cam lobes and fuel pump eccentric for wear ridges, pitting or scoring. Renew the camshaft if evident.
15 Renew the oil seals at the ends of the camshaft as a matter of course. On some models the distributor rotor arm is glued to the end of the camshaft and will be broken during removal, while on other models it can be removed without damage. Lubricate the lips of the new seals before fitting them, and store the camshaft so that its weight is not resting on the seals.
16 Examine the camshaft bearing surfaces in the cylinder head and bearing caps. Deep scoring or other damage means that the cylinder head must be renewed.
17 Inspect the tappet buckets and shims for scoring, pitting and wear ridges. Renew as necessary.

Refitting

18 Oil the tappets and fit them to the bores from which they were removed. Fit the correct shim, numbered side downwards, to each tappet.
19 Oil the camshaft bearings. Place the camshaft with its oil seals onto

34.11A Camshaft bearing cap and bolts

34.11B Removing the No 1 (flywheel end) camshaft bearing cap

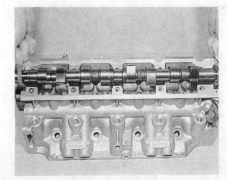

34.12 Lifting out the camshaft

34.13 Removing a tappet

the cylinder head. The oil seals must be positioned so that they are flush with the cylinder head faces.
20   Refit the camshaft bearing caps to their original locations, applying a little sealant to the end caps where they meet the cylinder head.
21   Apply sealant to the threads of the bearing cap bolts. Fit the bolts and tighten them progressively to the specified torque.
22   Refit the cylinder head backing plate.

23   Refit the camshaft sprocket with reference to Section 32.
24   Refit the fuel pump (Chapter 4).
25   Check and adjust the valve clearances as described in Section 29.
26   Refit the valve cover.
27   Refit the fuel vapour separator to the front of the engine and tighten the bolts.
28   Refit the air cleaner (Chapter 4).
29   Refit the rotor arm shield, rotor arm and distributor cap with reference to Chapter 5. Reconnect the HT leads.
30   Refit the timing belt with reference to Section 31.

35 Auxiliary shaft – removal, inspection and refitting

Removal
1   Remove the timing belt with reference to Section 31.
2   Remove the auxiliary shaft sprocket with reference to Section 32.
3   Unscrew the four bolts and withdraw the auxiliary shaft housing, then remove the gasket if fitted. Access may be easier from under the car.
4   From the top, unscrew the two bolts and withdraw the oil pump drivegear cover plate and gasket. Screw a suitable bolt into the oil pump drivegear or use a tapered wooden shaft and withdraw the drivegear from its location.
5   Unscrew the two bolts and washers and lift out the auxiliary shaft thrust plate and the auxiliary shaft (photos).

Inspection
6   Examine the auxiliary shaft and oil pump driveshaft for pitting,

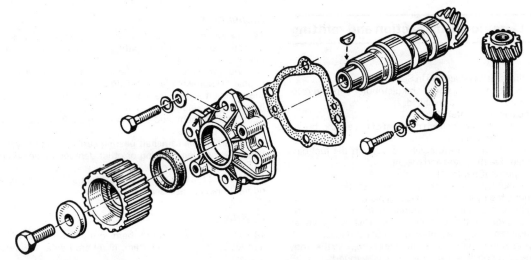

Fig. 2.26 Auxiliary shaft components (Sec 35)

35.5A Removing the auxiliary shaft thrust plate ...

35.5B ... and the auxiliary shaft itself

35.8 Auxiliary shaft housing and oil seal

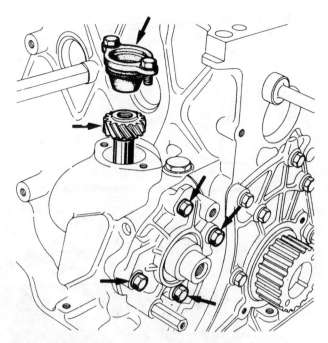

Fig. 2.27 Auxiliary shaft housing retaining bolt locations, oil pump driveshaft and cover plate (Sec 35)

35.11 Auxiliary shaft gasket positioned on the dowels

scoring or wear ridges on the bearing journals and for chipping or wear of the gear teeth. Renew as necessary.

7   Check the auxiliary shaft bearings in the cylinder block for wear and, if worn, have these renewed by your Renault dealer or suitably equipped engineering works. Wipe them clean if they are still serviceable.

Refitting

8   Clean off all traces of the old gasket from the auxiliary shaft housing and tap out the oil seal using a tube of suitable diameter (photo). Install the new oil seal using a block of wood and tap it in until it is flush with the outer face of the housing. The open side of the seal must be towards the engine.

9   Liberally lubricate the auxiliary shaft and slide it into its bearings.

10   Place the thrust plate in position with its curved edge away from

the crankshaft and refit the two retaining bolts, tightening them securely.

11   Place a new gasket in position over the dowels of the cylinder block (photo). If a gasket was not used previously, apply a bead of CAF 4/60 THIXO paste to the housing mating face.

12   Liberally lubricate the oil seal lips and then locate the housing in place. Refit and tighten the housing retaining bolts progressively in a diagonal sequence.

13   Lubricate the oil pump drivegear and lower the gear into its location.

14   Position a new O-ring seal on the drivegear cover plate, fit the plate and secure with the two retaining bolts.

15   Refit the auxiliary shaft sprocket with reference to Section 32.

36   Sump – removal and refitting

Removal

1   Apply the handbrake, then jack up the front of the car and support it on axle stands.

2   Drain the engine oil as described in Chapter 1, then refit and tighten the drain plug.

3   Unscrew the bolts and remove the flywheel or torque converter cover plate.

4   Where fitted, disconnect any electrical wiring at the sump sensors.

5   Unscrew and remove the bolts securing the sump to the crankcase. Tap the sump with a hide or plastic mallet to break the seal, then remove the sump.

6   Remove the gasket where fitted.

Refitting

7   Clean all traces of gasket or sealing compound from the mating faces of the sump and crankcase.

8   Where fitted, locate a new gasket on the sump, otherwise apply a bead of CAF 4/60 THIXO paste to the sump face.

9   If a gasket is not fitted, it is important that the sump is positioned correctly the first time and not moved around after the paste has touched the crankcase. Temporary long bolts or dowel rods may be used to help achieve this.

10   To prevent oil dripping from the oil pump and crankcase, wipe these areas clean before refitting the sump.

11   Lift the sump into position then insert the bolts and tighten them progressively to the specified torque.

12   Reconnect the electrical wiring where fitted.

13   Lower the car to the ground.

14   Fill the engine with fresh oil with reference to Chapter 1.

37   Oil pump – removal, inspection and refitting

Removal

1   Remove the sump as described in Section 36.

2   Unscrew the four retaining bolts at the ends of the pump body and withdraw the pump from the crankcase and drivegear.

Inspection

3   Unscrew the retaining bolts and lift off the pump cover.

4   Withdraw the idler gear and the drivegear/shaft. Mark the idler gear so that it can be refitted in its same position.

5   Extract the retaining clip and remove the oil pressure relief valve spring retainer, spring, spring seat and plunger.

6   Clean the components and carefully examine the gears, pump body and relief valve plunger for any signs of scoring or wear. Renew the pump complete if excessive wear is evident.

7   If the components appear serviceable, measure the clearance between the pump body and the gears and also the gear endfloat using feeler gauges. If the clearances exceed the specified tolerance, the pump must be renewed.

8   If the pump is satisfactory, reassemble the components in the reverse order of removal, fill the pump with oil, then refit the cover and tighten the bolts securely.

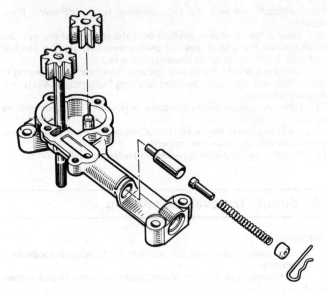

Fig. 2.28 Exploded view of the oil pump (Sec 37)

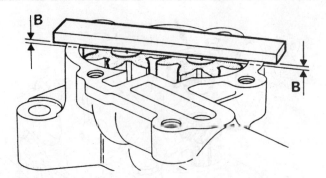

Fig. 2.29 Measuring the oil pump gear endfloat (B) (Sec 37)

Refitting

9   Wipe clean the mating faces of the oil pump and crankcase.
10   Lift the oil pump into position with its shaft engaged with the drivegear. Insert and fully tighten the retaining bolts (photo).

38 Crankshaft oil seals – renewal

Front/right-hand oil seal

1   Remove the timing belt and crankshaft sprocket with reference to Sections 31 and 32.
2   Remove the sump as described in Section 36.
3   Unscrew the bolts securing the front plate to the cylinder block and withdraw the plate, noting that it is located by dowels in the two lower bolt hole locations (photo).
4   Clean the front plate and scrape off all traces of sealant from the plate and cylinder block.
5   Prise out the old oil seal and clean the seating.
6   Fit a new seal so that it is flush with the outer face of the front plate using a block of wood. Ensure that the open side of the seal is fitted towards the engine.
7   Lubricate the oil seal lips. Apply a bead of CAF 4/60 THIXO paste to the mating face of the front plate, making sure that the oilway cavity is not blocked.
8   Refit the front plate and insert the retaining bolts. The two bolts around the oil seal opening at the 2 o'clock and 8 o'clock positions should also have a small quantity of the sealant paste applied to their threads, as they protrude into the crankcase. Progressively tighten the retaining bolts in a diagonal sequence.
9   Refit the sump as described in Section 36.
10   Refit the crankshaft sprocket and timing belt with reference to Sections 32 and 31.

Rear/left-hand oil seal

11   Remove the flywheel/driveplate as described in Section 40.
12   Prise out the old oil seal using a small screwdriver, taking care not to damage the surface of the crankshaft. Alternatively, the oil seal can be removed by drilling two small holes diagonally opposite each other and inserting self-tapping screws in them. A pair of grips can then be used to pull out the oil seal, by pulling on each side in turn.
13   Wipe clean the oil seal seating, then dip the new seal in fresh engine oil and locate it over the crankshaft with its closed side facing outwards. Make sure that the oil seal lip is not damaged as it is located on the crankshaft.
14   Using a metal tube, drive the oil seal squarely into the bore until flush. A block of wood cut to pass over the end of the crankshaft may be used instead.
15   Refit the flywheel with reference to Section 40.

37.10 Tightening the oil pump mounting bolts

38.3 Removing the front plate and oil seal

39 Engine mountings – renewal

Refer to Part A: Section 13.

40 Flywheel/driveplate – removal, inspection and refitting

Refer to Part A: Section 14.

Part D: Engine removal and general engine overhaul procedures

41 General information

Included in this part of Chapter 2 are the general overhaul procedures for the cylinder heads, cylinder block/crankcase and internal engine components.

The information ranges from advice concerning preparation for an overhaul and the purchase of replacement parts, to detailed step-by-step procedures covering removal, inspection, renovation and refitting of internal engine parts.

The following Sections have been compiled based on the assumption that the engine has been removed from the car. For information concerning in-car engine repair, as well as the removal and refitting of the external components necessary for the overhaul, refer to Part A (1390 cc engine), B (1397 cc engine), or C (1721 cc engine) of this Chapter and to Section 46 of this Part.

42 Engine overhaul – general information

It is not always easy to determine when, or if, an engine should be completely overhauled, as a number of factors must be considered.

High mileage is not necessarily an indication that an overhaul is needed, while low mileage does not preclude the need for an overhaul. Frequency of servicing is probably the most important consideration. An engine which has had regular and frequent oil and filter changes, as well as other required maintenance, will most likely give many thousands of miles of reliable service. Conversely, a neglected engine may require an overhaul very early in its life.

Excessive oil consumption is an indication that piston rings, valve seals and/or valve guides are in need of attention. Make sure that oil leaks are not responsible before deciding that the rings and/or guides are bad. Perform a cylinder compression check to determine the extent of the work required.

Check the oil pressure with a gauge fitted in place of the oil pressure sender, and compare it with the Specifications. If it is extremely low, the main and big-end bearings and/or the oil pump are probably worn out.

Loss of power, rough running, knocking or metallic engine noises, excessive valve gear noise and high fuel consumption may also point to the need for an overhaul, especially if they are all present at the same time. If a complete tune-up does not remedy the situation, major mechanical work is the only solution.

An engine overhaul involves restoring the internal parts to the specifications of a new engine. During an overhaul, the pistons and rings are replaced and the cylinder bores are reconditioned. New main bearings, connecting rod bearings and camshaft bearings are generally fitted, and if necessary, the crankshaft may be reground to restore the journals. The valves are also serviced as well, since they are usually in less than perfect condition at this point. While the engine is being overhauled, other components, such as the distributor, starter and alternator, can be overhauled as well. The end result should be a like-new engine that will give many trouble-free miles. **Note:** *Critical cooling system components such as the hoses, drivebelts, thermostat and water pump MUST be renewed when an engine is overhauled. The radiator should be checked carefully to ensure that it is not clogged or leaking. Also it is a good idea to renew the oil pump whenever the engine is overhauled.*

Before beginning the engine overhaul, read through the entire procedure to familiarize yourself with the scope and requirements of the job. Overhauling an engine is not difficult if you follow all of the instructions carefully, have the necessary tools and equipment and pay close attention to all specifications; however, it can be time consuming. Plan on the vehicle being tied up for a minimum of two weeks, especially if parts must be taken to an engineering works for repair or reconditioning. Check on the availability of parts and make sure that any necessary special tools and equipment are obtained in advance. Most work can be done with typical hand tools, although a number of precision measuring tools are required for inspecting parts to determine if they must be renewed. Often the engineering works will handle the inspection of parts and offer advice concerning reconditioning and renewal. **Note:** *Always wait until the engine has been completely*

disassembled and all components, especially the engine block have been inspected before deciding what service and repair operations must be performed by an engineering works. Since the condition of the block will be the major factor to consider when determining whether to overhaul the original engine or buy a reconditioned unit, do not purchase parts or have overhaul work done on other components until the block has been thoroughly inspected. As a general rule, time is the primary cost of an overhaul, so it does not pay to fit worn or substandard parts.

As a final note, to ensure maximum life and minimum trouble from a reconditioned engine, everything must be assembled with care in a spotlessly clean environment.

43 Engine removal – methods and precautions

If you have decided that an engine must be removed for overhaul or major repair work, several preliminary steps should be taken.

Locating a suitable place to work is extremely important. Adequate work space, along with storage space for the vehicle, will be needed. If a garage is not available, at the very least a flat, level, clean work surface is required.

Cleaning the engine compartment and engine before beginning the removal procedure will help keep tools clean and organized.

An engine hoist or A-frame will also be necessary. Make sure the equipment is rated in excess of the combined weight of the engine and transmission. Safety is of primary importance, considering the potential hazards involved in lifting the engine out of the vehicle.

If the engine is being removed by a novice, an assistant should be available. Advice and aid from someone more experienced would also be helpful. There are many instances when one person cannot simultaneously perform all of the operations required when lifting the engine out of the vehicle.

Plan the operation ahead of time. Arrange for or obtain all of the tools and equipment you will need prior to beginning the job. Some of the equipment necessary to perform engine removal and installation safely and with relative ease are (in addition to an engine hoist) a heavy duty floor jack, complete sets of spanners and sockets as described in the front of this manual, wooden blocks and plenty of rags and cleaning solvent for mopping up spilled oil, coolant and fuel. If the hoist must be hired, make sure that you arrange for it in advance, and perform all of the operations possible without it beforehand. This will save you money and time.

Plan for the vehicle to be out of use for quite a while. An engineering works will be required to perform some of the work which the do-it-yourselfer cannot accomplish without special equipment. These places often have a busy schedule, so it would be a good idea to consult them before removing the engine in order to accurately estimate the amount of time required to rebuild or repair components that may need work.

Always be extremely careful when removing and refitting the engine. Serious injury can result from careless actions. Plan ahead, take your time and you will find that a job of this nature, although major, can be accomplished successfully.

44 Engine (1397 cc) – removal and refitting (without transmission)

Note: *Only the 1397 cc engine may be removed on its own, leaving the transmission in situ. This engine may also be removed together with the transmission as described in Section 45*

Removal

1 Disconnect both battery leads.
2 Remove the bonnet with reference to Chapter 11.
3 Unbolt and remove the strengthening bar from between the front suspension unit turrets.
4 Remove the radiator with reference to Chapter 3.

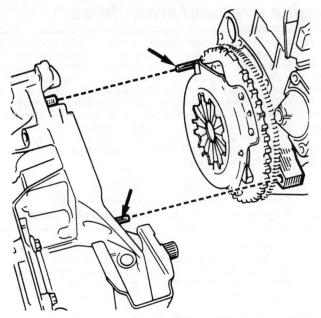

Fig. 2.30 Location studs (arrowed) on the gearbox and engine (Sec 44)

5 Remove the alternator/water pump drivebelt with reference to Chapter 1.

6 Apply the handbrake, then jack up the front of the car and support it on axle stands. Remove both front wheels.

7 Unbolt and remove the engine-to-gearbox tie-bar.

8 Unbolt and remove the cover from the bottom of the gearbox.

9 Using a socket on the crankshaft pulley bolt, turn the engine until the notch in the flywheel is aligned with the TDC mark on the bellhousing timing scale, and the distributor rotor is pointing towards the No 1 cylinder HT lead segment in the cap.

10 Using a socket or spanner, unscrew the crankshaft pulley retaining bolt. Lock the starter ring gear to prevent the engine turning by using a wide-bladed screwdriver inserted between the ring gear teeth and the crankcase, or alternatively apply the handbrake and engage top gear.

11 With the bolt removed, lift off the pulley and withdraw the pulley hub. If the hub is tight, carefully lever it off using two screwdrivers or use a two or three-legged puller. Take care not to loose the Woodruff key from the nose of the crankshaft.

12 Remove the starter motor with reference to Chapter 12.

13 Disconnect the accelerator and choke cables with reference to Chapter 4.

14 Refer to Chapter 4 and remove the air cleaner unit and its mounting.

15 Disconnect the heater, fuel and vacuum servo hoses.

16 Disconnect the wiring from the following components:

    (a) *Oil pressure switch*
    (b) *Temperature sender*
    (c) *Oil level sender*
    (d) *Alternator*
    (e) *King HT lead from the distributor*
    (f) *Fuel cut-off solenoid*
    (g) *Ignition AEI unit*

17 If necessary disconnect the main wiring harness connector blocks.

18 Disconnect the exhaust front pipe from the exhaust manifold with reference to Chapter 4.

19 On models fitted with power-assisted steering, remove the pump with reference to Chapter 10, although leave the hose attached and position the pump to one side.

20 On models fitted with air conditioning, remove the compressor with reference to Chapter 3, although leave the hose attached and position the pump to one side.

21 Unbolt the electronic ignition sensor unit from the top of the gearbox bellhousing.

22 Attach a suitable hoist to the engine lifting brackets, then raise the hoist to just take the weight of the engine.

23 Position a trolley jack under the gearbox and just take its weight.

24 Unscrew and remove the gearbox-to-engine nuts and bolts.

25 Unscrew and remove the location studs shown in Fig. 2.30.

26 Unscrew the lower nut from the right-hand front engine mounting.

27 Separate the engine from the gearbox until it is clear of the clutch.

28 With the help of an assistant, slowly lift the engine and at the same time check that the right-hand driveshaft is not dislocated.

29 Lift the engine from the engine compartment taking care not to damage any components on the surrounding panels. When high enough, lift it over the front body panel and lower the unit to the ground.

Refitting

30 Refitting is a reversal of removal, however note the following additional points:

    (a) *Apply a little high melting-point grease to the splines of the gearbox input shaft*
    (b) *Tighten all nuts and bolts to the specified torque*
    (c) *Refer to the applicable Chapters and Sections as for removal*

45 Engine – removal and refitting (with transmission)

Removal

1 Disconnect both battery leads.

2 Drain the cooling system with reference to Chapter 1.

3 Drain the engine and transmission oil with reference to Chapters 1 and 7 as applicable.

4 Remove the bonnet with reference to Chapter 11.

5 Unbolt and remove the strengthening bar from between the front suspension unit turrets.

6 Remove the radiator with reference to Chapter 3. Also disconnect the bottom hose from the cylinder block inlet elbow (photo).

7 Apply the handbrake, then jack up the front of the car and support on axle stands. Remove both front wheels.

8 Working beneath the right-hand side of the car, use a parallel pin punch to drive out the double roll pin securing the right-hand driveshaft to the transmission differential sun wheel stub shaft.

9 Unscrew and remove the two nuts and bolts securing the right-hand stub axle carrier to the suspension strut. Note that the nuts are on the brake caliper side.

10 Pull the top of the stub axle carrier outwards until the inner end of the driveshaft is released from the stub shaft.

11 Working on the left-hand side, remove the front brake caliper with reference to Chapter 9, but leave the hydraulic hose connected. Tie the caliper to the front suspension coil spring with wire or string taking care not to strain the hose.

12 Disconnect the steering track rod end from the left-hand stub axle carrier with reference to Chapter 10.

13 Unscrew the three bolts securing the driveshaft rubber gaiter retaining plate to the left-hand side of the transmission.

14 Unscrew and remove the two nuts and bolts securing the left-hand stub axle carrier to the suspension strut. Note that the nuts are on the brake caliper side.

15 Pull the top of the left-hand stub axle carrier outwards until the inner end of the driveshaft is released from the yoke. There may be some loss of oil from the transmission, so position a small container on the floor to catch it.

16 Refer to Chapter 4 and remove the air cleaner unit and its mounting.

17 Disconnect the heater, fuel and vacuum servo hoses.

18 Disconnect the wiring from the following components:

    (a) *Oil pressure switch (photo)*
    (b) *Temperature sender (photo)*
    (c) *Oil level sender*
    (d) *Starter motor*
    (e) *Alternator*
    (f) *King HT lead from the distributor*
    (g) *Fuel cut-off solenoid*
    (h) *Reversing light switch*
    (i) *Ignition AEI unit*

45.6 Disconnecting the bottom hose

45.18A Oil pressure switch on the front of the cylinder block (1390 cc engine)

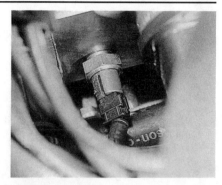

45.18B Temperature sender on the cylinder head (1390 cc engine)

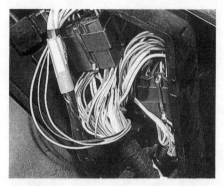

45.19 Main wiring harness connector blocks

45.30 Lifting the engine/transmission assembly from the engine compartment

19   If necessary disconnect the main wiring harness connector blocks (photo).
20   Disconnect the accelerator and choke cables with reference to Chapter 4.
21   Disconnect the speedometer cable with reference to Chapter 12.
22   Disconnect the engine earthing straps as applicable.
23   Disconnect the controls from the transmission with reference to Chapter 7.
24   On manual transmission models, disconnect the clutch cable with reference to Chapter 6.
25   Disconnect the exhaust front pipe from the exhaust manifold with reference to Chapter 4. On the 1390 cc engine, remove the front exhaust pipe completely.
26   On models fitted with power-assisted steering, remove the pump with reference to Chapter 10, although leave the hose attached and position the pump to one side.
27   On models fitted with air conditioning, remove the compressor with reference to Chapter 3, although leave the hose attached and position the pump to one side.
28   Attach a suitable hoist to the engine lifting brackets, then raise the hoist to just take the weight of the engine.
29   Disconnect the engine mountings with reference to Part A, Section 13.
30   With the help of an assistant, slowly lift the engine/transmission assembly from the engine compartment taking care not to damage any components on the surrounding panels (photo). When high enough, lift it over the front body panel and lower the unit to the ground.
31   To separate the gearbox from the engine, refer to Chapter 7.

Refitting

32   Refitting is a reversal of removal, however note the following additional points:

   (a) Refer to the applicable Chapters and Sections as for removal
   (b) Fit new roll pins to the right-hand driveshaft and seal the ends using a suitable sealant
   (c) Refit and tighten the brake caliper mounting bolts with reference to Chapter 9

   (d) Tighten all nuts and bolts to the specified torque
   (e) Refill the engine and transmission with oil with reference to Chapters 1 and 7
   (f) Refill the cooling system with reference to Chapter 1

46   Engine overhaul – dismantling sequence

1   It is much easier to disassemble and work on the engine if it is mounted on a portable engine stand. These stands can often be hired from a tool hire shop. Before the engine is mounted on a stand, the flywheel/driveplate should be removed from the engine so that the engine stand bolts can be tightened into the end of the cylinder block.
2   If a stand is not available, it is possible to disassemble the engine with it blocked up on a sturdy workbench or on the floor, although be extra careful not to tip or drop the engine when working without a stand.
3   If you are going to obtain a reconditioned engine, all external components must come off first in order to be transferred to the replacement engine (just as they will if you are doing a complete engine overhaul yourself). These components include:

   (a) Alternator and brackets
   (b) Distributor, HT leads and spark plugs
   (c) Thermostat and cover
   (d) Carburettor
   (e) Inlet and exhaust manifolds
   (f) Oil filter
   (g) Fuel pump
   (h) Engine mountings
   (i) Flywheel/driveplate

Note: *When removing the external components from the engine, pay close attention to details that may be helpful or important during refitting. Note the fitted position of gaskets, seals, spacers, pins, washers, bolts and other small items.*

4   If you are obtaining a short motor (which consists of the engine

47.2A Removing the split collets

47.2B Removing the spring seat

47.4 Removing an oil seal from the top of the valve guide

47.5A Valve components

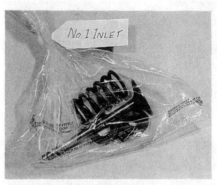
47.5B Store the valve components in a polythene bag after removal

cylinder block, crankshaft, pistons and connecting rods all assembled), then the cylinder head, sump, oil pump, and timing belt (where applicable) will have to be removed also.

5　If you are planning a complete overhaul, the engine can be disassembled and the internal components removed in the following order:

(a)　Inlet and exhaust manifolds
(b)　Timing belt/chain and sprockets
(c)　Cylinder head
(d)　Flywheel
(e)　Sump
(f)　Oil pump
(g)　Pistons
(h)　Crankshaft

6　Before beginning the disassembly and overhaul procedures, make sure that you have all of the correct tools necessary. Refer to the introductory pages at the beginning of this manual for further information.

47　Cylinder head – dismantling

Note: *New and reconditioned cylinder heads are available from the manufacturers and from engine overhaul specialists. Due to the fact that some specialist tools are required for the dismantling and inspection procedures, and new components may not be readily available, it may be more practical and economical for the home mechanic to purchase a reconditioned head rather than dismantle, inspect and recondition the original head*

1　On the 1721 cc engine, first withdraw the tappet buckets, complete with shims, from their bores in the head. Lay the buckets out on a sheet of cardboard numbered 1 to 8 with No 1 at the flywheel end. It is a good idea to write the shim thickness size on the card alongside each bucket

in case the shims are accidentally knocked off their buckets and mixed up. The size is etched on the shim bottom face.

2　Using a valve spring compressor, compress each valve spring in turn until the split collets can be removed. Release the compressor and lift off the cap, spring and spring seat (photos).

3　If, when the valve spring compressor is screwed down, the valve spring cap refuses to free and expose the split collets, gently tap the top of the tool, directly over the cap, with a light hammer. This will free the cap.

4　Withdraw the oil seal off the top of the valve guide, and then remove the valve through the combustion chamber (photo).

5　It is essential that the valves are kept in their correct sequence unless they are so badly worn that they are to be renewed. If they are going to be kept and used again, place them in labelled polythene bags, or alternatively put them in a sheet of card having eight holes numbered 1 to 8 – corresponding to the relative fitted positions of the valves (photos). Note that No 1 valve is nearest to the flywheel end of the engine.

48　Cylinder head and valves – cleaning, inspection and renovation

1　Thorough cleaning of the cylinder head and valve components, followed by a detailed inspection, will enable you to decide how much valve service work must be carried out during the engine overhaul.

Cleaning

2　Scrape away all traces of old gasket material and sealing compound from the cylinder head.

3　Scrape away the carbon from the combustion chambers and ports, then wash the cylinder head thoroughly with paraffin or a suitable solvent.

4　Scrape off any heavy carbon deposits that may have formed on the

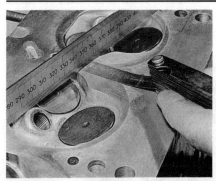

48.6 Checking the cylinder head surface for distortion

48.9 Checking the valve stem for excessive wear

48.11 Grinding in the valves

valves, then use a power-operated wire brush to remove deposits from the valve heads and stems.

Inspection

Note: *Be sure to perform all the following inspection procedures before concluding that the services of an engine overhaul specialist are required. Make a list of all items that require attention*

Cylinder head

5   Inspect the head very carefully for cracks, evidence of coolant leakage and other damage. If cracks are found, a new cylinder head should be obtained.

6   Use a straight-edge and feeler blade to check that the cylinder head surface is not distorted (photo). If it is, it may be possible to resurface it on the 1397 cc engine, however the manufacturers do not allow resurfacing on the other engine types.

7   Examine the valve seats in each of the combustion chambers. If they are severely pitted, cracked or burned then they will need to be renewed or recut by an engine overhaul specialist. If they are only slightly pitted, this can be removed by grinding the valve heads and seats together with coarse then fine grinding paste as described below.

8   If the valve guides are worn, indicated by a side-to-side motion of the valve, new guides must be fitted. This work is best carried out by an engine overhaul specialist, however they may be renewed using a suitable mandrel, making sure that they are at the correct height. A dial gauge may be used to determine the amount of side play of the valve.

Valves

9   Examine the heads of each valve for pitting, burning, cracks and general wear, and check the valve stem for scoring and wear ridges. Rotate the valve and check for any obvious indication that it is bent. Look for pits and excessive wear on the end of each valve stem. If the valve appears satisfactory at this stage, measure the valve stem diameter at several points using a micrometer (photo). Any significant difference in the readings obtained indicates wear of the valve stem. Should any of these conditions be apparent, the valve(s) must be renewed. If the valves are in satisfactory condition they should be

48.12 Checking the valve spring free length

ground (lapped) into their respective seats to ensure a smooth gas-tight seal.

10   Valve grinding is carried out as follows. Place the cylinder head upside down on a bench with a block of wood at each end to give clearance for the valve stems.

11   Smear a trace of coarse carborundum paste on the seat face and press a suction grinding tool onto the valve head. With a semi-rotary action, grind the valve head to its seat, lifting the valve occasionally to redistribute the grinding paste (photo). When a dull matt even surface is produced on both the valve seat and the valve, wipe off the paste and repeat the process with fine carborundum paste. A light spring placed under the valve head will greatly ease this operation. When a smooth unbroken ring of light grey matt finish is produced on both the valve and

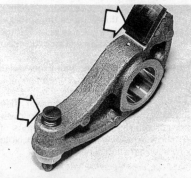

48.15A Check the rocker arm contact surfaces for wear (arrowed)

48.15B Checking the internal diameter of the rocker arms

48.15C Clean the oil spill holes using a length of wire

49.2 Pressing a valve seal onto its guide

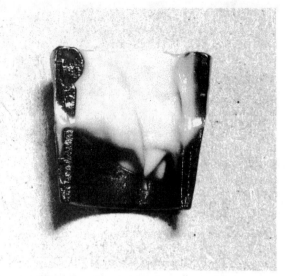

49.4 Use grease to hold the collets in place on reassembly

seat, the grinding operation is complete. Be sure to remove all traces of grinding paste using paraffin or a suitable solvent before reassembly of the cylinder head.

Valve components

12   Examine the valve springs for signs of damage and discoloration, and also measure their free length using vernier calipers (photo) or by comparing the existing spring with a new component.
13   Stand each spring on a flat surface and check it for squareness. If any of the springs are damaged, distorted or have lost their tension, obtain a complete new set of springs.
14   On the 1721 cc engine, inspect the tappet buckets and their shims for scoring, pitting, especially on the shims, and wear ridges. Renew any components as necessary. Note that some scuffing is to be expected and is acceptable provided that the tappets are not scored.

Rocker arm components – except 1721 cc engine

15   Check the rocker arm faces (the areas that contact the pushrod ends and valve stems) for pits, wear, score marks or any indication that the surface hardening has worn through. Check the rocker arm and rocker shaft pivot and contact areas in the same way. Measure the internal diameter of each rocker and check their fit on the shaft. Clean out the oil spill holes in each rocker using a length of wire (photos). Renew the rocker arm or the rocker shaft itself if any are suspect.
16   On 1397 cc engines, inspect the pushrod ends for scuffing and excessive wear. Roll each pushrod on a flat surface, such as a piece of plate glass and check for straightness.

49   Cylinder head – reassembly

1   Lubricate the stems of the valves and insert them into their original locations. If new valves are being fitted, insert them into the locations to which they have been ground.
2   Working on the first valve, dip the oil seal in engine oil then carefully locate it over the valve and onto the guide. Take care not to damage the seal as it is passed over the valve stem. Use a suitable socket or metal tube to press the seal firmly onto the guide (photo).
3   Locate the spring seat on the guide, followed by the spring and cap. Where applicable, the spring should be fitted with its closest coils towards the head.
4   Compress the valve spring and locate the split collets in the recess in the valve stem. Use a little grease to hold the collets in place (photo). Note that on the 1397 cc engine the collets are different for the inlet and exhaust valves, the latter type having two curved collars. Release the compressor, then repeat the procedure on the remaining valves.
5   With all the valves installed, place the cylinder head flat on the bench and, using a hammer and interposed block of wood, tap the end

of each valve stem to settle the components.
6   On the 1721 cc engine, lubricate the tappet buckets and insert them into their respective locations as noted during removal. Make sure that each bucket has its correct tappet shim in place on its upper face, and that the shim is installed with its etched size number facing downwards.

50   Camshaft and followers (1397 cc engine) – removal, inspection and refitting

Removal

1   Remove the cylinder head, distributor, timing chain and camshaft sprocket with reference to Part B.
2   Using a suitable bolt screwed into the distributor drivegear, or a length of tapered dowel rod, extract the drivegear from the distributor aperture.
3   Withdraw the camshaft followers from the top of the cylinder block, keeping them in strict order of removal.
4   Unscrew and remove the two bolts securing the camshaft retaining plate to the cylinder block and carefully withdraw the camshaft from its location.

Inspection

5   Examine the camshaft bearing surfaces, cam lobes and skew gear for wear ridges, pitting, scoring or chipping of the gear teeth. Renew the camshaft if any of these conditions are apparent.
6   If the camshaft is serviceable, temporarily refit the sprocket and secure with the retaining bolt. Using a feeler blade measure the clearance between the camshaft retaining plate and the outer face of the bearing journal. If the clearance (endfloat) exceeds the specified dimension, renew the retaining plate. To do this, remove the sprocket and draw off the plate and retaining collar using a suitable puller. Fit the new plate and a new collar using a hammer and tube to drive the collar into position.
7   Examine the condition of the camshaft bearings, and if renewal is necessary have this work carried out by a Renault dealer or engineering works.
8   Inspect the cam followers for wear ridges and pitting of their camshaft lobe contact faces, and for scoring on the sides of the follower body. Light scuff marks are normal, but there should be no signs of scoring or ridges. If the followers show signs of wear, renew them. Note that they must all be renewed if a new camshaft is being fitted.

Refitting

9   Lubricate the camshaft bearings and carefully insert the camshaft from the timing gear end of the engine.
10   Refit the retaining plate, then insert and tighten the bolts securely.

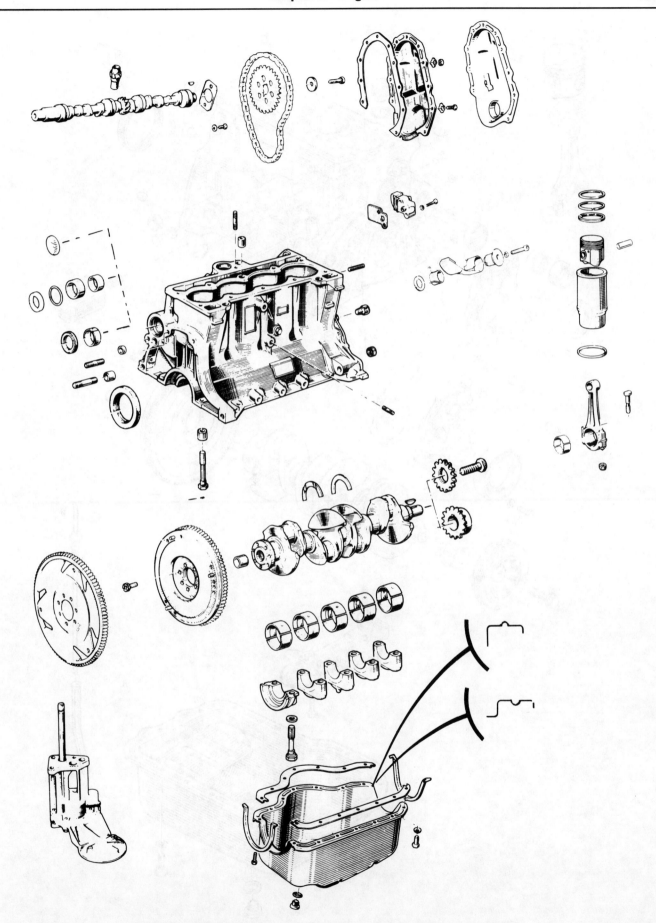

Fig. 2.31 Cylinder block components on the 1397 cc (C1J) engine (Secs 50 to 53)

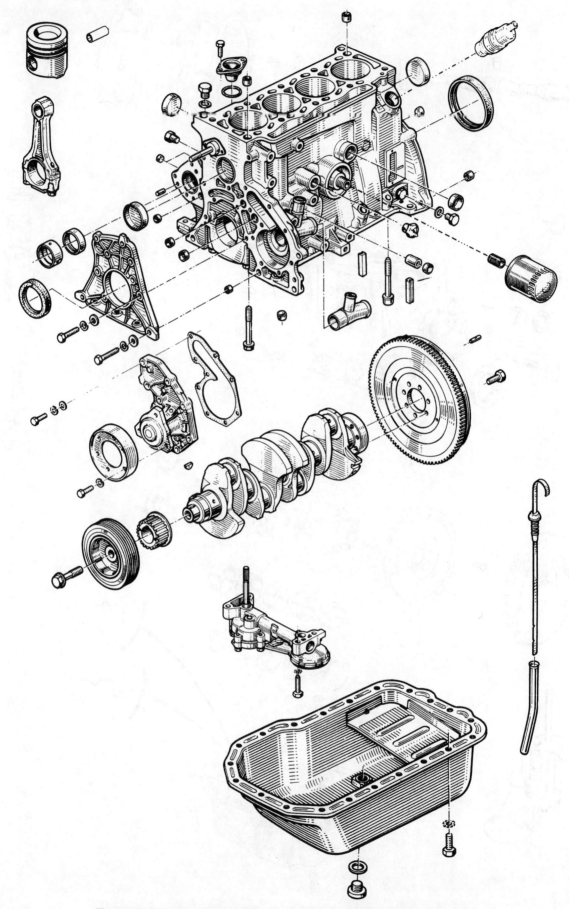

Fig. 2.32 Cylinder block components on the 1721 cc (F2N) engine (Secs 50 to 53)

50.14 Fit the distributor drivegear ...

50.15 ... so that the slot is at right-angles to the crankshaft centreline with its larger offset side facing the flywheel when fitted

Check that the camshaft rotates smoothly.

11 Lubricate the cam followers and insert them into their original bores in the cylinder block.

12 Refit the camshaft sprocket and timing chain, and cylinder head with reference to Part B.

13 Using a ring spanner on the crankshaft pulley bolt, turn the crankshaft until No 1 piston (flywheel end) is at the top of its compression stroke. This position can be established by placing a finger over No 1 plug hole and rotating the crankshaft until compression can be felt; continue turning the crankshaft until the piston reaches the top of its stroke. Use a screwdriver through the plug hole to feel the movement of the piston, but be careful not to damage the piston crown or the plug threads in the cylinder head.

14 Without moving the crankshaft, position the drivegear so that its slots are at the 2 o'clock and 8 o'clock positions with the larger offset side facing away from the engine (photo).

15 Now lower the drivegear into mesh with the camshaft and oil pump driveshaft. As the gear meshes with the camshaft it will rotate anti-clockwise and should end up with its slot at right-angles to the crankshaft centreline and with the larger offset towards the flywheel. It will probably be a tooth out on the first attempt and will take two or three attempts to get it just right (photo).

16 Refit the distributor with reference to Chapter 5.

51 Piston/connecting rod assemblies – removal

1 With the cylinder head, sump and oil pump removed, proceed as follows.

2 Rotate the crankshaft so that No 1 big-end cap (nearest the flywheel position) is at the lowest point of its travel. If the big-end cap and rod are not already numbered, mark them with a centre punch (photo). Mark both cap and rod in relation to the cylinder they operate in, noting that No 1 is nearest the flywheel end of the engine.

3 Before removing the big-end caps, use a feeler blade to check the amount of side play between the caps and the crankshaft webs (photo).

4 Unscrew and remove the big-end bearing cap nuts and withdraw the cap, complete with shell bearing from the connecting rod. If only the bearing shells are being attended to, push the connecting rod up and off the crankpin and remove the upper bearing shell. Keep the bearing shells and cap together in their correct sequence if they are to be refitted.

5 On 1390 cc and 1397 cc engines, remove the liner clamps and withdraw each liner, together with piston and connecting rod, from the top of the cylinder block. Mark the liners using masking tape, so that they may be refitted in their original locations.

51.2 Big-end caps marked with a centre punch

51.3 Checking the big-end cap side play

52.2 Checking the crankshaft endfloat with a dial gauge

52.3 Checking the crankshaft endfloat with a feeler blade – 1390 and 1397 cc engines

52.4 Identification numbers (arrowed) on the main bearings

52.7A Removing the thrust washers ...

52.7B ... and main bearing shell upper halves

6   Push the connecting rod up and remove the piston and rod from the bore. On 1390 cc and 1397 cc engines withdraw the piston from the bottom of the liner.

52 Crankshaft – removal

1   With the front cover and flywheel removed, proceed as follows.
2   Before the crankshaft is removed, check the endfloat using a dial gauge in contact with the end of the crankshaft (photo). Push the

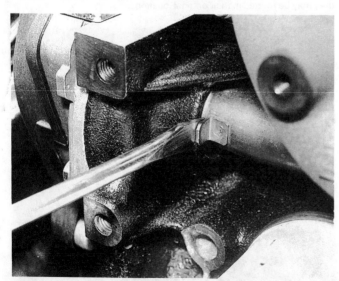

53.1A Removing the coolant pipe from the cylinder block (1390 cc engine)

crankshaft fully one way and then zero the gauge. Push the crankshaft fully the other way and check the endfloat. The result can be compared with the specified amount and will give an indication as to whether new thrust washers are required.
3   If a dial gauge is not available, feeler blades can be used. First push the crankshaft fully towards the flywheel end of the engine, then slip the feeler blade between the web of No 2 crankpin and the thrust washer of the centre main bearing (1390 cc and 1397 cc engines) (photo), or between the web of No 1 crankpin and the thrust washer of No 2 main bearing (1721 cc engine).
4   Identification numbers should be cast onto the base of each main bearing cap, but if not, number the cap and crankcase using a centre punch, similar to the connecting rods and caps (photo).
5   Unscrew and remove the main bearing cap retaining bolts and withdraw the caps, complete with bearing shells.
6   Carefully lift the crankshaft from the crankcase.
7   Remove the thrust washers at each side of the centre main bearing (1390 cc and 1397 cc engines) or No 2 main bearing (1721 cc engine), then remove the bearing shell upper halves from the crankcase (photos). Place each shell with its respective bearing cap.
8   Remove the oil seal from the rear of the crankshaft.

53 Cylinder block/crankcase – cleaning and inspection

Cleaning

1   For complete cleaning, the core plugs should be removed where fitted. Drill a small hole in them, then insert a self-tapping screw and pull out the plugs using a pair of grips or a slide-hammer. Also remove all external components and senders (photos).
2   Scrape all traces of gasket from the cylinder block, taking care not to damage the head and sump mating faces.
3   Remove all oil gallery plugs where fitted. The plugs are usually very

53.1B Removing the oil pressure switch from the cylinder block (1390 cc engine)

tight – they may have to be drilled out and the holes re-tapped. Use new plugs when the engine is reassembled.

4   If the block is extremely dirty, it should be steam cleaned.

5   After the block has been steam cleaned, clean all oil holes and oil galleries one more time. Flush all internal passages with warm water until the water runs clear, dry the block thoroughly and wipe all machined surfaces with a light rust preventive oil. If you have access to compressed air, use it to speed up the drying process and to blow out all the oil holes and galleries. **Warning:** *Wear eye protection when using compressed air!*

6   If the block is not very dirty, you can do an adequate cleaning job with hot soapy water and a stiff brush. Take plenty of time and do a thorough job. Regardless of the cleaning method used, be sure to clean all oil holes and galleries very thoroughly, dry the block completely and coat all machined surfaces with light oil.

7   The threaded holes in the block must be clean to ensure accurate torque readings during reassembly. Run the proper size tap into each of the holes to remove rust, corrosion, thread sealant or sludge and restore damaged threads. If possible, use compressed air to clear the holes of debris produced by this operation. Now is a good time to clean the threads on the head bolts and the main bearing cap bolts as well.

8   Refit the main bearing caps and tighten the bolts finger-tight.

9   After coating the mating surfaces of the new core plugs with suitable sealant refit them in the cylinder block. Make sure that they are driven in straight and seated properly or leakage could result. Special tools are available for this purpose, but a large socket, with an outside diameter that will just slip into the core plug will work just as well.

10   Apply suitable sealant to the new oil gallery plugs and insert them into the holes in the block. Tighten them securely.

11   If the engine is not going to be reassembled right away, cover it with a large plastic bag to keep it clean and prevent it rusting.

Inspection

12   Visually check the block for cracks, rust and corrosion. Look for stripped threads in the threaded holes. If there has been any history of internal water leakage, it may be worthwhile having an engine overhaul specialist check the block with special equipment. If defects are found, have the block repaired, if possible, or renewed.

13   Check the cylinder bores/liners for scuffing and scoring.

14   Measure the diameter of each cylinder at the top (just under the ridge area), centre and bottom of the cylinder bore, parallel to the crankshaft axis.

15   Next measure each cylinder's diameter at the same three locations across the crankshaft axis. If the difference between any of the measurements is greater than 0.20 mm, indicating that the cylinder is excessively out-of-round or tapered, then remedial action must be considered.

16   Repeat this procedure for the remaining pistons and cylinders.

17   If the cylinder walls are badly scuffed or scored, or if they are excessively out-of-round or tapered, have the cylinder block rebored (1721 cc engine) or obtain new cylinder liners (1390 cc and 1397 cc engines). Oversize pistons will also be required.

18   If the cylinders are in reasonably good condition then it may only be necessary to renew the piston rings.

19   If this is the case, the bores should be honed in order to allow the new rings to bed in correctly and provide the best possible seal. The conventional type of hone has spring-loaded stones and is used with a power drill. You will also need some paraffin or honing oil and rags. The hone should be moved up and down the cylinder to produce a crosshatch pattern and plenty of honing oil should be used. Ideally the crosshatch lines should intersect at approximately a 60° angle. Do not take off more material than is necessary to produce the required finish. If new pistons are being fitted, the piston manufacturers may specify a finish with a different angle, so their instructions should be followed. Do not withdraw the hone from the cylinder while it is still being turned, but stop it first. After honing a cylinder, wipe out all traces of the honing oil. If equipment of this type is not available, or if you are not sure whether you are competent to undertake the task yourself, an engine overhaul specialist will carry out the work at a moderate cost.

20   If new liners are being fitted, their protrusions must be checked as follows. Place the liner without its base O-ring in the cylinder block. Using a dial gauge or straight-edge and feeler blade, check that the protrusion of the liner above the upper surface of the cylinder block is between 0.02 and 0. 09 mm (photos). Check all of the liners in the same manner and record the protrusions. Note that the difference of

53.20A Checking the cylinder liner protrusion with a dial gauge ...

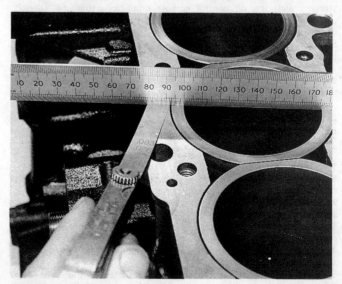

53.20B ... and with feeler blades

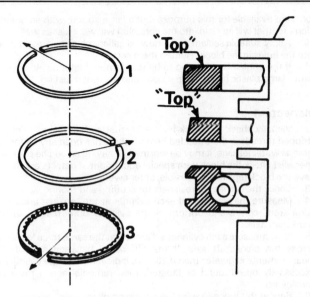

Fig. 2.33 Piston ring identification on the 1390 cc (E6J) engine (Sec 54)

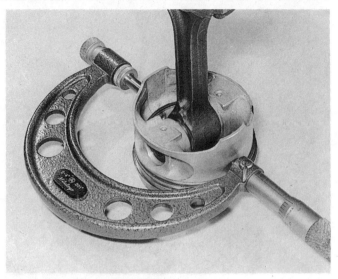

54.1 Measuring the pistons for ovality

protrusion between two adjacent liners must not exceed 0.05 mm, so it may be necessary to reposition them. The protrusions may be stepped upwards or downwards from the flywheel end of the engine.

54 Piston/connecting rod assemblies – inspection

1   Examine the pistons for ovality, scoring and scratches, and for wear of the piston ring grooves. Use a micrometer to measure the pistons (photo).
2   If the pistons or connecting rods are to be renewed it is necessary to have this work carried out by a Renault dealer or suitable engine overhaul specialist who will have the necessary tooling to remove the gudgeon pins.
3   If new rings are to be fitted to the original pistons, expand the old rings over the top of the pistons. The use of two or three old feeler blades will be helpful in preventing the rings dropping into empty grooves (photo).
4   Before fitting the new rings, ensure that the ring grooves in the piston are free of carbon by cleaning them using an old ring. Break the ring in half to do this.
5   Install the new rings by fitting them over the top of the piston, starting with the oil control scraper ring. Note that the second compression ring is tapered and must be fitted with the word 'TOP' uppermost.
6   With all the rings in position, space the ring gaps at 120° to each other.
7   Note that if new piston and liner assemblies have been obtained, each piston is matched to its respective liner and they must not be interchanged.

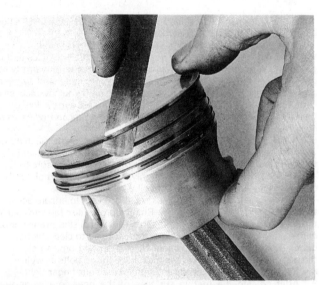

54.3 Using an old feeler blade to remove the piston rings

55 Crankshaft – inspection

1   Clean the crankshaft and dry it with compressed air if available. **Warning:** *Wear eye protection when using compressed air!* Be sure to clean the oil holes with a pipe cleaner or similar probe.
2   Check the main and big-end bearing journals for uneven wear, scoring, pitting and cracking.
3   Rub a penny across each journal several times (photo). If a journal picks up copper from the penny, it is too rough and must be reground.
4   Remove all burrs from the crankshaft oil holes with a stone, file or scraper.
5   Using a micrometer, measure the diameter of the main and connecting rod journals and compare the results with the Specifications

55.3 Using a penny to check the crankshaft journals for scoring

55.5 Using a micrometer to check the crankshaft journals

56.1 Typical marking on the back metal of a bearing shell

at the beginning of this Chapter (photo). By measuring the diameter at a number of points around each journal's circumference, you will be able to determine whether or not the journal is out-of-round. Take the measurement at each end of the journal, near the webs, to determine if the journal is tapered. If any of the measurements vary by more than 0.0254 mm, the crankshaft will have to be reground and undersize bearings fitted.

6   Check the oil seal journals as applicable at each end of the crankshaft for wear and damage. If the seal has worn an excessive groove in the journal, consult an engine overhaul specialist who will be able to advise if a repair is possible, or whether a new crankshaft is necessary.

56   Main and big-end bearings – inspection

1   Even though the main and big-end bearings should be renewed during the engine overhaul, the old bearings should be retained for close examination, as they may reveal valuable information about the condition of the engine. The size of the bearing shells is stamped on the back metal and this information should be given to the supplier of the new shells (photo).

2   Bearing failure occurs because of lack of lubrication, the presence of dirt or other foreign particles, overloading the engine, and corrosion. Regardless of the cause of bearing failure, it must be corrected before the engine is reassembled to prevent it from happening again.

3   When examining the bearings, remove them from the engine block, the main bearing caps, the connecting rods and the rod caps and lay them out on a clean surface in the same general position as their location in the engine. This will enable you to match any bearing problems with the corresponding crankshaft journal.

4   Dirt and other foreign particles get into the engine in a variety of ways. It may be left in the engine during assembly, or it may pass through filters or the crankcase ventilation system. It may get into the oil, and from there into the bearings. Metal chips from machining operations and normal engine wear are often present. Abrasives are sometimes left in engine components after reconditioning, especially when parts are not thoroughly cleaned using the proper cleaning methods. Whatever the source, these foreign objects often end up embedded in the soft bearing material and are easily recognized. Large particles will not embed in the bearing and will score or gouge the bearing and journal. The best prevention for this cause of bearing failure is to clean all parts thoroughly and keep everything spotlessly clean during engine assembly. Frequent and regular engine oil and filter changes are also recommended.

5   Lack of lubrication (or lubrication breakdown) has a number of interrelated causes. Excessive heat (which thins the oil), overloading (which squeezes the oil from the bearing face) and oil leakage (from excessive bearing clearances, worn oil pump or high engine speeds) all

contribute to lubrication breakdown. Blocked oil passages, which usually are the result of misaligned oil holes in a bearing shell, will also oil starve a bearing and destroy it. When lack of lubrication is the cause of bearing failure, the bearing material is wiped or extruded from the steel backing of the bearing. Temperatures may increase to the point where the steel backing turns blue from overheating.

6   Driving habits can have a definite effect on bearing life. Full throttle, low speed operation (labouring the engine) puts very high loads on bearings, which tends to squeeze out the oil film. These loads cause the bearings to flex, which produces fine cracks in the bearing face (fatigue failure). Eventually the bearing material will loosen in pieces and tear away from the steel backing. Short trip driving leads to corrosion of bearings because insufficient engine heat is produced to drive off the condensed water and corrosive gases. These products collect in the engine oil, forming acid and sludge. As the oil is carried to the engine bearings, the acid attacks and corrodes the bearing material.

7   Incorrect bearing installation during engine assembly will lead to bearing failure as well. Tight fitting bearings leave insufficient bearing oil clearance and will result in oil starvation. Dirt or foreign particles trapped behind a bearing shell result in high spots on the bearing which lead to failure.

57   Engine overhaul – reassembly sequence

1   Before reassembly begins ensure that all new parts have been obtained and that all necessary tools are available. Read through the entire procedure to familiarise yourself with the work involved, and to ensure that all items necessary for reassembly of the engine are at hand. In addition to all normal tools and materials, a thread-locking compound will be needed. A tube of RTV sealing compound will also be required for the joint faces that are fitted without gaskets. It is recommended that CAF 4/60 THIXO paste, obtainable from Renault dealers is used, as it is

Fig. 2.34 Typical bearing failures (Sec 56)

specially formulated for this purpose.

2   In order to save time and avoid problems, engine reassembly can be carried out in the following order:

(a)   *Crankshaft*
(b)   *Pistons*
(c)   *Oil pump*
(d)   *Sump*
(e)   *Flywheel*
(f)   *Cylinder head*
(g)   *Timing belt/chain and sprockets*
(h)   *Engine external components*

58   Crankshaft – refitting and main bearing running clearance check

1   Before fitting the crankshaft and main bearings on the 1721 cc engine, it is necessary to determine the correct thickness of side seals to be fitted to No 1 main bearing cap. To do this, place the bearing cap in position without any seals and secure it with the two retaining bolts. Locate a twist drill, dowel rod or any other suitable implement which will just fit in the side seal groove. Now measure the implement and this dimension is the side seal groove size. If the dimension is less than or equal to 5 mm, a 5.10 mm thick side seal is needed. If the dimension is more than 5 mm, a 5.3 mm thick side seal is required. Having determined the side seal size and obtained the necessary seals, proceed as follows for the other types of engine as well. Note that silicone is used instead of side seals when the engine is originally assembled at the factory.

Main bearing running clearance check

2   Clean the backs of the bearing shells and the bearing recesses in both the cylinder block and main bearing caps.
3   Press the bearing shells without oil holes into the caps, ensuring that the tag on the shell engages in the notch in the cap.
4   Press the bearing shells with the oil holes/grooves into the recesses in the cylinder block. Note the following points:

(a)   *On the 1390 cc engine No 5 upper main bearing shell is different from the rest in that it has an oil pump pinion lubricating chamfer which must face the timing belt end of the crankshaft (photo).*
(b)   *On the 1397 cc engine the upper shells for Nos 1 and 3 main bearings are identical, as are the shells for Nos 2, 4 and 5 main bearings are identical*
(c)   *On all engines, if the original main bearing shells are being re-used these must be refitted to their original locations in the block and caps*

5   Before the crankshaft can be permanently installed, the main bearing running clearance should be checked; this can be done in either of two ways. One method is to fit the main bearing caps to the cylinder block, with the bearing shells in place. With the cap retaining bolts tightened to the specified torque, measure the internal diameter of each assembled pair of bearing shells using a vernier dial indicator or internal micrometer. If the diameter of each corresponding crankshaft journal is measured and then subtracted from the bearing internal diameter, the result will be the main bearing running clearance. The second (and more accurate) method is to use an American product known as Plastigage. This consists of a fine thread of perfectly round plastic which is compressed between the bearing cap and the journal. When the cap is removed, the plastic is deformed and can be measured with a special card gauge supplied with the kit. The running clearance is determined from this gauge. Plastigage is sometimes difficult to obtain in the UK, but enquiries at one of the larger specialist chains of quality motor factors should produce the name of a stockist in your area. The procedure for using Plastigage is as follows.

6   With the upper main bearing shells in place, carefully lay the crankshaft in position. Do not use any lubricant; the crankshaft journals and bearing shells must be perfectly clean and dry.
7   Cut several pieces of the appropriate size Plastigage (they should be slightly shorter than the width of the main bearings) and place one piece on each crankshaft journal axis (photo).

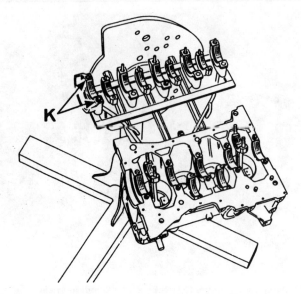

Fig. 2.35 Apply a thin coating of CAF 4/60 THIX0 sealant to the outer corners of No 1 main bearing cap (K) on the 1390 cc (E6J) engine (Sec 58)

8   With the bearing shells in position in the caps, fit the caps to their numbered or previously noted locations. Take care not to disturb the Plastigage.
9   Starting with the centre main bearing and working outward, tighten the main bearing cap bolts progressively to their specified torque setting. Don't rotate the crankshaft at any time during this operation.
10   Remove the bolts and carefully lift off the main bearing caps, keeping them in order. Don't disturb the Plastigage or rotate the crankshaft. If any of the bearing caps are difficult to remove, tap them from side-to-side with a soft-faced mallet.
11   Compare the width of the crushed Plastigage on each journal to the scale printed on the Plastigage envelope to obtain the main bearing running clearance (photo).
12   If the clearance is not as specified, the bearing shells may be the wrong size (or excessively worn if the original shells are being re-used). Before deciding that different size shells are needed, make sure that no dirt or oil was trapped between the bearing shells and the caps or block when the clearance was measured. If the Plastigage was wider at one end than at the other, the journal may be tapered.
13   Carefully scrape away all traces of the Plastigage material from the crankshaft and bearing shells using a fingernail or something similar which is unlikely to score the shells.

Final crankshaft refitting

14   Carefully lift the crankshaft out of the cylinder block once more.
15   Using a little grease, stick the thrust washers to each side of the centre main bearing (1390 cc and 1397 cc engines) or No 2 main bearing (1721 cc engine). Ensure that the oilway grooves on each thrust washer face outwards.
16   Lubricate the lips of the new crankshaft rear oil seal and carefully slip it over the crankshaft rear journal. Do this carefully as the seal lips are very delicate. Ensure that the open side of the seal faces the engine.
17   Liberally lubricate each bearing shell in the cylinder block and lower the crankshaft into position. Check that the rear oil seal is positioned correctly (photo).
18   Lubricate the bearing shells, then fit the bearing caps in their numbered, or previously noted locations. Note the following points:

(a)   *On the 1390 cc engine apply a thin coating of CAF 4/60 THIXO sealant to the outer corners of No 1 main bearing cap as shown in Fig. 2.35 (photo)*
(b)   *On the 1397 cc engine apply Loctite FRENETANCH to the bearing faces of No 1 main bearing cap*
(c)   *On the 1721 cc engine fit the side seals to No 1 main bearing cap with their seal grooves facing outwards. Position the seals so that approximately 1.2 mm (0.008 in) of seal protrudes at the bottom facing side (the side towards the crankcase).*

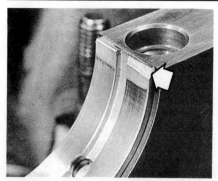

58.4 Oil pump lubricating chamfer (arrowed) on No 5 upper main bearing shell on the 1390 cc engine

58.7 Thread of Plastigage (arrowed) placed on a crankshaft main journal

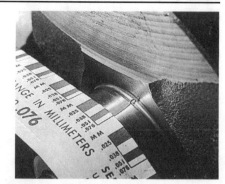

58.11 Measuring the Plastigage width with the special gauge

58.17 Rear oil seal located on the crankshaft

58.18 Applying sealant to No 1 main bearing cap on the 1390 cc engine

Lubricate the seals with a little oil, and apply a little CAF 4/60 THIXO sealant to the bottom corners of the cap prior to fitting it. When the cap is being fitted, use the bolts as a guide by just starting them in their threads, then pressing the cap firmly into position.

19   Fit the main bearing cap bolts and tighten them progressively to the specified torque.
20   Check that the crankshaft is free to turn, then check the endfloat with reference to Section 52.

59 Piston/connecting rod assemblies – refitting and big-end bearing running clearance check

1   Clean the backs of the big-end bearing shells and the recesses in the connecting rods and big-end caps. If new shells are being fitted, ensure that all traces of the protective grease are cleaned off using paraffin. Wipe the shells and connecting rods dry with a lint-free cloth.
2   Press the big-end bearing shells into the connecting rods and caps in their correct positions. Make sure that the location tabs are engaged with the cut-outs in the connecting rods (photo).

1390 cc and 1397 cc engines

Big-end bearing running clearance check

3   Lay the four liners face down in a row on the bench, in their correct order. Turn them as necessary so that the flats on the edges of liners 1 and 2 are towards each other, and the flats on liners 3 and 4 are towards each other also. Refit the O-rings to the base of each liner (photo).
4   Lubricate the pistons and piston rings then lay each piston and connecting rod assembly with its respective liner.
5   Starting with assembly No 1, make sure that the piston ring gaps are still spaced at 120° to each other and clamp the piston rings using a piston ring compressor.

6   Insert the piston and connecting rod assembly into the bottom of the liner ensuring that the arrow on the piston crown faces the flywheel end of the engine (photos). Using a block of wood or hammer handle against the end of the connecting rod, tap the piston into the liner until the top of the piston is approximately 25 mm (1.0 in) away from the top of the liner.
7   Repeat the procedure for the remaining three piston and liner assemblies.
8   Turn the crankshaft so that No 1 crankpin is at the bottom of its travel.
9   With the liner O-ring in position, place No 1 liner, piston and connecting rod assembly into its location in the cylinder block. Ensure that the arrow on the piston crown faces the flywheel end of the engine and the flat on the liner is positioned as described previously.
10   To measure the big-end bearing running clearance, refer to the information contained in Section 58 as the same general procedures apply. If the Plastigage method is being used, ensure that the crankpin journal and the big-end bearing shells are clean and dry then pull the connecting rod down and engage it with the crankpin. Lay the Plastigage strip on the crankpin, check that the marks made on the cap and rod during removal are opposite the camshaft side of the engine then refit the cap and retaining nuts. Tighten the nuts to the specified torque. Do not rotate the crankshaft during this operation. Remove the cap and check the running clearance by measuring the Plastigage as previously described.
11   With the liner/piston assembly installed, retain the liner using a bolt and washer screwed into the cylinder head bolt holes or using liner clamps (photo).
12   Repeat the above procedures for the remaining piston and liner assemblies.

Final connecting rod refitting

13   Having checked the running clearance of all the crankpin journals and taken any corrective action necessary, clean off all traces of Plastigage from the bearing shells and crankpin.
14   Liberally lubricate the crankpin journals and big-end bearing shells

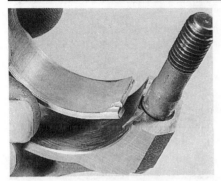

59.2 Engaging the shell tab with the cut-out in the connecting rods

59.3 Fitting the liner base O-rings

59.6A Use a piston ring compressor when inserting the pistons in the liners

59.6B The arrow on the piston crown must be facing the flywheel end of the engine

59.11 Liner clamp to hold the liners in place

59.14 Checking the gap between the liners

and refit the bearing caps once more, ensuring correct positioning as previously described. Tighten the bearing cap bolts to the specified torque and turn the crankshaft each time to make sure that it is free before moving on to the next assembly. On completion check that all the liners are positioned relative to each other so that a 0.1 mm feeler blade can pass freely through the gaps between the liners (photo). If this is not the case, it may be necessary to interchange one or more of the complete piston/liner assemblies to achieve this clearance.

1721 cc engine

Big-end bearing running clearance check

15   Lubricate No 1 piston and piston rings and check that the gaps are spaced at 120° intervals to each other.

16   Fit a ring compressor to No 1 piston then insert the piston and connecting rod into No 1 cylinder. With No 1 crankpin at its lowest point, drive the piston carefully into the cylinder with the wooden handle of a hammer and at the same time guide the connecting rod onto the crankpin. Make sure that the arrow on the piston crown faces the flywheel end of the engine.

17   To measure the big-end bearing running clearance, refer to the information contained in Section 58 as the same general procedures apply. If the Plastigage method is being used, ensure that the crankpin journal and the big-end bearing shells are clean and dry then engage the connecting rod with the crankpin. Lay the Plastigage strip on the crankpin, fit the bearing cap in its previously noted position then tighten the nuts to the specified torque. Do not rotate the crankshaft during this operation. Remove the cap and check the running clearance by measuring the Plastigage as previously described.

18   Repeat the above procedures on the remaining piston/connecting rod assemblies.

Final connecting rod refitting

19   Having checked the running clearance of all the crankpin journals and taken any corrective action necessary, clean off all traces of Plastigage from the bearing shells and crankpin.

20   Liberally lubricate the crankpin journals and big-end bearing shells and refit the bearing caps once more, ensuring correct positioning as

previously described. Tighten the bearing cap bolts to the specified torque and turn the crankshaft each time to make sure that it is free before moving on to the next assembly.

60   Engine – initial start-up after overhaul

1   With the engine refitted in the vehicle, double-check the engine oil and coolant levels.

2   With the spark plugs removed and the ignition system disabled by connecting the coil HT lead to ground with a jumper lead, crank the engine over on the starter until the oil pressure light goes out.

3   Refit the spark plugs and connect all the HT leads.

4   Start the engine, noting that this may take a little longer than usual due to the fuel pump and carburettor being empty.

5   While the engine is idling, check for fuel, water and oil leaks. Do not be alarmed if there are some odd smells and smoke from parts getting hot and burning off oil deposits.

6   Keep the engine idling until hot water is felt circulating through the top hose, then switch it off.

7   After a few minutes, recheck the oil and water levels and top up as necessary.

8   There is no requirement to re-tighten the cylinder head bolts on 1390 cc and 1721 cc engines, however on the 1397 cc engine the following procedure must be adopted.
   (a)   *Run the engine for 20 minutes, then switch it off and allow to cool for 2½ hours*
   (b)   *Remove the rocker cover and re-torque the cylinder head bolts in the sequence shown in Fig. 2.5. Slacken each bolt in turn half a turn then retighten it to the specified torque before moving on to the next bolt. After retightening, adjust the valve clearances again, as described in Part B of this Chapter*

9   If new pistons, rings or crankshaft bearings have been fitted, the engine must be run-in for the first 500 miles (800 km). Do not operate the engine at full throttle or allow it to labour in any gear during this period. It is recommended that the oil and filter be changed at the end of this period.

Chapter 3 Cooling, heating and air conditioning systems

Contents

Specifications

System type .... Pressurised, with front mounted radiator and electric cooling fan

Thermostat
Type .... Wax
Start-to-open temperature:
    1390 cc (E6J) and 1397 cc (C1J) .... 86°C
    1721 cc (F2N) .... 89°C
Fully open temperature:
    1390 cc (E6J) and 1397 cc (C1J) .... 98°C
    1721 cc (F2N) .... 101°C
Stroke .... 7.5 mm

Expansion tank cap
Pressure .... 1.2 bar

1 General information

The cooling system is of the pressurised type consisting of a belt-driven pump, aluminium crossflow radiator, expansion tank, electric cooling fan and a thermostat. The system functions as follows. Cold coolant in the bottom of the radiator passes through the bottom hose to the water pump where it is pumped around the cylinder block and head passages. After cooling the cylinder bores, combustion surfaces and valve seats, the coolant reaches the underside of the thermostat, which is initially closed. The coolant passes through the heater and inlet manifold and is returned to the water pump.

When the engine is cold the coolant circulates only through the cylinder block, cylinder head, heater and inlet manifold. When the coolant reaches a predetermined temperature, the thermostat opens and the coolant passes through the top hose to the radiator. As the coolant circulates through the radiator it is cooled by the inrush of air when the car is in forward motion. Airflow is supplemented by the action of the electric cooling fan when necessary. Upon reaching the bottom of the radiator, the coolant is now cooled and the cycle is repeated.

When the engine is at normal operating temperature the coolant expands and some of it is displaced into the expansion tank. This coolant collects in the tank and is returned to the radiator when the system cools.

The electric cooling fan, mounted behind the radiator, is controlled by a thermostatic switch located in the side of the radiator. At a predetermined coolant temperature the switch contacts close, thus actuating the fan.

When an air conditioning system is fitted, it is necessary to observe special precautions whenever dealing with any part of the system, its associated components and any items which necessitate disconnection of the system. If for any reason the system must be disconnected, entrust this task to your Renault dealer or a refrigeration engineer. The layout of the air conditioning system is shown in Fig. 3.9. **Warning:** *The refrigeration circuit contains a liquid refrigerant (Freon) and it is therefore dangerous to disconnect any part of the system without specialised knowledge and equipment.*

Fig. 3.1 Cooling system layout for the 1390 cc (E6J) engine (Sec 1)

1 *Engine*
2 *Radiator*
3 *Expansion tank*
4 *Heater*
5 *Inlet manifold*
14 *3 mm jet*
A *Bleed screw*
T *Thermostat*
X *Cooling fan thermostatic switch*

The refrigerant must not be allowed to come in contact with a naked flame otherwise a poisonous gas will be created. Do not allow the fluid to come in contact with the skin or eyes.

2 Electric cooling fan assembly – removal and refitting

Removal

1 Remove the radiator as described in Section 5.
2 Remove the shroud/fan bracket from the radiator by unscrewing the bolts or where necessary by drilling the heads off the rivets (photo).
3 Unscrew the nut or extract the retaining clip and slide the fan off the motor shaft.
4 The motor can now be removed by drilling out the retaining rivets.

Refitting

5 Refitting is a reversal of removal, using new rivets obtainable from Renault parts stockists.

2.2 Electric cooling fan mounting bolts on the radiator (arrowed)

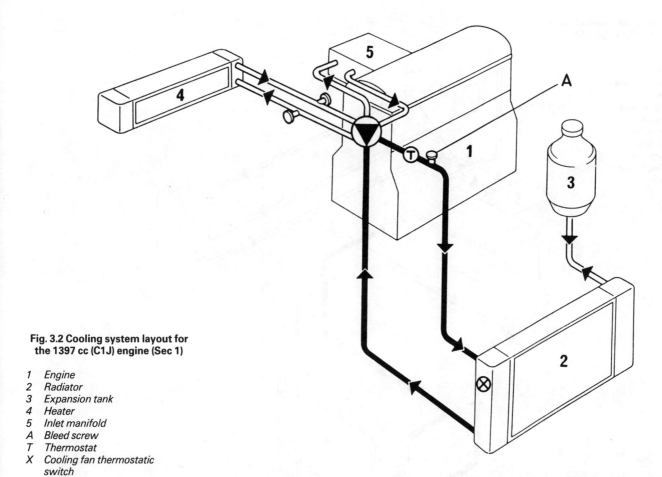

Fig. 3.2 Cooling system layout for the 1397 cc (C1J) engine (Sec 1)

1 Engine
2 Radiator
3 Expansion tank
4 Heater
5 Inlet manifold
A Bleed screw
T Thermostat
X Cooling fan thermostatic
   switch

3 Electric cooling fan thermostatic switch – testing, removal and refitting

Testing

1   The thermostatic switch is located on the left-hand side of the

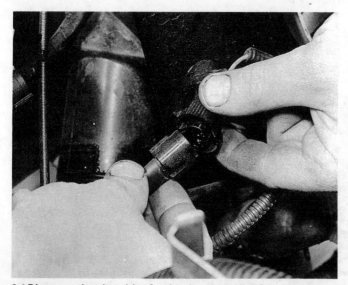

3.4 Disconnecting the wiring for the electric cooling fan thermostatic switch

radiator on the 1390 cc (E6J) engine but on the right-hand side of the radiator on 1397 cc (C1J) and 1721 cc (F2N) engines. If it develops a fault it is most likely to fail open-circuit. This will result in the fan motor remaining stationary even though the coolant temperature exceeds the switch-on point. The coolant may even reach boiling point.
2   To test for a faulty thermostatic switch, disconnect the two switch wires and join them together with a suitable length of wire. If the fan now operates with the ignition switched on, the thermostatic switch is proved faulty and must be renewed. If the fan is still inoperative this proves that there is a fault in the fan motor or associated wiring.

Removal

3   To remove the switch, disconnect the battery negative terminal and drain the cooling system, as described in Chapter 1.
4   Disconnect the two wires and then unscrew the switch from the radiator (photo). Remove the sealing washer.

Refitting

5   Refitting is a reversal of removal, but fit a new sealing washer and fully tighten the switch. Refill the cooling system as described in Chapter 1.

4 Temperature gauge sender unit – removal and refitting

Removal

1   Unscrew the expansion tank filler cap. If the engine is hot, place a cloth over the cap and unscrew it slowly allowing all the pressure to escape before removing the cap completely.

Fig. 3.3 Cooling system for the 1721 cc (F2N) engine (Sec 1)

1   Engine
2   Radiator
3   Expansion tank
4   Heater
5   Inlet manifold
14 3 mm jet
15 8 mm jet
A   Bleed screw
T   Thermostat
X   Cooling fan thermostatic switch

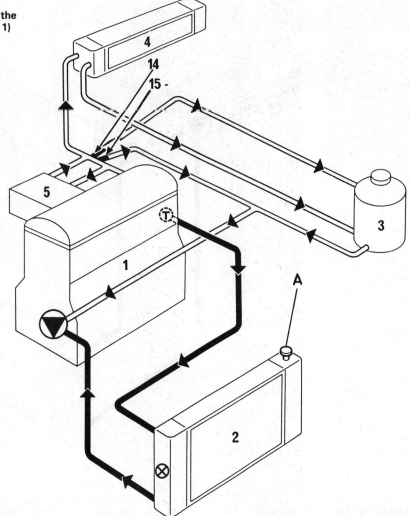

2   Place a suitable container beneath the radiator bottom hose outlet. Disconnect the bottom hose and drain approximately 1 litre (1.76 pints) of the coolant. Reconnect the hose and tighten the clip.
3   Disconnect the wire from the sender unit located on top of the water pump on the 1397 cc (C1J) engine, and on the left-hand end of the cylinder head on the 1390 cc (E6J) and 1721 cc (F2N) engines.
4   Unscrew the sender unit from its location.

Refitting

5   Refitting is a reversal of removal, but fully tighten the unit. Refill the cooling system with reference to Chapter 1.

5   Radiator – removal, inspection, cleaning and refitting

Removal

1   Disconnect the battery leads.
2   Drain the cooling system as described in Chapter 1.
3   On the 1721 cc (F2N) engine, disconnect the air duct leading from the radiator to the carburettor.
4   Loosen the clip and disconnect the top hose from the radiator (photo).

5.4 Disconnecting the top hose from the radiator

5.6 Disconnecting the wiring for the electric cooling fan

5.8A Unscrew the mounting bolts ...

5.8B ... and remove the radiator mounting brackets

5.9A Lift the radiator from the lower locating rubber bushes ...

5.9B ... and withdraw it from the engine compartment

5   Disconnect the wiring from the thermostatic switch, located on the left-hand side of the radiator on 1390 (E6J) engine, or the right-hand side of the radiator on 1397 cc (C1J) and 1721 cc (F2N) models.
6   Disconnect the wiring from the cooling fan connector, and release it from the plastic clip (photo).
7   On automatic transmission models, place a container beneath the radiator to catch any spilled fluid, then unscrew the fluid cooling pipe unions. Plug the ends of the pipes.
8   Unscrew the two mounting bolts from the engine compartment cross panel. Move the radiator to the rear and remove the mounting brackets (photos).
9   Lift the radiator up from the lower locating rubber bushes, then withdraw it from the engine compartment (photos).

Inspection and cleaning

10   Radiator repair is best left to a specialist, but minor leaks may be sealed using a radiator sealant such as Holts Radweld. Clear the radiator matrix of flies and small leaves with a soft brush, or by hosing.
11   If the radiator is to be left out of the car for more than 48 hours, special precautions must be taken to prevent the brazing flux used during manufacture from reacting with the chloride elements remaining from the coolant. This reaction could cause the aluminium core to oxidize causing leakage. To prevent this, either flush the radiator thoroughly with clean water, dry with compressed air and seal all outlets, or refill the radiator with coolant and temporarily plug all outlets.

Refitting

12   Refitting is a reversal of removal, but check the mounting bushes and if necessary renew them. Refill the cooling system with reference to Chapter 1. On automatic transmission models check and if necessary top up the automatic transmission fluid level.

6   Thermostat – removal, testing and refitting

Removal

1   On the 1390 cc (E6J) engine the thermostat is located in the cylinder head outlet elbow on the left-hand side of the engine (photo).
2   On the 1397 cc (C1J) engine the thermostat is located in the end of

6.1 Cylinder head outlet elbow containing the thermostat on the 1390 cc (E6J) engine (arrowed)

the radiator top hose at the water pump and is retained by a hose clip.
3   On the 1721 cc (F2N) engine the thermostat is located in a housing bolted to the left-hand side of the cylinder head beneath the distributor.
4   First partially drain the cooling system so that the coolant level is below the thermostat location.
5   Loosen the clip and disconnect the hose.
6   On the 1397 cc (E6J) engine withdraw the thermostat from inside the hose. On other engines unbolt the cover and remove the thermostat, then remove the sealing ring (photos).

Testing

7   To test whether the unit is serviceable, suspend it on a string in a saucepan of cold water, together with a thermometer. Heat the water and note the temperature at which the thermostat begins to open.

6.6A Removing the thermostat on the 1397 cc (C1J) engine

6.6B Removing the thermostat on the 1390 cc (E6J) engine

6.6C Removing the thermostat on the 1721 cc (F2N) engine

7.3A Unscrew the mounting bolts ...

7.3B ... and remove the water pump on the 1390 cc (E6J) engine

7.9 Unscrew the mounting bolts by inserting a socket through the holes in the pulley on the 1397 cc (C1J) engine

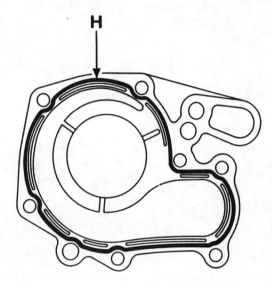

Fig. 3.4 Apply sealant (H) as shown on the 1390 cc (E6J) engine (Sec 7)

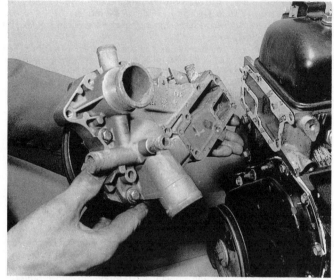

7.10 Removing the water pump on the 1397 cc (C1J) engine

Continue heating the water until the thermostat is fully open and then remove it from the water.

8   The temperature at which the thermostat should start to open is stamped on the unit. If the thermostat does not start to open at the specified temperature, or does not fully open in boiling water or fully close when removed from the water, then it must be discarded and a new one fitted.

Refitting

9   Refitting is a reversal of removal, but where applicable renew the sealing ring. On the 1397 cc engine make sure that the thermostat bleed hole is in the slot on the end of the water pump outlet. Refill the cooling system with reference to Chapter 1.

7 Water pump – removal and refitting

Removal

1390 cc (E6J) engine

1   Disconnect the battery leads, then drain the cooling system with reference to Chapter 1.

2   Remove the timing belt with reference to Chapter 2.

3   Unbolt the water pump from the front of the cylinder block (photos).

1397 cc (C1J) engine

4   Disconnect the battery leads and then refer to Chapter 1 and drain the cooling system.

5   Refer to Section 8 and remove the drivebelt.

6   Unscrew the bolt securing the alternator adjusting arm to the pump body, remove the bolt and swing the arm clear.

7   Slacken the hose clips and disconnect the hoses from the pump.

8   Disconnect the lead from the coolant temperature switch on top of the pump body.

9   Unscrew and remove the bolts securing the water pump to the cylinder head. Access to the bolt behind the pulley can be gained by inserting a socket and extension bar through the holes in the pulley (photo).

10   With all the bolts removed, withdraw the pump from the cylinder head (photo). If it is stuck, strike it sharply with a plastic or hide mallet.

1721 cc (F2N) engine

11   Disconnect the battery leads, then refer to Chapter 1 and drain the cooling system.

12   Remove the alternator drivebelt with reference to Section 8.

13   Unscrew the three bolts and remove the pump pulley (photo).

14   Unscrew the bolts securing the water pump to the cylinder block and withdraw the pump from its location (photos). If it is stuck, strike it sharply with a plastic or hide mallet. Remove the gasket.

Refitting

1390 cc (E6J) engine

15   Clean the mating faces of the water pump and cylinder block, then apply a bead of sealant 0.6 to 1.0 mm wide around the inner perimeter of the water pump sealing face on the water pump.

16   Locate the water pump on the cylinder block then insert the bolts and tighten them evenly.

7.13 Water pump and pulley on the 1721 cc (F2N) engine

7.14A Unscrew the mounting bolts (arrowed) ...

7.14B ... and remove the water pump on the 1721 cc (F2N) engine

17   Refit the timing belt with reference to Chapter 2.
18   Refill the cooling system and re-connect the battery leads.

1397 cc (C1J) engine

19   Refitting is a reversal of removal, but use new gaskets. Adjust the drivebelt tension and refill the cooling system as described in Chapter 1.

1721 cc (F2N) engine

20   Clean the mating faces of the water pump and cylinder block.
21   Locate the water pump on the cylinder block together with a new gasket and insert the bolts. Tighten the bolts.
22   Refit the pump pulley and tighten the bolts.
23   Refit and tension the alternator drivebelt with reference to Section 8.
24   Refill the cooling system (Chapter 1) then re-connect the battery leads.

8   Water pump/alternator drivebelt – renewal and adjustment

1   To remove the drivebelt, slacken the alternator pivot bolt and also the adjustment bolt, if applicable.
2   Move the alternator towards the engine and slip the drivebelt off the pulleys. On the 1721 cc (F2N) engine turn the nut on the adjustment rod as required.

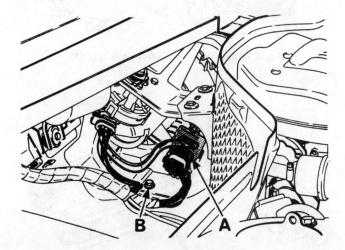

Fig. 3.5 Heater blower motor wiring (A) and mounting bolts (B) (Sec 9)

3   Fit the new drivebelt over the pulleys then adjust its tension with reference to Chapter 1.

9   Heater unit – removal and refitting

Removal

1   Disconnect the battery leads with reference to Chapter 12.
2   Remove the complete facia panel with reference to Chapter 11.
3   Remove the upper seal from the water box to the rear of the engine compartment. Also remove the external air inlet grilles.
4   Disconnect the wiring from the heater blower motor.
5   Remove the heater blower motor with reference to Section 10.
6   Drain the cooling system with reference to Chapter 1.
7   Loosen the two clips and disconnect the hoses from the heater radiator matrix.
8   Unbolt the heater unit and remove it from inside the car.

Refitting

9   Check that the seals are in good condition, then locate the unit on the bulkhead.
10   Position the blower motor over the heater and insert the bolts finger-tight. Also insert the heater mounting bolts.
11   Check and if necessary adjust the heater control cables.
12   Connect the hoses to the heater unit and tighten the clips.
13   Tighten the heater and blower motor mounting bolts, then reconnect the wiring to the blower motor.
14   Refit the upper seal to the water box and also refit the external air inlet grilles.
15   Refit the facia panel with reference to Chapter 11.
16   Refill the cooling system with reference to Chapter 1.
17   Reconnect the battery leads with reference to Chapter 12.

10   Heater blower unit – removal and refitting

Removal

1   Remove the water box upper seal and the external air inlet grille.
2   Disconnect the wiring from the blower unit (photo).
3   Unscrew the two mounting bolts, then remove the unit from the left-hand side of the bulkhead (photos). It is necessary to turn the unit on its side to do this.
4   Release the clips, then separate the two half-casings of the unit and remove the motor assembly (photo). If the unit has not previously been separated from new, the two casings will be hot-crimped together and it will be necessary to split them apart with a knife.

Refitting

5   Locate the motor assembly in the two half-casings making sure that the wiring connector can be fitted without stress.

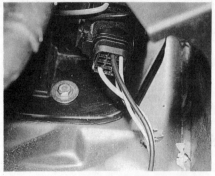

10.2 Heater blower unit wiring connector

10.3A Removing the heater blower unit

10.3B View of the heater air inlet with the blower unit removed

10.4 Prise off the clips to separate the two half-casings and gain access to the heater motor

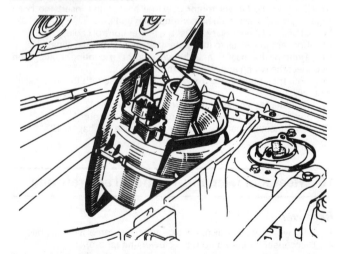

Fig. 3.6 Removing the heater blower motor (Sec 10)

6   Fit the casings together and secure with clips which are available in a kit from Renault dealers. The kit also contains a new seal for fitting to the unit. Do not refit the original seal, since if it does not seal correctly, there is a risk of excessive entry of water into the passenger compartment.
7   Refit the unit and tighten the mounting bolts.
8   Reconnect the wiring to the blower unit.
9   Refit the external air inlet grille and the water box upper seal.

11   Heater matrix – removal and refitting

Removal
1   Remove the heater unit with reference to Section 9.
2   Prise out the retaining clips, then pull out the matrix. Take care not to damage the air control flaps.

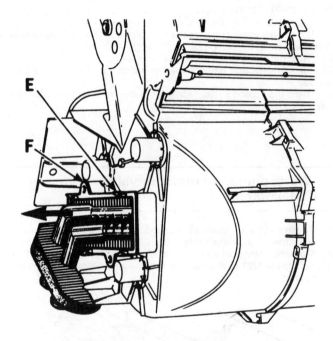

Fig. 3.7 Removing the heater matrix (Sec 11)

E   Retaining clips   *F   Mounting screw*

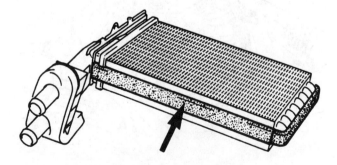

Fig. 3.8 Heater matrix sealing foam (Sec 11)

Refitting

3   Check that the sealing foam is in good condition, then insert the matrix and retain with the clips. If the clips have been broken during removal, fit two screws instead.
4   Refit the heater unit with reference to Section 9.

12   Heater resistor unit – removal and refitting

Removal

1   Remove the water box upper seal and external air inlet grille.
2   Unplug the wiring connector, then unscrew the two mounting screws.
3   Pull the clips apart and remove the resistor unit.

Refitting

4   If the resistor unit is being removed because it has been damaged, check that the heater fan motor turns freely before refitting it.
5   Refitting is a reversal of removal.

13   Heater control panel – removal and refitting

Removal

1   Unscrew the two screws securing the central lower cover beneath the heater control panel.
2   Unscrew the two mounting screws, then remove the control panel by releasing it at the bottom and removing the four clips (photo).
3   Disconnect the cables by releasing the clips.

Refitting

4   Refitting is a reversal of removal.

14   Heater control cables – removal and refitting

Removal

1   Remove the control panel as described in the previous Section.
2   Remove the air deflector (two screws).
3   Remove the cable to be renewed by releasing the clip and turning it through a quarter turn in order to release the flap control lever.

Refitting

4   Refit the cable so that it is flush with the sheath stop.
5   Turn the control knobs to the 'ventilation' and 'cold' positions.
6   Refit the control panel.
7   Place the control flaps in the 'ventilation' and 'cold' positions, then align the marks on the flap control sections.
8   Refit the mixer flap return spring (air mixer control), then the air deflector and lower cover. Note that the control cables are of different lengths – the longer one controls the mixer flap.

15   Air conditioning system components – removal and refitting

Warning: *The system should be professionally discharged before carrying out any of the following work. Cap or plug the pipe lines as soon as they are disconnected to prevent the entry of moisture. Refer to the precautions given in Section 1 before proceeding*

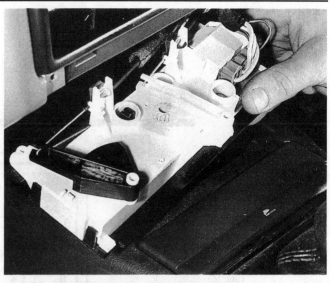

13.2 Removing the heater control panel

Blower unit and fan motor

1   Disconnect the battery leads.
2   Unbolt and remove the strengthening bar from between the front suspension turrets.
3   Remove the ignition module from the bulkhead.
4   Remove the water box bulkhead.
5   Disconnect the lines from the relief valve.
6   Unscrew the screws and separate the air conditioner from the ventilation body.
7   Remove the casing and then unscrew the mounting screw.
8   Remove the two mounting bolts from the ventilation unit under the facia panel on the left-hand side.
9   Pull the rubber cover from the blower unit, then unsolder the wiring.
10   Prise off the clips and separate the two half-casings.
11   Using a screwdriver, push back the rubber beads holding the motor in the casing.
12   Pull the fan motor directly from the casings.
13   Refitting is a reversal of removal, but make sure that the foam seals are in good condition and renew them if necessary. Have the system refilled by a refrigeration specialist.

Evaporator

14   Remove the blower unit as described in Section 10.
15   Prise the clips from the half-casings and also remove the three screws.
16   Remove the relief valve and take out the evaporator.
17   Refitting is a reversal of removal, but make sure that the foam seals are in good condition and renew them if necessary. Have the system refilled by a refrigeration specialist.

Compressor

18   Disconnect the battery leads and remove the alternator with reference to Chapter 12.
19   Remove the screw and disconnect the lines from the compressor.
20   Unbolt and remove the compressor from the engine.
21   Refitting is a reversal of removal. If a new compressor is being fitted, it will already have the correct amount of oil in it. However, if the old unit is being refitted check the oil level as follows. Withdraw the dipstick and wipe it dry, then re-insert it and withdraw it again. Check that the level is between 14 and 16 mm on the dipstick. When reconnecting the lines, check that the seals are in good condition and renew them if necessary. Tension the drivebelt as described in Chapter 1. Have the system refilled by a refrigeration specialist.

Condenser

22   Drain the cooling system with reference to Chapter 3.
23   Disconnect the lines from the condenser while holding the unions with a further spanner.

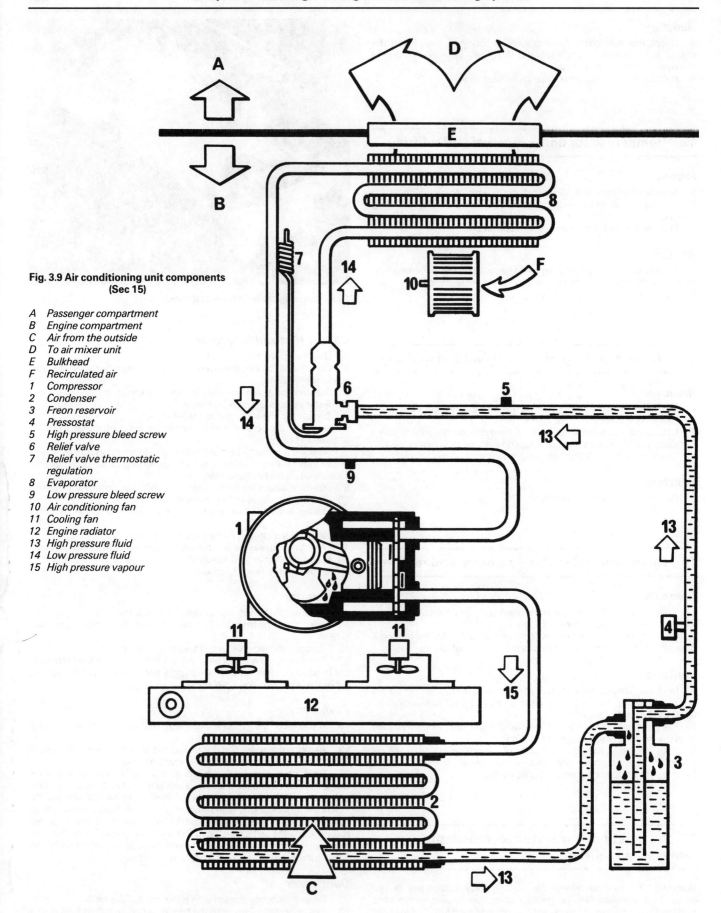

**Fig. 3.9 Air conditioning unit components
(Sec 15)**

A   Passenger compartment
B   Engine compartment
C   Air from the outside
D   To air mixer unit
E   Bulkhead
F   Recirculated air
1   Compressor
2   Condenser
3   Freon reservoir
4   Pressostat
5   High pressure bleed screw
6   Relief valve
7   Relief valve thermostatic
    regulation
8   Evaporator
9   Low pressure bleed screw
10 Air conditioning fan
11 Cooling fan
12 Engine radiator
13 High pressure fluid
14 Low pressure fluid
15 High pressure vapour

24   Disconnect the wiring from the cooling fan motor.
25   Remove the radiator upper mountings.
26   Lift the radiator and condenser assembly upwards from the engine compartment.
27   Remove the screws and separate the condenser from the radiator.
28   Refitting is a reversal of removal, but when reconnecting the lines to the condenser, oil them and hold the unions with a spanner to prevent any damage to the condenser.

Fan control module

29   Remove the water box bulkhead then remove the two screws and remove the module.
30   Refitting is a reversal of removal.

Temperature sensor

31   Remove the water box bulkhead, then bend up the tab and disconnect the wiring from the sensor.
32   Turn the sensor 90° clockwise and remove it from the casing.
33   Refitting is a reversal of removal.

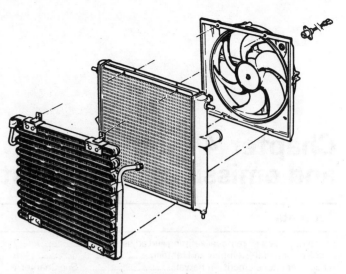

Fig. 3.10 Air conditioning condenser, radiator and electric cooling fan (Sec 15)

Chapter 4 Fuel, exhaust and emission control systems

Contents

Specifications

Fuel grade
Fuel octane requirement .... 95 RON unleaded or 97 RON leaded

Fuel pump
Type .... Mechanical, operated by eccentric on camshaft
Delivery pressure (static, with no fuel movement):
   Minimum .... 0.170 bar
   Maximum .... 0.325 bar

Carburettor (general)
Type .... Single or twin choke downdraught
Application/Identification:
   1390 cc (E6J) engine .... Weber 32 TLDR
   1397 cc (C1J) engine .... Zenith 32 IF2
   1721 cc (F2N) engine .... Solex 32 x 34 Z13
Choke type .... Manual

Weber 32 TLDR carburettor data
Idle speed .... 750 ± 50 rpm
Idle mixture CO content.. 1.5 ± 0.5 %
Needle valve .... 1.75 mm
Float level .... 31 mm
Accelerator pump injector 55
Positive throttle opening .... 0.65 mm (18°)
Pneumatic initial opening at 290 mbars .... 3.0 ± 0.5 mm
Mechanical initial opening .... 4.5 ± 0.5 mm

	Primary	Secondary
Choke tube	23	24
Main jet	122	160
Air correction jet	175	210
Idling jet	50	40
Auxiliary venturi	3.5R	3.5R
Emulsion tube	F3	F56
Enrichener	60	40

Zenith 32 IF2 carburettor data

Idle speed	700 ± 50 rpm
Idle mixture CO content	1.5 ± 0.5 %
Choke tube	24
Main jet	130
Idling jet	53
Air correction jet	90 x 160
Pneumatic enrichener	74
Accelerator pump travel	28.3 mm
Accelerator pump injector	50
Accelerator pump tube height	60 mm
Needle valve	1.25 mm
Float level	13.65 ± 0.1 mm
Auxiliary jet	110
Auxiliary tube height	0.6 mm
Degassing valve dimension	2.0 mm minimum
Positive throttle opening	0.9 mm
Pneumatic opening (upper choke opening after starting)	2.6 mm

Solex 32 x 34 Z13 carburettor data

Idle speed	800 ± 50 rpm
Idle mixture CO content	1.5 ± 0.5 %
Fast idling speed:	
Models with power steering:	
Front wheels straight-ahead	975 ± 50 rpm
Front wheels on full lock	700 to 730 rpm
Models with air conditioning or PAS and A/C	950 rpm
Needle valve	1.8 mm
Float level	33.5 ± 0.5 mm
Positive throttle opening	0.75 mm (22° 30')
Mechanical initial opening	3.5
Degassing valve dimension	0.3 mm

	Primary	Secondary
Choke tube	24	27
Main jet	115	137.5
Air correction jet	165	190
Idling jet	43	50
Econostat	–	120
Enrichener	50	–
Accelerator pump injector	40	35
Fast idling throttle valve setting:		
Power steering and air conditioning	13°	–
Power steering or air conditioning	11° 15'	–

1 General information and precautions

The fuel system consists of a fuel tank mounted under the rear of the car, a mechanical fuel pump and a single or twin choke downdraught carburettor. The mechanical fuel pump is operated by an eccentric on the camshaft and is mounted on the forward side of the cylinder block on the 1397 cc (C1J) engine, or rear side of the cylinder head on the 1390 cc (E6J) and 1721 cc (F2N) engines. A degassing chamber is located in the fuel line on the 1721 cc (F2N) engine (photo). The air cleaner contains a disposable paper filter element and incorporates a flap valve air temperature control system. This system allows cold air from the outside of the car and warm air from the exhaust manifold to enter the air cleaner in the correct proportions according to ambient air temperatures. The flap is controlled automatically by a temperature sensitive wax capsule.

Carburettors may be of Zenith, Solex or Weber manufacture according to model. The Zenith carburettor incorporates a water-heated lower body to improve fuel atomization, particularly when the engine is cold. On engines fitted with the Solex and Weber carburettors the inlet manifold is heated by the cooling system coolant. Mixture enrichment for cold starting is by a manually-operated choke control on all models.

The exhaust system is in three sections; the front downpipe (attached to the exhaust manifold by a spring-tensioned flange), intermediate section and resonator (attached to the downpipe by a clamped flange), and the tailpipe and silencer (attached to the intermediate section by a clamped flange). The system is suspended throughout its entire length by rubber mountings.

1.1 Degassing chamber (arrowed) on the 1721 cc (F2N) engine

2.2 Removing the air cleaner housing securing clip – 1390 cc (E6J) engine

2.3 Air inlet hose removal – 1390 cc (E6J) engine

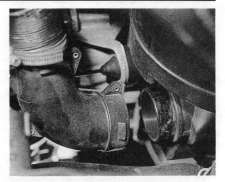

2.4 Hot air hose and elbow removal from the air cleaner housing – 1390 cc (E6J) engine

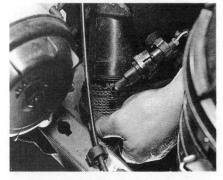

2.5 Disconnecting the fresh air hose from the front inlet elbow – 1390 cc (E6J) engine

2.6 Removing the air cleaner housing – 1390 cc (E6J) engine

2.10A Carburettor cooling duct attachment to the radiator support ...

2.10B ... and engine compartment strengthening bar – 1721 cc (F2N) engine

2.11 Disconnecting the hot air hose from the air cleaner housing and exhaust manifold shroud – 1721 cc (F2N) engine

2.13 Disconnecting the crankcase ventilation hose – 1721 cc (F2N) engine

Warning: *Many of the procedures in this Chapter require the removal of fuel lines and connections which may result in some fuel spillage. Before carrying out any operation on the fuel system refer to the precautions given in Safety first! at the beginning of this Manual and follow them implicitly. Petrol is a highly dangerous and volatile liquid and the precautions necessary when handling it cannot be overstressed.*

2 Air cleaner housing assembly – removal and refitting

Removal

1   Remove the air cleaner filter element as described in Chapter 1.

1390 cc (E6J) engine

2   Using a screwdriver loosen the clip securing the air cleaner body to the support bracket (photo). Remove the clip.
3   Loosen the clip and remove the air inlet hose from the duct on the carburettor (photo).
4   Disconnect the hot air hose and elbow from the side of the air cleaner body (photo).
5   Disconnect the fresh air hose from the inlet elbow on the front left-hand corner of the engine compartment, below the rear of the headlamp (photo).
6   Withdraw the air cleaner body from the support bracket (photo).

1397 cc (C1J) engine

7   Disconnect the air inlet hose and hot air hose from the air cleaner inlet.
8   Unscrew and remove the mounting bolts, noting the arrangement of the rubber spacers, washers and sleeves.
9   Withdraw the air cleaner body from the engine.

2.14A Air cleaner housing mounting –
1721 cc (F2N) engine

2.14B Removing the air cleaner housing –
1721 cc (F2N) engine

2.15 Air cleaner housing rubber mounting
(arrowed) – 1721 cc (F2N) engine

1721 cc (F2N) engine

10   For better access, unbolt the carburettor cooling duct from the radiator support and from the engine compartment strengthening bar (photos).

11   Loosen the clips and disconnect the hot air hose from the air cleaner body and from the shroud on the exhaust manifold (photo).

12   Disconnect the fresh air hose from the bottom of the air cleaner and from the front left-hand corner of the engine compartment.

13   Disconnect the crankcase ventilation hose from the air cleaner and from the T-piece near the bulkhead (photo).

14   Unscrew the mounting nuts and withdraw the air cleaner body from the engine compartment (photos).

15   Check the condition of the rubber mountings where applicable and renew them as necessary (photo). Also check the hoses and hose clips for condition.

Refitting

16   Refitting is a reversal of removal.

3   Fuel pump – testing, removal and refitting

Note: *Refer to the warning note in Section 1 before proceeding*

Testing

1   To test the fuel pump on the engine, temporarily disconnect the outlet pipe which leads to the carburettor, and hold a wad of rag over the pump outlet while an assistant spins the engine on the starter. *Keep the*

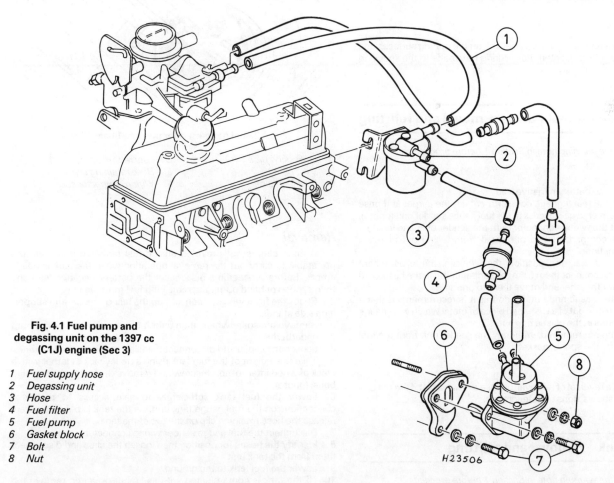

Fig. 4.1 Fuel pump and degassing unit on the 1397 cc (C1J) engine (Sec 3)

1   *Fuel supply hose*
2   *Degassing unit*
3   *Hose*
4   *Fuel filter*
5   *Fuel pump*
6   *Gasket block*
7   *Bolt*
8   *Nut*

H23506

hands away from the electric cooling fan. Regular spurts of fuel should be ejected as the engine turns.

2   The pump can also be tested by removing it. With the pump outlet pipe disconnected but the inlet pipe still connected, hold the wad of rag by the outlet. Operate the pump lever by hand; if the pump is in a satisfactory condition a strong jet of fuel should be ejected. On the 1390 cc (E6J) and 1397 cc (C1J) engines the pump lever should be moved up and down, whereas on the 1721 cc (F2N) engine the plunger should be pushed in and out.

3   If a suitable pressure gauge is available, a more accurate test may be carried out. Before connecting the gauge to the fuel system, run the engine at idling speed for several minutes in order to completely fill the carburettor float chamber. With the engine switched off, disconnect the fuel supply pipe at the carburettor end and then connect the pressure gauge to it. The gauge connection pipe should be transparent and short. Using a hose clamp, pinch the return pipe leading to the fuel tank. Hold the gauge as high as possible with the pipe vertical, then start the engine and allow it to idle. Lower the gauge until the level of fuel in the transparent pipe is level with the fuel pump diaphragm, then check that the pump static pressure is as given in the Specifications (note that the engine must be idling but there is no fuel movement as the gauge is connected to the outlet). Check the return pipe for obstruction by removing the clamp from the return hose and checking that the pressure then drops to between 0.01 and 0.02 bar – if the pressure is higher than this, blow through the return hose to clear the obstruction.

Removal

4   Disconnect the battery negative lead.
5   Identify the fuel pump inlet and outlet hoses for position then disconnect and plug them.
6   Unscrew the nuts/bolts securing the pump to the cylinder block (1397 cc/C1J) or cylinder head (1390 cc/E6J and 1721 cc/F2N) and remove the washers.
7   Withdraw the fuel pump from the engine and remove the gasket block. On the 1721 cc (F2N) engine note the number and location of the gaskets.

Refitting

8   Refitting is a reversal of removal, but clean the mating surfaces and fit a new gasket block. Tighten the securing nuts/bolts to the specified torque.

4   Fuel gauge sender unit – removal and refitting

Note: *Refer to the warning note in Section 1 before proceeding*

Removal

1   Disconnect the battery negative lead.
2   Working in the rear luggage compartment, lift the carpet and prise out the rubber cover to gain access to the fuel gauge sender unit (photo).
3   Disconnect the wiring connector from the sender unit, and locate it in the luggage compartment to prevent it from falling out of reach beneath the rear floor.
4   Identify the hoses for position then loosen the clips where applicable and disconnect them from the sender unit. Tie the hoses and wiring connector together and move them to one side.
5   Unscrew the plastic ring nut. To do this it is recommended that a removal tool is made out of a U-shaped piece of metal which will engage with the serrations in the plastic ring nut.
6   With the ring nut removed, withdraw the sender unit from the fuel tank, followed by the special gasket.

Refitting

7   Refitting is a reversal of removal, but use a new gasket if the old one is damaged or shows signs of deterioration.

5   Fuel tank – removal and refitting

Note: *Refer to the warning note in Section 1 before proceeding*

4.2 Fuel gauge sender unit and connections

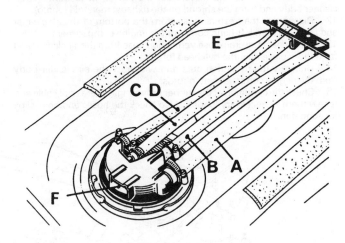

Fig. 4.2 Fuel gauge sender unit and hoses (Sec 4)

A Degassing pipe	D Fuel return pipe
B Vent pipe	E Hose retaining clip
C Fuel feed pipe	F Wiring connector socket

Removal

1   A drain plug is not provided on the fuel tank and it is therefore preferable to carry out the removal operation when the tank is nearly empty. Before proceeding, disconnect the battery negative lead and then syphon or hand pump the remaining fuel from the tank.
2   Chock the front wheels, then jack up the rear of the car and support it on axle stands.
3   Remove the spare wheel, then unbolt the spare wheel carrier from the underbody.
4   Loosen the clip(s) and disconnect the filler hose from the fuel tank.
5   Take the weight of the fuel tank using a trolley jack together with a block of wood interposed. Unscrew and remove the fuel tank mounting bolts. (photo).
6   Lower the fuel tank sufficiently to gain access to the hose connections on the fuel gauge tank unit. As the tank is being lowered, release the hose retaining clip on the top of the tank.
7   Disconnect the fuel gauge sender wiring connector.
8   Identify the hoses for position then loosen the clips and disconnect them from the tank unit.
9   Lower the fuel tank to the ground.
10   If the tank is contaminated with sediment or water, remove the

Fig. 4.3 Fuel tank hoses (Sec 5)

A   *Degassing pipe*
B   *Vent pipe*
C   *Fuel feed pipe*
D   *Fuel return pipe*
E   *Pipe retaining clip*

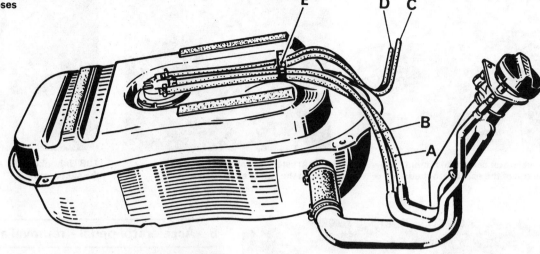

5.5 Fuel tank mounting bolt (arrowed)

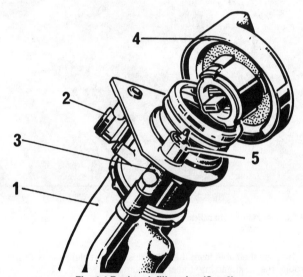

Fig. 4.4 Fuel tank filler pipe (Sec 6)

1	*Filler pipe*	4	*Cap*
2	*Safety valve*	5	*Plunger*
3	*Filling limiter*		

sender unit as described in Section 4 and swill the tank out with clean fuel. If the tank is damaged or leaks, it should be repaired by a specialist, or alternatively, renewed.

Refitting

11   Refitting is a reversal of removal, but make sure that the hoses are not trapped as the tank is lifted into place.

6   Fuel tank filler pipe – removal and refitting

Note: *Refer to the warning note in Section 1 before proceeding*

Removal

1   A drain plug is not provided on the fuel tank and it is therefore preferable to carry out the removal operation when the tank is nearly empty. Before proceeding, disconnect the battery negative lead and then syphon or hand pump the remaining fuel from the tank.
2   Chock the front wheels, then jack up the rear of the car and support it on axle stands.
3   Loosen the clip and disconnect the filler hose from the filler pipe.
4   Identify the degassing and vent pipes for position, then disconnect them from the filler pipe.
5   Open the fuel filler flap and remove the cap.

6   Unscrew the cross-head screws located inside the filler flap recess, and remove the filler pipe assembly.

Refitting

7   Refitting is a reversal of removal.

7   Accelerator cable – removal, refitting and adjustment

Removal

1   Remove the air cleaner assembly (1397 cc/C1J engine) or the air duct (1390 cc/E6J and 1721 cc/F2N engines) from the carburettor.
2   Working inside the car, release the cable end fitting which is a push fit in the accelerator pedal rod (photo).
3   At the carburettor, open the throttle and unhook the end of the accelerator cable from the sector arm (photos).
4   Pull the adjustment ferrule from the bracket on the valve cover and feed the cable through the bracket (photo).

7.2 Accelerator cable attachment (arrowed) to the top of the accelerator pedal

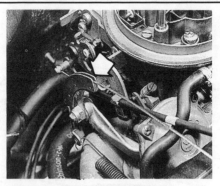

7.3A Accelerator cable fitted to the sector arm on the carburettor (arrowed)

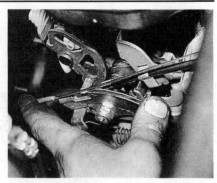

7.3B Unhooking the accelerator cable from the sector arm

7.4 Accelerator cable adjustment ferrule

5   Release the cable from the cable ties/support clips and withdraw it through the bulkhead into the engine compartment.

Refitting and adjustment

6   Refitting is a reversal of removal, but if necessary adjust it as follows. With the pedal fully released, check that there is a small amount of slack in the cable with the throttle sector on its stop. Have an assistant fully depress the accelerator pedal, then check that the throttle sector is in its fully open position. If adjustment is required, remove the spring clip from the adjustment ferrule, reposition the ferrule as necessary, then insert the clip in the next free groove on the ferrule.

8   Accelerator pedal – removal and refitting

Removal

1   Working inside the car, release the accelerator cable end fitting which is a push fit in the pedal rod.
2   Unscrew the bolt securing the pedal assembly to the bulkhead and withdraw it from inside the car.

Refitting

3   Refitting is a reversal of removal, but check the accelerator cable adjustment as described in Section 7.

9   Choke cable – removal, refitting and adjustment

Removal

1   Disconnect the battery negative lead.
2   Remove the carburettor inlet air duct.
3   Using a screwdriver or pair of pliers, disconnect the coiled end of the choke cable from the lever on the carburettor (photo).
4   Prise out the clip securing the choke outer cable to the bracket on the side of the carburettor (photo).
5   Working inside the car, remove the screw and withdraw the choke control knob panel from the facia (photos).
6   Disconnect the warning lamp wiring from the knob (photo).
7   Release the cable from the cable ties/support clips in the engine compartment, then withdraw it through the bulkhead into the car interior.

Refitting and adjustment

8   Refitting is a reversal of removal, but adjust the cable as follows.

9.3 Disconnecting the choke cable from the lever on the carburettor

9.4 Releasing the choke outer cable securing clip

9.5A Remove the screw ...

9.5B ... and withdraw the choke control knob panel from the facia

9.6 Disconnecting the choke control knob warning lamp wiring

11.1A Rear view of the Weber 32 TLDR

11.1B Front view of the Weber 32 TLDR

With the control knob pulled out approximately 2.0 mm and the choke lever on the carburettor in its rest position (ie choke fully open), fit the clip over the outer cable and attach it to the support bracket. Check that

the choke control lever is in its rest position with the knob pushed home, and fully closed (ie the choke valve is shut) with the knob pulled out.

10 Unleaded petrol – general information and usage

All engines covered by this manual can run on either unleaded fuel (octane rating 95) or 4-star leaded fuel (octane rating 97). No adjustments are necessary to the ignition timing.

11 Carburettor – general information

The carburettors may be of Weber (photos), Zenith or Solex manufacture according to model. All types are downdraught, however the carburettor is single choke on the 1397 cc (C1J) engine but twin choke on other engines. On the 1721 cc (F2N) engine, the carburettor may be fitted with a step-up solenoid valve in order to increase the engine speed when the power-assisted steering pump or air conditioning compressor is operating.

12 Carburettor – removal and refitting

Removal
1 Unbolt the strengthening bar from between the front suspension strut turrets. On the 1721 cc (F2N) engine it will also be necessary to remove the carburettor cooling duct.
2 On the 1397 cc (C1J) engine, drain the cooling system as described in Chapter 1, then disconnect the coolant hoses from the carburettor.
3 Remove the air cleaner or inlet duct from the top of the carburettor and place to one side. Remove the gasket (photos).
4 Disconnect the accelerator and choke cables from the carburettor as described in the relevant Sections of this Chapter.
5 Disconnect the fuel inlet hose and plug its end (photos).
6 On the 1390 cc (E6J) and 1721 cc (F2N) engines disconnect the crankcase ventilation hose (photo).
7 On the 1721 cc (F2N) engine disconnect the wiring for the anti run-on solenoid and, where applicable, the step-up valve, carburettor temperature sender and carburettor heater (photos).
8 Unscrew the mounting nuts/bolts, remove the washers and withdraw the carburettor from the inlet manifold. On the 1390 cc (E6J) and 1721 cc (F2N) engines a Torx key will be required to unscrew the bolts (photos). Recover the set of gaskets and, where applicable, the heat shield.

12.3A Carburettor air inlet duct on the – 1390 cc (E6J) engine

12.3B Unscrew the nuts ...

12.3C ... and remove the air inlet duct ...

12.3D ... and gasket from the carburettor – 1721 cc (F2N) engine

12.5A Fuel inlet hose (arrowed) – 1390 cc (E6J) engine

12.5B Disconnecting the fuel inlet hose – 1721 cc (F2N) engine

12.6 Disconnecting the crankcase ventilation hose – 1721 cc (F2N) engine

12.7A Disconnecting the wiring from the anti run-on solenoid – 1721 cc (F2N) engine

12.7B Disconnecting the step-up valve wiring connector by the carburettor – 1721 cc (F2N) engine

12.7C Carburettor temperature sender – 1721 cc (F2N) engine

12.8A Carburettor mounting bolts (arrowed) – 1390 cc (E6J) engine

12.8B Removing the carburettor – 1390 cc (E6J) engine

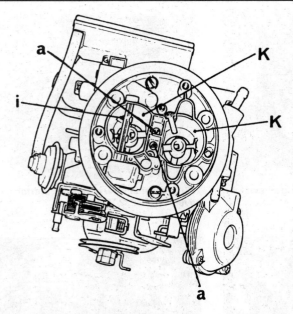

Fig. 4.5 Weber 32 TLDR main body components (Sec 13)

a   Air correction jet   K   Choke tube
i   Accelerator pump injector

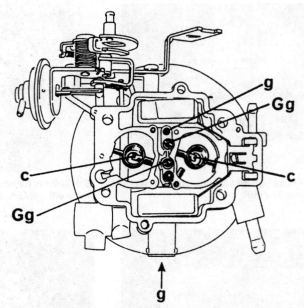

Fig. 4.6 Weber 32 TLDR cover components (Sec 13)

c   Auxiliary venturi   Gg   Main jet
g   Idling jet

Refitting

9   Refitting is a reversal of removal, but make sure that the mating surfaces of the carburettor and inlet manifold are clean and fit a new set of gaskets. Adjust the accelerator and choke cables as described in Sections 7 and 9. On the 1397 cc (C1J) engine, refill the cooling system as described in Chapter 1. Adjust the idling speed and mixture with reference to Chapter 1.

13 Carburettor – fault diagnosis, overhaul and adjustments

Fault diagnosis

1   Faults with the carburettor are usually associated with dirt entering the float chamber and blocking the jets, causing a weak mixture or power failure within a certain engine speed range. If this is the case, then a thorough clean will normally cure the problem. If the carburettor is well worn, uneven running may be caused by air entering through the throttle valve spindle bearings. All the carburettors fitted to the Renault 19 are fitted with manually-operated chokes which do not normally cause any problems.

Overhaul and adjustments

2   The following paragraphs describe cleaning and adjustment procedures which can be carried out by the home mechanic after the carburettor has been removed from the inlet manifold. If the carburettor is worn or damaged, it should either be renewed or overhauled by a specialist who will be able to restore the carburettor to its original calibration.

Weber 32 TLDR

3   Disconnect the vacuum hose from the choke pull-off vacuum capsule (photo).
4   Unscrew and remove the two slotted screws from the top of the carburettor cover and lift the cover from the main body (photo). Remove the gasket from the cover.
5   The various jets are shown in the accompanying illustrations (photo). Each jet should be removed and identified for position, then the float chamber can be cleaned of any sediment. Clean the main body and the cover thoroughly with fuel, and blow through the carburettor internal channels and jets using air from an air line or foot pump.

6   With the jets refitted and a new gasket located on the cover, check the float level setting as follows. Hold the cover vertical so that the floats hang down and close the needle valve without causing the valve ball to be depressed. Measure the distance between the gasket and the nearest point of the float, and compare with the dimension given in the Specifications. If adjustment is necessary, bend the tag on the float arm and make the check again.
7   Reassembly is a reversal of dismantling.

Zenith 32 IF2

8   Unscrew and remove the screws and lift the cover off of the main body. Remove the gasket.
9   Refer to the accompanying illustration for the location of each jet. Remove each jet and identify it for position. Using fuel, thoroughly clean the float chamber, main body and cover. Blow through the carburettor internal channels and jets using air from an air line or foot pump.
10   To check the float level setting, turn the cover upside down. Measure the distance between the upper face of the needle valve body washer and the end of the needle valve. If the measured dimension is greater than specified, tighten the needle valve body to compress the washer until the dimension is correct. If the measured dimension is less than specified, renew the washer and tighten the needle valve body until the correct dimension is obtained.
11   Reassembly is a reversal of dismantling, but fit a new gasket.

Solex 32 x 34 Z13

12   Remove the screws securing the carburettor cover to the main body (photo).
13   Lift the cover, and at the same time disengage the degassing valve plunger from the operating lever (photo).
14   Refer to the accompanying illustration for the location of the various jets (photo). Remove each jet and identify it for location. Using fuel, thoroughly clean the float chamber, main body and cover. Blow through the carburettor internal channels and jets using air from an air line or foot pump.
15   Note how the needle valve is attached to the float arm, then push out the fulcrum pin, remove the float assembly and valve, and remove the gasket. Renew the gasket and refit the float assembly (photo).
16   To check the float level setting hold the cover vertical so that the floats hang down. The needle valve should be closed but the spring-tensioned ball in the end of the valve should not be depressed. Measure the distance between the gasket and the floats and compare with the dimension given in the Specifications (photo). If adjustment is necessary, bend the tag on the float arm and make the check again.
17   Reassembly is a reversal of dismantling.

13.3 Choke pull-off vacuum hose (arrowed) – Weber 32 TLDR

13.4 Carburettor cover retaining screws (arrowed) – Weber 32 TLDR

13.5 Underside view of the carburettor cover – Weber 32 TLDR

13.12 Removing the carburettor cover retaining screws – Solex 32 x 34 Z13

13.13 Disengaging the degassing valve plunger (A) from the operating lever (B) – Solex 32 x 34 Z13

13.14 View of the carburettor main body with the cover removed – Solex 32 x 34 Z13

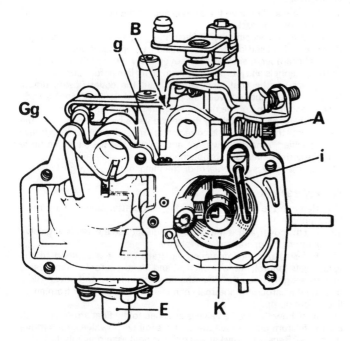

Fig. 4.7 Zenith 32 IF2 main body components (Sec 13)

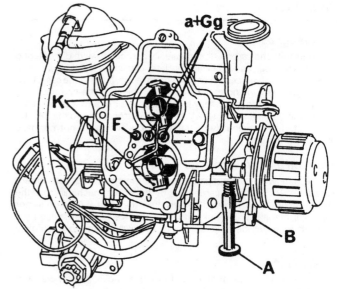

Fig. 4.8 Solex 32 x 34 Z13 main body components (Sec 13)

A	Idling speed air screw	Gg	Main jet
B	Idling speed mixture screw	i	Accelerator pump jet
E	Pneumatic richener	K	Choke tube
g	Idling jet		

a	Air correction jet	F	Idling speed fuel circuit filter
A	Idling volume screw		
B	Idling mixture screw	Gg	Main jet
		K	Choke tube

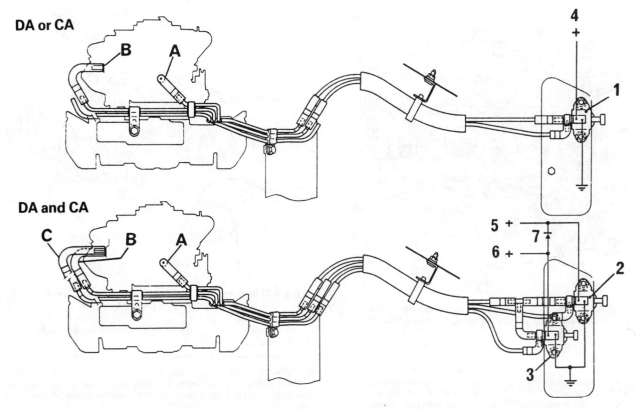

Fig. 4.9 Fast idling system for models fitted with power-assisted steering or air conditioning (Sec 13)

DA = Power-assisted steering
CA = Air conditioning
A Carburettor connection (red ring)
B Actuator connection (blue ring) on DA or CA models

C Connection on actuator (grey ring) on CA and DA + CA models
D Throttle actuator
E DA adjusting screw
F CA adjusting screw

1 DA or CA solenoid valve
2 DA solenoid valve
3 CA solenoid valve
4 DA pressure switch or CA compressor

5 DA pressure switch
6 CA compressor
7 Diode

18 Models fitted with this carburettor may be equipped with power-assisted steering, air conditioning, or both, and on these models an idling step-up system is fitted to compensate for the extra load of the power-assisted steering pump and/or air conditioning compressor. The fast idling speed checking procedure is as follows, but before carrying it out the normal idling speed adjustment should be made as described in Chapter 1. The engine must be at its normal operating temperature and the adjustment must be made with the electric cooling fan stopped.
19 On models with power-assisted steering make sure that the front

wheels are pointing straight-ahead, then apply a vacuum of 600 mbar or manifold vacuum to the throttle step-up actuator (blue ring) on the carburettor. The engine speed should be as given in the Specifications at the beginning of this Chapter. If not, turn the adjustment screw shown in Fig. 4.10 (photo). On models with air conditioning, switch on the air conditioner to its maximum position before making the adjustment. On models with both power-assisted steering and air conditioning, carry out the power steering adjustment as described, then carry out the air conditioning adjustment in that order.

13.15 Underside view of the carburettor cover – Solex 32 x 34 Z13

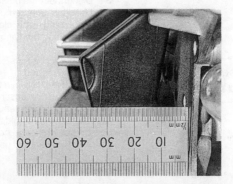

13.16 Checking the float level setting – Solex 32 x 34 Z13

13.19 Adjustment screw for the throttle step-up actuator – Solex 32 x 34 Z13

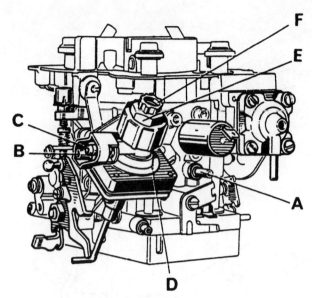

Fig. 4.10 Idling step-up system for models fitted with power-assisted steering and/or air conditioning (Sec 13)

A   Carburettor vacuum
    connection
B   Actuator vacuum
    connection (blue ring) for
    models with power
    steering or air conditioning
    (single stage)
C   Actuator vacuum
    connection (grey ring) for
    models with air
    conditioning and power
    steering (double stage)
D   Throttle actuator
E   Power steering adjusting
    screw
F   Air conditioning adjusting
    screw

14   Inlet manifold pre-heater (1721 cc/F2N engine) – removal and refitting

Removal

1   Unbolt the strengthening bar from between the front suspension strut turrets. It will also be necessary to remove the carburettor cooling duct.
2   Remove the air inlet duct from the top of the carburettor and move it to one side.
3   Pull the connector apart which connects the main wiring harness to the pre-heater wiring.
4   Unbolt the pre-heater from the bottom of the inlet manifold and lower it down through the aperture in the exhaust manifold.

Refitting

5   Refitting is a reversal of removal.

15   Inlet and exhaust manifold assembly (1397 cc/C1J engine) – removal and refitting

Removal

1   Remove the carburettor as described in Section 12.
2   Disconnect the brake servo vacuum hose and the crankcase ventilation hose from the inlet manifold.
3   Unbolt and remove the starter motor protective shield.
4   Remove the hot air ducting then unbolt the metal tube and air cleaner support bracket.
5   Unscrew the nut and withdraw the heat shield from the exhaust manifold.

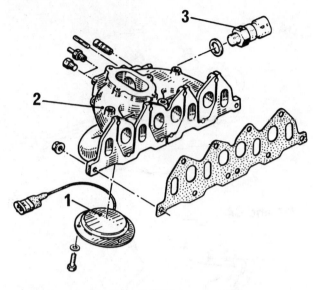

Fig. 4.11 Inlet/exhaust manifolds, and pre-heater on the 1721 cc (F2N) engine (Secs 14 and 16)

1   Pre-heater
2   Inlet/exhaust manifold
3   Temperature switch

6   Unscrew and remove the two nuts, then remove the washers, tension springs and sleeves securing the exhaust front pipe to the manifold. Slide the flange plate off the manifold studs and separate the joint.
7   Progressively unscrew the nuts securing the manifold assembly to the cylinder head and remove the washers.
8   Withdraw the manifold assembly from the studs on the cylinder head, then remove the gasket.

Refitting

9   Refitting is a reversal of removal. Ensure that the cylinder head and manifold mating faces are clean and use a new gasket. Refit the carburettor with reference to Section 12.

16   Inlet and exhaust manifolds (1721 cc/F2N engine) – removal and refitting

Removal

1   Remove the carburettor as described in Section 12.
2   Drain the cooling system as described in Chapter 1, then disconnect the coolant hoses from the inlet manifold.
3   Disconnect the brake servo vacuum hose from the inlet manifold.
4   Unscrew and remove the two nuts, then remove the washers, tension springs and sleeves securing the exhaust front pipe to the manifold. Slide the flange plate off the manifold studs and separate the joint.
5   Unscrew the nuts securing the hot air shroud to the manifold and remove the shroud.
6   Unbolt and remove the manifold support brackets.
7   Progressively unscrew the nuts and bolts securing the inlet and exhaust manifolds and withdraw them from the cylinder head. Although the manifolds are separate, they are retained by the same bolts since the bolt holes are split between the manifold flanges. Recover the manifold gasket.

Refitting

8   Refitting is a reversal of removal. Ensure that the cylinder head and manifold mating surfaces are clean and use a new gasket. Refit the carburettor with reference to Section 12. Refill the cooling system with reference to Chapter 1.

17   Inlet manifold (1390 cc/E6J engine) – removal and refitting

Removal

1   Remove the carburettor as described in Section 12. Alternatively the inlet manifold may be removed together with the carburettor, but if this method is used it will still be necessary to disconnect the accelerator and choke cables and the various hoses.
2   Drain the cooling system as described in Chapter 1, then disconnect the coolant hoses from the inlet manifold (photo).
3   Disconnect the brake servo vacuum hose (photo).
4   Progressively unscrew the nuts then withdraw the inlet manifold from the studs on the cylinder head. Remove the gasket (photos).

Refitting

5   Refitting is a reversal of removal. Ensure that the cylinder head and manifold mating surfaces are clean and use a new gasket. Where applicable, refit the carburettor with reference to Section 12. Refill the cooling system with reference to Chapter 1.

18   Exhaust manifold (1390 cc/E6J engine) – removal and refitting

Removal

1   Unscrew and remove the two nuts, then remove the washers, tension springs and sleeves securing the exhaust front pipe to the manifold (photo). Slide the flange plate off the manifold studs and separate the joint.
2   Loosen the clip and disconnect the hot air hose for the air cleaner from the exhaust manifold hot air shroud (photo).

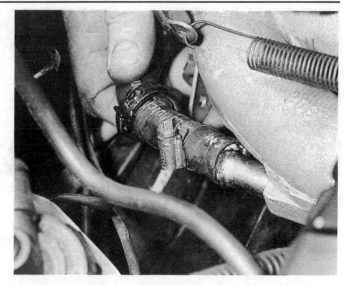

17.2 Disconnecting the coolant hoses from the inlet manifold – 1390 cc (E6J) engine

3   Unscrew the nuts and remove the hot air shroud from the manifold (photo).
4   Progressively unscrew the nuts and bolts securing the exhaust manifold then withdraw it from the cylinder head. Recover the manifold gasket (photos).

Refitting

5   Refitting is a reversal of removal. Ensure that the cylinder head and manifold mating surfaces are clean and use a new gasket.

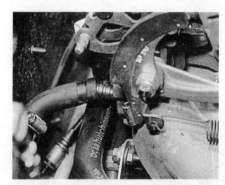

17.3 Disconnecting the brake servo vacuum hose – 1390 cc (E6J) engine

17.4A Removing the inlet manifold complete with carburettor – 1390 cc (E6J) engine

17.4B Removing the inlet manifold gasket – 1390 cc (E6J) engine

18.1 Unscrewing the exhaust front pipe to manifold joint nuts – 1390 cc (E6J) engine

18.2 Disconnecting the air cleaner hot air hose from the exhaust manifold shroud – 1390 cc (E6J) engine

18.3 Removing the hot air shroud from the exhaust manifold – 1390 cc (E6J) engine

18.4A Unscrew the nuts ...

18.4B ... and remove the exhaust manifold ...

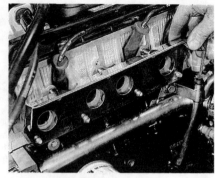

18.4C ... and gasket

Fig. 4.12 Exhaust system components for the 1390 cc (E6J) and 1397 cc (C1J) engines (Sec 19)

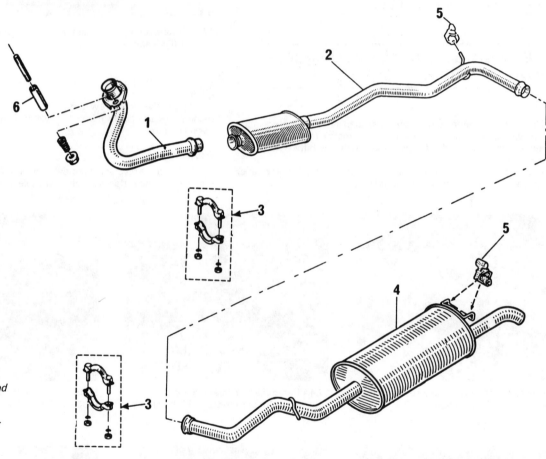

1   Downpipe
2   Intermediate pipe and
    resonator
3   Connecting clamp
4   Tailpipe and silencer
5   Exhaust rubber
    mounting
6   Spacer to limit
    tightening of downpipe nut

19 Exhaust system – general information and component renewal

1   The exhaust system components are shown in Figs. 4.12 and 4.13. The system consists of three sections. Both the front pipe and tail pipe can be removed leaving the remaining exhaust system in position, however to remove the intermediate section it is recommended that the tailpipe is removed first then disconnected from the front pipe.

2   To remove the system or part of the system, first jack up the front or rear of the car and support it on axle stands. Alternatively, position the car over an inspection pit or on car ramps.

3   To remove the front pipe unscrew and remove the two nuts, then remove the washers, tension springs and sleeves securing the exhaust front pipe to the manifold. Slide the flange plate off the manifold studs and separate the joint. Unscrew the nuts and remove the clamp securing the front pipe to the intermediate section. Pull the front pipe from the intermediate section. On the 1721 cc (F2N) engine, unbolt the heat guard if necessary. Refitting is a reversal of removal but tighten the nuts to the specified torque (photos).

4   To remove the tailpipe unscrew the nuts and remove the clamp

Fig. 4.13 Exhaust system components for the 1721 cc (F2N) engine (Sec 19)

1 Downpipe
2 Spherical joint
3 Intermediate pipe and
   expansion chamber
4 Tailpipe and silencer
5 Exhaust rubber mounting
6 Downpipe to intermediate pipe
   connecting clamp
7 Spacer to limit tightening of
   downpipe nut

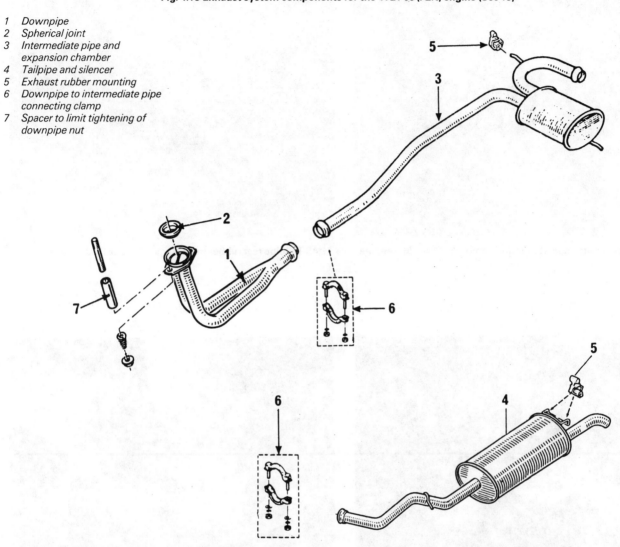

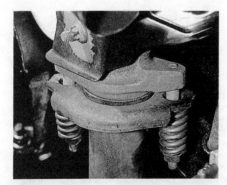

19.3A Exhaust front pipe to manifold joint flange – 1390 cc (E6J) engine

19.3B Exhaust front pipe to intermediate section clamp – 1390 cc (E6J) engine

19.3C Heat guard and bracket – 1721 cc (F2N) engine

19.4A Tailpipe to intermediate section clamp – 1390 cc (E6J) engine

19.4B Tailpipe rear rubber mountings – 1390 cc (E6J) engine

19.5A Exhaust intermediate section rubber mounting – 1390 cc (E6J) engine

19.5B Strengthening bracket fitted to the exhaust intermediate section – 1390 cc (E6J) engine

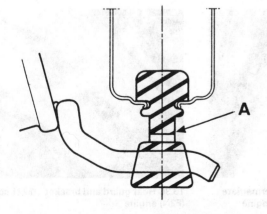

Fig. 4.14 Exhaust rubber mounting (A) (Sec 19)

securing the tailpipe to the intermediate section. Slide the rubber mountings off of the bars, and if necessary remove them from the underbody by turning them through 90°. Separate the tailpipe from the intermediate section (photos). On the 1721 cc (F2N) engine, unbolt the heat guard if necessary. Refitting is a reversal of removal, but tighten the clamp nuts securely and renew the rubber mountings if necessary.

5   To remove the intermediate section first remove the tailpipe as described in the previous paragraph. Unscrew the nuts and remove the clamp securing the front pipe to the intermediate section. Slide the rubber mountings off of the bars, and if necessary remove them from the underbody by turning them through 90°. Separate the intermediate section from the front pipe and if necessary unbolt the strengthening

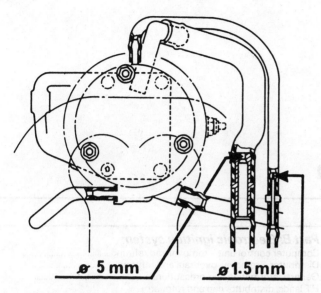

Fig. 4.15 Crankcase ventilation system for the 1390 cc (E6J) engine
(Sec 20)

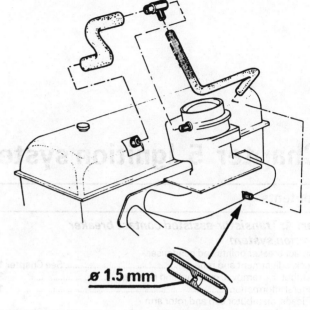

Fig. 4.16 Crankcase ventilation system for the 1397 cc (C1J) engine
(Sec 20)

bracket (photos). On the 1721 cc (F2N) engine, unbolt the heat guard if
necessary. Refitting is a reversal of removal, tighten the clamp nuts
securely and renew the rubber mountings if necessary.

20   Crankcase ventilation system – general information

1   The layout of the crankcase ventilation system, according to engine
type, is shown in the accompanying illustrations.
2   When the engine is idling, or under partial load conditions, the high
depression in the inlet manifold draws the crankcase fumes (diluted by
air from the air cleaner side of the throttle valve) through the calibrated
restrictor and into the combustion chambers.
3   The system ensures that there is always a partial vacuum in the
crankcase, and so prevents pressure which could cause oil
contamination, fume emission and oil leakage past seals.
4   The crankcase ventilation hoses should be periodically cleaned to
ensure correct operation of the system.

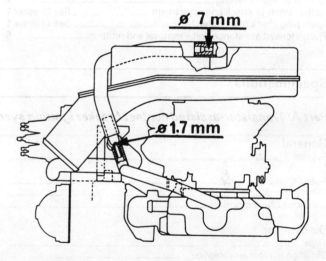

Fig. 4.17 Crankcase ventilation system for the 1721 cc (F2N) engine
(Sec 20)

Chapter 5 Ignition system

Contents

Specifications

Part A: Transistor-assisted contact breaker ignition system

General
System .... Coil, and distributor with contact breaker points and condenser, transistorised assistance unit in low tension circuit
Application .... 1397 cc (C1J) engine
Firing order 1–3–4–2
Location of No 1 cylinder.................................... Flywheel end

Distributor
Type .... Conventional, with contact breaker points and condenser
Direction of rotor arm rotation .... Clockwise

Ignition coil
Type .... Conventional, mounted on bulkhead
Primary resistance .... 1.45 ohms

Part B: Electronic ignition system

General
System type .... Renix AEI computer control unit with position/speed sensor, ignition coil attached to control unit, distributor only for HT spark distribution
Application .... 1390 cc (E6J) and 1721 cc (F2N) engines
Firing order 1–3–4–2
Location of No 1 cylinder.................................... Flywheel end

Distributor
Type .... Ducellier, rotor arm and cap only, rotor arm fixed to distributor shaft on 1390 cc (E6J) engine and to end of camshaft on 1721 cc (F2N) engine
Direction of rotor arm rotation .... Anti-clockwise

Ignition coil
Type .... Renix AEI, mounted on computer control unit
Primary resistance .... 0.4 to 0.8 ohms

Part A: Transistor-assisted contact breaker ignition system

1 General information

This type of ignition system consists of a basic conventional contact breaker ignition system but with the addition of a transistor assistance unit. The transistor assistance unit has two sockets on it, the top one for normal use which includes transistor assistance, and the bottom one for emergency use which bypasses the transistor unit and converts the system to a conventional contact breaker ignition system. The wiring plug is simply moved from one socket to the other as required. **Note:** *Some models may have a sealed unit without the two socket positions.*

In order that the engine may run correctly it is necessary for an electrical spark to ignite the fuel/air mixture in the combustion chamber at exactly the right moment in relation to engine speed and load.

Basically the conventional ignition system functions as follows. Low tension voltage from the battery is fed to the ignition coil where it is converted into high tension voltage. The high tension voltage is powerful enough to jump the spark plug gap in the cylinder many times a second under high compression pressure, provided that the ignition system is in good working order and that all adjustments are correct.

The ignition system consists of two individual circuits known as the low tension (LT) circuit and high tension (HT) circuit.

The low tension circuit (sometimes known as the primary circuit) consists of the battery, the lead to ignition switch, the lead to the low tension or primary coil windings, and the lead from the low tension coil windings to the contact breaker points and condenser in the distributor.

The high tension circuit (sometimes known as the secondary circuit) consists of the high tension or secondary coil winding, the heavily insulated lead from the centre of the coil to the centre of the distributor cap, the rotor arm, the spark plug leads and the spark plugs.

The complete ignition system operation is as follows. Low tension voltage from the battery is changed within the ignition coil to high tension voltage by the opening and closing of the contact breaker points in the low tension circuit. High tension voltage is then fed, via a contact in the centre of the distributor cap, to the rotor arm of the distributor. The rotor arm revolves inside the distributor cap, and each time it passes one of the four metal segments in the cap, the opening and closing of the contact breaker points causes the high tension voltage to build up, jump the gap from the rotor arm to the appropriate metal segment and so, via the spark plug lead, to the spark plug where it finally jumps the gap between the two spark plug electrodes, one being earthed.

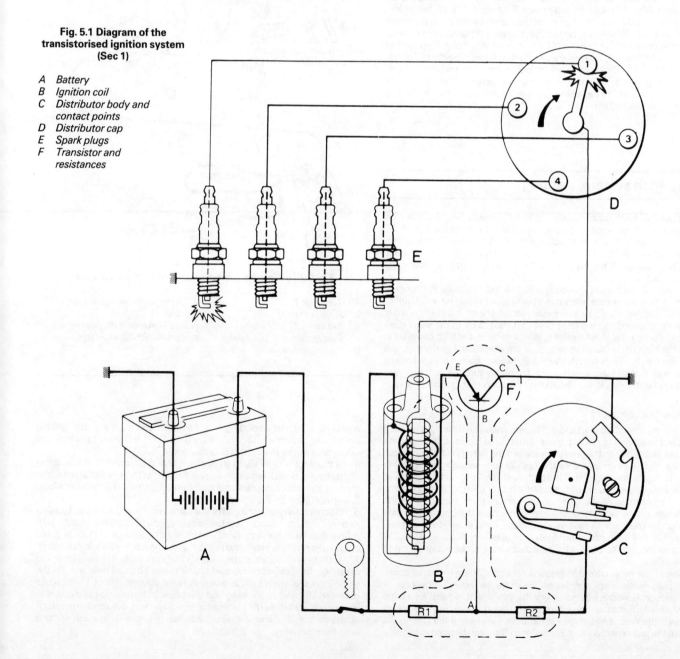

Fig. 5.1 Diagram of the transistorised ignition system (Sec 1)

A Battery
B Ignition coil
C Distributor body and contact points
D Distributor cap
E Spark plugs
F Transistor and resistances

The ignition timing is advanced and retarded automatically to ensure the spark occurs at just the right instant for the particular load at the prevailing engine speed.

The ignition advance is controlled both mechanically and by a vacuum-operated system. The mechanical governor mechanism consists of two weights which move out under centrifugal force from the central distributor shaft as the engine speed rises. As they move outwards they rotate the cam relative to the distributor shaft, and so advance the spark. The weights are held in position by two light springs, and it is the tension of these springs which is largely responsible for correct spark advancement.

The vacuum control consists of a diaphragm, one side of which is connected via a small-bore tube, to the carburettor and the other side to the contact breaker plate. Depression in the induction manifold and carburettor, which varies with engine speed and throttle opening, causes the diaphragm to move, so rotating the contact breaker plate and advancing or retarding the spark.

The function of the transistor-assistance unit is to relieve the contact points of carrying the full primary current and therefore extend their service life and provide a more reliable system. The contact points are used to switch a transistor on and off and it is the transistor which carries the full primary current.

The transistor operates as follows, noting that components mentioned relate to those shown in area F, of Fig. 5.1. With the points open, the base (B) and emitter (E) are of the same potential and therefore no current flows. When the points close, the base (B) becomes negative due to the voltage drop at point (A) and current then flows through the transistor collector (C). The resistances R1 and R2 are fitted in the circuit to provide a low control voltage, and this also greatly increases the life of the contact points as they only carry a small current. When the points open again the voltage increases at point (A) and the base (B), and the transistor is switched off.

2   Ignition system – testing

1   Should a fault occur in the ignition system, first bypass the transistor assistance unit by pulling the connector from the top of the unit then fitting it in the lower socket. If the fault disappears, the fault is proved to be in the transistor-assistance unit. If the fault remains, check the basic conventional system with reference to the following paragraphs.
2   There are two main symptoms indicating faults in the ignition system. Either the engine will not start or fire, or the engine is difficult to start and misfires. If it is a regular misfire (ie the engine is running on only two or three cylinders), the fault is almost sure to be in the secondary (high tension) circuit. If the misfiring is intermittent, the fault could be in either the high or low tension circuits. If the car stops suddenly, or will not start at all, it is likely that the fault is in the low tension circuit. Loss of power and overheating, apart from faulty carburation settings, are normally due to faults in the distributor or to incorrect ignition timing.

Engine fails to start

3   If the engine fails to start and the engine was running normally when it was last used, first check that there is fuel in the fuel tank. If the engine turns over normally on the starter motor and the battery is fully charged, then the fault may be in either the high or low tension circuits. First check the high tension circuit. If the battery is known to be fully charged, the ignition lights come on, but the starter motor fails to turn the engine, check the tightness of the leads on the battery terminals and also the secureness of the earth lead to its connection on the body. It is quite common for the leads to have worked loose, even if they look and feel secure. If one of the battery terminal posts gets very hot when trying to work the starter motor, this is a sure indication of a faulty connection to that terminal.
4   One of the most common reasons for bad starting is wet or damp spark plug leads and distributor. Remove the distributor cap. If condensation is visible internally, dry the cap with a rag and also wipe over the leads. Refit the cap. Alternatively, using a moisture dispersant such as Holts Wet Start can be very effective in starting the engine. To prevent the problem recurring, Holts Damp Start can be used to provide

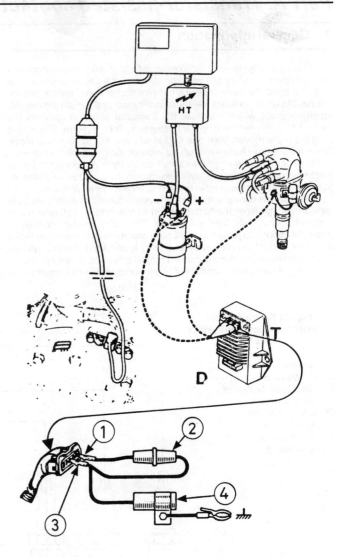

Fig. 5.2 Testing the transistorised ignition system (Sec 2)

1	Terminal 1	T	Transistorised assistance
2	Fuse (see text)		unit
3	Terminal 2		Note that Renault diagnostic
4	Condenser		equipment is shown in this
D	Connector plug		figure

a sealing coat, so excluding any further moisture from the ignition system. In extreme difficulty, Holts Cold Start will help to start a car when only a very poor spark occurs.
5   If the engine still fails to start, check that the current is reaching the plugs, by disconnecting each plug lead in turn at the spark plug end, and holding the end of the cable about 5 mm away from the cylinder block. Spin the engine on the starter motor.
6   Sparking between the end of the cable and the block should be fairly strong with a good, regular blue spark. Hold the lead with rubber-insulated pliers to avoid electric shocks. If current is reaching the plugs then remove, clean and regap them. The engine should now start.
7   If there is no spark at the plug leads, take off the HT lead from the centre of the distributor cap and hold it to the block as before. Spin the engine on the starter once more. A rapid succession of blue sparks between the end of the lead and the block indicates that the coil is in order and that either the distributor cap is cracked, the rotor arm faulty, or the carbon brush in the distributor cap is not making good contact with the rotor arm.

8   If there are no sparks from the end of the lead from the coil, check the connections at the coil end of the lead. If it is in order start checking the low tension circuit.

9   Either transfer the connector to the lower socket on the transistor-assistance unit, or remove the connector and interconnect pins 1 and 3 in the connector as shown in Fig. 5.2. The 5 amp fuse in the figure protects the Renault diagnostic equipment and does not need to be fitted if diagnostic equipment is not being used. As a precaution against a faulty condenser at the distributor, a known good condenser should be connected to earth as shown.

10   Use a 12V voltmeter or a 12V bulb and two lengths of wire. With the ignition switched on and the points open, test between the low tension wire to the coil positive (+) terminal and earth. No reading indicates a break in the supply from the ignition switch. Check the connections at the switch to see if any are loose. Refit them and the engine should run. If a reading is now indicated, this shows a faulty coil or condenser, or broken lead between the coil and the distributor.

11   Take the condenser wire off the points assembly, and with the points open test between the moving point and earth. If there is now a reading then the fault is in the condenser. Fit a new one, as described in Chapter 1, and the fault should clear.

12   With no reading from the moving point to earth, take a reading between earth and the coil negative (–) terminal. A reading here shows a broken wire between the coil and distributor. No reading confirms that the coil has failed and must be renewed, after which the engine should run. Remember to refit the condenser wire to the points assembly. For these tests it is sufficient to separate the points with a piece of paper while testing with the points open.

Engine misfires

13   If the engine misfires regularly, run it at a fast idle speed. Pull off each of the plug caps in turn and listen to the note of the engine. Hold the plug cap in a dry cloth or with a rubber glove as additional protection against a shock from the HT supply.

14   No difference in engine running will be noticed when the lead from the defective circuit is removed. Removing the lead from one of the good cylinders will accentuate the misfire.

15   Remove the plug lead from the end of the defective plug and hold it about 5 mm away from the block. Restart the engine. If the sparking is fairly strong and regular, the fault must lie in the spark plug.

16   The plug may be loose, the insulation may be cracked, or the

electrodes may have burnt away, giving too wide a gap for the spark to jump. Worse still, one of the electrodes may have broken off. Renew the spark plugs.

17   If there is no spark at the end of the plug lead, or if it is too weak and intermittent, check the ignition lead from the distributor to the plug. If the insulation is cracked or perished, renew the lead. Check the connections at the distributor cap.

18   If there is still no spark, examine the distributor cap carefully for tracking. This can be recognised by a very thin black line running between two or more electrodes, or between an electrode and some other part of the distributor. These lines are paths which now conduct electricity across the cap, thus letting it run to earth. The only answer is a new distributor cap.

19   Apart from the ignition timing being incorrect, other causes of misfiring have already been dealt with under the section dealing with the failure of the engine to start. To recap, these are that:

(a)   The coil may be faulty, giving an intermittent misfire
(b)   There may be a damaged wire or loose connection in the low tension circuit
(c)   The condenser may be short-circuiting
(d)   There may be a mechanical fault in the distributor (broken driving spindle or contact breaker spring)

20   If the ignition is too far retarded, it should be noted that the engine will tend to overheat, and there will be quite a noticeable drop in power. If the engine is overheating and the power is down, and the ignition timing is correct, then the carburettor should be checked, as it is likely that this is where the fault lies.

3   Distributor – removal, overhaul and refitting

Removal

1   Mark the spark plug HT leads to aid refitting and pull them off the ends of the plugs. Release the distributor cap retaining clips and place the cap and leads to one side.

2   Remove No 1 spark plug (nearest the flywheel end of the engine).

3   Place a finger over the plug hole and turn the engine in the normal direction of rotation (clockwise from the crankshaft pulley end) until pressure is felt in No 1 cylinder. This indicates that the piston is commencing its compression stroke. The engine can be turned with a socket or spanner on the crankshaft pulley bolt.

4   Continue turning the engine until the mark on the flywheel is aligned with the TDC notch on the clutch bellhousing.

5   Using a dab of paint or a small file, make a reference mark between the distributor base and the cylinder block.

6   Detach the vacuum advance pipe and disconnect the LT lead at the wiring connector. Release the wiring loom from the support clip on the distributor body.

7   Unscrew the distributor clamp retaining nut and lift off the clamp. Withdraw the distributor from the engine and recover the seal.

Overhaul

8   Renewal of the contact breaker assembly, condenser, rotor and distributor cap should be regarded as the limit of overhaul on these units, as few other spares are available separately. Refer to Chapter 1 for these procedures. It is possible to renew the vacuum unit, but this must then be set up to suit the advance curve of the engine by adjustment of the serrated cam on the baseplate; this is best left to a Renault dealer or automotive electrician.

9   When the distributor has seen extended service and the shaft, bushes and centrifugal mechanism become worn it is advisable to purchase a new distributor.

Refitting

10   To refit the distributor, first check that the engine is still at the TDC position with No 1 cylinder on compression. If the engine has been turned while the distributor was removed, return it to the correct position as previously described. Also make sure that the seal is in position on the base of the distributor.

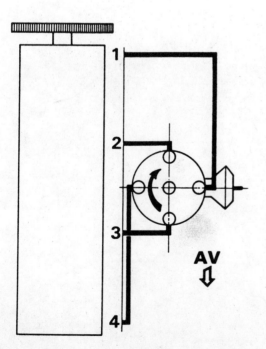

Fig. 5.3 HT spark plug lead connection diagram (Sec 3)

11   With the rotor arm pointing directly away from the engine and the vacuum unit at approximately the 5 o'clock position, slide the distributor into the cylinder block and turn the rotor arm slightly until the offset peg on the distributor drive dog positively engages with the drivegear.

12   Align the previously made reference marks on the distributor base and cylinder block. If a new distributor is being fitted, position the distributor body so that the rotor arm points toward the No 1 spark plug HT lead segment in the cap. With the distributor in this position, refit the clamp and secure with the retaining nut.

13   Reconnect the LT lead at the connector, refit the vacuum advance pipe and secure the wiring loom in the support clip.

14   Refit the No 1 spark plug, the distributor cap and the spark plug HT leads.

15   Check and if necessary adjust the ignition timing as described in Chapter 1.

4   Ignition coil – removal and refitting

Removal

1   Where fitted, remove the cover from the top of the coil. Disconnect the HT lead from the coil.

2   Identify the LT leads for position then disconnect them from the terminals on the coil.

3   Loosen the mounting nut and slide the coil and bracket from the mounting stud.

Refitting

4   Refitting is a reversal of removal, but if necessary wipe clean the top of the coil to prevent any tracking of the HT current.

5   Transistorised assistance unit – removal and refitting

Removal

1   Disconnect the wiring plug from the transistorised assistance unit located on the bulkhead.

2   Unscrew the mounting nuts and remove the unit.

Refitting

3   Refitting is a reversal of removal.

Part B: Electronic ignition system

6 General information and precautions

The electronic ignition system operates on an advanced principle whereby the main functions of the distributor are replaced by a computer control unit.

The system consists of three main components, namely the computer control unit which incorporates an ignition coil and a vacuum advance unit, the distributor which directs the HT voltage received from the coil to the appropriate spark plug, and an angular position sensor which determines the position and speed of the crankshaft by sensing special segments in the flywheel.

The computer control unit receives information on crankshaft position relative to TDC and BDC and also engine speed from the angular position sensor, and receives information on engine load from the vacuum advance unit. From these constantly changing variables, the computer calculates the precise instant at which HT voltage should be supplied and triggers the coil accordingly. The voltage then passes from the coil to the appropriate spark plug, via the distributor in the conventional way. The function of the centrifugal and vacuum advance mechanisms as well as the contact breaker points normally associated with a distributor, are all catered for by the computer control unit, so that the sole purpose of the distributor is to direct the HT voltage from the coil to the appropriate spark plug.

Due to the sophisticated nature of the electronic ignition system the following precautions must be observed to prevent damage to the components and reduce risk of personal injury.

(a) Ensure that the ignition is switched off before disconnecting any of the ignition wiring
(b) Ensure that the ignition is switched off before connecting or disconnecting any ignition test equipment, such as a timing light
(c) Do not connect a suppression condenser or test lamp to the ignition coil negative terminal
(d) Do not connect any test appliance or stroboscopic timing light requiring a 12 volt supply to the ignition coil positive terminal
(e) Do not allow an HT lead to short out or spark against the computer control unit body
(f) Do not earth the coil primary or secondary circuits

Warning: *The voltages produced by the electronic ignition system are considerably higher than those produced by conventional systems. Extreme care must be taken when working on the system with the ignition switched on. Persons with surgically-implanted cardiac pacemaker devices should keep well clear of the ignition circuits, components and test equipment.*

7 Ignition system – testing

1 There are two main symptoms indicating faults in the ignition

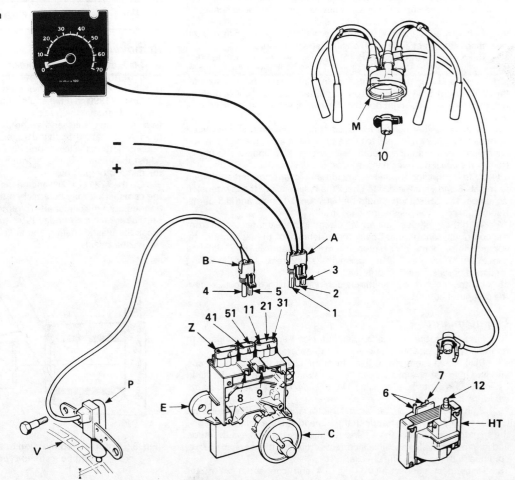

Fig. 5.4 Electronic ignition system components (Sec 6)

1 Positive (+) supply
2 Earth (−)
3 Tachometer
4 Position/speed sensor terminal
5 Position/speed sensor terminal
6 Coil positive (+) terminal and interference suppression capacitor terminal
7 Coil negative (−) terminal
8 Coil positive (+) terminal on the control unit (joined internally to 11)
9 Coil negative (−) terminal on the control unit
10 Rotor arm
11 Positive (+) supply from battery (joined internally to 8)
12 Coil HT terminal
21 Negative (−) lead to battery
31 Tachometer output
41 Position/speed sensor signal
51 Position/speed sensor signal
A Supply connector
B Position/speed sensor connector
C Vacuum capsule
E Computer control unit
HT Ignition coil
M Distributor cap
P Magnetic position/speed sensor
V Flywheel
Z Socket for temperature ignition timing correction on the 1721 cc (F2N) engine

system. Either the engine will not start or fire, or the engine is difficult to start and misfires. Each of these possibilities is covered separately in the following paragraphs.

Engine fails to start

2   First check the HT leads, distributor cap and spark plugs with reference to the relevant sections of this Chapter.
3   Remove the two connectors from the bottom of the computer control unit and check the terminals for corrosion. If necessary, remove and refit the connectors several times in order to clean the terminals. If they are very dirty, scrape the terminals with a suitable instrument.
4   Using a voltmeter, check that the voltage between the coil positive (+) terminal at the interference suppression condenser output and earth, with the ignition switched on, is at least 9.5 volts.
5   Disconnect connector (A) Fig. 5.4 and connect a voltmeter between terminal 1 and earth. Switch on the ignition and attempt to start the engine. The reading on the voltmeter should be at least 9.5 volts. If not, check the battery voltage and recharge if necessary. Also check the computer control unit supply wiring.
6   With connector (A) still disconnected and the ignition switched off, connect an ohmmeter between terminal 2 and the vehicle earth. If the reading is not zero, check the earth wiring from the connector for a possible loose connection.
7   With connector (A) still disconnected and the ignition switched off, connect an ohmmeter between the coil terminal 6 and the computer control unit terminal 11. If the reading is not zero, renew the control unit.
8   Reconnect connector (A) and switch on the ignition. Connect a voltmeter between terminal 6 and the vehicle earth. If the reading is not at least 9.5 volts, shake the connector and observe if the reading increases. If it is still incorrect, check the coil terminal contacts for corrosion. If still incorrect, renew the connector (A).
9   With the ignition switched off, disconnect the connector (B) in Fig. 5.4. Check the resistance of the position/speed sensor by connecting an ohmmeter across terminals 4 and 5. The reading should be 200 ohms ± 50 ohms. If the reading is incorrect, renew the position/speed sensor.
10   Using a feeler blade, check that the clearance between the end of the position/speed sensor (P) and the flywheel (V) is 1.0 ± 0.5 mm. If the clearance is incorrect, renew the position/speed sensor.
11   Reconnect both connectors (A) and (B) then remove the ignition coil as described in Section 9. Connect a 12 volt test light between terminals 8 and 9 on the computer control unit (ie the coil terminals on the control unit). Spin the engine on the starter motor and check that the test light flashes. If the light does not flash, renew the computer control unit.
12   With the ignition coil still removed, connect an ohmmeter between terminals 7 and 12 on the coil to check the resistance of the high tension windings. The resistance should be between 2000 and 12 000 ohms. Renew the coil if the resistance is incorrect.
13   With the ignition coil still removed, connect an ohmmeter between terminals 6 and 7 on the coil to check the resistance of the low tension windings. The resistance should be between 0.4 ohms and 0.8 ohms. Renew the coil if the resistance is incorrect.
14   With the ignition switched off, disconnect the connector (A) from the computer control unit. Check the resistance of the tachometer by connecting an ohmmeter between terminals 2 and 3. The resistance should be 20 000 ohms. If the resistance is incorrect, check the wiring for a fault or renew the tachometer.
15   If after making the previous checks there is still no HT spark, renew the computer control unit.

Engine misfires

16   First check the HT leads, distributor cap and spark plugs with reference to the relevant sections of this Chapter.
17   Disconnect the main HT lead from the coil at the distributor cap end and hold the end of the lead 20 mm away from the cylinder head using a well insulated pair of pliers. *Do not allow the HT lead to touch the computer control unit.*
18   Spin the engine on the starter motor and check that there are regular strong HT sparks between the HT lead and the cylinder head. If the sparking is good, but the engine still misfires, check the carburation and ignition timing for possible incorrect settings. If there are no sparks, continue with the following checks.
19   Disconnect connector (A) Fig. 5.4 and connect a voltmeter between terminal 1 and earth. Switch on the ignition and attempt to start the engine. The reading on the voltmeter should be at least 9.5

volts. If not, check the battery voltage and recharge if necessary. Also check the computer control unit supply wiring.
20   With the ignition switched off, disconnect the connector (B) Fig. 5.4. Check the resistance of the position/speed sensor by connecting an ohmmeter across terminals 4 and 5. The reading should be 200 ohms ± 50 ohms. If the reading is incorrect, renew the position/speed sensor.
21   Using a feeler blade, check that the clearance between the end of the position/speed sensor (P) and the flywheel (V) is 1.0 ± 0.5 mm. If the clearance is incorrect, renew the position/speed sensor. If it is correct, remove the sensor and clean the magnetic end of the sensor of any oil, dirt or grease. Refit the sensor, but if the misfire still persists renew the sensor.
22   To check the condition of the vacuum capsule on the computer control unit, reconnect all plugs then start the engine and hold its speed steady at 3000 rpm. Pull the vacuum pipe from the capsule and check if the engine speed falls. If it does, the capsule is operating correctly, however if the speed remains constant check the vacuum pipes and the vacuum capsule. If the misfire still persists, renew the computer control unit.
23   On 1721 cc (F2N) engined models there is an additional connector fitted to the computer control unit at position Z, which is linked to the electric cooling fan temperature switch. When the switch is off (ie at coolant temperatures less than 90° C) there should be no voltage at the connector terminals, and the ignition timing is unaffected. If the coolant temperature is greater than 90° C there should be 12 volts at the terminals, and in this state the ignition timing is retarded by 3° ± 2° between engine speeds of 1200 and 4700 rpm and at a vacuum of between 0 to 270 mbar. The ignition timing correction protects the engine against pinking under severe operating conditions.

---

8   Distributor – removal, overhaul and refitting

Removal

1   Mark the spark plug HT leads to aid refitting and pull them off the ends of the plugs. Unscrew the retaining screws and place the distributor cap and leads to one side (photo).
2   On the 1390 cc (E6J) engine, pull the rotor arm off of the distributor shaft and remove the plastic shield, then use a Torx key to unscrew the two mounting bolts and withdraw the distributor from the cylinder head. Note that although the upper mounting bolt hole in the distributor body is slotted, the lower bolt hole is not slotted, so it is not possible to adjust the position of the distributor. Remove the seal from the base of the distributor (photos).
3   On the 1721 cc (F2N) engine the rotor arm is connected directly onto the camshaft. It may be attached by a circlip or alternatively it may be bonded onto the camshaft. To remove the circlip type, prise it carefully off. To remove the bonded type, twist it using a pair of grips – this will break the plastic coating and enable the arm to be removed. Remove the plastic shield.

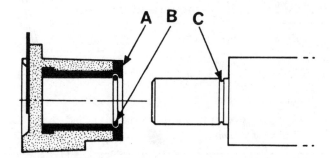

Fig. 5.5 Rotor arm connection to the camshaft on the 1721 cc (F2N) engine – circlip type connection (Sec 8)

A   *Insert*   B   *Circlip*   C   *Groove in the camshaft*

8.1 Unscrewing the distributor cap retaining screws

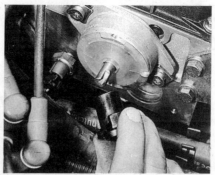

8.2A Removing the rotor arm

8.2B Distributor mounting bolts (arrowed)

8.2C Removing the distributor

8.2D Removing the seal from the base of the distributor

Overhaul

4   Check the rotor arm and distributor cap with reference to Chapter 1 and renew them if necessary.
5   On the 1390 cc (E6J) engine check the amount of play between the distributor shaft and body. This should not be excessive unless the engine has covered a high mileage, however if it is excessive, the complete distributor should be renewed. Check the condition of the seal for the distributor base and renew it if necessary.

Refitting

6   Refitting is a reversal of removal. On the 1721 cc (F2N) engine, do not attempt to bond a rotor arm to a camshaft designed to accept a rotor arm with a circlip.

9 Ignition coil – removal and refitting

Removal

1   Disconnect the HT wire from the coil.
2   Remove the four screws and withdraw the coil from the computer control unit, at the same time disconnecting the LT wiring terminals.

Refitting

3   Refitting is a reversal of removal, but make sure that the wires are fitted securely.

10 Computer control unit – removal and refitting

Removal

1   Disconnect the HT wire from the coil.

10.3 Vacuum hose for the vacuum capsule (arrowed)

2   Disconnect the two 1390 cc (E6J) or three 1721 cc (F2N) connectors from the bottom of the unit.
3   Disconnect the hose from the vacuum advance capsule (photo).
4   Unbolt and remove the computer control unit from the bulkhead.

Refitting

5   Refitting is a reversal of removal.

11   Position/speed sensor – removal and refitting

Removal

1   Disconnect the position/speed sensor wire from the bottom of the computer control unit.
2   Unbolt and remove the ignition position/speed sensor from the aperture at the top of the gearbox bellhousing (photo).

Refitting

3   Refitting is a reversal of removal. It is important to use only the special shouldered bolts to attach the sensor to the gearbox bellhousing as these determine its correct clearance from the flywheel.

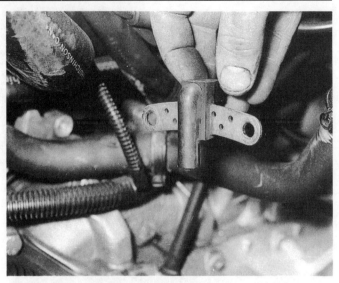

11.2 Removing the position/speed sensor from the top of the gearbox bellhousing

Chapter 6 Clutch

Contents

Specifications

Type .... Single dry plate, self-adjusting cable operation

Clutch disc
Diameter:
    1390 cc (E6J) and 1397 cc (C1J) engines .... 181.5 mm
    1721 cc (F2N) engine .... 200.0 mm
Lining thickness (new, and in compressed position) .... 7.7 mm

Torque wrench settings	**Nm**	**lbf ft**
Clutch cover bolts:		
1390 cc (E6J) and 1397 cc (C1J) engines	18	13
1721 cc (F2N) engine	25	19

1 General information

All manual transmission models are equipped with a cable-operated single dry plate diaphragm spring clutch assembly. The unit consists of a steel cover which is dowelled and bolted to the rear face of the flywheel, and contains the pressure plate and diaphragm spring.

The clutch disc is free to slide along the splined gearbox input shaft and is held in position between the flywheel and the pressure plate by the pressure of the diaphragm spring. Friction lining material is riveted to the clutch disc which has a spring cushioned hub to absorb transmission shocks and help ensure a smooth take-up of the drive.

The clutch is actuated by a cable controlled by the clutch pedal. The clutch release mechanism consists of a release arm and bearing which are in permanent contact with the fingers of the diaphragm spring.

Depressing the clutch pedal actuates the release arm by means of the cable. The arm pushes the release bearing against the diaphragm fingers, so moving the centre of the diaphragm spring inwards. As the centre of the spring is pushed in, the outside of the spring pivots out, so moving the pressure plate backwards and disengaging its grip on the clutch disc.

When the pedal is released, the diaphragm spring forces the pressure plate into contact with the friction linings on the clutch disc. The disc is now firmly sandwiched between the pressure plate and the flywheel, thus transmitting engine power to the gearbox.

Wear of the friction material on the clutch disc is automatically

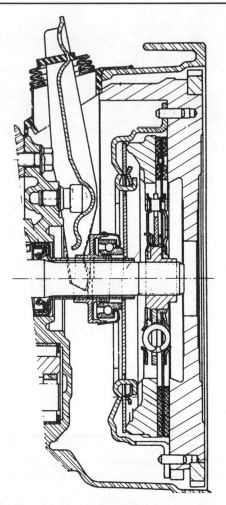

Fig. 6.1 Cross-section of the clutch components (Sec 1)

Alternative types shown

compensated for by a self-adjusting mechanism attached to the clutch pedal. The mechanism consists of a serrated quadrant, a notched cam and a tension spring. One end of the clutch cable is attached to the quadrant which is free to pivot on the pedal, but is kept in tension by the spring. As the pedal is depressed the notched cam contacts the quadrant thus locking it and allowing the pedal to pull the cable and operate the clutch. As the pedal is released the tension spring causes the quadrant to move free of the notched cam and rotate slightly, thus taking up any free play that may exist in the cable.

2   Clutch cable – removal and refitting

Removal

1   Disconnect the battery negative terminal.
2   Disengage the outer cable from the bracket on the bellhousing then slip the cable end out of the release fork (photo).
3   Working inside the car remove the transverse ventilation ducting from under the facia on the right-hand side by cutting the plastic ties and disconnecting the ducting from the heater and outlet.
4   Press the clutch pedal to the floor, and then release it and free the cable end from the serrated quadrant on the self-adjusting mechanism (photo).
5   Remove the cable from the quadrant and then push the outer cable out of its location in the bulkhead using a screwdriver.
6   Pull the cable through into the engine compartment, detach it from the support clips and remove it from the car.

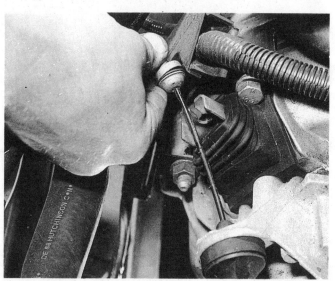

2.2 Disengaging the outer cable from the bracket on the bellhousing

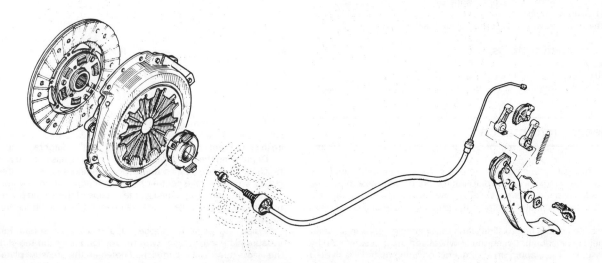

Fig. 6.2 Clutch cable and pedal components (Sec 1)

2.4 Clutch cable end (arrowed) in the quadrant on the self-adjusting mechanism

Fig. 6.3 Checking the clutch inner cable slack at the release fork end (Sec 2)

Refitting

7   To refit the cable thread it through from the engine compartment, lay it over the self-adjusting cam and connect the cable end to the quadrant.
8   Slip the other end of the cable through the bellhousing bracket and into the release fork.
9   Depress the clutch pedal to draw the outer cable into its locating hole in the bulkhead, ensuring that it locates properly.
10   Depress the clutch pedal several times in order to allow the self-adjusting mechanism to set the correct free play.
11   Refit the transverse ventilation ducting under the facia and secure with new plastic ties.
12   When the self-adjusting mechanism on the clutch pedal is functioning correctly there should be a minimum of 20.0 mm slack in the cable. To check this dimension, pull out the inner cable near the release fork on the gearbox as shown in Fig. 6.3. If there is less than the minimum slack in the cable, the self-adjusting mechanism should be checked. Also check that the movement at the top of the release fork is between 17.0 and 18.0 mm as shown in Fig. 6.4. This movement ensures that the clutch pedal stroke is correct. Make sure that the serrated quadrant and support arms are free to turn on their respective pivots, and that the spring has not lost its tension. If necessary check the free length of the spring against a new one. Also check that the inner cable is not seizing in the outer cable.

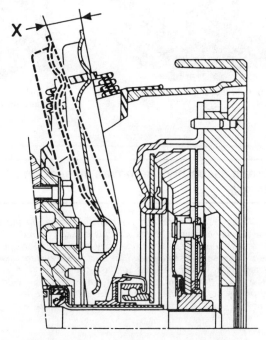

Fig. 6.4 Checking the clutch release fork movement (X) (Sec 2)

3   Clutch pedal – removal and refitting

Removal

1   Disconnect the battery negative terminal.
2   Disconnect the clutch cable at the transmission end by slipping the cable end out of the release fork and disengaging the outer cable from the bracket on the bellhousing.
3   Working inside the car, detach the moulded plastic cover from the pedal bracket assembly.
4   If necessary, the air duct at the base of the facia can be removed to provide greater access by detaching it from the heater unit and vent tube.
5   Press the clutch pedal to the floor and then release it to free the cable end from the serrated quadrant on the pedal self-adjusting mechanism. Lift the cable out of the quadrant and self-adjusting cam on the pedal.
6   Prise off the retaining clips on both ends of the pedal cross-shaft. Slide the shaft out of the pedal bracket, towards the right-hand side of the car, and withdraw the clutch pedal.
7   With the pedal removed, inspect the two bushes and renew them if worn.

Refitting

8   To refit the pedal, place it in position in the pedal bracket and slide the cross-shaft through. Refit the retaining clips at both ends.
9   Lay the clutch cable over the self-adjusting cam and connect the cable end to the quadrant.
10   Slip the other end of the cable through the bellhousing bracket and into the release fork.
11   Turn the quadrant on the self-adjusting mechanism towards the front of the car to introduce some slack in the cable, then depress the clutch pedal several times so that the mechanism self-adjusts.
12   Refit the air duct at the base of the facia, refit the cover over the pedal bracket and reconnect the battery.

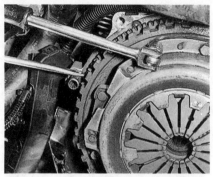

4.2 Unscrewing the clutch cover retaining bolts, showing a screwdriver engaged with the starter ring gear

4.3 Removing the clutch cover and disc from the flywheel

4.5 Clutch disc, showing linings and torsion springs

4.6A Inner view of the clutch pressure plate assembly

4.6B Outer view of the clutch pressure plate assembly

4.15 Using a clutch alignment tool to centralise the clutch disc

4   Clutch assembly – removal, inspection and refitting

Warning: *Dust created by clutch wear and deposited on the clutch components may contain asbestos which is a health hazard. DO NOT blow it out with compressed air or inhale any of it. DO NOT use petrol or petroleum based solvents to clean off the dust. Brake system cleaner or methylated spirit should be used to flush the dust into a suitable receptacle. After the clutch components are wiped clean with rags, dispose of the contaminated rags and cleaner in a sealed, marked container*

Removal

1   Access to the clutch may be gained in one of two ways. Either the engine/transmission unit can be removed, as described in Chapter 2, and the transmission separated from the engine, or the engine may be left in the car and the transmission unit removed independently, as described in Chapter 7.
2   Having separated the transmission from the engine, unscrew and remove the clutch cover retaining bolts, working in a diagonal sequence and slackening the bolts only a few turns at a time. Hold the flywheel stationary by positioning a screwdriver over the front location dowel on the cylinder block and engaging it with the starter ring gear (photo).
3   Ease the clutch cover off its locating dowels and be prepared to catch the clutch disc which will drop out as the cover is removed. Note which way round the disc is fitted (photo).

Inspection

4   With the clutch assembly removed, clean off all traces of asbestos dust using a dry cloth. This is best done outside or in a well-ventilated area; asbestos dust is harmful, and must not be inhaled.
5   Examine the linings of the clutch disc for wear and loose rivets, and

the disc rim for distortion, cracks, broken torsion springs and worn splines (photo). The surface of the friction linings may be highly glazed, but, as long as the friction material pattern can be clearly seen, this is satisfactory. If there is any sign of oil contamination, indicated by a continuous, or patchy, shiny black discoloration, the disc must be renewed and the source of the contamination traced and rectified. This will be either a leaking crankshaft oil seal or gearbox input shaft oil seal, or both. The renewal procedure for the former is given in Chapter 2,

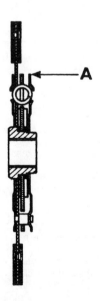

Fig. 6.5 Clutch disc offset (A) (Sec 4)

4.16 Tightening the clutch cover bolts

however renewal of the gearbox input shaft oil seal should be entrusted to a Renault garage as it involves dismantling the gearbox and the renewal of the clutch release bearing guide tube using a press. The disc must also be renewed if the lining thickness has worn down to, or just above, the level of the rivet heads.

6   Check the machined faces of the flywheel and pressure plate. If either is grooved, or heavily scored, renewal is necessary. The pressure plate must also be renewed if any cracks are apparent, or if the diaphragm spring is damaged or its pressure suspect (photos).

7   With the gearbox removed it is advisable to check the condition of the release bearing, as described in Section 5.

Refitting

8   It is important that no oil or grease is allowed to come into contact with the friction material of the clutch disc or the pressure plate and flywheel faces. It is advisable to refit the clutch assembly with clean hands and to wipe down the pressure plate and flywheel faces with a clean dry rag before assembly begins.

9   Begin reassembly by placing the clutch disc against the flywheel with the side having the larger offset facing away from the flywheel.

10   Place the clutch cover over the dowels, refit the retaining bolts and tighten them finger-tight so that the clutch disc is gripped, but can still be moved.

11   The clutch disc must now be centralised so that, when the engine and transmission are mated, the splines of the gearbox input shaft will pass through the splines in the centre of the clutch disc hub.

12   Centralisation can be carried out quite easily by inserting a round bar through the hole in the centre of the clutch disc so that the end of the bar rests in the hole in the end of the crankshaft.

13   Using the support bearing as a fulcrum, moving the bar sideways or up and down will move the clutch disc in whichever direction is necessary to achieve centralisation.

14   Centralisation is easily judged by removing the bar and viewing the clutch disc hub in relation to the support bearing. When the support bearing appears exactly in the centre of the clutch disc hub, all is correct.

15   An alternative and more accurate method of centralisation is to use a commercially available clutch aligning tool obtainable from most accessory shops (photo).

16   Once the clutch is centralised, progressively tighten the cover bolts in a diagonal sequence to the torque setting given in the Specifications (photo).

17   The transmission can now be refitted to the engine by referring to the relevant Chapter of this manual.

5   Clutch release bearing – removal, inspection and refitting

Removal

1   To gain access to the release bearing it is necessary to separate the engine and transmission either by removing the transmission unit individually, or by removing both units as an assembly and separating them after removal. Depending on the method chosen, the appropriate procedures will be found in Chapter 2 or Chapter 7.

2   With the transmission removed from the engine, tilt the release fork and slide the bearing assembly off the gearbox input shaft guide tube.

3   To remove the bearing from its holder, release the four tags of the spring retainer, lift off the retainer and remove the bearing.

4   To remove the release fork, disengage the rubber cover and then pull the fork upwards to release it from its ball pivot stud.

Inspection

5   Check the bearing for smoothness of operation and renew it if there is any roughness or harshness as the bearing is spun.

Refitting

6   Refitting the release fork and release bearing is the reverse sequence to removal, but note the following points:

(a)   *Lubricate the release fork pivot ball stud and the release bearing-to-diaphragm spring contact areas sparingly with molybdenum disulphide grease*

(b)   *Ensure that the release fork spring retainer locates behind the flat shoulder of the ball pivot stud*

Chapter 7 Transmission

Contents

Specifications

Part A: Manual gearbox

Type .... Four or five forward speeds (all synchromesh) and reverse. Final drive differential integral with main gearbox

Designation:
    Four-speed units .... JB0 or JB4
    Five-speed units .... JB1, JB3 or JB5

Gearbox ratios

JB0 and JB4:
    1st .... 3.7 : 1
    2nd .... 2.1 : 1
    3rd .... 1.3 : 1
    4th .... 0.9 : 1
    Reverse .... 3.6 : 1
JB1, JB3 and JB5:
    1st .... 3.7 : 1
    2nd .... 2.1 : 1
    3rd .... 1.3 : 1
    4th .... 1.0 : 1
    5th .... 0.8 : 1
    Reverse .... 3.6 : 1

Final drive ratios

JB0 .... 3.5 : 1
JB4, JB3 and JB5 .... 3.6 : 1
JB1 .... 4.1 : 1

Torque wrench settings

	Nm	lbf ft
Gearbox mounting bolts	40 to 50	30 to 37
Gearchange casing nuts	15	11
Link rod clevis bolt	30	22

Part B: Automatic transmission

Type .... Three forward speeds and reverse. Final drive differential integral with transmission

Designation MB1

Ratios

1st	2.50 : 1
2nd	1.50 : 1
3rd	1.00 : 1
Reverse	2.00 : 1
Final drive	3.87 : 1

Torque wrench settings

	Nm	lbf ft
Driveplate to crankshaft	65	48
Driveplate to torque converter	25	19
Gauze filter	9	7
Sump	6	4
Fluid cooler	40	30
Transmission mounting bolts	40	30

Part A: Manual gearbox

1 General information

The manual gearbox is either of four or five-speed type with one reverse gear. Baulk ring synchromesh gear engagement is used on all the forward gears. The final drive (differential) unit is integral with the main gearbox and is located between the mechanism casing and the clutch and differential housing. The gearbox and differential both share the same lubricating oil.

Gearshift is by means of a floor-mounted lever connected by a remote control housing and gearchange rod to the gearbox fork contact shaft.

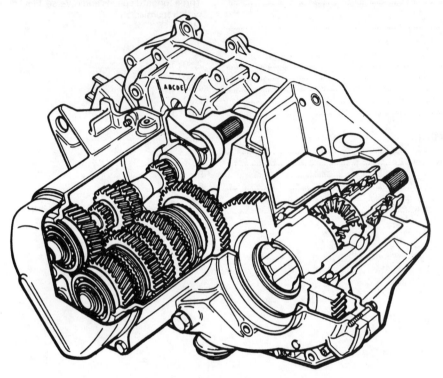

Fig. 7.1 Cutaway view of the four-speed gearbox (Sec 1)

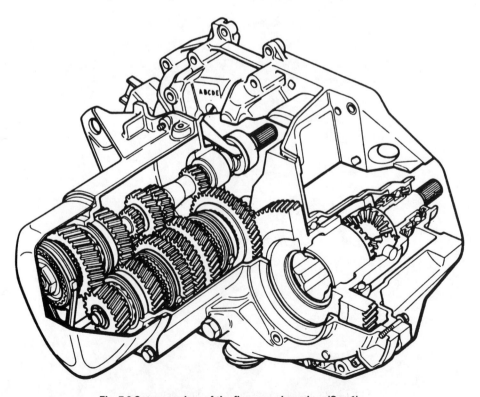

Fig. 7.2 Cutaway view of the five-speed gearbox (Sec 1)

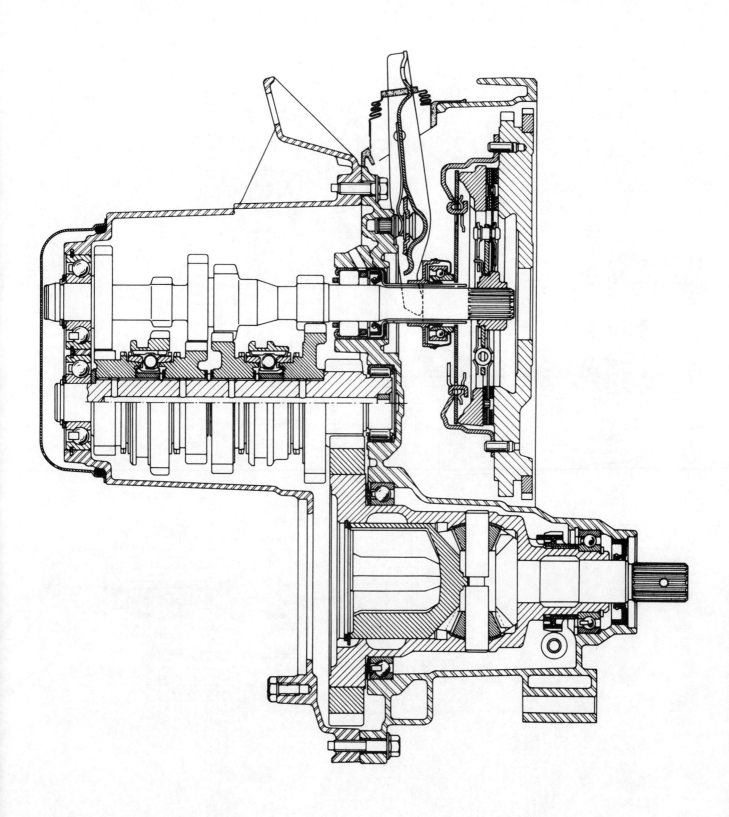

Fig. 7.3 Sectional view of the four-speed gearbox (Sec 1)

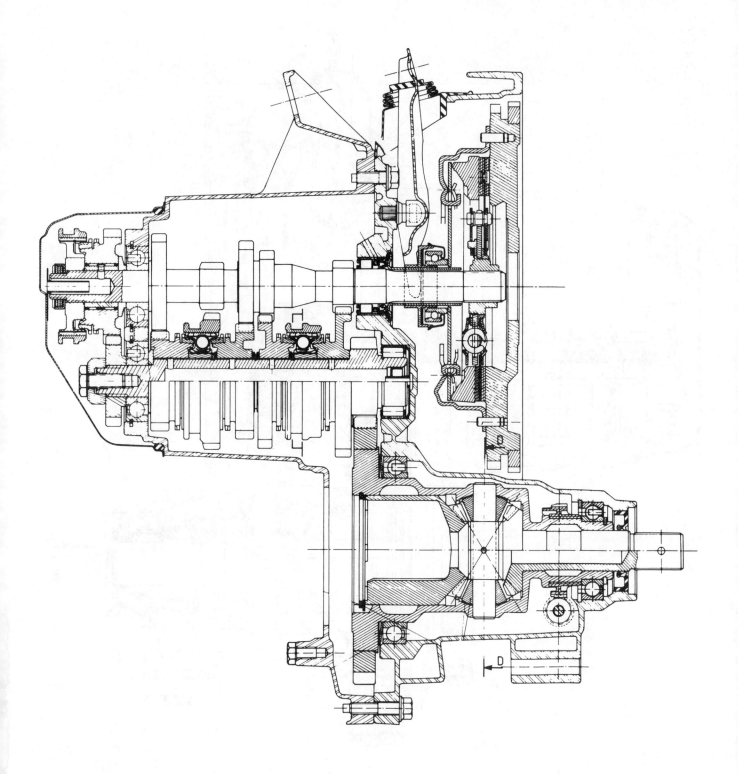

Fig. 7.4 Sectional view of the five-speed gearbox (Sec 1)

**Fig. 7.5 Gearchange linkage/
mechanism components
(Sec 2 and 3)**

1 Link rod
2 Spring returning 3rd/4th
   plane
3 Casing
4 Pad
5 Gear lever assembly
6 Gear lever boot
7 Knob
8 Circlip
9 Bush
10 Sleeve

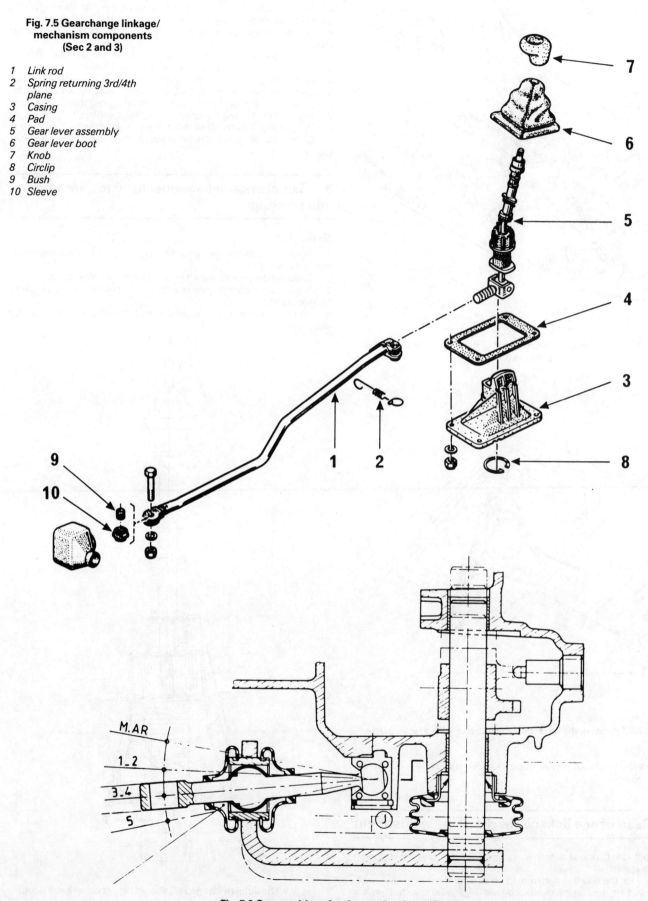

Fig. 7.6 Gear positions for the gearbox lever (Sec 2)

Fig. 7.7 Using the special Renault tool to hold the gearbox lever in position (Sec 2)

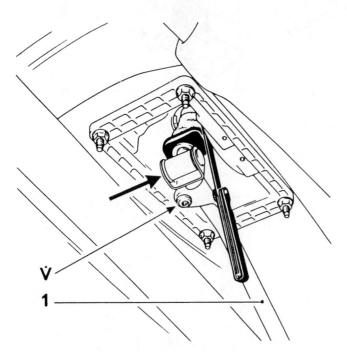

Fig. 7.8 Adjusting the gear lever mechanism with a feeler blade (Sec 2)

1 Link rod   *Arrow indicates direction of pressure*
V Pinch bolt

2   Gearchange linkage/mechanism – adjustment

1   Apply the handbrake then jack up the front of the car and support it on axle stands.
2   Unhook the return spring from the gear lever clevis.
3   Select 1st gear on the gearbox by moving the lever with reference to Fig. 7.6. Renault technicians use a special tool to hold the lever in

position and take up any free play, however a suitable alternative tool can be made from flat metal bar or wood.
4   Loosen the link rod clevis bolt so that the rod can be moved on the clevis.
5   Locate the link rod on the gear lever clevis so that there is approximately 5 mm between the rod and clevis body.
6   Move the gear lever so that the lower latch is against the inclined plane on the casing, then insert a 2 mm feeler blade between the latch and plane. Hold the lever in this position, then tighten the clevis bolt.
7   Remove the holding bar and refit the return spring.
8   Refer to Fig. 7.9 and check that the gap 'Y' is between 2 and 5 mm.
9   Check that all gears can be selected, then lower the car to the ground.

3   Gearchange linkage/mechanism – removal and refitting

Removal

1   Working inside the car, prise the gear lever boot from the centre console (photo).
2   Unscrew the screws and lift off the centre console (photos).
3   Apply the handbrake, then jack up the front of the car and support it on axle stands.
4   Working beneath the car disconnect the flexible exhaust pipe mountings.

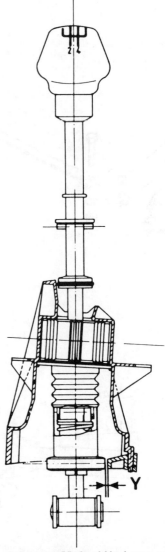

Fig. 7.9 The adjustment gap (Y) should be between 2 and 5 mm (Sec 2)

3.1 Removing the gear lever boot from the centre console

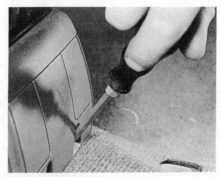

3.2A Remove the centre console rear screws ...

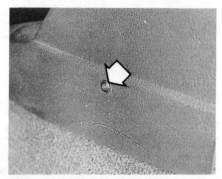

3.2B ... and side screws (arrowed)

3.2C View of the gear lever and casing with the centre console removed

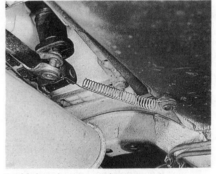

3.5 Link rod return spring

5   Unhook the return spring from the link rod (photo).
6   Pull back the rubber boot from the front end of the link rod, then unscrew and remove the bolt and disconnect the rod from the gearbox lever. Recover the bush and sleeve.
7   Unscrew and remove the nuts securing the casing assembly to the body, then lower the assembly while pulling the exhaust system to one side.
8   Mark the link rod and gear lever clevis in relation to each other. Unscrew the pinch bolt and remove the rod from the clevis.
9   Grip the gear lever in a vice, then remove the knob and gear lever boot. The knob is bonded to the lever and may be hard to remove.
10   Extract the circlip from the bottom of the gear lever and withdraw the lever and latch from the casing.

Refitting

11   Refitting is a reversal of removal, but lubricate the pivot points with grease and use suitable adhesive to bond the knob to the lever. Finally adjust the gear shift as described in Section 2.

4   Speedometer drive – removal and refitting

Removal

1   Remove the left-hand driveshaft with reference to Chapter 8.
2   Extract the circlip and thrust washer, then withdraw the left-hand differential sunwheel. The sunwheel also acts as the driveshaft spider housing.
3   Turn the differential until the planet wheels are in a vertical plane so that the speedometer drive gear is visible.
4   Pull out the clip and disconnect the speedometer cable from the outside of the gearbox.

5   Using long-nosed pliers, extract the speedometer drivegear shaft vertically from the outside of the gearbox.
6   Using the same pliers, extract the speedometer drivegear from inside the differential housing being very careful not to drop it.
7   Examine the drivegear teeth for wear and damage and renew it if necessary. Note that if the drivegear teeth on the differential are worn or damaged, it will be necessary to dismantle the gearbox, and this work should be entrusted to a Renault dealer.

Refitting

8   Using the pliers, insert the speedometer drivegear into its location.

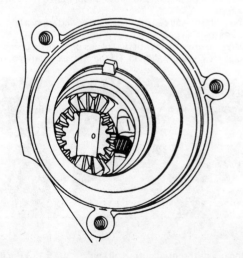

Fig. 7.10 View of the speedometer drive gear with the differential sun wheel removed (Sec 4)

9   From outside the gearbox, refit the drivegear shaft making sure that it engages with the gear location notches correctly.
10   Refit the speedometer cable and secure with the clip.
11   Insert the differential sunwheel, then refit the thrust washer and circlip.
12   Refit the left-hand driveshaft with reference to Chapter 8.

5 Differential output oil seal (right-hand side) – renewal

1   Apply the handbrake then jack up the front of the car and support it on axle stands. Remove the roadwheel on the appropriate side.
2   Remove the engine splash guard, where applicable.
3   Position a suitable container beneath the gearbox, then unscrew the drain plug and allow the oil to drain. When most of the oil has drained, clean and refit the drain plug, tightening it securely.
4   Using a suitable punch, drive out the double roll pins securing the inner end of the right-hand driveshaft to the splined differential side gear.
5   Unscrew the nut securing the steering tie-rod end to the steering arm, then use a balljoint removal tool to separate the balljoint taper.
6   Refer to Chapter 9 and unbolt the brake caliper from the stub axle carrier. Do not disconnect the hydraulic hose from the caliper. Tie the caliper to the suspension coil spring without straining the hydraulic hose.
7   Loosen only the lower bolt securing the stub axle carrier to the bottom of the suspension strut. Unscrew and remove the upper bolt, then tilt the stub axle carrier and disconnect the driveshaft. Take care not to damage the driveshaft rubber bellows.
8   Wipe clean the old oil seal and measure its fitted depth below the casing edge. This is necessary to determine the correct fitted position of the new oil seal if the special Renault fitting tool is not being used.
9   Remove the old oil seal by first using a small drift to tap the outer edge of the seal inwards so that the opposite edge of the seal tilts out of the casing (photo). A pair of pliers or grips can then be used to pull the oil seal out of the casing. Take care not to damage the splines of the differential side gear.
10   Wipe clean the oil seal seating in the casing.
11   Before fitting the new oil seal it is necessary to cover the splines on the side gear to prevent damage to the oil seal lips. Ideally a close-fitting plastic cap should be located on the splines, however if this is not available wrap some adhesive tape over them to serve the same purpose.
12   Smear a little grease on the lips of the new oil seal and on the protective cap or tape.
13   Carefully locate the new oil seal over the side gear and enter it squarely into the casing. Using a piece of metal tube or a socket tap the oil seal into position to its correct depth as previously noted (photos). Renault use a special tool to ensure that the oil seal is fitted to the correct depth, and it may be possible to hire this tool from a Renault garage or tool hire shop.
14   Remove the plastic cap or adhesive tape and apply a little grease to the splines of the side gear.
15   Engage the driveshaft with the splines on the side gear so that the roll pin holes are correctly aligned. Tilt the stub axle carrier and slide the

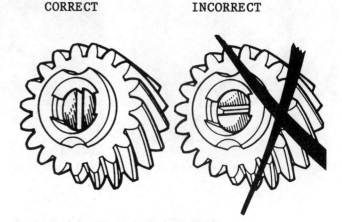

Fig. 7.11 Engagement of the speedometer drivegear shaft with the gear location notches (Sec 4)

driveshaft onto the side gear, making sure that it enters the oil seal centrally.
16   With the holes aligned, tap the double roll pins into position to secure. Seal the ends of the roll pins with a suitable sealant.
17   Refit the upper bolt securing the stub axle carrier to the bottom of the suspension strut, then tighten both upper and lower bolts to the specified torque (see Chapter 10).
18   Refit the brake caliper to the stub axle carrier and tighten the bolts to the specified torque with reference to Chapter 9.
19   Clean the track rod arm balljoint taper and the steering arm, then refit the balljoint to the arm and tighten the nut to the specified torque (see Chapter 10).
20   Refill the gearbox with the correct quantity and grade of oil with reference to Chapter 1.
21   Refit the engine splash guard, where applicable.
22   Refit the roadwheel and lower the car to the ground.

6 Reversing lamp switch – removal and refitting

Removal

1   Apply the handbrake then jack up the front of the car and support it on axle stands.
2   Where applicable, remove the engine splash guard.
3   Position a suitable container beneath the gearbox, then unscrew the drain plug and allow the oil to drain. When all of the oil has drained, clean and refit the drain plug, tightening it securely.
4   Disconnect the wiring from the reversing lamp switch.
5   Unscrew the switch from the bottom left-hand side of the gearbox and remove the washer.

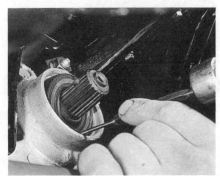

5.9 Tap the old differential output oil seal with a small drift to remove it

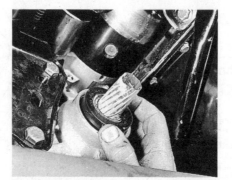

5.13A Position the new differential output oil seal on the gearbox ...

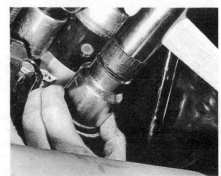

5.13B ... and drive it in with a socket or metal tube

7.4 Unscrewing the gearbox oil drain plug

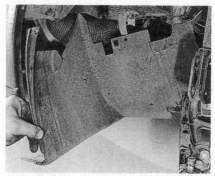

7.9 Removing the left-hand inner wing protective cover

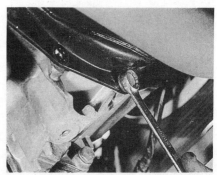

7.15 Unscrew the engine-to-gearbox tie-rod bracket bolts at the gearbox ...

7.16 ... and at the engine

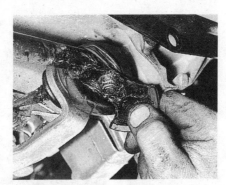

7.17A Pull back the rubber boot ...

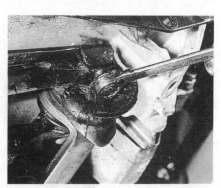

7.17B ... then unbolt the gear lever rod from the lever on the gearbox

7.19 Reversing light switch (arrowed)

7.24 Unscrewing the engine-to-gearbox nuts and bolts

Refitting

6 Clean the location in the gearbox and the threads of the switch.
7 Insert the switch together with a new washer and fully tighten it.
8 Reconnect the wiring.
9 Refill the gearbox with the correct quantity and grade of oil with reference to Chapter 1.
10 Refit the engine splash guard, where applicable.
11 Lower the car to the ground.

7 Manual gearbox – removal and refitting

Note: *This Section describes the removal of the gearbox leaving the engine in position in the car, however if an adequate lifting hoist is available it may be easier to remove both the engine and the gearbox together as described in Chapter 2 and then to separate the gearbox from the engine on the bench*

Removal

1 The manual gearbox is removed upwards from the engine compartment after disconnecting it from the engine. Due to the weight of the unit, it will be necessary to have some form of lifting equipment available, such as an engine crane or suitable hoist to enable the unit to be removed in this way.
2 Apply the handbrake then jack up the front of the car and support it on axle stands. Remove both the front roadwheels.
3 Where applicable, remove the engine splash guard.
4 Position a suitable container beneath the gearbox, then unscrew the drain plug and allow the oil to drain (photo). When all of the oil has drained, clean and refit the drain plug, tightening it securely.
5 Disconnect the battery negative lead.
6 Unscrew the nut securing the left-hand steering tie-rod end to the steering arm, then use a balljoint removal tool to separate the balljoint taper.
7 Working in the engine compartment, unscrew the three bolts securing the left-hand driveshaft inner rubber boot to the gearbox.

7.26 Removing the left-hand front engine mounting assembly

7.27 Engine earth strap (arrowed)

7.30 Radiator moved to the right-hand side for the removal of the gearbox

7.31 Using two nuts to unscrew the gearbox location studs

7.35 Lifting the gearbox from the engine compartment

8   Refer to Chapter 9 and unbolt the left-hand brake caliper from the stub axle carrier. Do not disconnect the hydraulic hose from the caliper. Tie the caliper to the suspension coil spring without straining the hydraulic hose.
9   Unbolt the front left-hand inner wing protective cover. There are two Torx screws and one self-tapping screw (photo).
10   Unscrew and remove the pinch bolt securing the front lower balljoint to the bottom of the stub axle carrier.
11   Support the weight of the stub axle carrier and driveshaft on a trolley jack, then unscrew the two bolts and separate the knuckle from the bottom of the suspension strut.
12   Withdraw the left-hand driveshaft and stub axle carrier from the gearbox. Make sure that the tripod components remain in position on the inner end of the driveshaft, otherwise they may fall into the gearbox.
13   Working on the right-hand side driveshaft, use a suitable punch to drive out the roll pins.
14   Loosen only the lower bolt securing the right-hand stub axle carrier to the bottom of the suspension strut. Unscrew and remove the upper bolt, then tilt the stub axle carrier and disconnect the driveshaft.
15   Unscrew and remove the bolts securing the engine-to-gearbox tie-rod bracket to the gearbox (photo).
16   Loosen the tie-rod mounting bolts on the engine, or alternatively remove them and remove the tie-rod completely (photo).
17   Cut the plastic tie and pull back the rubber boot, then disconnect the gear lever rod from the lever on the gearbox by unscrewing the nut and removing the bolt (photos). Recover the bush from inside the lever.
18   Disconnect the wiring from the starter motor (except on the 1390 cc/ E6J engine).
19   Pull the wiring connector from the reversing light switch (photo).
20   Refer to Chapter 1 and remove the air cleaner unit and its mounting.
21   Unbolt and remove the ignition position/speed sensor from the aperture at the top of the gearbox bellhousing and position the lead to one side.
22   Pull the clutch inner cable out from the outer cable, then disconnect the cable from the release lever and withdraw it from the

bracket on the gearbox. Position it to one side.
23   Disconnect the speedometer cable by pulling out the pin and pulling the cable up from the gearbox.
24   Unscrew and remove the gearbox-to-engine nuts and bolts from around the gearbox and from the starter motor (photo). There is no need to remove the starter motor.
25   Connect a suitable hoist to the engine and lift it slightly. Alternatively the engine may be supported on a trolley jack so that the hoist can be used to remove the gearbox.
26   Unbolt the left-hand front engine mounting assembly from the gearbox and from the front crossmember (photo).
27   Unbolt the engine earth strap from the body, beneath the left-hand front wing (photo).
28   Unscrew the bolts securing the rear centre engine mounting bracket to the gearbox and move it to the rear as far as possible. The bracket may be removed completely if necessary, by moving the engine forward and withdrawing the bracket upwards.
29   Slightly raise the gearbox using a further trolley jack.
30   The radiator must now be moved to one side, although it is not necessary to drain the coolant or disconnect any of the hoses. First disconnect the wiring from the cooling fan motor and the thermostatic switch. Unscrew the radiator mountings and move the radiator to the right-hand side (photo). Use a piece of cardboard to protect the radiator matrix from damage as it is quite fragile.
31   Remove the gearbox location studs by using a nut and locknut to unscrew each of them from their locations on the front and rear of the bellhousing (photo). The front stud protrudes to the left-hand side and the rear stud protrudes to the right-hand side at the rear of the engine. (See Fig. 2.30)
32   On models with power-assisted steering, remove the two clips holding the PAS hose to the body panel and crossmember.
33   Support the weight of the gearbox on a trolley jack. Disconnect the gearbox from the engine while sliding the 5th speed housing between the engine crossmember and the side panel beneath the left-hand front wing. Careful use of a wide-blade screwdriver may be necessary to free the bellhousing from the location dowels.

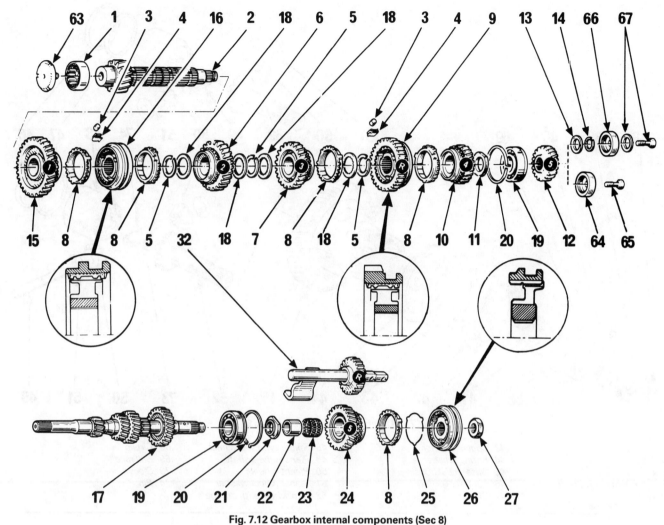

Fig. 7.12 Gearbox internal components (Sec 8)

1 Roller race	10 4th speed gear	19 Ball race	32 Reverse shaft and gear
2 Output shaft	11 Washer	20 Circlip	63 Oil baffle
3 Roller	12 5th speed gear	21 Washer	64 Thrust washer
4 Spring	13 Washer	22 5th speed ring	65 5th speed end bolt on
5 Circlip	14 5th speed circlip	23 Needle race	output shaft
6 2nd speed gear	15 1st speed gear	24 5th speed gear (primary)	66 Shouldered washer
7 3rd speed gear	16 1st/2nd gear hub	25 5th speed spring	67 Retaining bolt and washer
8 Synchro ring	17 Input shaft	26 5th speed gear hub	
9 3rd/4th gear hub	18 Splined ring	27 5th speed nut	

34 Raise the engine slightly and move it to the rear, then turn the gearbox to the front and release it from the engine.

35 Attach a hoist to the gearbox. Connect one end to the clutch cable mounting lug, and connect the other end to a bolt temporarily fitted to the gearbox. Lift the gearbox from the engine compartment (photo).

Refitting

36 Refitting is a reversal of removal but note the following additional points:

(a) *Make sure that the location studs are correctly positioned in the gearbox. Note that their positions are different for the different engine types*

(b) *Apply a little high melting-point grease to the splines of the gearbox input shaft. Do not apply too much otherwise there is the possibility of the grease contaminating the clutch friction disc. Make sure that the clutch release bearing is correctly located on the release arm*

(c) *Fit new roll pins to the right-hand driveshaft and seal the ends using a suitable sealant*

(d) *Refit and tighten the brake caliper mounting bolts with reference to Chapter 9*

(e) *Replenish the gearbox with oil and check the level with reference to Chapter 1*

(f) *Tighten all nuts and bolts to the specified torque*

8 Manual gearbox overhaul – general information

Overhauling a manual gearbox is a difficult and involved job for the DIY home mechanic. In addition to dismantling and reassembling many small parts, clearances must be precisely measured and, if necessary, changed by selecting shims and spacers. Gearbox internal components are also often difficult to obtain and in many instances, extremely expensive. Because of this, if the gearbox develops a fault or becomes noisy, the best course of action is to have the unit overhauled by a

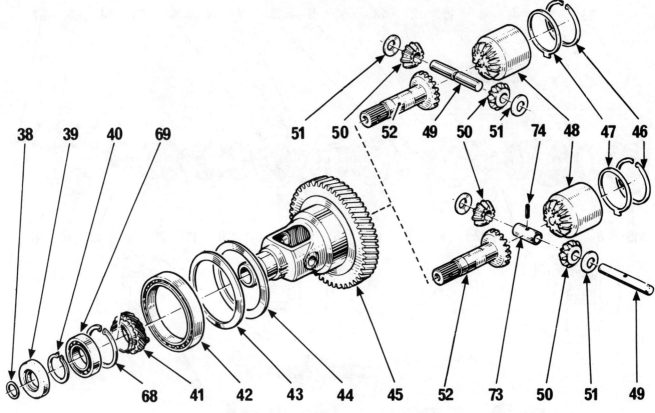

Fig. 7.13 Differential components (Sec 8)

38 O-ring	43 Spacer washer	48 Spider type sun wheel	68 Circlip
39 Oil seal	44 Spring washer	49 Planet wheel shaft	69 Ball race
40 Circlip	45 Differential housing	50 Planet wheels	73 Sleeve
41 Speedometer drive gear	46 Circlip	51 Planet wheel washer	74 Pin
42 Ball race	47 Shim	52 Sun wheel with tail shaft	

specialist repairer or to obtain an exchange reconditioned unit.

Nevertheless, it is not impossible for the more experienced mechanic to overhaul a gearbox if the special tools are available and the job is done in a deliberate step-by-step manner so that nothing is overlooked.

The tools necessary for an overhaul include internal and external circlip pliers, bearing pullers, a slide-hammer, a set of pin punches, a dial test indicator and possibly a hydraulic press. In addition, a large, sturdy workbench and a vice will be required.

During dismantling of the gearbox, make careful notes of how each component is fitted to make reassembly easier and accurate.

Before dismantling the gearbox, it will help if you have some idea what area is malfunctioning. Certain problems can be closely related to specific areas in the gearbox which can make component examination and replacement easier. Refer to the Fault diagnosis Section at the beginning of this manual for more information.

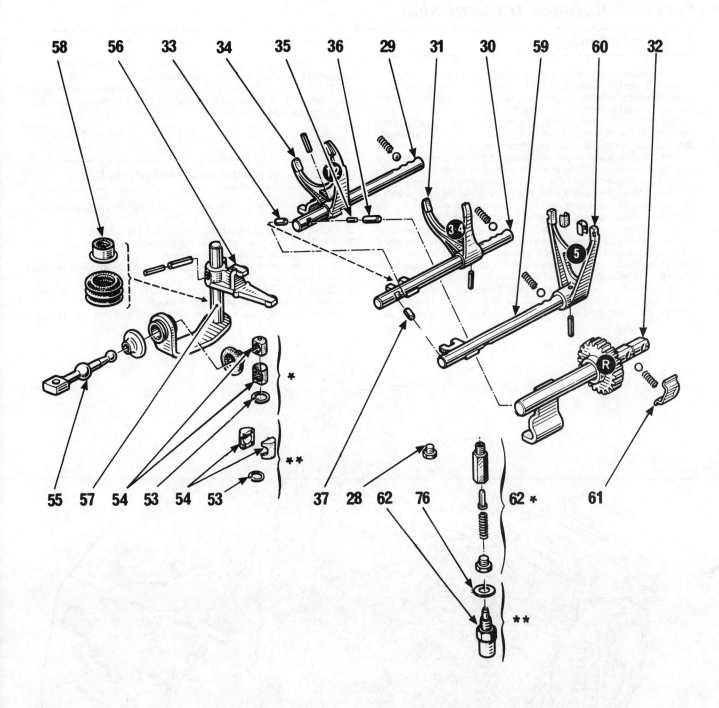

Fig. 7.14 Gear selector components (Sec 8)

Note: * = 1st type,
         ** = 2nd type
28 Threaded stop (four-speed)
29 1st/2nd shift rod
30 3rd/4th shift rod
31 3rd/4th gear fork
32 Reverse shaft

33 Plunger between 1st/2nd
     and 3rd/4th
34 1st/2nd shift fork
35 1st/2nd plunger
36 Plunger between 1st/2nd
     and reverse
37 5th speed plunger
     (five-speed)

53 Circlip
54 Link support
55 Link
56 Selector finger
57 Input shaft
58 Bush
59 5th speed rod (five-speed)

60 5th speed shift fork
     (five-speed)
61 Reverse stirrup
62 5th speed detent assembly
     (five-speed)
76 5th speed detent shim
     washer

Part B: Automatic transmission

9 General information

A three-speed fully automatic transmission is available as an option on the 1. 4 litre GTS and TSE models. The transmission consists of a torque converter, an epicyclic geartrain, hydraulically-operated clutches and brakes, and an electronic control unit.

The torque converter provides a fluid coupling between engine and transmission which acts as an automatic clutch, and also provides a degree of torque multiplication when accelerating.

The epicyclic geartrain provides either of the three forward or one reverse gear ratios according to which of its component parts are held stationary or allowed to turn. The components of the geartrain are held or released by brakes and clutches which are activated by a hydraulic control unit. An oil pump within the transmission provides the necessary hydraulic pressure to operate the brakes and clutches.

Impulses from switches and sensors connected to the transmission throttle and selector linkage are directed to a computer module which determines the ratio to be selected from the information received. The computer activates solenoid valves which in turn open or close ducts within the hydraulic control unit. This causes the clutches and brakes to hold or release the various components of the geartrain and provide the correct ratio for the particular engine speed or load. The information from the computer module can be overridden by use of the selector lever and a particular gear can be held if required, regardless of engine speed.

The automatic transmission fluid is cooled by passing it through a sealed tank within the cooling system radiator.

Due to the complexity of the automatic transmission any repair or overhaul work must be left to a Renault dealer with the necessary special equipment for fault diagnosis and repair.

10 Selector mechanism – adjustment

1   Apply the handbrake, then jack up the front of the car and support it on axle stands.
2   Move the selector lever inside the car to the D position.
3   Working under the car remove the protective cover from under the selector lever, then disconnect the cable end fitting from the lever.
4   Check that the transmission is in the D position and if necessary move the lever accordingly.
5   Refer to Fig. 7.19 and check that the dimension between the cable end fitting and the outer cable location bracket is 131 mm. If this is not the case, loosen the two bracket mounting nuts and move the bracket

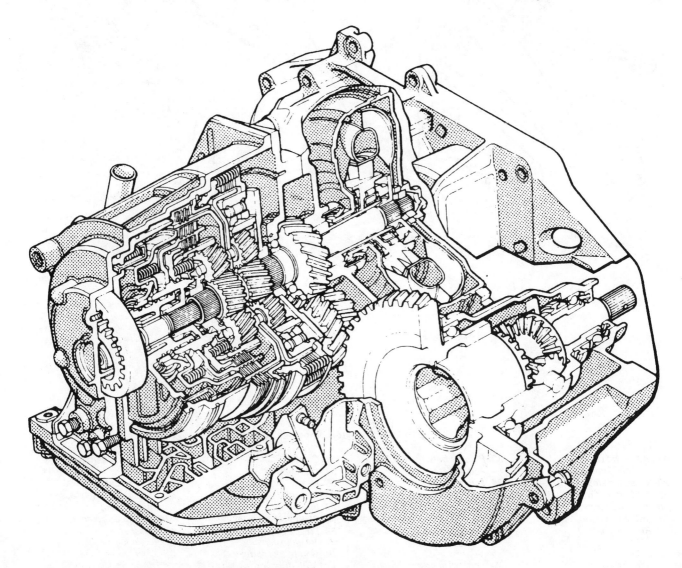

Fig. 7.15 Cutaway view of the automatic transmission (Sec 9)

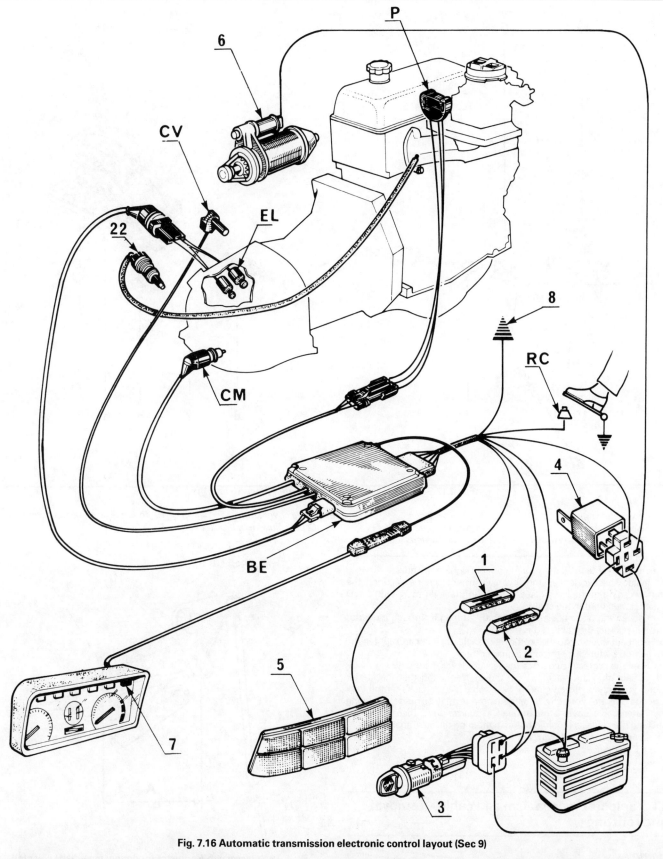

Fig. 7.16 Automatic transmission electronic control layout (Sec 9)

1 Fuse – reversing lamp (5 amp)	5 Reversing lamps	22 Vacuum capsule	EL Solenoid valves
2 Fuse (1.5 amp)	6 Starter	BE Computer module	RC Kick-down switch
3 Ignition switch	7 Automatic transmission warning lamp	CM Multi-function switch	P Load potentiometer
4 Starter relay	8 Automatic transmission earth	CV Speed sensor	

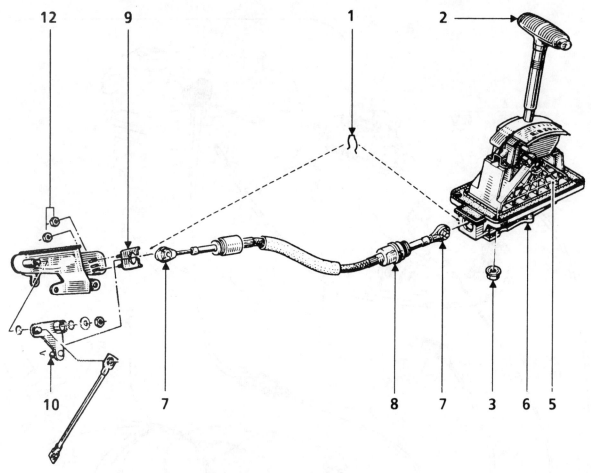

Fig. 7.17 Selector mechanism components (Secs 10 and 11)

1 Cable retaining clips	5 Control casing	8 Cable cover stop	10 Intermediate selector lever
2 Selector lever	6 Protective cover	9 Cable adjustment bracket	12 Nuts
3 Assembly mounting nuts	7 Cable end fittings		

as necessary until the dimension is correct. Tighten the nuts.

6   Inside the car, loosen the four adjustment screws securing the control casing to the lower assembly. Align the lever mark with the D position then tighten the screws.

7   Loosen the outer cable cover stop by turning it through a quarter turn. Check that the cable slides freely.

8   Connect the cable to the bottom of the selector lever and tighten the cover stop by turning it through a quarter turn.

9   Refit the protective cover to the selector lever assembly.

10   Check that the selector lever moves freely and that the starter motor will only operate with P or N selected. Also check that the Park function operates correctly. Small adjustments may be made by turning the outer cable cover stop through a quarter turn, then pulling or pushing the cable as required before tightening the stop again.

11   Lower the car to the ground.

11   Selector mechanism and cable – removal and refitting

Removal

1   Apply the handbrake, then jack up the front of the car and support it on axle stands.

2   Inside the car, move the selector lever to position D.

3   Remove the selector lever by pulling it hard upwards.

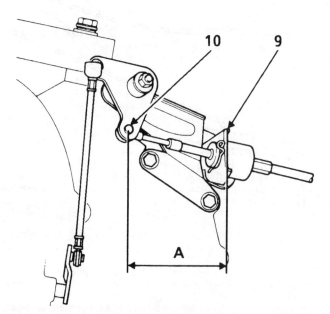

Fig. 7.18 Selector cable adjustment dimension with D selected (Sec 10)

A = 131 mm	10 Cable end fitting centre
9 Cable adjustment bracket	point

4   Working under the car remove the protective cover from under the selector lever.
5   Disconnect the cable end fittings from the bottom of the selector lever and from the intermediate lever on the transmission.
6   Unscrew the four nuts securing the selector lever assembly to the underbody, then lower the assembly.
7   Extract the clips and withdraw the cable from the selector lever assembly and from the transmission.

Refitting

8   Refitting is a reversal of removal, but adjust the cable as described in Section 10.

12   Speedometer drive – removal and refitting

Refer to Section 4.

13   Differential output oil seal (right-hand side) – renewal

Refer to Section 5.

14   Multi-function switch – removal and refitting

Refer to Section 6, but top up the transmission fluid with reference to Chapter 1.

15   Automatic transmission – removal and refitting

Removal

1   Disconnect the battery negative lead.
2   Drain the cooling system as described in Chapter 1.
3   Drain the automatic transmission fluid as described in Chapter 1.
4   For better access, remove the bonnet with reference to Chapter 11.
5   Remove the radiator and expansion tank as described in Chapter 3.
6   Remove the electronic ignition unit with reference to Chapter 5.
7   Remove the air cleaner assembly as described in Chapter 4.
8   Unbolt and remove the strengthening bar from between the front suspension strut turrets.
9   Remove the front wheels.
10   Remove the left-hand brake caliper with reference to Chapter 9, but leave the hydraulic hose connected. Tie the caliper to the front suspension coil with wire or string, taking care not to strain the hose.
11   Disconnect the left-hand steering track rod end from the stub axle carrier with reference to Chapter 10.
12   Unscrew the three bolts which attach the left-hand driveshaft inner gaiter retaining plate to the transmission.
13   Unscrew and remove the two bolts securing the left-hand stub axle carrier to the suspension strut. Note that the nuts are on the brake caliper side.
14   Unscrew the nut and withdraw the clamp bolt securing the left-hand lower suspension arm balljoint to the base of the stub axle carrier.
15   Release the stub axle carrier from the strut and then lift it out together with the driveshaft taking care not to damage the constant velocity joints. Push down on the suspension arm to disengage the lower balljoint.
16   Working on the right-hand side of the car, use a parallel pin punch to drive out the double roll pin securing the inner driveshaft joint yoke to

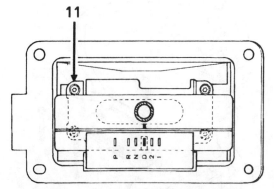

Fig. 7.19 Control casing on the selector assembly (Sec 10)

11   Adjustment nuts

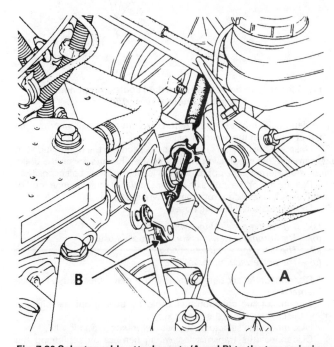

Fig. 7.20 Selector cable attachments (A and B) to the transmission (Sec 15)

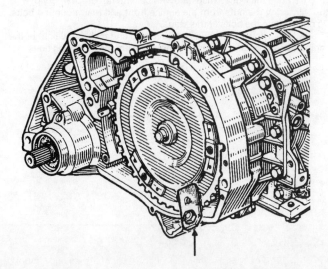

Fig. 7.21 Torque converter retaining plate (arrowed) attached to the transmission (Sec 15)

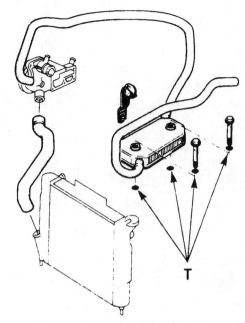

Fig. 7.22 Automatic transmission fluid cooler components and sealing O-rings (T) (Sec 15)

the differential sunwheel stub shaft. Drive out the small inner roll pin first, then drive out the outer roll pin.

17   Unscrew the two nuts from the bolts securing the right-hand stub axle carrier to the suspension strut. Note that the nuts are on the brake caliper side. Remove the upper bolt, but leave the lower bolt in position.

18   Pull the top of the stub axle carrier outwards until the inner end of the driveshaft is released from the sun wheel stub shaft.

19   Disconnect the following hoses:

   (a)   The heater hoses at the water pump
   (b)   The automatic transmission fluid cooler hoses
   (c)   The fuel supply and return hoses
   (d)   The brake vacuum servo hose

20   Disconnect the accelerator cable and choke cables with reference to Chapter 4.

21   Disconnect the speedometer cable by pulling out the pin and pulling the cable up from the gearbox.

22   Disconnect the selector cable with reference to Section 11.

23   Disconnect the transmission wiring harness by separating the connector at the bulkhead. Also detach the earth cables.

24   Remove the strap securing the electronic unit to the transmission.

25   Remove the front exhaust downpipe with reference to Chapter 4.

26   Unscrew the nuts from the engine front and rear mounting bolts. Do not remove the bolts at this stage.

27   Attach a hoist to the engine lifting eyes and take the weight of the engine/transmission assembly. Remove the engine mounting bolts.

28   Lift the engine/automatic transmission assembly from the engine compartment taking care not to damage the surrounding components. Lower the assembly onto the ground or onto a workbench.

29   To separate the automatic transmission from the engine first remove the starter motor with reference to Chapter 12.

30   Unbolt the protection plate from the bottom of the transmission.

31   Unscrew and remove the bolts securing the drive plate to the torque converter while holding the starter ring gear stationary with a wide-bladed screwdriver engaged with the ring gear teeth. Turn the ring gear as required to bring each of the bolts into view.

32   Refer to Fig. 7.22 and attach a home-made retaining plate to the transmission in order to keep the torque converter in position while pulling the transmission from the engine. This is important because the torque converter could be seriously damaged if it is dropped. The retaining plate will also be necessary when refitting the transmission, in order to keep the torque converter engaged with the transmission pump.

33   Unscrew and remove the transmission-to-engine nuts and bolts, and withdraw the transmission from the engine.

34   If necessary unbolt the fluid cooler from the transmission and remove the sealing O-rings.

Refitting

35   Refitting is a reversal of removal but note the following additional points:

   (a)   *Tighten all nuts and bolts to the specified torques (where applicable)*
   (b)   *Refer to Chapter 9 when refitting the front brake caliper*
   (c)   *Make sure that the torque converter is fully engaged with the transmission pump before refitting the transmission to the engine*
   (d)   *If necessary adjust the selector cable with reference to Section 10*
   (e)   *When refitting the fluid cooler, check and if necessary renew the sealing O-rings*
   (f)   *Fill the automatic transmission with fluid with reference to Chapter 1*
   (g)   *Fill the cooling system with reference to Chapter 1*
   (h)   *Adjust the accelerator and choke cables with reference to Chapter 4*

16   Automatic transmission overhaul – general information

In the event of a fault occurring on the transmission, it is first necessary to determine whether it is of an electrical, mechanical or hydraulic nature, and to do this special test equipment is required. It is therefore essential to have the work carried out by a Renault dealer if a transmission fault is suspected, or if the transmission warning lamp on the instrument panel illuminates.

Do not remove the transmission from the car for possible repair before professional fault diagnosis has been carried out, since most tests require the transmission to be in the vehicle.

Chapter 8 Driveshafts

Contents

Specifications

Type .... Equal length solid driveshafts with spider-and-yoke or six-ball constant velocity joints

Lubrication

Lubricant type/specification .... Mobil CVJ 825 Black star or Mobil EXF57C (supplied with new Renault gaiters)

Lubricant quantity:
    Outer constant velocity joint:
        GE 86 .... 295 g
        GE 76 .... 180 g
    Inner constant velocity joint:
        GI 62 .... 130 g
        RC 490 .... 160 g

Torque wrench settings

	Nm	lbf ft
Driveshaft nut	250	185
Left-hand driveshaft gaiter retaining plate bolts	25	19

1 General information

Drive is transmitted from the differential to the front wheels by means of two, equal length, solid steel driveshafts.

Both driveshafts are fitted with a constant velocity joint at their outer ends which may be of spider-and-yoke type or of six-ball coupling type. The constant velocity joint consists of the stub axle member which is splined to engage with the front wheel hub, and either a spider containing needle roller bearings and cups, or six balls within a cage, which engage with the driveshaft yoke. The complete assembly is protected by a rubber gaiter secured to the driveshaft and stub axle member.

At the driveshaft inner ends a different arrangement is used on each side. On the right-hand side the driveshaft is splined to engage with a spider, also containing needle roller bearings and cups. The spider is free to slide within the joint yoke which is splined and retained by a roll pin to the differential sun wheel stub shaft. As on the outer joints, a rubber gaiter secured to the driveshaft and yoke protects the complete assembly.

On the left-hand side the driveshaft also engages with a spider, but the yoke in which the spider is free to slide is an integral part of the differential sun wheel. On this side the rubber gaiter is secured to the transmission casing with a retaining plate and to a ball-bearing on the driveshaft with a retaining clip. The bearing allows the driveshaft to turn within the gaiter, which does not revolve.

The design and construction of the driveshaft components is such

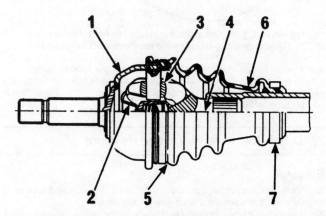

Fig. 8.1 Sectional view of the spider-and-yoke type outer constant velocity joint (Sec 1)

1	Stub axle member	5	Retaining clip
2	Starplate	6	Gaiter
3	Spider	7	Retaining clip
4	Yoke		

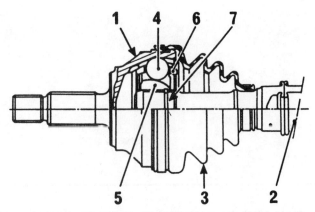

Fig. 8.2 Sectional view of the six-ball type outer constant velocity joint (Sec 1)

1	Stub axle member	5	Hub
2	Driveshaft	6	Ball cage
3	Gaiter	7	Retaining clip
4	Balls		

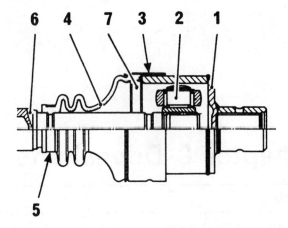

Fig. 8.3 Sectional view of the inner constant velocity joint – right-hand side shown (Sec 1)

1	Yoke	5	Retaining clip
2	Spider	6	Driveshaft
3	Metal cover	7	Metal insert
4	Gaiter		

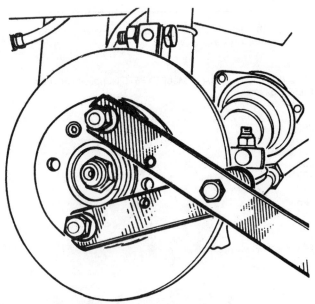

Fig. 8.4 Using two lengths of metal bar to hold the front hub stationary when unscrewing the driveshaft nut (Sec 2)

Fig. 8.5 Using an extractor to push the driveshaft out of the front hub (Sec 2)

that the only repairs possible are renewal of the rubber gaiters and renewal of the inner joint spiders. Wear or damage to the outer constant velocity joints or the driveshaft splines can only be rectified by fitting a complete new driveshaft assembly.

2 Driveshaft – removal and refitting

Removal

1   Apply the handbrake, then jack up the front of the car and support it on axle stands. Remove the appropriate roadwheel.
2   Remove the front brake caliper with reference to Chapter 9, but leave the hydraulic hose connected. Tie the caliper to the front suspension coil spring with wire or string, taking care not to strain the hose (photo).
3   Hold the front hub stationary by using two roadwheel bolts to attach a length of metal bar to the hub as shown in Fig. 8.4, then unscrew the driveshaft nut using a socket and extension bar (photo), and remove the washer. Alternatively have an assistant firmly depress the footbrake

pedal to hold the hub and disc stationary while the nut is being unscrewed.
4   Disconnect the steering track rod end from the stub axle carrier with reference to Chapter 10.
5   Unscrew the two nuts from the bolts securing the stub axle carrier to the suspension strut (photo). Note that the nuts are on the brake caliper side. Remove the upper bolt, but leave the lower bolt in position at this stage.

Left-hand driveshaft

6   Drain the gearbox oil or automatic transmission fluid with reference to Chapter 1.
7   Unscrew the three bolts securing the rubber gaiter retaining plate to the side of the gearbox/transmission (photo).

Right-hand driveshaft

8   Using a parallel pin punch, drive out the double roll pin securing the inner joint yoke to the differential sun wheel stub shaft. Drive out the

2.2 Front brake caliper tied to the front coil spring with wire

2.3 Removing the driveshaft nut

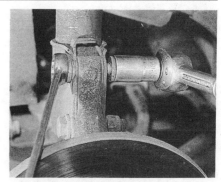

2.5 Unscrewing the stub axle carrier-to-suspension strut bolts

2.7 Removing the left-hand driveshaft inner retaining plate from the gearbox/transmission

2.8 Use a parallel pin punch to drive out the double roll pin securing the right-hand inner joint yoke to the differential sun wheel stub shaft

2.9A Pull out the right-hand side drive-shaft ...

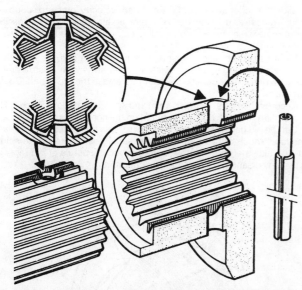

Fig. 8.6 Showing the correct fitting of the right-hand driveshaft roll pins (Sec 2)

small inner roll pin first, then drive out the outer roll pin. Access to the roll pin is gained from under the car and the driveshaft must be turned until the roll pin is visible (photo).

Both driveshafts

9   Pull the top of the stub axle carrier outwards until the inner end of the driveshaft is released from the yoke (left-hand side) or sun wheel

stub shaft (right-hand side). On the left-hand side there may be some loss of oil so position a small container beneath the transmission. After disconnecting the right-hand side driveshaft, remove the O-ring from the sun wheel stub shaft (photos).

10   Remove the lower bolt securing the stub axle carrier to the suspension strut, then withdraw the driveshaft outer joint stub axle from the hub, if necessary using a soft metal drift or suitable extractor to release the stub axle from the splines. Locking fluid is used on the splines during assembly, so the stub axle is likely to be tight inside the splines. Take care not to damage the rubber gaiter during the removal procedure.

Refitting

11   All new driveshafts supplied by Renault are equipped with cardboard or plastic protectors to prevent damage to the gaiters. Even the slightest knock to the gaiter can puncture it and cause the entry of water or dirt at a later date which may lead to the premature failure of the joint. If the original driveshaft is being refitted it is worthwhile making up some cardboard protectors as a precaution. They can be held in position with elastic bands. The protectors should be left on the driveshafts until the end of the refitting procedure.

Left-hand driveshaft

12   Insert the tripod spider into the differential yoke sun wheel while keeping the driveshaft as horizontal as possible.

13   Wipe clean the side of the gearbox/transmission, then insert the three bolts securing the rubber gaiter retaining plate and tighten to the specified torque. Keep the driveshaft as horizontal as possible during this procedure to ensure that the gaiter is not twisted.

14   Refill the gearbox or automatic transmission with oil/fluid with reference to Chapter 1.

Right-hand driveshaft

15   Lubricate the splines on the sun wheel stub shaft with molybdenum disulphide grease. Fit a new O-ring over the sun wheel stub splines.

2.9B ... and disconnect it from the splines on the sun wheel stub shaft

2.9C Disconnecting the left-hand side driveshaft from the yoke

2.9D Removing the O-ring from the right-hand side sun wheel stub shaft

2.17 Sealing the ends of the roll pins with sealing compound

2.22 Tightening the driveshaft nut with a torque wrench

16   Engage the inner end of the driveshaft with the sun wheel making sure that the roll pin holes are in alignment. Slide the driveshaft onto the sun wheel until the roll pin holes are aligned with each other.
17   Drive in new roll pins with their slots 90° apart then seal the ends of the pins with sealing compound (Renault recommend CAF 4/60 THIXO paste) (photo). The holes in the sun wheel are chamfered to assist the fitting of new roll pins.

Both driveshafts

18   Apply locking fluid to the splines on the driveshaft outer joint stub axle.
19   Move the top of the stub axle carrier inwards and at the same time engage the end of the driveshaft with the hub splines. Slide the hub fully onto the splines.
20   Insert the stub axle carrier bolts the correct way round and reconnect the steering track rod end. Tighten the nuts to the specified torque (Chapter 10).
21   Refit the front brake caliper with reference to Chapter 9.
22   Fit the driveshaft nut and washer and tighten the nut to the specified torque using the metal bar (paragraph 3). Alternatively have an assistant firmly depress the footbrake pedal while the nut is being tightened (photo).
23   Remove the cardboard protectors from the driveshaft rubber gaiter.
24   Refit the roadwheel then lower the car to the ground. Depress the brake pedal several times to re-set the disc pads.

3   Outer constant velocity joint (spider-and-yoke) rubber gaiter – renewal

1   Remove the driveshaft as described in Section 2.
2   Cut through the metal bands with snips taking care not to damage the grooves in the stub axle casing or the driveshaft itself.

3   Slide the gaiter away from the constant velocity joint and scoop out as much grease as possible from the joint (at this stage it will be possible to determine which type of constant velocity joint is fitted, if not already known).
4   Mount the stub axle in a soft-jawed vice then pull the driveshaft from it while prising up the starplate retainer arms with a screwdriver. Prising up one arm should be sufficient to release the driveshaft. Do not twist the arms.
5   Recover the thrust plunger, shim and spring from the stub axle. The original shim must be refitted to maintain the correct end play.
6   Cut the old gaiter from the driveshaft. Clean the driveshaft yoke and remove as much of the remaining grease as possible from the spider and stub axle member. Do this using a wooden spatula or old rags; do not use any cleaning solvent, petrol or paraffin.

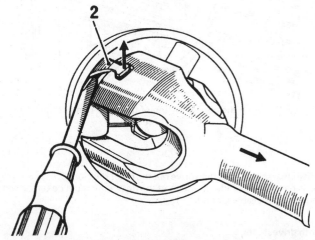

Fig. 8.7 Prising up the starplate retainer arms on the spider-and-yoke outer constant velocity joint (2) (Sec 3)

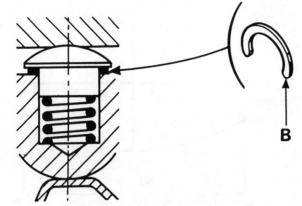

Fig. 8.8 Thrust plunger, spring and shim (B) on the spider-and-yoke outer constant velocity joint (Sec 3)

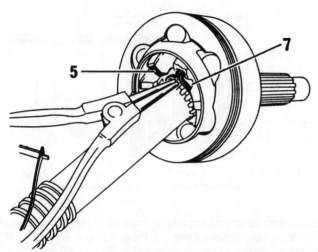

Fig. 8.10 Removing the internal circlip (7) on the six-ball outer constant velocity joint in order to separate the driveshaft from the hub (5) (Sec 4)

7   Obtain a new rubber gaiter, retaining clips and a small quantity of the special lubricating grease. All these parts are available in the form of a repair kit obtainable through Renault parts stockists.
8   In order to fit the new gaiter a special tool is required to expand the small end of the gaiter and allow it to slide over the driveshaft yoke. The manufacturer's tool is shown in the Fig. 8.9, but a suitable alternative can be made by bending a sheet of tin in conical fashion and then bonding the seams using superglue or pop rivets. An old 5 litre oil container is quite useful for this purpose. Make sure that the seam is well protected with tape to prevent it cutting the new gaiter.
9   Before fitting the new gaiter, generously lubricate the expander tool and the inside of the gaiter with clean engine oil.
10   Position the small end of the gaiter over the small end of the tool and move it up and down the expander two or three times to make the rubber more pliable. Hold the gaiter with a cloth rag in order to grip it.
11   Mount the driveshaft in a soft-jawed vice with the yoke angled upwards.
12   Position the large end of the expander tool against the driveshaft yoke and pull the gaiter up the expander and onto the yoke. Make sure that the end of the gaiter does not tuck under as it is being fitted, and use plenty of lubricant.
13   When the small end of the gaiter is in place over the yoke, remove the tool and slide the gaiter up the driveshaft.
14   Insert the spring and thrust plunger in the stub axle and make sure that the spider rollers are fully on the trunnions.
15   Fit the starplate retainer with the arms central between the rollers.
16   With the stub axle mounted in the vice offer the driveshaft and yoke to it. Move the driveshaft from side to side until one of the retainer

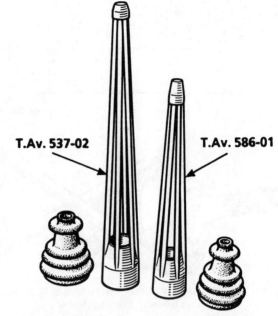

Fig. 8.9 Special Renault tools for fitting new rubber gaiters to the spider-and-yoke outer constant velocity joint (Sec 3)

arms can be engaged in its cut-out, then press the driveshaft firmly over the spider and insert the remaining arms. A slotted screwdriver will facilitate lifting the arms into position.
17   Move the driveshaft in the direction of one of the spider trunnions. This will cause the thrust plunger to lift, and the shim can then be inserted beneath the plunger head.
18   Remove the driveshaft from the vice then articulate the joint through all angles and check that it moves freely.
19   Distribute the grease supplied in the repair kit evenly around the spider and the grooves in the driveshaft yoke. If all of the old grease was not completely removed, leave some of the new grease in the sachet as it is important that the joint only has the correct amount of grease equal to the amount in the sachet.
20   Position the large end of the gaiter on the stub axle housing making sure that the two lips are correctly located in the two grooves. Position the small end so that the gaiter convolutions are neither stretched nor compressed.
21   With the stub axle and driveshaft aligned, lift the small end of the gaiter temporarily to equalise the air pressure.
22   Fit the metal band clips on the ends of the gaiter and secure by squeezing the raised portion. Ideally a crimping tool should be used, but alternatively pincers or pliers may be used.
23   Wipe away any external grease then refit the driveshaft as described in Section 2.

4   Outer constant velocity joint (six-ball) rubber gaiter – renewal

1   Remove the driveshaft as described in Section 2.
2   Slit the gaiter and rubber collar with a knife and remove them from the driveshaft (at this stage it will be possible to determine which type of constant velocity joint is fitted, if not already known).
3   Scoop out as much grease as possible using a wooden spatula or old rags; do not use any cleaning solvent, petrol or paraffin.
4   Obtain a new rubber gaiter and a small quantity of the special lubricating grease. All these parts are available in the form of a repair kit obtainable through Renault parts stockists.
5   Using circlip pliers expand the joint internal circlip, then at the same time tap the exposed face of the ball hub with a mallet and separate the coupling from the driveshaft.
6   Wipe clean the driveshaft then locate the new rubber collar and rubber gaiter on it.

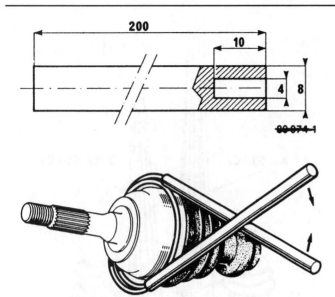

Fig. 8.11 Using two lengths of hollow metal tubing to fit the large spring onto the outer coupling (Sec 4)

7   Slide the constant velocity joint coupling onto the driveshaft until the internal circlip locates in the groove.

8   Spread all the grease supplied with the repair kit inside the rubber gaiter and inside the coupling joint. If all of the old grease was not completely removed, leave some of the new grease in the sachet as it is important that the joint only has the correct amount of grease equal to the amount in the sachet.

9   Locate the lips of the rubber gaiter in the grooves of the coupling and driveshaft. With the coupling aligned with the driveshaft, lift the lip of the gaiter to equalise the air pressure.

10   Locate the rubber collar on the inner end of the gaiter, then locate the large spring on the outer end using two lengths of hollow metal tubing to ease the spring into position as shown in Fig. 8.11.

11   Wipe away any external grease then refit the driveshaft as described in Section 2.

5   Right-hand driveshaft inner joint (GI 62) rubber gaiter – renewal

1   Remove the driveshaft from the car, as described in Section 2.

2   As applicable, slip off the retaining spring or cut free the clip securing the gaiter to the yoke.

3   Slit the gaiter and rubber collar with a knife and remove them from the driveshaft.

4   Using pliers, carefully bend up the anti-separation plate tags at their corners and then slide the yoke off the spider (photo). It is only necessary to bend up the corners of two of the tags. Be prepared to hold

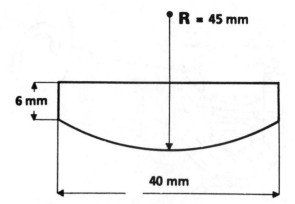

Fig. 8.12 Former plate dimensions for the right-hand driveshaft inner joint anti-separation tags (Sec 5)

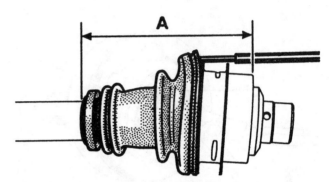

Fig. 8.13 Rubber gaiter fitting dimension for the right-hand driveshaft inner joint (GI 62) (Sec 5)

A   153 ± 1 mm

the rollers in place otherwise they may fall off the spider trunnions as the yoke is withdrawn. If necessary, secure the rollers in place using tape after removal of the yoke. The rollers are matched to their trunnions and it is most important that they are not interchanged.

5   Extract the circlip securing the spider to the driveshaft using circlip pliers (photo). On some models the spider may be staked in position. Using a dab of paint or a small file mark, identify the position of the spider in relation to the driveshaft, as a guide to refitting.

6   The spider can now be removed (photo). If it is tight, use one of the following methods. Preferably using a press or by improvisation with a puller, support the spider under the rollers and press out the driveshaft. If a press is not available support the spider under its central boss, using suitable half-round packing pieces, and drive the shaft out using a hammer and brass drift. It is important, if this method is used, that only the central boss of the spider is supported and not the rollers. The shock loads imposed could easily damage the inner faces of the rollers and spider and also the small needle roller bearings.

5.4 Bend up the anti-separation plate tags with pliers

5.5 Extracting the circlip from the inner end of the right-hand side driveshaft

5.6 Removing the spider from the inner end of the right-hand side driveshaft

Fig. 8.14 Removing the metal casing from the right-hand driveshaft inner joint (RC 490) (Sec 6)

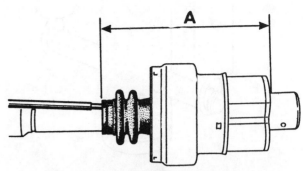

Fig. 8.15 Rubber gaiter fitting dimension for the right-hand driveshaft inner joint (RC 490) (Sec 6)

A   156 ± 1 mm

7   Clean the driveshaft and remove as much of the grease as possible from the spider and yoke using a wooden spatula or old rags. Do not use any cleaning solvent, petrol or paraffin.
8   Examine the spider, rollers and yoke for any signs of scoring or wear and for smoothness of movement of the rollers on the spider trunnions. If wear is evident the spider and rollers can be renewed, but it is not possible to obtain a replacement yoke. Obtain a new rubber gaiter, retaining clips and a quantity of the special lubricating grease. These parts are available in the form of a repair kit available from Renault parts stockists.
9   Begin reassembly by lubricating the driveshaft and the inside of the gaiter generously with engine oil.
10   Place the rubber retaining collar over the driveshaft and then fit the gaiter.
11   Place the spider on the driveshaft splines in the same relative position as noted prior to removal.
12   Drive the spider fully onto the driveshaft using a hammer and tubular drift, then refit the retaining circlip. Where there is no circlip, stake the end of the driveshaft in three places at intervals of 120° to secure the spider.
13   Evenly distribute the special grease contained in the repair kit around the spider and inside the yoke. If all of the old grease was not completely removed, leave some of the new grease in the sachet as it is important that the joint only has the correct amount of grease equal to the amount in the sachet.
14   Slide the yoke into position over the spider.
15   Carefully tap the corners of the anti-separation tags flat. If the tags have been bent excessively, it will be necessary to fit a former behind them to ensure that they are returned to their original shape. Using a piece of 2.5 mm (0.1 in) thick steel or similar material, make up a former plate to the dimensions shown in Fig. 8.12.
16   Position the former under each anti-separation plate tag in the yoke in turn, and tap the tag down onto the former plate. Remove the plate when all the tags have been returned to their original shape.
17   Slide the gaiter up the driveshaft and locate the gaiter in its respective grooves in the driveshaft and in the yoke.
18   Slip the rubber retaining collar into place over the gaiter.
19   Insert a thin blunt instrument, such as a knitting needle, under the lip of the gaiter to allow all trapped air to escape. With the instrument in position, compress the joint until the dimension from the small end of the gaiter to the flat end face of the yoke is as shown in Fig. 8.13. Hold the yoke in this position and withdraw the instrument.
20   Slip a new retaining spring into place to secure the gaiter. Make sure that the retaining spring is not stretched. All of the coils should be touching after the spring has been fitted.
21   Refit the driveshaft as described in Section 2.

6   Right-hand driveshaft inner joint (RC 490) rubber gaiter – renewal

1   Remove the driveshaft from the car, as described in Section 2.
2   Using a pair of grips bend up the three points where the metal plate contacts the inner joint.

3   Cut the small gaiter retaining collar. Cut open the gaiter and remove as much grease as possible.
4   Remove the yoke by tapping the metal casing off it, using a brass or copper drift, and separating it from the spider. Be careful that the rollers do not fall off the trunnions – they must not be interchanged.
5   Remove the circlip (if fitted) which secures the spider to the driveshaft. Make identification marks between the spider and the shaft for use when refitting.
6   Press or pull the spider off the driveshaft.
7   Remove the gaiter, metal casing and insert. Clean and examine the shaft and spider. Obtain a new rubber gaiter, retaining clips and a quantity of the special lubricating grease. These parts are available in the form of a repair kit available from Renault parts stockists.
8   Fit a new retaining clip to the driveshaft, followed by a new gaiter, the insert and the metal casing.
9   Refit the spider, observing the alignment marks, and press it home.
10   Refit the securing circlip, if one was found on dismantling. On versions without a circlip, secure the spider by peening the splines in three places.
11   Using the grease supplied in the repair kit, lubricate the yoke, the spider and the inside of the gaiter. If all of the old grease was not completely removed, leave some of the new grease in the sachet as it is important that the joint only has the correct amount of grease, equal to the amount in the sachet.
12   Fit the yoke to the spider. Fit the gaiter and insert to the metal casing, then slide the casing onto the yoke until the guide plate is flush with the yoke. Secure the casing by staking it in three places.
13   Insert a thin blunt instrument, such as a knitting needle, between the end of the gaiter and the driveshaft so that air can escape. Move the joint in or out to achieve the dimension 'A' shown in Fig. 8.15.
14   Without disturbing the joint or the gaiter, remove the knitting needle and fit the new retaining clip.
15   Refit the driveshaft as described in Section 2.

7   Left-hand driveshaft inner rubber gaiter and bearing – renewal

1   Remove the driveshaft as described in Section 2.
2   Using circlip pliers, extract the circlip securing the spider to the driveshaft. Using a dab of paint or a small file, mark the position of the spider in relation to the driveshaft, as a guide to refitting.
3   The spider can now be removed in one of the following ways. Preferably using a press or by improvisation with an hydraulic puller, support the spider under the rollers and press out the driveshaft. Alternatively support the spider under its central boss, using suitable half-round packing pieces, and drive the shaft out using a hammer and brass drift. It is important, if this method is used, that only the central boss of the spider is supported and not the rollers. The shock loads imposed could easily damage the inner faces of the rollers and spider and also the small needle roller bearings.
4   Now support the bearing at the small end of the gaiter and press or drive the shaft out of the gaiter and bearing assembly.

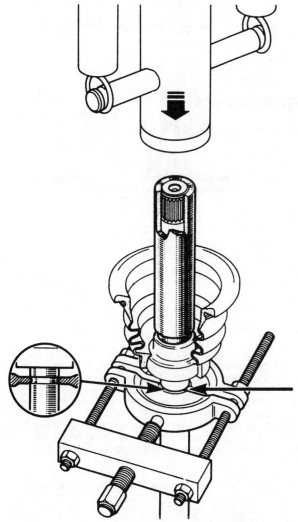

Fig. 8.16 Pressing the bearing/gaiter onto the left-hand driveshaft (Sec 7)

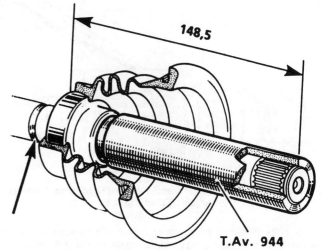

Fig. 8.17 Gaiter/bearing fitting dimension for the left-hand driveshaft inner joint (Sec 7)

press is being used. The gaiter and bearing must be positioned so that the distance from the end of the driveshaft to the flat face at the small diameter end of the gaiter is 148.5 mm (5.85 in) – see Fig. 8.17.
8   Now place the spider on the driveshaft in the same position as noted during removal. Drive or press the spider onto the shaft and refit the circlip.
9   Refit the driveshaft to the car, as described in Section 2.

8   Thermo-plastic gaiter – renewal

1   The rubber-type gaiters described in the previous Sections have been superseded by gaiters made of a thermoplastic material. The later gaiter cannot be expanded over the driveshaft outer joint yoke on the tripod-type constant velocity joint, so it is necessary to remove the inner gaiter first in order to renew the outer gaiter. By doing this the outer gaiter can be fitted from the inner end of the driveshaft. It is recommended that both the inner and outer gaiters are renewed at the same time when renewing the outer gaiter. Renewal of the inner gaiter alone is as described in Sections 5, 6 or 7, and renewal of the outer gaiter on the six-ball type is as described in Section 4. This Section, however, describes renewal of the gaiter on the tripod-type outer constant velocity joint.
2   Remove the driveshaft as described in Section 2.
3   Remove the gaiter from the inner end of the driveshaft as described in Sections 5, 6 or 7.
4   Where a vibration/torque damper is fitted, use a puller or press to remove it from the inner end of the driveshaft (photo). It will be necessary to pull on the inner rubber bush of the unit otherwise it will distort and break away from the outer metal housing.
5   Cut free the small clip from the inner end of the gaiter (photo).

5   Carefully inspect the spider and rollers for signs of wear or deterioration. The rollers should be free from any signs of scoring and they should turn smoothly on the spider trunnions. Renew the spider assembly if necessary. Obtain a new gaiter which is supplied complete with the small bearing.
6   Owing to the lip type seal used in the bearing, the bearing and gaiter must be refitted using a press or by improvising using an hydraulic puller. There is a very great risk of distorting the seal if a hammer and tubular drift are used to drive the assembly onto the driveshaft.
7   Fig. 8.16 shows the arrangement for fitting the gaiter and bearing if a

8.4 Pulling the vibration/torque damper from the driveshaft

8.5 Cutting free the gaiter clips

8.8A Driveshaft gaiter kit

8.8B Packing the outer coupling joint with grease

8.9 Fitting the new gaiter onto the outer joint

6 Using a hacksaw cut through the large outer clip taking care not to damage the groove in the stub axle casing.

7 Slit the gaiter and remove it from the driveshaft, then scoop out as much grease as possible from the joint. Wipe clean the driveshaft and stub axle casing.

8 The new gaiter comes complete with clips and a sachet of grease (photo). Spread all the grease supplied with the repair kit inside the rubber gaiter and inside the coupling joint ([photo]). If all of the old grease was not completely removed, leave some of the new grease in the sachet as it is important that the joint only has the correct amount of grease, equal to the amount in the sachet.

9 Slide the new gaiter over the inner end of the driveshaft and onto the outer joint, making sure that it locates correctly in the grooves (photo).

10 Fully articulate the joint to ensure that the gaiter is correctly seated and to ensure that any excess air is forced out.

11 Fit and tighten the two clips. The type of clip fitted may vary. With one type it is necessary to compress an external tag using pliers. The Renault type ideally requires the use of a special tool although it is just possible to use pincers (photos).

12 Wipe clean the driveshaft and gaiter then refit the unit to the car as described in Section 2.

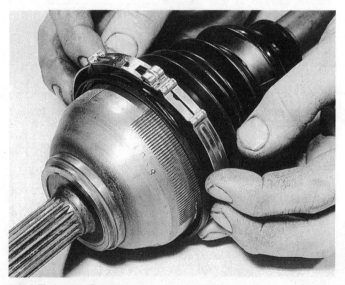

8.11A Fitting the Renault type outer gaiter clip

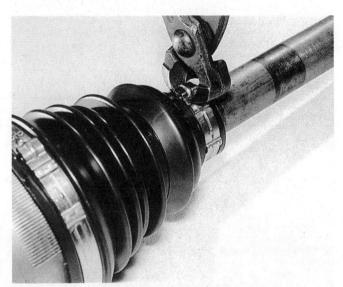

8.11B Tightening the inner gaiter clip with pincers

Chapter 9 Braking system

Contents

Specifications

System type ....

Dual hydraulic circuit split diagonally on non-ABS models, and front to rear on ABS models. Disc front brakes. Drum rear brakes except on ABS models, which have rear disc brakes. Vacuum servo assistance on non-ABS models. ABS system is load sensitive. Cable-operated handbrake on rear brakes

Front brakes

Type	Disc
Make	Bendix or Girling single piston sliding calipers
Disc diameter	238.0 mm
Disc thickness:	
Plain discs (all models except GTX and TXE fitted with non-ABS brakes):	
New	12.0 mm
Minimum after machining..	10.5 mm
Ventilated discs (GTX and TXE fitted with non-ABS brakes):	
New	20.0 mm
Minimum after machining..	18.0 mm
Maximum disc run-out	0.07 mm
Minimum disc pad thickness (including backplate).....................	6.0 mm

Rear drum brakes

Drum diameter:	
New	180.5 mm
Maximum drum diameter after machining	181.25 mm
Brake shoe lining thickness (including shoe):	
New	6.5 mm
Minimum	2.5 mm

Rear disc brakes

Disc diameter	238.0 mm
Disc thickness:	
New	12.0 mm
Minimum disc thickness after machining............................	10.5 mm
Maximum disc run-out	0.07 mm
Minimum disc pad thickness (including backplate)...................	6.0 mm

Torque wrench settings

	Nm	lbf ft
Front brake disc	25	19
Rear drum brake backplate	45	33
Bleed screw	7	5
Flexible hose union	13	10
Brake pipe union nut	13	10
Girling caliper guide bolts	35	26
Caliper mounting bolt	100	74
Bendix caliper body to reaction frame.	65	48
Master cylinder to servo	13	10
Servo to bulkhead	20	15

1   General information

The braking system is of dual hydraulic circuit type, comprising a master cylinder (or hydraulic unit on ABS models) and wheel cylinders. On all non-ABS (anti-lock braking system) models the circuit is split diagonally, whereas on ABS models the circuit is split front to rear.

Under normal conditions both circuits operate in unison, however in the event of failure of one circuit the remaining circuit will provide adequate braking to stop the car in an emergency.

Disc brakes are fitted to the front wheels. Drum brakes are fitted to the rear wheels except on models with ABS, which are fitted with rear disc brakes.

The rear wheel cylinders (rear drum brakes) incorporate integral brake pressure compensators which control the hydraulic pressure to the rear brakes. The compensators prevent rear wheel lock-up during emergency braking.

The cable-operated handbrake operates independently on the rear wheels. A vacuum servo unit is fitted to non-ABS models – on ABS models, pedal pressure assistance is provided automatically through the hydraulic unit and high pressure pump.

Warning: *Dust created by the braking system may contain asbestos, which is a health hazard. Never blow it out with compressed air and don't inhale any of it. An approved filtering mask should be worn when working on the brakes. DO NOT use petroleum-based solvents to clean brake parts. Use brake cleaner or methylated spirit only.*

2   Brake pedal – removal and refitting

Removal

1   Working inside the car, remove the lower facia panel from beneath the steering column for access to the pedal bracket.
2   Extract the split pin, washer and clevis pin securing the servo unit pushrod to the brake pedal.
3   Prise the spring clip from the inner end of the pivot shaft and remove the washer.
4   Slide out the pivot shaft until the brake pedal can be withdrawn.
5   Examine the bushes for wear and renew them if necessary. If the shaft is worn excessively, the clutch pedal will have to be removed as described in Chapter 6, and the shaft renewed.

Refitting

6   Refitting is a reversal of removal, but lubricate the bushes, pivot shaft and pushrod clevis pin with molybdenum disulphide grease.

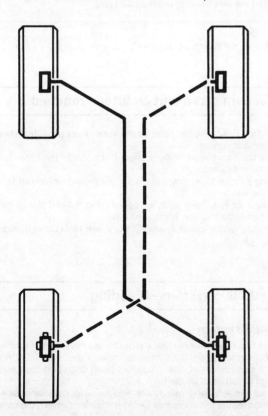

Fig. 9.1 Diagonally split hydraulic system, incorporating wheel cylinders with integral compensators (Sec 1)

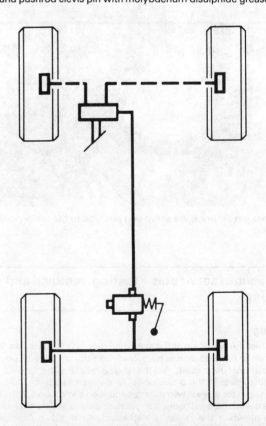

Fig. 9.2 Front/rear split hydraulic system on ABS models, incorporating a load dependent compensator (Sec 1)

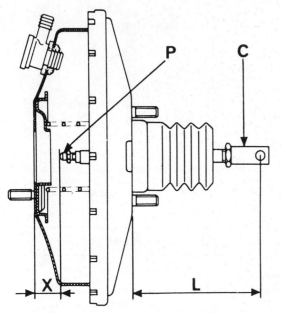

Fig. 9.3 Vacuum servo adjustment dimensions (Secs 3 and 8)

C = Pushrod clevis   P = Stud
L = 117.5 mm   X = 22.3 mm

3.6 Clevis pin securing the servo unit pushrod to the brake pedal (arrowed)

3   Vacuum servo unit – testing, removal and refitting

Testing

1   To test the operation of the servo unit depress the footbrake four or five times to exhaust the vacuum, then start the engine while keeping the footbrake depressed. As the engine starts there should be a noticeable 'give' in the brake pedal as vacuum builds up. Allow the engine to run for at least two minutes and then switch it off. If the brake pedal is now depressed again, it should be possible to detect a hiss from the servo when the pedal is depressed. After about four or five applications no further hissing will be heard and the pedal will feel considerably firmer.

Removal

2   Disconnect the battery negative terminal.
3   Refer to Section 8 and remove the master cylinder.
4   Disconnect the vacuum hose at the servo non-return valve.
5   Working inside the car, remove the lower facia panel from beneath the steering column.
6   Extract the split pin, washer and clevis pin securing the servo unit pushrod to the brake pedal (photo).
7   Unscrew the four nuts and remove the washers securing the servo to the bulkhead and withdraw the unit into the engine compartment.
8   Note that the servo unit cannot be dismantled for repair or overhaul and, if faulty, must be renewed.

Refitting

9   Before refitting the servo unit, check the dimensions shown in Fig. 9.3 for the pushrod and clevis positions and if necessary adjust them. Make sure that the locknuts are tight after making an adjustment.
10   Refitting is a reversal of removal with reference to Section 8 when refitting the master cylinder.

4   Vacuum servo unit non-return valve – removal, testing and refitting

Removal

1   Slacken the clip and disconnect the vacuum pipe from the non-return valve on the front face of the servo unit.
2   Withdraw the valve from its rubber sealing grommet by pulling and twisting. Remove the sealing grommet from the servo unit.

Testing

3   Examine the non-return valve and sealing grommet for damage and signs of deterioration and renew if necessary. The valve may be tested by blowing through it in both directions – it should only be possible to blow from the servo end to the manifold end.

Refitting

4   Refitting is a reversal of removal.

5   Vacuum servo unit air filter – renewal

1   Working inside the car, remove the lower facia panel from beneath the steering column.
2   Ease the convoluted rubber cover off the rear of the servo unit and move it up the pushrod.
3   Using a screwdriver or scriber, hook out the old air filter and remove it from the servo.
4   Make a cut in the new filter, as shown in Fig. 9.4 and place it over the pushrod and into position in the servo end.
5   Refit the rubber cover, then refit the lower facia panel beneath the steering column.

6   Hydraulic system – bleeding

Non-ABS system

1   If the master cylinder or brake pipes/hoses have been disconnected and reconnected, then the complete system (both circuits) must be bled. If a component of one circuit has been disturbed then only that particular circuit need be bled.
2   Bleed the left-hand rear brake and its diagonally opposite front brake, then repeat this sequence on the remaining circuit if the complete system is to be bled.
3   There are a variety of do-it-yourself brake bleeding kits available from motor accessory shops, and it is recommended that one of these

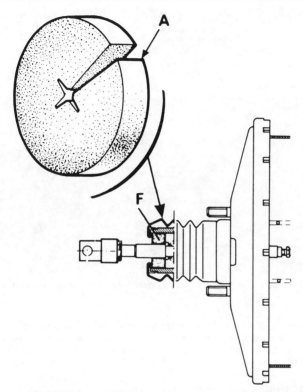

Fig. 9.4 Vacuum servo unit air filter renewal (Sec 5)

A   Cut the new filter as   F   Air filter fitted in the servo
    shown   unit

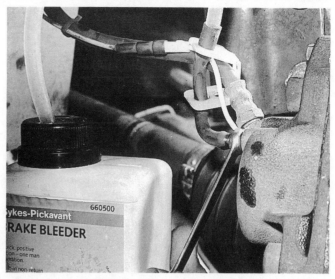

6.9 Bleeding a front brake caliper

kits is used wherever possible as they greatly simplify the bleeding operation. Follow the kit manufacturer's instructions in conjunction with the following procedure.

4   During the bleeding operation do not allow the brake fluid level in the reservoir to drop below the minimum mark, and only use new fluid for topping-up. *Never re-use fluid bled from the system.*

5   Before starting, check that all rigid pipes and flexible hoses are in good condition and that all hydraulic unions are tight. Take great care not to allow hydraulic fluid to come into contact with the vehicle paintwork, otherwise the finish will be seriously damaged. Wash off any spilt fluid immediately with cold water.

6   If a brake bleeding kit is not being used, gather together a clean jar, a suitable length of clear plastic or rubber tubing which is a tight fit over the bleed screw and a new tin of the specified brake fluid (see *'Lubricants, fluids and capacities'* at the beginning of this manual).

7   Clean the area around the bleed screw on the left-hand rear brake and remove the dust cap. Connect one end of the tubing to the bleed screw and immerse the other end in the jar containing sufficient brake fluid to keep the end of the tube submerged.

8   Open the bleed screw half a turn and have an assistant depress the brake pedal to the floor and then slowly release it. Tighten the bleed screw at the end of each downstroke to prevent the expelled air fluid from being drawn back into the system. Continue this procedure until clean brake fluid, free from air bubbles, can be seen flowing into the jar, and then finally tighten the bleed screw.

9   Remove the tube, refit the dust cap and repeat this procedure on the diagonally opposite front brake caliper (photo).

10   Repeat the procedure on the remaining circuit.

ABS system

Note: *Due to the complex nature of the ABS it is highly recommended that this work is carried out by a Renault garage.*

11   A pressure bleeding kit must be used to bleed the hydraulic circuit on the ABS system. A kit can be obtained from a motor accessory shop, and it is usually operated by air pressure from the spare tyre.

12   By connecting a pressurised container to the master cylinder fluid reservoir, bleeding is then carried out by simply opening each bleed screw in turn and allowing the fluid to run out, rather like turning on a tap, until no air is visible in the expelled fluid. The container has a large reserve of hydraulic fluid sufficient for complete bleeding.

13   The pressure accumulator must be emptied first as follows. Make sure that the ignition is switched off then depress the brake pedal twenty times so that the brake pedal pressure becomes noticeably hard.

14   The hydraulic circuit is split front and rear, and the front circuit must be bled first.

15   Before starting, check that all rigid pipes and flexible hoses are in good condition and that all hydraulic unions are tight. Take great care not to allow hydraulic fluid to come into contact with the vehicle paintwork, otherwise the finish will be seriously damaged. Wash off any spilt fluid immediately with cold water.

16   Ensure that the fluid reservoir is full, and open the compressed air valve on the bleeding equipment.

17   Clean the area around the bleed screw on the front right-hand brake and remove the dust cap. Connect one end of the tubing to the bleed screw and direct the other end into the jar.

18   Open the bleed screw, wait for approximately 20 seconds for the hydraulic fluid to drain out, then close the bleed screw. Refit the dust cap.

19   Repeat this procedure for the left-hand front brake.

20   The rear hydraulic circuit must now be bled. Ensure that the pressure accumulator is empty and that the ignition is switched off.

21   Clean the area around the bleed screw on the right-hand rear brake and remove the dust cap. Connect one end of the tubing to the bleed screw, and direct the other end into the jar containing enough brake fluid to cover the open end of the tube.

22   It is most important to ensure that the following operations are carried out in the order given.

23   Open the bleed screw. Have an assistant press down lightly on the brake pedal. Switch on the ignition.

24   Wait for a continuous stream of hydraulic fluid, free from air bubbles, to flow into the container, then release the brake pedal.

25   Tighten the bleed screw. Switch off the ignition.

26   Repeat the procedure on the left-hand rear brake.

27   Pressurise the pressure accumulator by switching on the ignition and waiting for the pump to stop.

28   If necessary, top up the brake fluid level.

7   Hydraulic pipes and hoses – inspection, removal and refitting

Inspection

1   The hydraulic pipes, hoses, hose connections and pipe unions should be regularly examined.

2   First check for signs of leakage at the pipe unions, then examine the

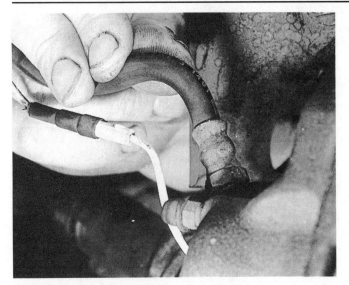

7.2 Checking a brake hydraulic hose for cracking

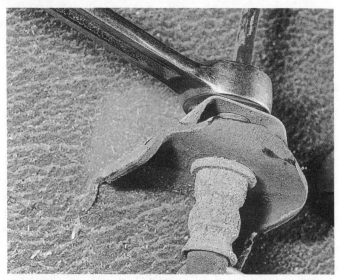

7.5 Using a split ring spanner to unscrew a hydraulic pipe union nut

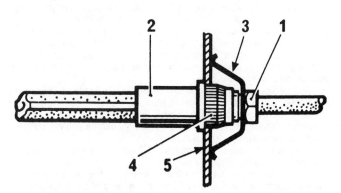

Fig. 9.5 Hydraulic pipe connection to a flexible hose (Sec 7)

1 Union nut	4 Splined end fitting
2 Flexible hose	5 Bodywork
3 Spring clip support	

flexible hoses for signs of cracking, chafing and fraying (photo).

3   The brake pipes should be examined carefully for signs of dents, corrosion or other damage. Corrosion should be scraped off, and if the depth of pitting is significant, the pipes renewed. This is particularly likely in those areas underneath the vehicle body where the pipes are exposed and unprotected.

Removal

4   If any section of pipe or hose is to be removed, the loss of fluid may be reduced by removing the hydraulic fluid reservoir filler cap, placing a piece of polythene over the filler neck, then refitting and tightening the filler cap. If a section of pipe is to be removed from the master cylinder, the reservoir should be emptied by syphoning out the fluid or drawing out the fluid with a pipette.

5   To remove a section of pipe, unscrew the union nuts at each end of the pipe and release it from the clips attaching it to the body. Where the union nuts are exposed to the full force of the weather, they can sometimes be quite tight. If an open-ended spanner is used, burring of the flats on the nuts is not uncommon, and for this reason it is preferable to use a split ring spanner which will engage all the flats (photo). If such a spanner is not available, self-locking grips may be used although this is not recommended.

6   To remove a flexible hose first clean the ends of the hose and the surrounding area, then unscrew the union nut(s) from the hose end(s). Recover the spring clip and withdraw the hose from the serrated mounting in the support bracket. Where applicable, unscrew the hose from the caliper.

7   Brake pipes with flared ends and union nuts in place can be obtained individually or in sets from Renault dealers or accessory shops. The pipe is then bent to shape, using the old pipe as a guide, and is ready for fitting to the car.

Refitting

8   Refitting the pipes and hoses is a reversal of removal. Make sure that brake pipes are securely supported in their clips and ensure that the hoses are not kinked. Check also that the hoses are clear of all suspension components and underbody fittings and will remain clear during movement of the suspension and steering. After refitting, remove the polythene from the reservoir and bleed the brake hydraulic system as described in Section 6.

8   Master cylinder (non-ABS models) – removal and refitting

Removal

1   Remove the air cleaner duct from the carburettor with reference to Chapter 4.

2   Unbolt and remove the strengthening bar from between the front suspension turrets.

3   Syphon the brake fluid from the reservoir or alternatively place a container beneath the master cylinder and cover the surrounding components with rags.

4   Pull the reservoir direct from the top of the master cylinder.

5   Identify the brake pipes for position then unscrew the union nuts and disconnect them. Tape over the pipe ends to prevent the entry of dust and dirt.

6   Unscrew the mounting nuts and withdraw the master cylinder from the servo unit. Note the position of the vacuum hose support bracket (photo).

7   It is not possible to obtain seals or internal components for the master cylinder, therefore if it is faulty it should be renewed complete. The reservoir locating seals may be renewed if necessary, and the seal between the master cylinder and the vacuum servo should be renewed as a matter of course whenever the unit is removed, as a leak at this point will allow atmospheric pressure into the servo unit.

Refitting

8   Before refitting the master cylinder, clean the mounting faces and check that the thrust rod protrusion is as shown in Fig. 9.3. If necessary, adjust the protrusion by repositioning the thrust rod extension.

9   Refitting is a reversal of removal, but tighten the nuts to the specified torque. Fit a new seal, and when offering the master cylinder

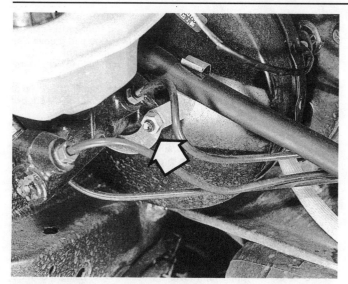

8.6 Master cylinder mounting nut and vacuum hose support bracket (arrowed)

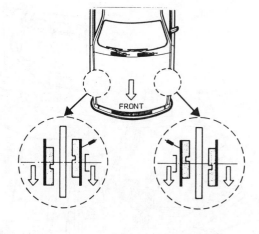

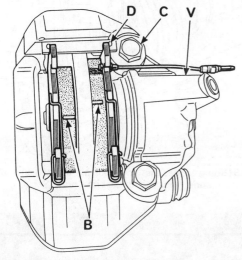

Fig. 9.7 Correct fitting of Bendix off-set brake pads (Sec 9)

B	Grooves	D	Spring clip location
C	Bracket bolt	V	Bleed screw

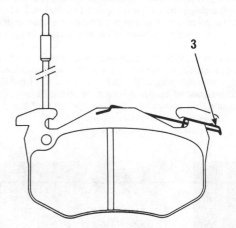

Fig. 9.6 Anti-rattle spring (3) fitted to the Bendix brake pad (Sec 9)

to the servo, make sure that it is correctly aligned so that the pushrod enters the piston centrally. Finally bleed the hydraulic system as described in Section 6.

9 Front brake pads – renewal

Warning: *Disc brake pads must be renewed on both front wheels at the same time – never renew the pads on only one wheel as uneven braking may result. Also, the dust created by wear of the pads may contain asbestos, which is a health hazard. Never blow it out with compressed air and don't inhale any of it. An approved filtering mask should be worn when working on the brakes. DO NOT use petroleum based solvents to clean brake parts. Use brake cleaner or methylated spirit only*

1   Apply the handbrake then jack up the front of the car and support it on axle stands. Remove the front roadwheels.

Bendix calipers

2   Disconnect the brake pad wear warning light wire at the connector.
3   Push the piston into its bore by pulling the caliper outwards.
4   Extract the small spring clip and then withdraw the retaining key (photos).
5   Using pliers if necessary, withdraw the pads from the caliper, and remove the anti-rattle spring from each pad (photos). If required, the thickness of the pad linings can be checked at this stage using a steel rule.

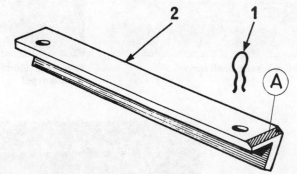

Fig. 9.8 Bendix disc pad retaining key (2) and spring (1) showing filed chamfer (A) (Sec 9)

6   With the pads removed, check that the caliper is free to slide on the guide sleeves and that the rubber dust excluders around the piston and guide sleeves are undamaged. If attention to these components is necessary refer to Section 10.
7   To refit the pads, move the caliper sideways as far as possible towards the centre of the car. Fit the anti-rattle spring to the innermost pad making sure that this pad is the one with the wear warning light wire, then locate the pad in position , with the backing plate against the piston.
8   Note that the pads are of the offset type, having only one cutaway

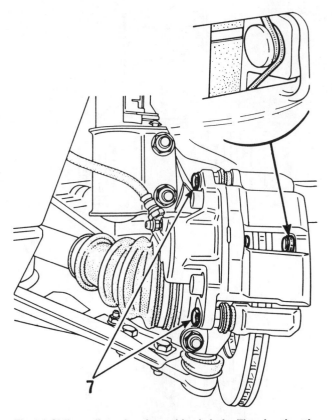

Fig. 9.9 Girling caliper showing guide pin bolts (7) and anti-rattle spring location on the brake pads (Sec 9)

on their outer edge, compared with the two cutaways on the symmetrical type. Looking at the pads from the front of the car, the innermost pad groove must be higher than the outer pad groove (see Fig. 9.7). Make sure that the pads are fitted correctly (photo).

9   Move the caliper outwards then fit the anti-rattle spring to the outer pad and locate the pad in the caliper.

10   Slide the retaining key into place and refit the small spring clip at the inner end. It may be necessary to file an entry chamfer on the edge of the retaining key to enable it to be fitted without difficulty.

11   Reconnect the brake pad wear warning light wire, refit the roadwheel and repeat the renewal procedure on the other front brake.

12   On completion check the hydraulic fluid level in the reservoir then depress the brake pedal two or three times to bring the pads into contact with the disc, and lower the car to the ground.

Girling calipers

13   Pull the caliper body outwards away from the centre of the car. This will push the piston back into its bore to facilitate removal and refitting of the pads.

14   Disconnect the brake pad wear warning light at the connector (photo).

15   Unscrew the upper and lower guide pin bolts using a suitable spanner while holding the guide pins with a second spanner (photos).

16   With the guide pins removed, lift the caliper off the brake pads and carrier bracket, and tie it up in a convenient place under the wheelarch. Do not allow the caliper to hang unsupported on the flexible brake hose.

17   Withdraw the two brake pads from the carrier bracket. If required, the thickness of the pads can be checked at this stage using a steel rule (photos).

18   Before refitting the pads, check that the guide pins are free to slide in the carrier bracket and check that the rubber dust excluders around the guide pins are undamaged. Brush the dust and dirt from the caliper and piston but **do not** *inhale it as it is injurious to health*. Inspect the dust excluder around the piston for damage and inspect the piston for evidence of fluid leaks, corrosion or damage. If attention to any of these components is necessary, refer to Section 10.

9.4A Extract the small spring ...

9.4B ... and withdraw the retaining key (Bendix type)

9.5A Removing the outer brake pad ...

9.5B ... and inner brake pad (Bendix type)

9.8 Showing the offset of the Bendix brake pads

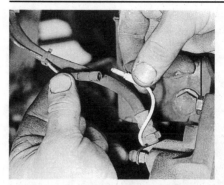

9.14 Disconnecting the brake pad wear warning light wiring (Girling type)

9.15A Unscrewing the guide pin bolts while holding the guide pins with a second spanner (Girling type)

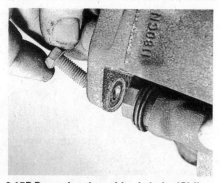

9.15B Removing the guide pin bolts (Girling type)

9.17A Removing the outer brake pad from the carrier bracket (Girling type)

9.17B Checking the thickness of the brake pad linings (Girling type)

19   To refit the pads, place them in position on the carrier bracket noting that the pad with the warning light must be nearest to the centre of the car. The anti-rattle springs must be located as shown in Fig. 9.9.

20   Make sure that the caliper piston is fully retracted in its bore. If not, carefully push it in using a flat bar or screwdriver as a lever, or preferably use a G-clamp.

21   Position the caliper over the pads then fit the lower guide pin bolt having first coated its threads with locking fluid. Apply locking fluid to the upper guide pin bolt, press the caliper into position, and fit the bolt. Tighten the bolts to the specified torque, starting with the lower bolt.

22   Reconnect the brake pad wear warning light wire, refit the roadwheel and repeat the renewal procedure on the other front brake.

23   On completion check the hydraulic fluid level in the reservoir then depress the brake pedal two or three times to bring the pads into contact with the disc, and lower the car to the ground.

10 Front brake caliper – removal, overhaul and refitting

Removal

1   Apply the handbrake, then jack up the front of the car and support it on axle stands. Remove the appropriate roadwheel.

2   Fit a brake hose clamp to the flexible brake hose leading to the front brake caliper. This will minimise brake fluid loss during subsequent operations.

3   Loosen only the union on the caliper end of the flexible brake hose.

4   Remove the brake pads as described in Section 9.

5   Remove the Bendix type caliper by unscrewing the two bolts securing the caliper assembly to the stub axle carrier.

6   With the flexible brake hose still attached to the caliper, have an assistant very slowly depress the brake pedal until the piston has been ejected just over halfway out of its bore.

7   Unscrew the caliper from the brake hose, then plug or tape over the end of the hose to prevent dirt entry.

8   On the Girling type caliper unbolt the caliper frame from the stub axle carrier (photos).

Overhaul

9   With the caliper on the bench, wipe away all traces of dust and dirt, but *avoid inhaling the dust as it is injurious to health*.

10   On the Bendix type caliper unscrew the two bolts securing the caliper body to the reaction frame and lift off the body. Also remove the guide sleeves and seals.

11   On the Girling type caliper remove the guide pins and seals from the frame.

12   Withdraw the partially ejected piston from the caliper body and remove the dust cover. On the Girling type also remove the clip.

13   Using a suitable blunt instrument such as a knitting needle or a thick feeler blade, carefully extract the piston seal from the caliper bore.

14   Clean all the parts in methylated spirit or clean brake fluid, and wipe dry using a lint-free cloth. Inspect the piston and caliper bore for signs of damage, scuffing or corrosion, and if these conditions are evident renew the caliper body assembly. Inspect the condition of the dust excluders over the guide sleeves/pins and renew these too if there is any sign of damage or deterioration. Check the guide sleeves/pins for damage or distortion and renew if necessary.

15   If the components are in satisfactory condition, a repair kit consisting of new seals and dust excluders should be obtained. The guide sleeves/pins are also obtainable as a separate kit.

16   Lubricate the piston and seal with clean brake fluid and carefully fit the seal to the caliper bore.

17   On the Bendix type caliper, insert the piston into its bore, fit the new dust cover and then push the piston fully into its bore.

18   On the Girling type caliper, position the dust cover over the innermost end of the piston so that the caliper bore sealing lip protrudes beyond the base of the piston. Using a blunt instrument if necessary, engage the sealing lip of the dust cover with the groove in the caliper.

10.8A Girling caliper frame mounting bolts (arrowed)

10.8B Unscrewing the Girling caliper frame mounting bolts

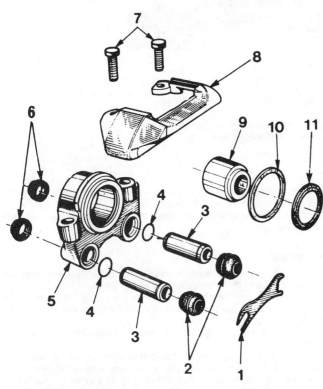

Fig. 9.10 Bendix type brake caliper components (Sec 10)

1 Retaining strip	7 Reaction frame retaining
2 Guide sleeve inner dust	bolts
excluders	8 Reaction frame
3 Guide sleeves	9 Piston
4 Guide sleeve seals	10 Piston seal
5 Caliper body	11 Piston dust excluder
6 Guide sleeve outer dust	
excluders	

Now push the piston into the bore until the other sealing lip of the dust cover can be engaged with the groove in the piston. Having done this, push the piston fully into its bore. Ease the piston out again slightly, and make sure that the cover lip is correctly seating in the piston groove. Fit the clip.

19   Smear the guide sleeves/pins with high melting-point grease and refit them together with the seals.

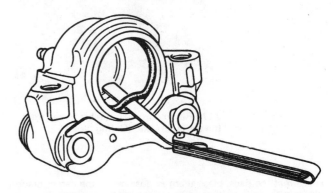

Fig. 9.11 Using a feeler blade to remove the piston seal from the Bendix type caliper (Sec 10)

20   On the Bendix type caliper refit the caliper body to the reaction frame and tighten the bolts to the specified torque.

Refitting

21   On the Girling type caliper refit the caliper frame to the stub axle carrier and tighten the bolts to the specified torque.
22   Hold the flexible brake hose and screw the caliper body back onto the hose.
23   Refit the Bendix type caliper to the stub axle carrier and tighten the bolts to the specified torque.
24   Refit the brake pads with reference to Section 9.
25   Fully tighten the flexible brake hose union to the caliper, making sure that it is not twisted or touching adjacent components.
26   Remove the brake hose clamp.
27   Bleed the hydraulic system with reference to Section 6. Note that providing the precautions described were taken to minimise brake fluid loss, it should only be necessary to bleed the relevant front brake.
28   Refit the roadwheel and lower the car to the ground.

11   Front brake disc – inspection, removal and refitting

Inspection

1   Apply the handbrake, then jack up the front of the car and support it on axle stands. Remove the appropriate front roadwheel.
2   Rotate the disc by hand and examine it for deep scoring, grooving or

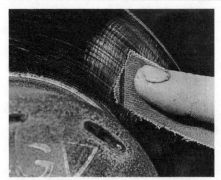

11.2A Using emery tape to remove light scoring from the disc

11.2B Checking the brake disc thickness with a micrometer

11.2C Checking the brake disc run-out with a dial test gauge

11.3 Girling brake caliper assembly suspended from the front suspension coil spring (pads removed)

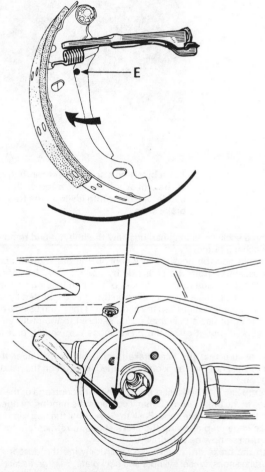

Fig. 9.12 Using a screwdriver inserted through the brake drum to release the handbrake operating lever (Sec 12)

E   *Handbrake operating lever stop peg*

cracks. Light scoring is normal and may be removed with emery tape, but, if excessive, the disc must be renewed. Any loose rust and scale around the outer edge of the disc can be removed by lightly tapping it with a small hammer while rotating the disc. Measure the disc thickness with a micrometer, if available. Disc run-out can be checked using a dial test gauge, although a less accurate method is to use a feeler blade together with a metal base block (photos).

Removal

3   Unscrew the two bolts securing the brake caliper assembly to the stub axle carrier. Withdraw the caliper, complete with pads, off the disc and suspend it from the front suspension coil spring (photo). Avoid straining the flexible brake hose. An alternative method on models with the Bendix caliper is to unbolt the reaction frame from the caliper body.
4   Using a Torx type socket bit or driver, unscrew the two screws securing the disc to the hub and withdraw the disc. If it is tight, lightly tap its rear face with a hide or plastic mallet.

Refitting

5   Refitting the disc is the reverse sequence to removal. If new discs are being fitted, first remove their protective coating. Ensure complete cleanliness of the hub and disc mating faces and tighten the screws to the specified torque. Coat the threads of the caliper or reaction frame bolts with locking fluid before fitting and tightening them. Finally depress the brake pedal two or three times to bring the pads into contact with the disc.

12   Rear brake drum – removal, inspection and refitting

Removal

1   Chock the front wheels then jack up the rear of the car and support it on axle stands. Remove the appropriate rear roadwheel and release the handbrake.
2   By judicious tapping and levering, remove the hub cap from the centre of the brake drum (photo).

12.2 Levering the hub cap from the centre of the brake drum

12.3A Removing the hub nut ...

12.3B ... and thrust washer

12.6A Inserting a screwdriver through one of the wheel bolt holes to depress the handbrake operating lever on the trailing brake shoe

12.6B Stop peg on the handbrake operating lever on the trailing brake shoe

3   Using a socket and long bar, unscrew the hub nut and remove the thrust washer (photos).

4   It should now be possible to withdraw the brake drum and hub bearing assembly from the stub axle by hand. It may be difficult to remove the drum due to the tightness of the hub bearing on the stub axle, or due to the brake shoes binding on the inner circumference of the drum. If the bearing is tight, tap the periphery of the drum using a hide or plastic mallet, or use a universal puller, secured to the drum with the wheel bolts, to pull it off. If the brake shoes are binding proceed as follows.

5   First ensure that the handbrake is fully off. From under the car slacken the locknut then back off the knurled adjuster on the handbrake primary rod.

6   Refer to Fig. 9.12 and insert a screwdriver through one of the wheel bolt holes in the brake drum so that it contacts the handbrake operating lever on the trailing brake shoe. Push the lever until the peg slips behind the brake shoe web allowing the brake shoes to retract (photos). The brake drum can now be withdrawn.

7   With the brake drum removed brush or wipe the dust from the drum, brake shoes, wheel cylinder and backplate. *Take great care not to inhale the dust as it is injurious to health. It is recommended that an approved filtering mask be worn during this operation.*

Inspection

8   Examine the internal surface of the brake drum for signs of scoring or cracks. If any deterioration of the surface finish is evident the drum may be skimmed to a maximum of 1.0 mm on the internal diameter, otherwise renewal is necessary. If the drum is to be skimmed it will be necessary to have the work carried out on both rear drums to maintain a consistent internal diameter on both sides.

Refitting

9   Slide the brake drum onto the stub axle and refit the thrust washer and hub nut. Tighten the hub nut to the specified torque and then tap the hub cap into place.

10   Depress the footbrake several times to operate the self-adjusting mechanism.

11   The handbrake should now be adjusted as described in Chapter 1, or after removing the brake drum on the other side if this is being done.

12   On completion, refit the roadwheel(s) and lower the car to the ground.

13   Rear brake shoes – renewal

Warning: *Drum brake shoes must be renewed on both rear wheels at the same time – never renew the shoes on only one wheel as uneven braking may result. Also, the dust created by wear of the shoes may contain asbestos, which is a health hazard. Never blow it out with compressed air and don't inhale any of it. An approved filtering mask should be worn when working on the brakes. DO NOT use petroleum based solvents to clean brake parts; use brake cleaner or methylated spirit only*

1   Remove the rear brake drum with reference to Section 12.

2   Note the fitted positions of the springs and the adjuster strut (photo).

3   Remove the shoe steady spring cups by depressing and turning them through 90° (photo). Remove the cups, springs and pins.

4   Pull the leading brake shoe from the bottom anchor and disconnect the lower return spring (photo).

5   Move the bottom ends of the brake shoes towards each other, then disconnect the tops of the shoes from the wheel cylinder (photo). Be careful not to damage the wheel cylinder rubber boots.

6   Disconnect the upper return spring from the brake shoes.

7   Remove the leading shoe and adjuster bolt from the adjuster strut (photo).

8   Unhook the handbrake cable from the handbrake operating lever on the trailing shoe (photo). Remove the trailing shoe.

13.2 Rear brake shoes fully assembled

13.3 Removing the rear brake shoe steady springs

13.4 Disconnecting the leading brake shoe from the bottom anchor

13.5 Disconnecting the rear brake shoes from the wheel cylinder

13.7 Removing the leading shoe and adjuster bolt from the adjuster strut

13.8 Unhook the handbrake cable from the handbrake operating lever on the trailing shoe

13.9 Rear brake trailing shoe and adjuster strut

13.10 Rear brake leading shoe and adjuster bolt

13.12 Apply a little high melting-point grease to the shoe contact points on the backplate

13.13 Spring components on the end of the adjuster strut

13.17 Reconnecting the upper return spring

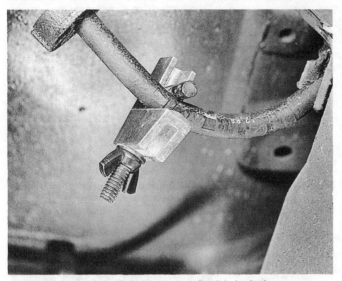

14.3 Brake hose clamp fitted to the rear flexible brake hose

14.5 Unscrewing the union nut from the rear of the wheel cylinder

9   Unhook the spring and remove the adjuster strut from the trailing shoe (photo).
10 Unhook the spring and remove the adjuster bolt from the leading shoe (photo).
11 Clean the adjuster strut, paying particular attention to the wheel and threads. Note that left-hand and right-hand struts are not interchangeable – they are marked 'G' (gauche) and 'D' (droit) respectively. Apply a little high melting-point grease to the threads of the adjuster.
12 Clean the backplate, then apply a little high melting-point grease to the shoe contact points on the backplate (photo).
13 Transfer the adjuster strut and bolt to the new shoes. Make sure that the spring components on the end of the strut are correctly fitted (photo). Position the adjuster wheel at the inner end of the adjuster bolt.
14 Locate the trailing shoe on the backplate and reconnect the handbrake cable to the operating lever. Refit the shoe steady spring to hold it in place.
15 Offer the leading shoe onto the backplate and insert the adjuster bolt into the adjuster strut. Refit the shoe steady spring to hold it in place.
16 Refit the lower return spring using a screwdriver to stretch the spring end into the location hole.
17 Refit the upper return spring using a screwdriver to stretch the spring end into the location hole (photo).
18 Turn the adjuster wheel until the diameter of the shoes is between 178.7 and 179.2 mm. This should allow the brake drum to just pass over the shoes.
19 Refit the brake drum with reference to Section 12.
20 Repeat the procedure on the remaining rear brake.

14   Rear wheel cylinder – removal and refitting

Removal

1   Remove the brake drum as described in Section 12.
2   Using pliers, detach the brake shoe upper return spring from both brake shoes.
3   Using a brake hose clamp or self-locking wrench with protected jaws, clamp the flexible brake hose just in front of the rear suspension transverse member (photo). This will minimise brake fluid loss during subsequent operations.
4   Wipe away all traces of dirt around the brake pipe union at the rear of the wheel cylinder.
5   Unscrew the union nut securing the brake pipe to the wheel cylinder (photo). Carefully ease out the pipe and plug or tape over its end to prevent dirt entry.
6   Unscrew the two bolts securing the wheel cylinder to the backplate. Move the brake shoes apart at the top and withdraw the cylinder from between the two shoes.

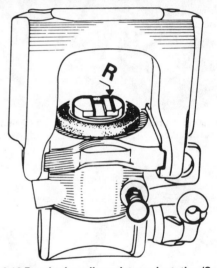

Fig. 9.13 Rear brake caliper piston orientation (Sec 15)

Line R to be nearest bleed screw

Refitting

7   Wipe clean the backplate, then spread the brake shoes and locate the wheel cylinder in position.
8   Engage the brake pipe and screw in the union nut two or three turns to ensure that the thread has started.
9   Insert the two wheel cylinder retaining bolts and tighten them securely. Now fully tighten the brake pipe union nut.
10 Remove the clamp from the flexible brake hose.
11 Refit the brake shoe upper return spring to the brake shoes using a screwdriver to stretch the spring into position.
12 Refit the brake drum with reference to Section 12.
13 Bleed the brake hydraulic system as described in Section 6. Providing suitable precautions were taken to minimise loss of fluid, it should only be necessary to bleed the relevant rear brake.

15   Rear brake pads – renewal

Warning: *Disc brake pads must be renewed on both rear wheels at the same time – never renew the pads on only one wheel as uneven braking may result. Also, the dust created by wear of the pads may contain asbestos, which is a health hazard. Never blow it out with compressed air and don't inhale any of it. An approved filtering mask should be worn* *when working on the brakes. DO NOT use petroleum based solvents to clean brake parts; use brake cleaner or methylated spirit only.*

1   Chock the front wheels, then jack up the rear of the car and support it on axle stands. Remove the rear wheels.
2   Disconnect the handbrake cable from the lever on the caliper.
3   Extract the two lockpins then tap out the two sliding keys.
4   Lift the caliper from the disc and tie it up out of the way.
5   Remove the disc pads and springs.
6   Clean the caliper by carefully brushing away the dust and dirt, *but avoid inhaling it as it is injurious to health*.
7   Retract the piston fully into its cylinder prior to fitting the new pads. Do this by turning the piston with the square section shaft of a screwdriver until the piston continues to turn but will not go in any further. As the piston goes in, the fluid level in the master cylinder reservoir will rise; anticipate this by syphoning out some fluid.
8   Finally, set the piston so that the line (R – Fig. 9.13) is nearest to the bleed screw.
9   Locate the springs onto the pads and fit the pads.
10   Fit the caliper by engaging one end of the caliper between the spring clip and the keyway on the bracket, compress the springs and engage the opposite end.
11   Insert the first key, then insert a screwdriver in the second key slot and use it as a lever until the slot will accept the key.
12   Fit new key lockpins.
13   Renew the pads on the opposite rear wheel.
14   Reconnect the handbrake cable.
15   Apply the brake pedal several times to position the pads against the discs.
16   Refit the wheels and lower the car to the ground.
17   Top up the brake fluid reservoir to the correct level.

16   Rear brake caliper – removal, overhaul and refitting

Removal

1   Chock the front wheels then jack up the rear of the car and support it on axle stands. Remove the rear wheel.
2   Disconnect the handbrake cable from the lever on the caliper.
3   Fit a brake hose clamp to the flexible hose leading to the caliper, then loosen only the hose union.
4   Extract the two lockpins then tap out the two sliding keys. Lift the caliper from the disc.
5   Unscrew the caliper from the hose and plug the end of the hose to prevent the entry of dirt.

Overhaul

6   Clean away external dirt from the caliper and grip it in the jaws of a vice fitted with jaw protectors.
7   Remove the dust excluder from around the piston and then unscrew the piston, using the square section shaft of a screwdriver. Once the piston turns freely but does not come out any further, apply low air pressure to the fluid inlet hole to eject the piston. Only low air pressure is required, such as that generated by a foot-operated tyre pump.
8   Inspect the surfaces of the piston and cylinder bore. If there is evidence of scoring or corrosion, renew the caliper cylinder.
9   To remove the cylinder, a wedge will have to be made in accordance with the dimensions shown in Fig. 9.14.
10   Drive the wedge in to slightly separate the support bracket arms and then slide out the cylinder after the spring-loaded locating pin has been depressed.
11   If the piston and cylinder are in good condition, then the cylinder will not have to be removed from the support bracket but overhauled in the following way.
12   Remove and discard the piston seal and wash the components in methylated spirit.
13   Obtain a repair kit which will contain all the necessary renewable items. Fit the new seal using the fingers to manipulate it into its groove.
14   Dip the piston in clean hydraulic fluid and insert the piston into the cylinder.
15   Using the square section shaft of a screwdriver, turn the piston until it turns but will not go in any further. Set the piston so that the line (R – Fig. 9.13) is nearest the bleed screw.
16   Fit a new dust excluder.
17   If the handbrake operating mechanism is worn or faulty, dismantle it in the following way before renewing the piston seal.
18   Grip the caliper in a vice fitted with jaw protectors.
19   Remove the dust excluder, the piston, dust cover, and circlip.
20   Compress the spring washers and pull out the shaft.
21   Remove the plunger cam, spring, adjusting screw, plain washer and spring washer.
22   Drive out the sleeve using a drift, and remove the sealing ring.
23   Clean all components and renew any that are worn.
24   Reassembly is a reversal of dismantling but observe the following points.

(a)   Drive in the sleeve until it is flush with face (A) in Fig. 9.15
(b)   Make sure that the spring washers are fitted as shown, convex face to convex face
(c)   Align the piston as previously described

Refitting

25   Refit the caliper after screwing it onto the hydraulic hose. Tighten the hose union. Refit the disc pads.
26   Reconnect the handbrake cable.
27   Bleed the hydraulic circuit (Section 6).

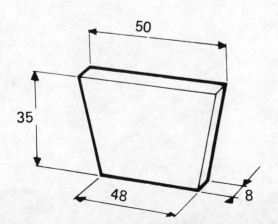

Fig. 9.14 Rear caliper support bracket arm wedge dimensions (mm) (Sec 16)

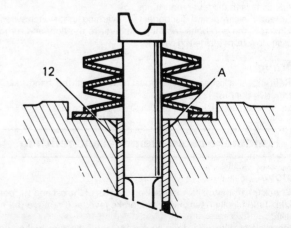

Fig. 9.15 Rear caliper sleeve (12) fitted flush with face (A) (Sec 16)

28   Refit the wheel and lower the car to the ground.
29   Apply the brake pedal several times and adjust the handbrake cable (Chapter 1).

17   Rear brake disc – inspection, removal and refitting

Inspection

1   Chock the front wheels, then jack up the rear of the car and support it on axle stands. Remove the appropriate rear roadwheel. Fully release the handbrake.
2   Rotate the disc by hand and examine it for deep scoring, grooving or cracks. Light scoring is normal, but, if excessive, the disc must be renewed. Any loose rust and scale around the outer edge of the disc can be removed by lightly tapping it with a small hammer while rotating the disc. Measure the disc thickness with a micrometer, if available. Disc run-out can be checked using a dial test gauge, although a less accurate method is to use a feeler blade together with a metal base block.

Removal

3   Remove the disc pads and disconnect the handbrake cable with reference to Sections 15 and 19. Tie the caliper up out of the way.
4   Unscrew and remove the two caliper bracket bolts and lift off the caliper bracket.
5   Using a Torx bit, unscrew and remove the two disc fixing screws and remove the disc.

Refitting

6   Refitting is a reversal of removal, but remove any protective coating from the new disc, and apply thread-locking fluid to the threads of the caliper bracket bolts. Apply the brake pedal several times and adjust the handbrake as described in Chapter 1. Refit the wheel and lower the car to the ground.

18   Handbrake lever – removal and refitting

Removal

1   Chock the front wheels then jack up the rear of the car and support it on axle stands. Fully release the handbrake lever.
2   Working under the car, unscrew the nut and remove the washer from the rear of the handbrake operating rod. Remove the cable compensator from the operating rod.
3   Release the primary rod from the support/guide block.
4   Working inside the car, remove the cover, then unbolt the two seat belt flexible stalk anchorages.
5   Make a slit in the carpet, just to the rear of the lever assembly to provide access to the lever mountings.
6   Spread the carpet and disconnect the warning light switch wires.
7   Unscrew the two bolts securing the lever to the floor and remove the assembly from inside the car (photo).

Refitting

8   Refitting is a reversal of removal, but adjust the handbrake as described in Chapter 1.

19   Handbrake cable – removal and refitting

Removal

1   Chock the front wheels then jack up the rear of the car and support it on axle stands. Fully release the handbrake lever and remove the rear wheel(s).
2   On models with rear drum brakes, remove the rear brake shoes from the appropriate side as described in Section 13.
3   On models with rear disc brakes, disconnect the cable from the caliper lever.

18.7 View of the handbrake lever mounting bolts from under the car (arrowed)

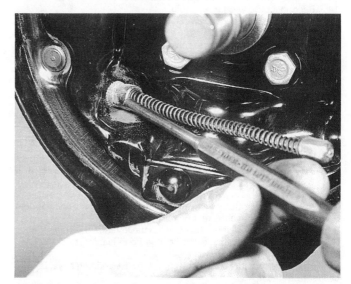

19.5 Driving the handbrake outer cable from the brake backplate

19.6 Handbrake cable support clip

4   Working under the car, unscrew the nut and remove the washer from the rear of the handbrake operating rod. Remove the cable compensator from the operating rod and disconnect the appropriate cable.
5   On models with rear drum brakes, using a narrow punch drive the outer cable from the brake backplate (photo).
6   Release the outer cable from the clip, then withdraw the cable from under the car. On some models it may be necessary to unbolt the clip and remove it together with the cable (photo).

Refitting

7   Refitting is a reversal of removal, however before refitting the drum, adjust the handbrake as described in Chapter 1.

20   Stop lamp switch – removal and refitting

Removal

1   The stop lamp switch is located on the pedal bracket beneath the facia (photo).
2   To remove the switch, pull off the wiring plug then unscrew it from the bracket.

Refitting

3   Refitting is a reversal of removal, but adjust the position of the switch so that the stop lamps operate after approximately 6.0 mm of pedal travel.

21   Anti-lock braking system – general information

The hydraulic components used in this system are similar to those

20.1 Stop lamp switch and wiring (arrowed)

used in a conventional braking system but the following additional items are fitted.

(a) A speed sensor on each wheel
(b) Four targets mounted at the front of the driveshafts and at the rear of the rear hubs
(c) An electronic computer comprising a self-monitoring system, a hydraulic unit which incorporates a pressure regulating valve, and a high pressure pump
(d) Two warning lamps are fitted to the instrument panel

The anti-lock braking system operates in the following way. As soon as the car roadspeed exceeds 3.7 mph (6.0 kph) the system becomes operational.
When the brakes are applied, the speed sensors detect the rapidly

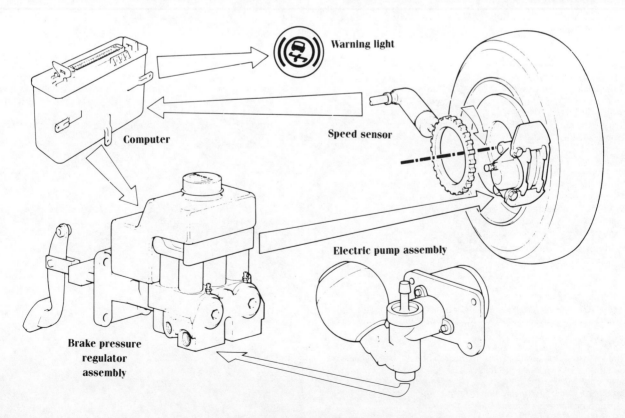

Fig. 9.16 Anti-lock braking system components (Sec 21)

falling speed of any roadwheel which happens if it starts to lock. The computer operates a regulator valve to prevent hydraulic braking pressure rising and to reduce it until the particular roadwheel deceleration ceases.

As soon as this deceleration ceases, a reverse phase commences to again raise the hydraulic pressure to normal.

The anti-lock cycle can be repeated up to ten times per second.

In order to maintain even braking, one rear wheel locking will subject the opposite brake to the same pressure variation cycle.

The warning lamp indicates to the driver the fact that the system is non-operational. Should this happen, the normal braking system remains fully operational, but the fault in the ABS must be repaired at the earliest opportunity.

If the warning lamp illuminates intermittently, check that the wheel sensor lead connections are clean and secure.

The warning switch in the fluid reservoir is a two-stage type which first activates the handbrake warning lamp on the instrument panel when the fluid drops below the normal minimum level. If the fluid level continues to drop, the switch then activates a second warning lamp on the instrument panel.

When the second warning lamp is illuminated due to a further drop in the fluid level, the ABS continues to operate on the rear wheels only, with normal braking to the front wheels.

In the event of both warning lamps operating simultaneously, it indicates that the pressure pump has a malfunction and is not working. Again the system will operate the rear wheel brakes only, with normal braking to the front wheel.

If a fault develops on the ABS system, it is recommended that the car be taken to a Renault garage for diagnosis and for replacement of any components.

At the time of writing no information was available covering these aspects of the system.

Chapter 10 Suspension and steering

Contents

Specifications

Front suspension

Type ....   Independent by MacPherson struts with inclined coil springs,
integral telescopic shock absorbers and anti-roll bar

Hub bearing endfloat ....   0 to 0.05 mm

Front underbody height (H1–H2):
  Enclosed bar rear suspension .... 87.0 ± 7.5 mm
  Open-bar rear suspension .... 93.0 ± 7.5 mm

Rear suspension

Type ....   Independent by trailing arms with transverse torsion bars (enclosed
or open according to model), telescopic shock absorbers and
anti-roll bar

Hub bearing endfloat ....   0 to 0.03 mm

Rear underbody height (H4–H5):
  Enclosed bar rear suspension .... 10 ± 7.5 mm
  Open-bar rear suspension .... 25 ± 7.5 mm

Rear wheel toe setting:
  Enclosed bar rear suspension .... -2 to -4 mm toe-in ($-20'$ to $-40'$)
  Open-bar rear suspension .... -3 to -5 mm toe-in ($-30'$ to $-50'$)

Steering

Type ....   Rack and pinion, power-assisted on some models

Turns lock-to-lock:
  Manual steering 3.9
  Power-assisted steering 3.5

Camber angle (nominal) .... $0° \pm 30'$

Camber angle at specified underbody height (H1–H2):
  22 mm .... $+1° 35' \pm 30'$
  59 mm .... $+0° 30' \pm 30'$
  86 mm .... $-0° 05' \pm 30'$
  115 mm .... $-0° 30' \pm 30'$
  149 mm .... $-0° 45' \pm 30'$

	Manual steering	Power steering
Maximum camber variation between sides	1°	
Castor angle (nominal):		
Manual steering	2° 30′	
Power-assisted steering	5°	
Castor angle at specified underbody height (H5–H2):		
21 mm	2° 55′	5°
40 mm	2° 25′	4° 30′
59 mm	1° 55′	4°
78 mm	1° 25′	3° 30′
97 mm	0° 55′	3°
Maximum castor variation between sides	1°	
Steering axis inclination at specified underbody height (H1–H2):		
22 mm	10° 45′ ± 30′	
59 mm	12° 5′ ± 30′	
86 mm	12° 55′ ± 30′	
115 mm	13° 40′ ± 30′	
149 mm	14° 15′ ± 30′	
Maximum steering axis inclination variation between sides	1°	
Toe setting	1.0 ± 1.0 mm (0° 10′ ± 10′) toe-out	

Roadwheels

Type	Pressed steel or aluminium alloy, according to model
Size	5B x 13, 5J x 13, 5 1/2 B x 13 and 5 1/2 J x 14 according to model
Maximum run-out at rim	1.2 mm
Maximum eccentricity on tyre bead locating surface	0.8 mm

Tyres

Tyre size	145 R 13S, 165/70 R 13T, 175/70 R 13T, 175/70 R 13H, 175/65 R 14T, and 175/65 R 14H, according to model

Tyre pressures (cold)*

	Front	Rear
Manual transmission models	2.0 bar (29 lbf/in²)	2.2 bar (32 lbf/in²)
Automatic transmission models	2.1 bar (31 lbf/in²)	2.2 bar (32 lbf/in²)

For latest information, consult vehicle handbook or tyre manufacturer's recommendations

Torque wrench settings

	Nm	lbf ft
Front suspension		
Strut upper mounting	25	19
Strut piston rod to mounting	60	44
Strut to stub axle carrier	110	81
Balljoint clamp bolt	55	41
Balljoint to lower arm	75	55
Lower arm inner pivot bolt	75	55
Anti-roll bar	35	26
Rear suspension		
Bearing bracket to underbody	80	59
Anti-roll bar to trailing arm (enclosed bar suspension)	45	33
Shock absorber lower mounting	60	44
Shock absorber upper mounting	20	15
Backplate to trailing arm	45	33
Hub nut	160	118
Steering		
Track rod end locknut	35	26
Track rod end to stub axle carrier	35	26
Steering gear mounting	50	37
Steering wheel nut	40	30
Intermediate shaft to pinion shaft pinch bolt	30	22
Roadwheels		
Wheel bolts	80	59

1   General information

The independent front suspension is of the MacPherson strut type incorporating inclined coil springs, integral telescopic shock absorbers and an anti-roll bar. The struts are attached to stub axle carriers at their lower ends, and the carriers are in turn attached to the lower suspension arm by balljoints. The anti-roll bar is attached to the subframe and lower suspension arms by rubber bushes.

The independent rear suspension is of the trailing arm type incorporating torsion bars. On models up to 90 bhp it is of tubular type and consists of two torsion bars within a tube and an external anti-roll bar. On other models it is of open four-bar type consisting of two torsion bars and an L-section metal cross bar. The torsion bars are connected at the centre with a link, and two half anti-roll bars are also connected at the central link.

A rack and pinion steering gear is fitted together with a conventional column and 'safety' intermediate shaft. Power-assisted steering is available on some models.

2   Front stub axle carrier – removal and refitting

Removal

1   Apply the handbrake, then jack up the front of the car and support it on axle stands. Remove the appropriate front roadwheel.

Fig. 10.1 Front suspension layout (Sec 1)

Fig. 10.2 Rear suspension layout (Sec 1)

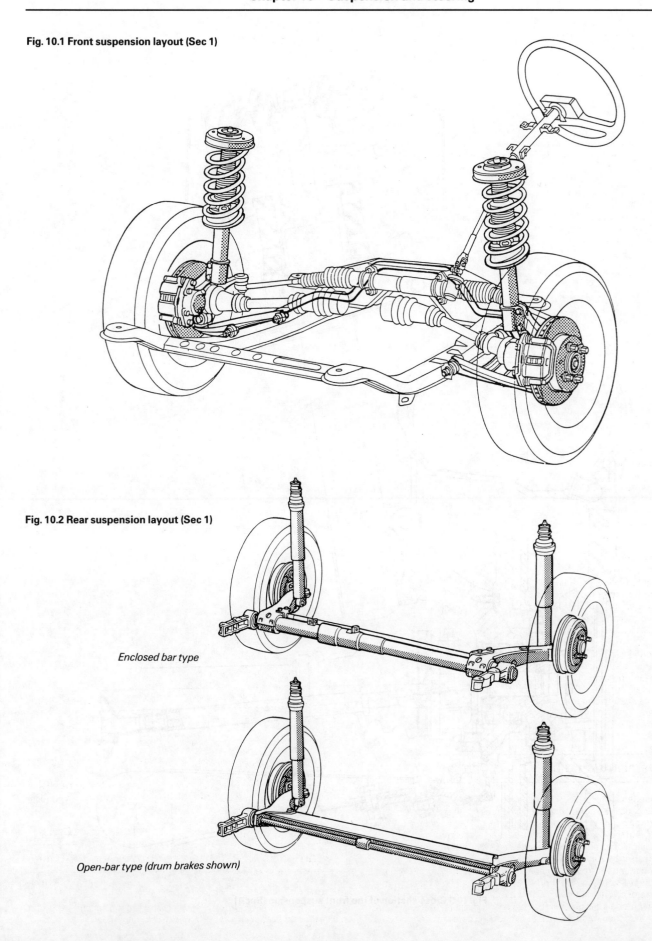

Enclosed bar type

Open-bar type (drum brakes shown)

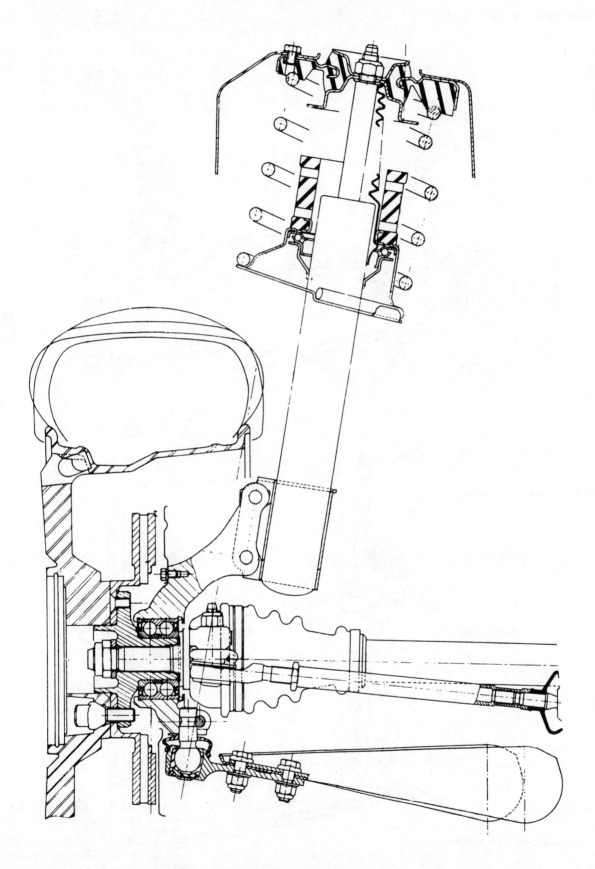

Fig. 10.3 Cross-section of the front suspension (Sec 1)

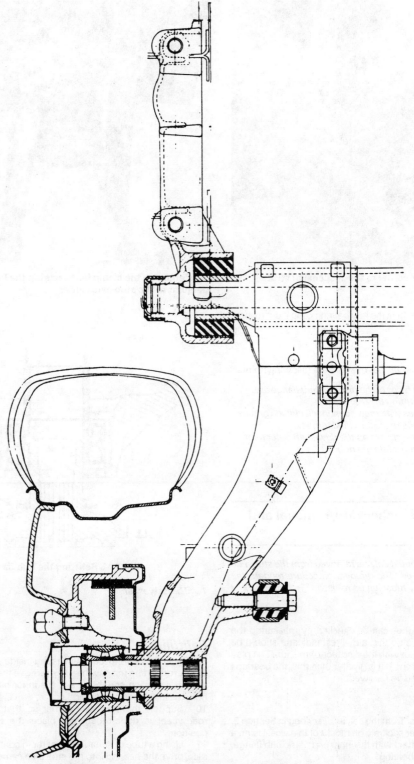

Fig. 10.4 Cross-section of the rear suspension – enclosed bar type shown (Sec 1)

2 Remove the front brake disc with reference to Chapter 9.

3 Hold the front hub stationary by using two roadwheel bolts to attach a length of metal bar to the hub, then unscrew the driveshaft nut using a socket and extension bar. Alternatively, have an assistant firmly depress the footbrake pedal to hold the hub and disc stationary while the nut is being unscrewed. Remove the washer.

4 Disconnect the steering track rod end balljoint from the stub axle carrier with reference to Section 25.

5 Unscrew and remove the two bolts securing the stub axle carrier to the suspension strut. Note that the nuts are on the brake caliper side (photo).

6 Unscrew the nut and withdraw the clamp bolt securing the lower suspension arm balljoint to the base of the stub axle carrier (photo).

7 Release the stub axle carrier from the strut and then lift it, while pushing down on the suspension arm, to disengage the lower balljoint. Withdraw the stub axle carrier from the driveshaft and remove it from

2.5 Bolts holding the stub axle carrier to the suspension strut

2.6 Removing the clamp bolt securing the lower suspension arm balljoint to the stub axle carrier

the car. If the driveshaft is a tight fit in the hub bearings, tap it out using a plastic mallet, or use a suitable puller.

Refitting

8   Refitting is a reversal of removal, but observe the following points:

    (a) *Ensure that the mating faces of the disc and hub flange are clean and flat before refitting the disc*
    (b) *Lubricate the hub splines with molybdenum disulphide grease*
    (c) *Tighten all nuts and bolts to the specified torque*
    (d) *Apply locking fluid to the splines on the driveshaft outer joint stub axle before inserting it into the hub*

3   Front hub bearings – checking, removal and refitting

Note: *The front hub bearings should only be removed from the stub axle carrier if they are to be renewed. The removal procedure renders the bearings unserviceable and they must not be re-used*

Checking

1   Wear in the front hub bearings can be checked by measuring the amount of side play present. To do this, a dial test indicator should be fixed so that its probe is in contact with the disc face of the hub. The play should be between 0 and 0.05 mm. If it is greater than this, the bearings are worn excessively and should be renewed.

Removal

2   Remove the stub axle carrier from the car, as described in Section 2.
3   Support the stub axle carrier securely on blocks or in a vice. Using a tube of suitable diameter in contact with the inner end of the hub flange, drive the hub flange out of the bearing.
4   The bearing will come apart as the hub flange is removed and one of the bearing inner races will remain on the hub flange. To remove it, support the flange in a vice and lever off the inner race using a two or three-legged puller. Recover the thrust washer from the hub flange after removal of the inner race.
5   Extract the bearing retaining circlip from the inner end of the stub axle carrier.
6   Support the stub axle carrier on blocks or in a vice so that the side nearest the roadwheel is uppermost.
7   Place the previously removed inner race back in position over the ball cage. Using a tube of suitable diameter in contact with the inner race, drive the complete bearing assembly out of the stub axle carrier.

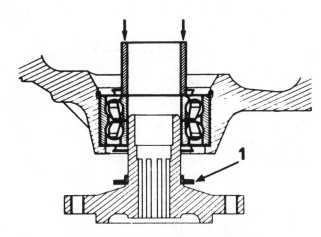

Fig. 10.5 Refitting the hub flange (Sec 3)

1   *Thrust washer*

Refitting

8   Clean the bearing location seating inside the hub.
9   Before fitting the new bearing, remove the plastic covers protecting the seals at each end, but leave the inner plastic sleeve in position to hold the inner races together.
10   Support the stub axle carrier so that the side away from the roadwheel is uppermost, and place the new bearing squarely in position.
11   Using a tube of suitable diameter in contact with the bearing outer race, drive the bearing into the stub axle carrier. Ensure that the bearing does not tip slightly and bind as it is being fitted. If this happens the outer race and housing may be damaged, so take great care to keep it square.
12   With the bearing in position, lubricate the lips of the two seals with multi-purpose grease. Remove the plastic retaining sleeve.
13   Place the thrust washer over the hub flange and lay it on the bench, flat face down.
14   Locate the stub axle carrier and bearing inner race over the hub flange and drive the bearing onto the flange using a tube in contact with the bearing's inner race.
15   Fit a new bearing retaining circlip to the stub axle carrier and then refit the assembly to the car, as described in Section 2.

4.3 Front suspension strut upper mounting bolts (arrowed)

4 Front suspension strut – removal and refitting

Removal

1   Apply the handbrake, then jack up the front of the car and support it on axle stands. Remove the appropriate front roadwheel.
2   Unscrew and remove the two nuts and bolts securing the suspension strut to the upper part of the stub axle carrier. Note that the nuts are on the brake caliper side.
3   From within the engine compartment unscrew the two bolts securing the strut upper mounting to the turret (photo). Note that there are two sets of holes – one for manual steering models and the other for power-assisted steering models.
4   Release the strut from the stub axle carrier and withdraw it from under the wheelarch while pressing on the lower suspension arm to prevent damage to the driveshaft gaiter.

Refitting

5   Refitting is a reversal of removal. Ensure that the strut-to-stub axle carrier bolts are fitted with the nuts on the brake caliper side and tighten all the retaining bolts to the specified torque. Make sure that the strut upper mounting bolts are fitted in their correct holes.

5 Front suspension strut – dismantling, examination and reassembly

Note: *Before attempting to dismantle the front suspension strut, a tool to hold the coil spring in compression must be obtained. The Renault tool is shown in Fig. 10.7, however careful use of conventional coil spring compressors will prove satisfactory*

Dismantling

1   With the strut removed from the car, clean away all external dirt then mount it upright in a vice.
2   Fit the spring compressor tool and compress the coil spring until all tension is relieved from the upper mounting (photo).
3   Withdraw the plastic cap over the strut upper mounting nut, hold the strut piston with an Allen key and unscrew the nut with a ring spanner (photo).
4   Lift off the washer, upper mounting and spring seat assembly followed by the spring and compressor tool. Do not remove the tool from the spring unless the spring is to be renewed. Finally, remove the bump stop, convoluted rubber cone, and the lower spring seat and bearing components.

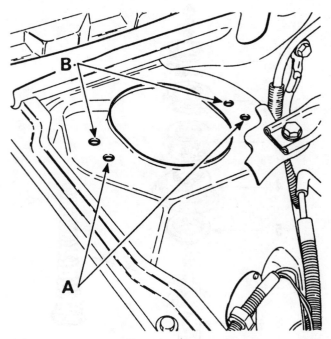

Fig. 10.6 Front suspension strut upper mounting bolt holes (Sec 4)

A   *Manual steering models*   B   *Power-assisted steering models*

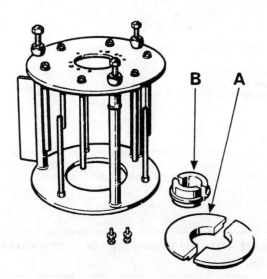

Fig. 10.7 Renault spring compressor tool (Sec 5)

A   *Thrust cup*   B   *Retaining shell*

Examination

5   With the strut assembly now completely dismantled, examine all the components for wear, damage or deformation and check the bearing for smoothness of operation. Renew any of the components as necessary.
6   Examine the strut for signs of fluid leakage. Check the strut piston for signs of pitting along its entire length and check the strut body for signs of damage or elongation of the mounting bolt holes. Test the operation of the strut, while holding it in an upright position, by moving the piston through a full stroke and then through short strokes of 50 to 100 mm. In both cases the resistance felt should be smooth and continuous. If the resistance is jerky, or uneven, or if there is any visible sign of wear or damage to the strut, renewal is necessary.

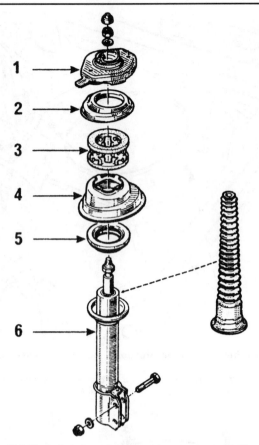

Fig. 10.8 Exploded view of the front suspension strut (Sec 5)

1   Upper mounting   4   Lower spring seat
2   Upper spring seat   5   Bearing
3   Bump stop   6   Strut

Reassembly

7   Reassembly is a reversal of dismantling, however make sure that the spring ends are correctly located in the upper and lower seats and tighten the upper nut to the specified torque.

5.2 Using spring compressors to compress the front suspension coil spring

5.3 Unscrewing the front suspension strut upper mounting nut while holding the strut piston with an Allen key

6   Front suspension anti-roll bar – removal and refitting

Removal

1   Apply the handbrake, then jack up the front of the car and support it on axle stands.
2   Remove the exhaust downpipe with reference to Chapter 4.
3   Disconnect the gearchange linkage from the transmission with reference to Chapter 7.
4   Unscrew the nuts and remove the clamp bolts holding the ends of the anti-roll bar to the lower suspension arms. Remove the clamps.
5   Unscrew the nuts and remove the clamp bolts from the mountings on the subframe (photo). Remove the clamps.
6   Lower the anti-roll bar from the rear of the subframe.
7   Check the bar for damage and the rubber bushes for wear and deterioration. If the bushes are in need of renewal, slide them off the bar and fit new ones after lubricating them with rubber grease.

Refitting

8   Refitting is a reversal of removal, but delay fully tightening the clamp bolts until the unladen weight of the car is on the suspension.

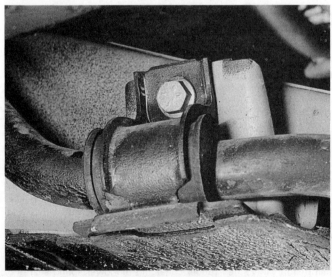

6.5 Front suspension anti-roll bar mounting on the subframe

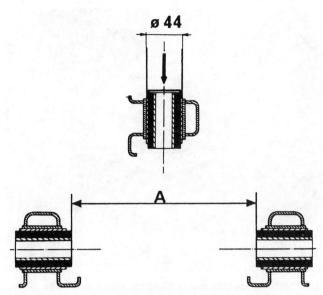

Fig. 10.9 Front suspension lower arm pivot bush fitting dimension (Sec 7)

A 147.0 ± 0.5 mm

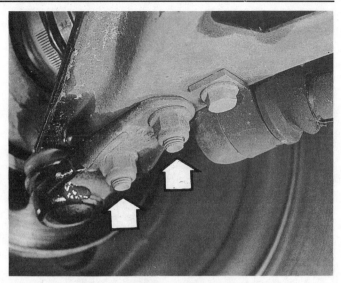

8.4A Front suspension balljoint bolts (arrowed) on the lower suspension arm

7 Front suspension lower arm – removal and refitting

Removal

1   Apply the handbrake, then jack up the front of the car and support it on axle stands. Remove the appropriate roadwheel.
2   Unscrew the nuts and remove the clamp bolts holding the ends of the anti-roll bar to the lower suspension arms. Remove the clamps, then loosen the mounting clamp bolts and pull the anti-roll bar downwards.
3   Unscrew the nut and remove the clamp bolt securing the lower suspension balljoint to the stub axle carrier. Note which way round the bolt is fitted.
4   Unscrew the nuts and remove the spacers and pivot bolts from the inner end of the suspension arm then withdraw the arm from the subframe and stub axle carrier. If the balljoint stub is seized in the stub axle carrier, lever or drive it out with a mallet. Recover the plastic protector from the balljoint boot.
5   If the inner pivot bushes are to be renewed, this can be done using suitable lengths of tube and a press or wide-opening vice. Renew the bushes one at a time so that the distance between the bush inner edges is maintained at 146.5 to 147.5 mm.

Refitting

6   Refitting is a reversal of removal. Make sure that the plastic protector is positioned over the balljoint boot. Tighten the balljoint clamp bolt to the specified torque. Tighten the pivot bolts and anti-roll bar mounting bolts to the specified torque with the unladen weight of the car on the suspension.

8 Front suspension balljoint – renewal

1   Apply the handbrake, then jack up the front of the car and support it on axle stands. Remove the roadwheel.
2   Unscrew the nut and remove the clamp bolt securing the lower suspension balljoint to the stub axle carrier.
3   Loosen the lower suspension arm inner pivot bolts, then pull the arm down from the stub axle carrier. If necessary, lever the arm down.
4   Unscrew the two nuts and bolts securing the balljoint to the lower suspension arm and withdraw the balljoint. Recover the plastic protector from the balljoint boot (photos).

8.4B Removing the plastic protector from the front suspension balljoint

5   Fit the new balljoint using a reversal of the removal procedure, but tighten the nuts to the specified torque. Delay tightening the suspension arm inner pivot bolts until the weight of the car is on the suspension.

9 Rear hub bearings – checking, removal and refitting

Checking

1   Chock the front wheels, then jack up the rear of the car and support it on axle stands. Remove the appropriate rear roadwheel and fully release the handbrake.
2   Wear in the rear hub bearings can be checked by measuring the amount of side play present. To do this, a dial test indicator should be fixed so that its probe is in contact with the hub. The play should be between 0 and 0.03 mm. If it is greater than this, the bearings are worn excessively and should be renewed.

Removal

3   On models with rear drum brakes, remove the brake drum with reference to Chapter 9.

9.5A Extract the circlip ...

9.5B ... then drive out the rear hub bearing with a metal tube

Fig. 10.10 Exploded view of the rear hub bearing (Sec 9)

4   On models with rear disc brakes, remove the brake disc with reference to Chapter 9, then lever or tap off the grease cap from the centre of the hub. Using a socket and long bar, unscrew the hub nut and remove the thrust washer. Pull the hub bearing assembly from the stub axle.
5   With the hub removed, extract the circlip and drive out the bearing using a tube of suitable diameter inserted through the inside of the hub and in contact with the bearing outer race (photos).
6   Clean the bearing seating inside the hub.

Refitting

7   Place the bearing in the hub and drive it fully home, again using a tube in contact with the bearing outer race. Take great care to keep the bearing square as it is installed, otherwise it may jam in the hub bore.
8   With the bearing in position, refit the retaining circlip.
9   Check that the bearing inner spacer/thrust washer is located on the stub axle. Smear a little SAE 80W oil onto the stub axle to help the bearings slide into position.
10   Slide the brake drum or disc (as applicable) onto the stub axle and refit the thrust washer and hub nut. Tighten the hub nut to the specified torque and then tap the hub cap into place.
11   On rear disc brake models secure the brake disc with reference to Chapter 9.
12   Depress the footbrake several times. If necessary, adjust the handbrake as described in Chapter 1.
13   Refit the roadwheel and lower the car to the ground.

10   Rear shock absorber – removal, testing and refitting

Removal

1   Chock the front wheels, then jack up the rear of the car and support it on axle stands. Remove the appropriate roadwheel.
2   Using a trolley jack, lift the trailing arm until the shock absorber is compressed slightly then unscrew and remove the lower mounting bolt (photo).
3   Working inside the luggage compartment, pull off the rubber cover then unscrew the upper mounting nut (photo). If necessary, hold the piston rod stationary with a further spanner.
4   Withdraw the shock absorber from under the car.

Testing

5   Mount the shock absorber in a vice and test it as described in Section 5 for the front suspension strut. Also check the mounting

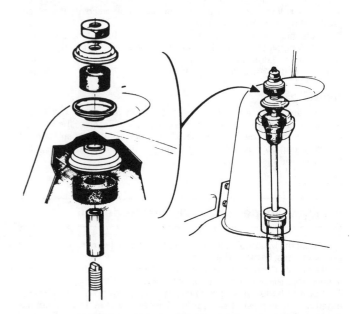

Fig. 10.11 Exploded view of the rear shock absorber upper mounting (Sec 10)

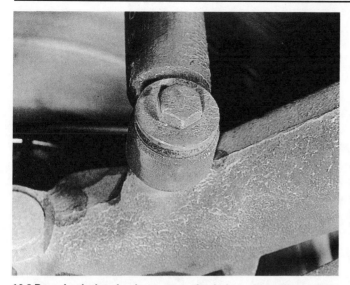

10.2 Rear shock absorber lower mounting bolt on the trailing arm

10.3 Rear shock absorber upper mounting nut in the luggage compartment

rubbers for damage and deterioration. Renew the complete unit if any damage or excessive wear is evident.

Refitting

6 Before refitting the shock absorber, mount it upright in the vice and operate it fully through several strokes in order to prime it.
7 Refitting is a reversal of removal, but delay fully tightening the nut and bolt to the specified torque until the weight of the car is on the suspension.

11 Rear suspension anti-roll bar (enclosed bar rear axle) – removal and refitting

Removal

1 Chock the front wheels then jack up the rear of the car and support it on axle stands.
2 From each end of the anti-roll bar unscrew the through-bolts securing the brackets to the rear suspension trailing arms. Note the location of the handbrake cable brackets. Recover the plates with the trapped nuts.
3 Withdraw the anti-roll bar from under the car. If the bar is to be refitted, identify it for position to ensure correct positioning when refitting.

Refitting

4 Refitting is a reversal of removal, but tighten the through-bolts to the specified torque. Note that the cutaway sides of the brackets must be towards the front of the car.

12 Rear suspension torsion bar – removal and refitting

Removal

1 Chock the front wheels then jack up the rear of the car and support it on axle stands. Remove the appropriate roadwheel.
2 On models with the enclosed bar rear axle, remove the anti-roll bar as described in Section 11.
3 Remove the rear shock absorber as described in Section 10.
4 Lower the trailing arm until all the tension in the torsion bar is released.
5 Prise the cap from the trailing arm bearing bracket.
6 Mark the position of the torsion bar in relation to the bearing bracket, and on the open-bar rear axle, in relation to the centre link block.

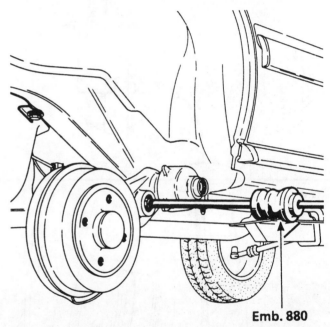

Emb. 880

Fig. 10.12 Using the special Renault tool to remove the torsion bar on the open-bar rear suspension (Sec 12)

7 The torsion bar can now be withdrawn outwards using a slide-hammer such as Renault tool Emb.880 or a suitable alternative. It is possible to improvise by screwing a long bolt with a flat washer into the torsion bar and placing the jaws of a spanner against the washer. Striking the spanner sharply with a hammer should free the torsion bar.
8 Once the splines of the torsion bar are free, the bar can be withdrawn completely from its location. Note that the torsion bars are not interchangeable from side to side and are marked with symbols on their ends for identification as shown in Fig. 10.13.

Refitting

9 If the original torsion bar is being refitted, insert it so that the marks made in paragraph 6 are aligned. However, if a new bar is being fitted, the trailing arm must be positioned to provide the dimension shown in Fig. 10.14. A tool similar to that shown will hold the trailing arm in position, or the arm can be positioned with the trolley jack.
10 With the trailing arm supported in this position lubricate the torsion bar splines with molybdenum disulphide grease and insert the bar into the bracket. The number of splines at each end of the bar is

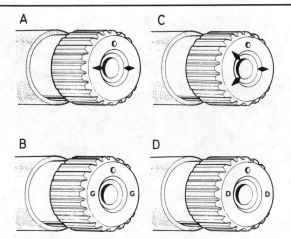

Fig. 10.13 Rear suspension torsion bar identification (Sec 12)

A & B – Left-hand torsion bar
C & D – Right-hand torsion bar

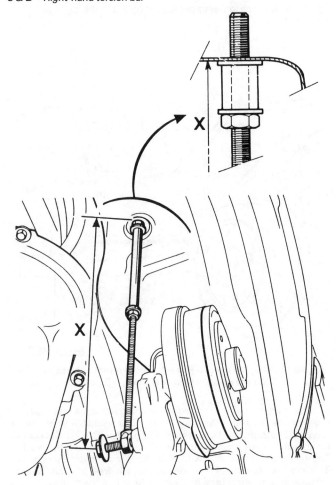

Fig. 10.14 Rear suspension setting dimension (Sec 12)

x = 590 mm (enclosed bar suspension), or
645 mm (open-bar suspension)

different so it will be necessary to turn it to find the point where both sets of splines enter freely. Having found this, tap the bar fully home using a hammer and soft metal drift.
11   Refit the cap to the bearing bracket.
12   Refit the rear shock absorber (Section 10), the rear anti-roll bar on models with the enclosed bar rear axle (Section 11), and the rear roadwheel. Lower the car to the ground.

13.8 Rear suspension trailing arm bracket mounting bolts

13   It is now necessary to check the rear underbody height, noting that the fuel tank should be full, or an equivalent weight placed in the luggage compartment, and the tyres correctly inflated. Refer to Section 17 for further information.

13   Rear suspension trailing arm (enclosed bar rear axle) – removal and refitting

Removal

1   Chock the front wheels, then jack up the rear of the car and support it on axle stands. Remove the appropriate rear roadwheel.
2   Remove the anti-roll bar and the shock absorber lower mounting bolt with reference to Sections 11 and 10 respectively. Remove the torsion bar on the side concerned, as described in Section 12.
3   Remove the rear brake drum/hub with reference to Chapter 9.
4   With the drum removed, detach the handbrake cable from the operating lever on the trailing brake shoe and withdraw the cable from the brake backplate.
5   Using a brake hose clamp, clamp the appropriate flexible brake hose just in front of the rear axle. This will minimise brake fluid loss during subsequent operations. Clean the union on the trailing arm then unscrew the union nut and withdraw the hose from the bracket. Recover the clip then tape over the ends of the hose and pipe to prevent the entry of dirt.
6   Support the weight of the trailing arm with a trolley jack.
7   Working inside the luggage compartment, lift the carpet and remove the trim to gain access to the trailing arm mounting bolt heads.
8   Unscrew the nuts from beneath the car then tap the bolts through the bearing bracket with a suitable drift (photo).
9   Lower the jack as necessary to allow the trailing arm to clear the sill.
10   Pull the trailing arm from the remaining arm. If it is tight, it may be necessary to use a puller.
11   With the arm removed, the brake backplate can be unbolted if required and the spacer removed from the stub axle (photo).

Refitting

12   To refit the arm, push it onto the other arm having first lubricated the inner bushes with grease. If it is tight, use a rope as a tourniquet between the two arms. Temporarily position the anti-roll bar over the mounting holes to determine how far the bars should be interlocked.
13   Raise the trolley jack to lift the arm, and insert the mounting bolts, tightening their nuts securely. Refit the trim inside the luggage compartment.
14   Refit the brake backplate. Use locking fluid on the retaining bolts and tighten them to the specified torque setting. Refit the stub axle spacer.

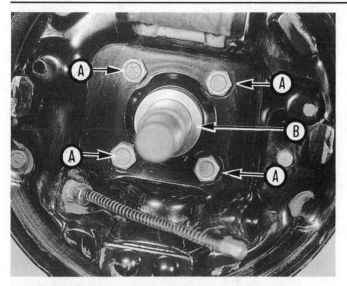

13.11 Rear brake backplate mounting bolts (A) and bearing spacer (B)

15   Refit the flexible brake hose and rigid pipe together with the clip and tighten the union nut.
16   Remove the brake hose clamp.
17   Refit the handbrake cable and drum with reference to Chapter 9.
18   Refit the torsion bar (Section 12), shock absorber (Section 10), and anti-roll bar (Section 11).
19   Bleed the brake hydraulic system as described in Chapter 9, noting that it should only be necessary to bleed the relevant rear brake, providing the hose was clamped as described.
20   Finally refit the roadwheel and lower the car to the ground.

14 Rear suspension trailing arm bearings (enclosed bar rear axle) – renewal

1   Remove both trailing arms with reference to Section 13.
2   Mount the left-hand trailing arm in a vice.
3   To remove the bearings it will be necessary to obtain the Renault tool shown in Fig. 10.15 or to make up a similar tool using the Renault tool as a pattern, as follows. First note the exact position of the bearings.
4   Obtain a threaded rod long enough to reach the inner bearing, a tube of suitable diameter as shown, one thick washer of diameter equal to that of the bearing, a washer of diameter greater than the tube, and two nuts. Cut two sides off the smaller washer so that just a flat strip with a hole in the centre remains. This will form the swivelling end part shown on the Renault tool. Pass the threaded rod through the hole in the strip and screw on a nut. Feed the strip and rod through the bearing so that the strip locates behind the bearing. Place the tube over the rod and in contact with the edge of the arm. Place the large washer over the end of the tube and then screw on the remaining nut. Hold the rod with grips and tighten the nut to draw out the bearing, then repeat this operation to remove the remaining bearing.
5   Clean the inside of the arm then drive in the new bearings using suitable tubing.
6   Mount the right-hand trailing arm in the vice.
7   Note the exact position of the bearing inner tracks. Cut or grind almost through the bearing inner tracks taking care not to damage the tube. Using a cold chisel, split the tracks and remove them from the tube. Also cut and remove the seal from the tube.
8   Clean the arm and fit the new seal.
9   Press on the new inner tracks making sure that the lead chamfer goes on first. When doing this, if the load is being taken on the axle support assemblies make sure that the torsion bars are correctly located in the anchor points.
10   It is not necessary to grease the bearing needle races as they are supplied already greased.
11   Reassemble and refit the trailing arms with reference to Section 13.

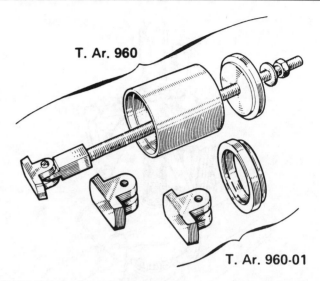

Fig. 10.15 Renault tool for removing the rear suspension trailing arm bearings on the enclosed bar rear axle (Sec 14)

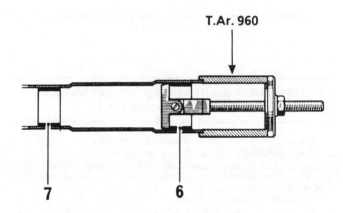

Fig. 10.16 Using the Renault tool to remove the rear suspension trailing arm bearings (Sec 14)

6   Outer bearing   7   Inner bearing

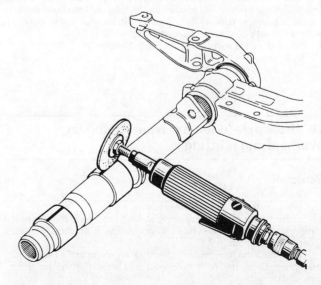

Fig. 10.17 Removing the bearing inner tracks by grinding (Sec 14)

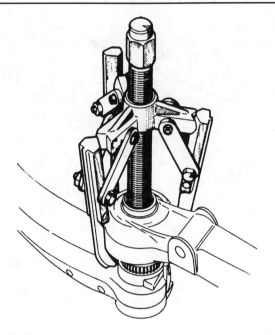

Fig. 10.18 Using a puller to remove the rear suspension bearing bracket (Sec 15)

15   Rear suspension bearing bracket bushes (enclosed bar rear axle) – renewal

1   Remove the trailing arm as described in Section 13.
2   Apply brake fluid to the bush to soften the rubber.
3   Using a two or three-legged puller draw the bearing bracket from the trailing arm. The rubber will tear during this process leaving the inner part of the bush on the arm.
4   Remove the remaining part of the bush by cutting with a hacksaw taking care not to damage the trailing arm tube. Also remove the outer remains of the bush from the bearing bracket. Clean the tube and bracket.
5   The fitted position of the new bush must be flush with the end of the trailing arm tube so mark the inner part of the tube to indicate the final position of the bush.
6   Press or drive the new bush fully into the bearing bracket.
7   Position the bracket as shown in Fig. 10.19 in relation to the trailing arm then press or drive the bracket on the tube until the bush reaches the mark made in paragraph 5. Check that the dimension between bracket bolt hole centres is as shown in Fig. 10.20.
8   Refit the trailing arm with reference to Section 13.

16   Rear axle (open bar type) – removal, overhaul and refitting

Removal

1   Chock the front wheels, then jack up the rear of the car and support it on axle stands. Remove both rear roadwheels.
2   Support both rear trailing arms so that the shock absorbers are compressed slightly, then unscrew and remove both shock absorber lower mounting bolts.
3   Disconnect the handbrake cables from each rear brake caliper with reference to Chapter 9. Also disconnect the cables from the underbody clips (photo).
4   Using brake hose clamps, clamp both rear flexible hoses then

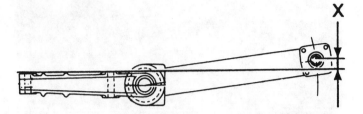

Fig. 10.19 Correct assembling dimension of the rear suspension bearing bracket and trailing arm (Sec 15)

x = 15 mm

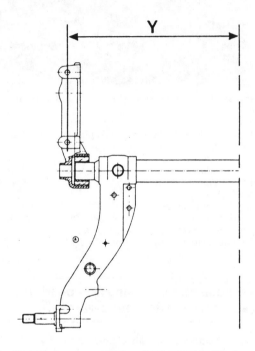

Fig. 10.20 Rear suspension bearing bracket bolt hole centre dimension (Sec 15)

y = 1268 ± 1 mm

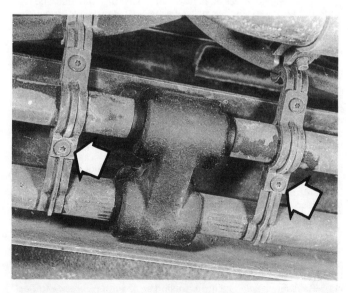

16.3 Handbrake cable supports (arrowed) on the open bar rear axle

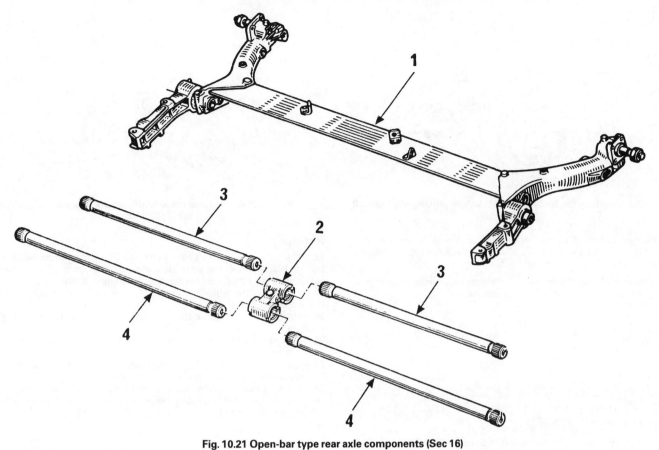

Fig. 10.21 Open-bar type rear axle components (Sec 16)

1 Integral trailing arms and   2 Link block   3 Anti-roll bars   4 Torsion bars
   flexible bar

---

disconnect them by unscrewing the union nuts. Recover the clips and tape over the ends of the hoses and pipes to prevent the entry of dirt.
5   Support the weight of the rear axle on a trolley jack.
6   Unscrew the nuts securing the bearing brackets to the underbody (photo). If necessary, hold the bolt heads by lifting the carpet and removing the trim inside the luggage compartment.
7   Lower the rear axle from the underbody and remove it.

Overhaul

8   Remove the two torsion bars with reference to Section 12.
9   If required, remove the bearings using the method described for the enclosed bar rear axle in Section 14.
10   Mark the anti-roll bars in relation to the trailing arms and link block, then extract them using a slide-hammer such as Renault tool Emb.880 or a suitable alternative.
11   Examine all the components for damage and wear. Check the splines on the torsion bars, anti-roll bars, link block and trailing arms. If the trailing arms or L-shaped section is damaged, it will be necessary to obtain a new rear axle (supplied with the bearing brackets already fitted, but requiring the original torsion bars and anti-roll bars to be fitted). If the bearing bracket bushes require renewal use the procedure described in Section 15.
12   Commence reassembly by placing the rear axle upside-down on blocks of wood positioned under the L-shaped section so that the bearing brackets are free.
13   If the old anti-roll bars are being refitted, grease the splines and refit them in their original positions.
14   If new anti-roll bars are being fitted, use a ruler as shown in Fig. 10.22 and mark each trailing arm between the centres of the torsion bar and anti-roll bar holes. Make the mark by the bottom of a spline. Clean the anti-roll bar splines and grease them well. Insert one anti-roll bar with the marked spline aligned with the mark already made (Fig. 10.23). Fit the link block with the centre section parallel with the

16.6 Rear axle bearing bracket and mounting bolt on the open bar rear axle

L-shaped wide section. Insert the remaining anti-roll bar from the opposite side with the marked spline aligned with the mark made previously.
15   It is now necessary to adjust the centre link in order to avoid any contact with the L-section cross bar during deflection of the rear suspension. Move the centre link up and down and measure the total

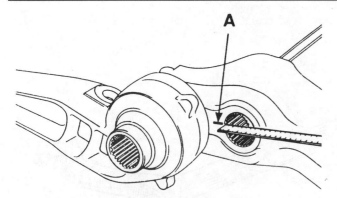

Fig. 10.22 Marking the trailing arms (A) before refitting the anti-roll bars (Sec 16)

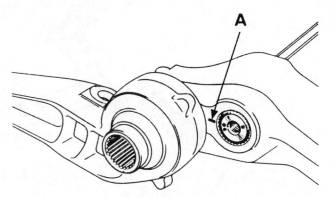

Fig. 10.23 Anti-roll bar fitted with its mark aligned with mark (A) (Sec 16)

movement in relation to the cross bar. This should be no more than 2.0 mm. Refer to the following table and determine the amount of correction in terms of splines necessary.

Amount of play measured (mm)	Number of splines to compensate
2 to 4	1
5 to 6	2
7 to 8	3
9 to 10	4
11 to 12	5
13 to 14	6
15 to 16	7
17 to 18	8
19 to 20	9

16   To correct the position of the centre link, remove one of the anti-roll bars, then slide off the link and move it by the determined amount of splines away from the L-section bar.
17   Refit the remaining bar, but this time offset the centre link by the determined amount of splines in the opposite direction. This action will effectively pre-tension the anti-roll bars and prevent them moving excessively.
18   Using a G-clamp, press the centre link down until it is parallel with the L-section cross bar, then insert the torsion bars on their correct sides until fully entered in the link block. Try them in different positions to find the point where both sets of splines enter freely.

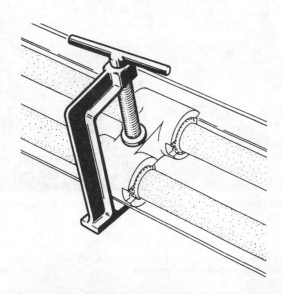

Fig. 10.24 Using a G-clamp to press the centre link down until parallel with the L-section cross bar (Sec 16)

Refitting

19   Place the rear axle on a trolley jack and lift it into position with the bearing brackets over the bolts. Refit the nuts and tighten them to the specified torque, then refit the luggage compartment trim.
20   Reconnect the brake lines and tighten the union nuts. Remove the brake hose clamps.
21   Reconnect the handbrake cables, referring to Chapter 9 if necessary.
22   Refit the torsion bars with reference to Section 12, then remove the G-clamp.
23   Support the rear trailing arms, then reconnect the rear shock absorbers and tighten the lower mounting bolts.
24   Refit the rear roadwheels and lower the car to the ground.
25   Check the rear underbody height and adjust if necessary with reference to Section 17.

17   Underbody height – checking and adjustment

1   Position the car on a level surface with the tyres correctly inflated and the fuel tank full.

Enclosed bar rear suspension

2   It is only possible to adjust the rear suspension height in multiples of 3.0 mm. First measure and record the dimensions H4 and H5 as shown in Fig. 10.25, noting that the H5 dimension is taken between the centre of the torsion bar to the ground. Deduct H5 from H4 and check that the result is 10.0 ± 7.5 mm.
3   If adjustment is necessary, determine the amount of splines the torsion bar must be moved noting that one spline is equal to 3.0 mm of height. For example, if the height needs adjusting by 10.0 mm the torsion bar should be moved by three splines.
4   To make the adjustment, support the trailing arm on a trolley jack and remove the shock absorber lower mounting bolt. Remove the torsion bar with reference to Section 12, then reposition the trailing arm so that the bar can be refitted with the required spline adjustment. Refit and tighten the shock absorber lower mounting bolt.
5   After making an adjustment, it may be necessary to adjust the headlight beam alignment with reference to Chapter 1.

Open-bar rear suspension

6   First measure and record the dimensions H4 and H5 as shown in Fig. 10.25, noting that the H5 dimension is taken between the centre of the torsion bar to the ground. Deduct H5 from H4 and check that the result is 25.0 ± 7.5 mm.
7   If the side-to-side height difference is excessive, the anti-roll bar must be re-positioned on the lower side to bring that side up to the height of the highest side. First remove both rear torsion bars and the anti-roll bar on the lower side after marking their positions. Determine the position of the trailing arm where the anti-roll bar can be refitted in

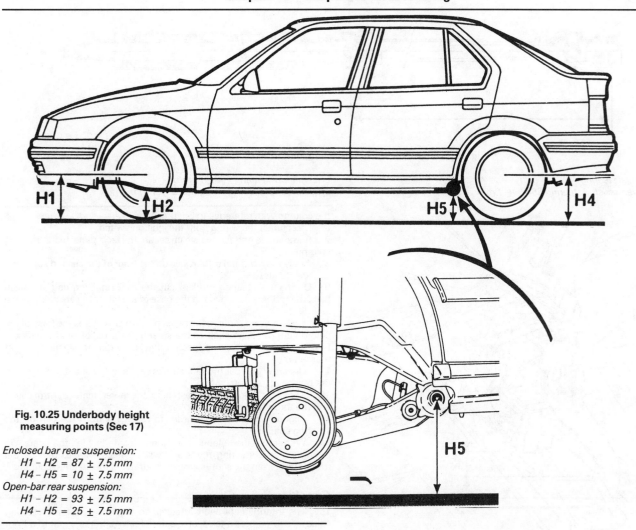

Fig. 10.25 Underbody height measuring points (Sec 17)

Enclosed bar rear suspension:
$H1 - H2 = 87 \pm 7.5\,mm$
$H4 - H5 = 10 \pm 7.5\,mm$
Open-bar rear suspension:
$H1 - H2 = 93 \pm 7.5\,mm$
$H4 - H5 = 25 \pm 7.5\,mm$

its original location freely, then lower the arm by the side-to-side difference previously noted and insert the anti-roll bar again, this time turning it as required to find the position where both sets of splines enter freely. The following table shows the anti-roll bar spline offset to compensate for various height adjustments.

Height to be taken up (mm)	Number of splines to compensate
5	2
10	4
15	6
20	8
25	10
30	12
35	14
40	16
45	18
50	20

After making the adjustment, finally refit the torsion bars. Lower the car to the ground and if necessary adjust the headlight beam alignment with reference to Chapter 1.

8   If the height is incorrect, remove the torsion bar from the appropriate side after marking its position. Determine the position of the trailing arm where the torsion bar can be refitted in its original location freely, then adjust the arm up or down as necessary by the difference of height required, and insert the torsion bar again, this time turning it as required to find the position where both sets of splines enter freely. Refer to the table in the previous paragraph to determine the amount of torsion bar spline offset to compensate for various height adjustments. After refitting the torsion bar, lower the car to the ground and if necessary adjust the headlight beam alignment with reference to Chapter 1.

18   Steering wheel – removal and refitting

Removal

1   Set the front wheels in the straight-ahead position, and release the steering lock by inserting the ignition key.
2   Ease off the steering wheel pad to provide access to the retaining nut (photo).

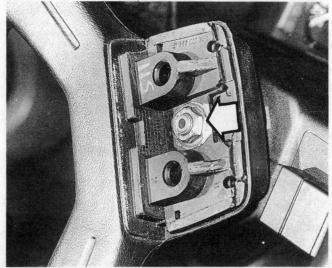

18.2 Steering wheel retaining nut (arrowed)

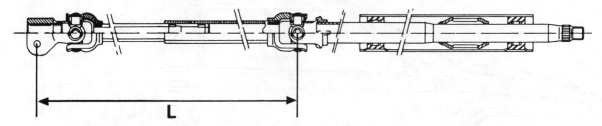

Fig. 10.26 Intermediate shaft checking dimension – L (Sec 19)

RHD manual steering 406 ± 1 mm
RHD power-assisted steering 354.5 ± 1 mm

LHD manual steering 408 ± 1 mm
LHD power-assisted steering 355.5 ± 1 mm

the column with reference to Chapter 12.
6   Disconnect the wiring from the ignition switch.
7   Remove the two screws which secure the facia panel to the steering column.
8   Apply the handbrake, then jack up the front of the car and support it on axle stands.
9   On manual steering models, cut the PVC retaining ring and push back the rubber boot covering the base of the intermediate shaft by the scuttle.
10   Unscrew and remove the pinch bolt which secures the base of the column intermediate shaft to the steering gear pinion shaft. Mark the two shafts in relation to each other in order to ensure correct reassembly.
11   Unscrew the four mounting bolts securing the steering column to the bulkhead (photo).
12   Remove the lower facia fastening, the lower heater control cover, and the three facia mounting bolts.
13   Slightly lift the facia in order to release it from the clip on the steering column.
14   Withdraw the steering column from inside the car. On power-assisted steering models it will be necessary to release the rubber boot from the scuttle when withdrawing the steering column.

Checking

15   The intermediate shaft attached to the bottom of the steering column incorporates a telescopic safety feature. In the event of a front end crash, the shaft collapses and prevents the steering wheel injuring the driver. Before refitting the steering column, the length of the intermediate shaft must be checked. Refer to Fig. 10.26 and make sure that the applicable length is as given. If the length is shorter than specified, the complete steering column must be renewed. An indication of damage to the intermediate shaft will be apparent if it is found that the pinch bolt at its base cannot be inserted freely when refitting the column.

Fig. 10.27 Checking the height-adjustable steering column lever (Sec 19)

1   *Lever clamp nut*   *x = 30 mm*
3   *Locking lever*

3   Using a socket, unscrew and remove the retaining nut.
4   Mark the steering wheel and steering column shaft in relation to each other and withdraw the wheel from the shaft splines. If it is tight, tap it upwards near the centre, using the palm of your hand, or twist the steering wheel from side-to-side to release it from the splines.

Refitting

5   Refitting is a reversal of removal, but align the previously made marks and tighten the retaining nut to the specified torque.

19   Steering column – removal, checking and refitting

Removal

1   Disconnect the battery leads with reference to Chapter 12.
2   Remove the steering wheel as described in Section 18.
3   Remove the lower facia panel from under the steering wheel.
4   Remove the screws and withdraw the steering column upper and lower shrouds.
5   Remove the steering column combination switch assembly from

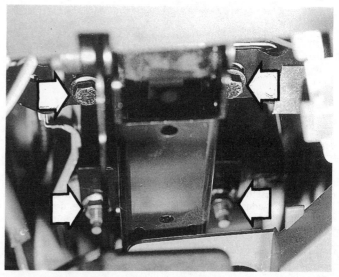

19.11 Steering column mounting bolts/nuts (arrowed)

Refitting

16   Refitting is a reversal of removal, but tighten all nuts and bolts to the specified torque. Before tightening the mounting bolts check that there is a clearance between the direction indicator return finger and the light control mounting. On manual steering models, use a new PVC ring to secure the rubber boot to the scuttle. On models with a height-adjustable steering column, check if the locking lever operates easily or whether it is partially concealed and difficult to operate. If necessary, the lever may be adjusted by removing the lever clamp nut, lowering the column, then locking the column by tightening the nut located on the same shaft as the lever clamp nut. Position the locking lever 30 mm from the column support, then refit the serrated nut.

20   Steering gear rubber gaiter – renewal

1   Remove the track rod end balljoint as described in Section 25.
2   Release the clip(s) and slide the gaiter off the rack and pinion housing and track rod.
3   Scrape off all grease from the old gaiter and apply to the track rod inner joint. Wipe clean the seating areas on the rack and pinion housing and track rod.
4   Slide the new gaiter onto the housing and track rod and tighten the clip(s) .
5   Refit the track rod end balljoint as described in Section 25.

21   Steering gear (manual steering) – removal and refitting

Removal

1   Apply the handbrake, then jack up the front of the car and support on axle stands. Remove both front roadwheels.
2   On each side unscrew the nuts securing the track rod end balljoint to the stub axle carrier and use a separator tool to release the balljoints.
3   Cut the PVC retaining ring and push back the rubber boot covering the base of the intermediate shaft by the scuttle.
4   Unscrew and remove the pinch bolt which secures the base of the column intermediate shaft to the steering gear pinion shaft. Mark the two shafts in relation to each other in order to ensure correct reassembly.
5   Unscrew and remove the two mounting nuts and bolts, then withdraw the steering gear sideways at the same time releasing the pinion from the intermediate shaft splines (photo).
6   If necessary, remove the track rod end balljoints as described in Section 25.

Refitting

7   Refitting is a reversal of removal, but tighten all nuts and bolts to the specified torque. Use a new PVC ring to secure the rubber boot to the scuttle. Finally check and adjust the front wheel alignment as described in Section 26.

22   Steering gear (power-assisted steering) – removal and refitting

Removal

1   Apply the handbrake, then jack up the front of the car and support it on axle stands. Remove both front roadwheels.
2   On each side unscrew the nuts securing the track rod end balljoint to the stub axle carrier and use a separator tool to release the balljoints.
3   Unscrew and remove the pinch bolt which secures the base of the column intermediate shaft to the steering gear pinion shaft. Mark the two shafts in relation to each other in order to ensure correct reassembly.
4   Using brake hose clamps, clamp both the supply and return hoses

21.5 Steering gear mounting (arrowed)

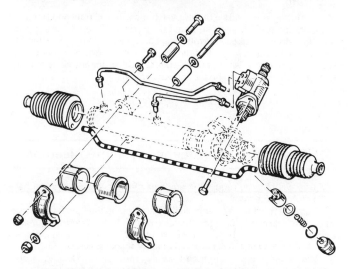

Fig. 10.28 Power-assisted steering gear components (Sec 22)

near the fluid reservoir. This will prevent unnecessary loss of fluid during subsequent operations.
5   Remove the air cleaner assembly as described in Chapter 4.
6   Unscrew the union nuts for the hydraulic fluid supply and return lines at the steering gear. Also unbolt the fluid line mounting brackets. Be prepared for some loss of fluid by placing a suitable container beneath the line unions.
7   Loosen the clips, then disconnect the short length of hose from the low pressure return line. Completely remove the low pressure line.
8   Remove the exhaust front downpipe with reference to Chapter 4.
9   With the container in place beneath the steering gear, unscrew the union nuts connecting the secondary pipes to the rack and pinion housing. To prevent dirt and dust entering the hydraulic circuit, fit plugs to the apertures in the steering gear and in the ends of the pipes.
10   Unscrew and remove the mounting bolts then withdraw the steering gear from the side of the car.
11   If necessary, remove the track rod end balljoints as described in Section 25.

Refitting

12   Refitting is a reversal of removal, but tighten all nuts and bolts to the specified torque. Make sure that the pipes are located correctly so that they do not foul any surrounding components. On completion fill the system with the specified fluid up to the maximum level mark, and bleed the system as described in Section 24. Check for any signs of fluid leakage from the system hoses and connections. Finally check and adjust the front wheel alignment as described in Section 26.

23 Power-assisted steering pump – removal and refitting

Removal

1   Remove the alternator and drivebelt as described in Chapter 12.
2   Using brake hose clamps, clamp both the supply and return hoses leading from the fluid reservoir. This will prevent unnecessary loss of fluid during subsequent operations. Also position a suitable container beneath the pump to catch spilled fluid.
3   Unbolt and remove the alternator tensioner support bracket.
4   Disconnect the pressure switch plug, then unbolt the bracket support for the high pressure line.
5   Disconnect the supply hose from the top of the pump.
6   Unscrew the union nut and disconnect the high pressure line from the pump. Remove the sealing washer.
7   Unbolt the pump support and remove the pump/support assembly.
8   To remove the pulley, first measure the dimension from the end of the shaft and the pulley to ensure correct refitting, then use a puller or press to remove the pulley from the shaft.
9   Unbolt the pump support.

Refitting

10   Refitting is a reversal of removal, but tighten all nuts and bolts to the specified torque. Make sure that the pipes are located correctly so that they do not foul any surrounding components. On completion fil' the system with the specified fluid up to the maximum level mark, and bleed the system as described in Section 24. Check for any signs of fluid leakage from the system hoses and connections.

25.2 Track rod end balljoint locknut (arrowed)

24 Power-assisted steering system – bleeding

1   This will only be required if any part of the hydraulic system has been disconnected.
2   Remove the fluid reservoir filler cap and top up the fluid level to the maximum mark using only the specified fluid. Refer to *'Lubricants, fluids and capacities'* at the beginning of this manual for fluid specifications, and Chapter 1 for details of the two types of fluid reservoir.
3   With the engine stopped, slowly move the steering from lock-to-lock several times to purge out the internal air, then top up the level in the fluid reservoir.
4   Repeat this procedure with the engine running and again top up the level.

25.3 Using a balljoint separator tool to release the track rod end tapered shank from the stub axle carrier steering arm

25 Track rod end balljoint – removal and refitting

Removal

1   Apply the handbrake, then jack up the front of the car and support it on axle stands. Remove the appropriate front roadwheel.
2   Using a suitable spanner, slacken the balljoint locknut on the track rod by a quarter of a turn (photo). Hold the track rod stationary with another spanner engaged with the flats at its inner end to prevent it from turning.
3   Unscrew and remove the nut securing the balljoint to the stub axle carrier arm and then release the tapered shank using a balljoint separator tool (photo).
4   Count the number of exposed threads between the end of the balljoint and the locknut and record this figure.
5   Unscrew the balljoint from the track rod while counting the number of turns necessary to remove it.
6   If a new balljoint is to be fitted, unscrew the locknut from the old balljoint.

Refitting

7   If removed, screw the locknut onto the new balljoint and position it so that the same number of exposed threads are visible as was noted during removal.
8   Screw the balljoint into the track rod the number of turns noted during removal until the locknut just contacts the track rod. Now tighten the locknut while holding the track rod as before.
9   Engage the shank of the balljoint with the stub axle carrier arm and refit the locknut. Tighten the locknut to the specified torque. If the balljoint shank turns while the locknut is being tightened, place a jack under the balljoint. The tapered fit of the shank will lock it and prevent rotation as the nut is tightened.
10   Refit the roadwheel and lower the car to the ground.
11   Finally check and if necessary adjust the front wheel alignment with reference to Section 26.

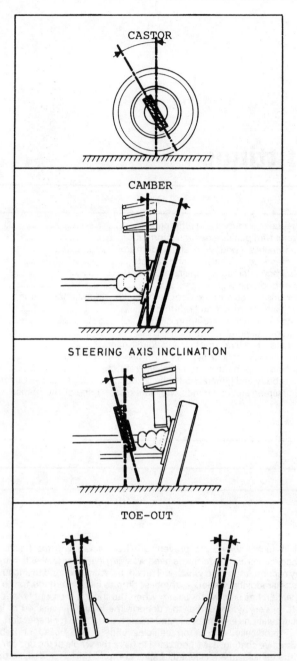

CASTOR

CAMBER

STEERING AXIS INCLINATION

TOE-OUT

Fig. 10.29 Wheel alignment and steering angles (Sec 26)

26 Wheel alignment and steering angles – general information

1   Accurate front wheel alignment is essential to provide positive steering and prevent excessive tyre wear. Before considering the steering/suspension geometry, check that the tyres are correctly inflated, that the front wheels are not buckled, and that the steering linkage and suspension joints are in good order, without slackness or wear.

2   Wheel alignment consists of four factors: *Camber* is the angle at which the front wheels are set from the vertical when viewed from the front of the car. 'Positive camber' is the amount (in degrees) that the wheels are tilted outward at the top of the vertical. *Castor* is the angle between the steering axis and a vertical line when viewed from each side of the car. 'Positive castor' is when the steering axis is inclined rearward at the top. *Steering axis inclination* is the angle (when viewed from the front of the car) between the vertical and an imaginary line drawn through the suspension strut upper mounting and the lower suspension arm balljoint. *Toe setting* is the amount by which the distance between the front inside edges of the roadwheels (measured at hub height) differs from the diametrically opposite distance measured between the rear inside edges of the front roadwheels.

3   With the exception of the toe setting, all other steering angles are set during manufacture and no adjustment is possible. It can be assumed, therefore, that unless the car has suffered accident damage all the preset steering angles will be correct. Should there be some doubt about their accuracy it will be necessary to seek the help of a Renault dealer, as special gauges are needed to check the steering angles.

4   Two methods are available to the home mechanic for checking the toe setting. One method is to use a gauge to measure the distance between the front and rear inside edges of the roadwheels. The other method is to use a scuff plate, in which each front wheel is rolled across a movable plate which records any deviation, or scuff, of the tyre from the straight-ahead position as it moves across the plate. Relatively inexpensive equipment of both types is available from accessory outlets to enable these checks, and subsequent adjustments to be carried out at home.

5   If, after checking the toe setting using whichever method is preferable, it is found that adjustment is necessary, proceed as follows.

6   Turn the steering wheel onto full left lock and record the number of exposed threads on the right-hand track rod end. Now turn the steering onto full right lock and record the number of threads on the left-hand side. If there are the same number of threads visible on both sides then subsequent adjustment can be made equally on both sides. If there are more threads visible on one side than the other it will be necessary to compensate for this during adjustment. *After adjustment there must be the same number of threads visible on each track rod end. This is most important.*

7   To alter the toe setting, slacken the locknut on the track rod end and turn the track rod using a self-grip wrench to achieve the desired setting. When viewed from the side of the car, turning the rod clockwise will increase the toe-in, turning it anti-clockwise will increase the toe-out. Only turn the track rods by a quarter of a turn each time and then recheck the setting using the gauges, or scuff plate.

8   After adjustment tighten the locknuts and reposition the steering gear rubber gaiter to remove any twist caused by turning the track rods.

Chapter 11 Bodywork and fittings

Contents

Specifications

Torque wrench setting	Nm	lbf ft
Seat belt anchorages	20	15

1 General information

The bodyshell and underframe is of all-steel welded construction, incorporating progressive crumple zones at the front and rear and a rigid centre safety cell. The assembly and welding of the main body unit is completed by computer-controlled robots, and is checked for dimensional accuracy using computer and laser technology. All major body panels are protected with an electrolytic zinc coating and are given a zinc phosphate bath.

The front and rear bumpers are of collapsible cellular construction to minimise minor accident damage and the front wings are bolted in position to facilitate accident damage repair. The plastic side panels are also designed to absorb light impact without damage.

2 Maintenance – bodywork and underframe

The general condition of a vehicle's bodywork is the one thing that significantly affects its value. Maintenance is easy but needs to be regular. Neglect, particularly after minor damage, can lead quickly to further deterioration and costly repair bills. It is important also to keep watch on those parts of the vehicle not immediately visible, for instance the underside, inside all the wheelarches and the lower part of the engine compartment.

The basic maintenance routine for the bodywork is washing – preferably with a lot of water, from a hose. This will remove all the loose solids which may have stuck to the vehicle. It is important to flush these off in such a way as to prevent grit from scratching the finish. The wheelarches and underframe need washing in the same way to remove any accumulated mud which will retain moisture and tend to encourage rust. Paradoxically enough, the best time to clean the underframe and wheel arches is in wet weather when the mud is thoroughly wet and soft. In very wet weather the underframe is usually cleaned of large accumulations automatically and this is a good time for inspection.

Periodically, except on vehicles with a wax-based underbody protective coating, it is a good idea to have the whole of the underframe of the vehicle steam cleaned, engine compartment included, so that a thorough inspection can be carried out to see what minor repairs and renovations are necessary. Steam cleaning is available at many garages and is necessary for the removal of the accumulation of oily grime which sometimes is allowed to become thick in certain areas. If steam cleaning facilities are not available, there are one or two excellent grease solvents available such as Holts Engine Cleaner or Holts Foambrite, which can be brush applied. The dirt can then be simply hosed off. Note that these methods should not be used on vehicles with wax-based underbody protective coating or the coating will be removed. Such vehicles should be inspected annually, preferably just prior to winter, when the underbody should be washed down and any damage to the wax coating repaired using Holts Undershield. Ideally, a completely fresh coat should be applied. It would also be worth considering the use of such wax-based protection for injection into door panels, sills, box sections, etc, as an additional safeguard against rust damage where such protection is not provided by the vehicle manufacturer.

After washing paintwork, wipe off with a chamois leather to give an unspotted clear finish. A coat of clear protective wax polish like the many excellent Turtle Wax polishes, will give added protection against chemical pollutants in the air. If the paintwork sheen has dulled or oxidised, use a cleaner/polisher combination such as Turtle Extra to restore the brilliance of the shine. This requires a little effort, but such dulling is usually caused because regular washing has been neglected. Care needs to be taken with metallic paintwork, as special non-abrasive cleaner/polisher is required to avoid damage to the finish. Always check that the door and ventilator opening drain holes and pipes are completely clear so that water can be drained out. Brightwork should be treated in the same way as paintwork. Windscreens and windows can be kept clear of the smeary film which often appears by the use of proprietary glass cleaner like Holts Mixra. Never use any form of wax or other body or chromium polish on glass.

3 Maintenance – upholstery and carpets

Mats and carpets should be brushed or vacuum cleaned regularly to keep them free of grit. If they are badly stained remove them from the vehicle for scrubbing or sponging and make quite sure they are dry before refitting. Seats and interior trim panels can be kept clean by wiping with a damp cloth and Turtle Wax Carisma. If they do become stained (which can be more apparent on light coloured upholstery) use a little liquid detergent and a soft nail brush to scour the grime out of the grain of the material. Do not forget to keep the headlining clean in the same way as the upholstery. When using liquid cleaners inside the vehicle do not over-wet the surfaces being cleaned. Excessive damp could get into the seams and padded interior causing stains, offensive odours or even rot. If the inside of the vehicle gets wet accidentally it is worthwhile taking some trouble to dry it out properly, particularly where carpets are involved. *Do not leave oil or electric heaters inside the vehicle for this purpose.*

4 Minor body damage – repair

Note: *For more detailed information about bodywork repair, the Haynes Publishing Group publish a book by Lindsay Porter called The Car Bodywork Repair Manual. This incorporates information on such aspects as rust treatment, painting and glass-fibre repairs, as well as details on more ambitious repairs involving welding and panel beating.*
The photographic sequence on pages 230 and 231 illustrates the operations detailed in the following sub-sections.

Repairs of minor scratches in bodywork

If the scratch is very superficial, and does not penetrate to the metal of the bodywork, repair is very simple. Lightly rub the area of the scratch with a paintwork renovator like Turtle Wax New Color Back, or a very fine cutting paste like Holts Body + Plus Rubbing Compound, to remove loose paint from the scratch and to clear the surrounding bodywork of wax polish. Rinse the area with clean water.

Apply touch-up paint such as Holts Dupli-Color Color Touch or a paint film like Holts Autofilm, to the scratch using a fine paint brush; continue to apply fine layers of paint until the surface of the paint in the scratch is level with the surrounding paintwork. Allow the new paint at least two weeks to harden, then blend it into the surrounding paintwork by rubbing the scratch area with a paintwork renovator or a very fine cutting paste such as Holts Body + Plus Rubbing Compound or Turtle Wax New Color Back. Finally apply wax polish from one of the Turtle Wax range of wax polishes.

Where the scratch has penetrated right through to the metal of the bodywork, causing the metal to rust, a different repair technique is required. Remove any loose rust from the bottom of the scratch with a penknife, then apply rust inhibiting paint such as Turtle Wax Rust Master, to prevent the formation of rust in the future. Using a rubber or nylon applicator fill the scratch with bodystopper paste like Holts Body + Plus Knifing Putty. If required, this paste can be mixed with cellulose thinners, such as Holts Body + Plus Cellulose Thinners, to provide a very thin paste which is ideal for filling narrow scratches. Before the stopper-paste in the scratch hardens, wrap a piece of smooth cotton rag around the top of a finger. Dip the finger in cellulose thinners and quickly sweep it across the surface of the stopper-paste in the scratch; this will ensure that the surface of the stopper-paste is slightly hollowed. The scratch can now be painted over as described earlier in this Section.

Repairs of dents in bodywork

When deep denting of the vehicle's bodywork has taken place, the first task is to pull the dent out, until the affected bodywork almost attains its original shape. There is little point in trying to restore the original shape completely, as the metal in the damaged area will have stretched on impact and cannot be reshaped fully to its original contour. It is better to bring the level of the dent up to a point which is about 3 mm below the level of the surrounding bodywork. In cases where the dent is very shallow anyway, it is not worth trying to pull it out at all. If the underside of the dent is accessible, it can be hammered out gently from behind, using a mallet with a wooden or plastic head. Whilst doing this, hold a suitable block of wood firmly against the outside of the panel to absorb the impact from the hammer blows and thus prevent a large area of the bodywork from being 'belled-out'.

Should the dent be in a section of the bodywork which has a double skin or some other factor making it inaccessible from behind, a different technique is called for. Drill several small holes through the metal inside the area – particularly in the deeper section. Then screw long self-tapping screws into the holes just sufficiently for them to gain a good purchase in the metal. Now the dent can be pulled out by pulling on the protruding heads of the screws with a pair of pliers.

The next stage of the repair is the removal of the paint from the damaged area, and from an inch or so of the surrounding 'sound' bodywork. This is accomplished most easily by using a wire brush or abrasive pad on a power drill, although it can be done just as effectively by hand using sheets of abrasive paper. To complete the preparation for filling, score the surface of the bare metal with a screwdriver or the tang of a file, or alternatively, drill small holes in the affected area. This will provide a really good 'key' for the filler paste.

To complete the repair see the Section on filling and respraying.

Repairs of rust holes or gashes in bodywork

Remove all paint from the affected area and from an inch or so of the surrounding 'sound' bodywork, using an abrasive pad or a wire brush on a power drill. If these are not available a few sheets of abrasive paper will do the job most effectively. With the paint removed you will be able to judge the severity of the corrosion and therefore decide whether to renew the whole panel (if this is possible) or to repair the affected area. New body panels are not as expensive as most people think and it is often quicker and more satisfactory to fit a new panel than to attempt to repair large areas of corrosion.

Remove all fittings from the affected area except those which will act as a guide to the original shape of the damaged bodywork (eg headlamp shells etc). Then, using tin snips or a hacksaw blade, remove all loose metal and any other metal badly affected by corrosion. Hammer the edges of the hole inwards in order to create a slight depression for the filler paste.

Wire brush the affected area to remove the powdery rust from the surface of the remaining metal. Paint the affected area with rust inhibiting paint like Turtle Wax Rust Master; if the back of the rusted area is accessible treat this also.

Before filling can take place it will be necessary to block the hole in some way. This can be achieved by the use of aluminium or plastic mesh, or aluminium tape.

Aluminium or plastic mesh or glass fibre matting, such as the Holts Body + Plus Glass Fibre Matting, is probably the best material to use for a large hole. Cut a piece to the approximate size and shape of the hole to be filled, then position it in the hole so that its edges are below the level of the surrounding bodywork. It can be retained in position by several blobs of filler paste around its periphery.

Aluminium tape should be used for small or very narrow holes. Pull a piece off the roll and trim it to the approximate size and shape required, then pull off the backing paper (if used) and stick the tape over the hole; it can be overlapped if the thickness of one piece is insufficient. Burnish down the edges of the tape with the handle of a screwdriver or similar, to ensure that the tape is securely attached to the metal underneath.

Bodywork repairs – filling and respraying

Before using this Section, see the Sections on dent, deep scratch, rust holes and gash repairs.

Many types of bodyfiller are available, but generally speaking those proprietary kits which contain a tin of filler paste and a tube of resin hardener are best for this type of repair, like Holts Body + Plus or Holts

No Mix which can be used directly from the tube. A wide, flexible plastic or nylon applicator will be found invaluable for imparting a smooth and well contoured finish to the surface of the filler.

Mix up a little filler on a clean piece of card or board – measure the hardener carefully (follow the maker's instructions on the pack) otherwise the filler will set too rapidly or too slowly. Alternatively, Holts No Mix can be used straight from the tube without mixing, but daylight is required to cure it. Using the applicator apply the filler paste to the prepared area; draw the applicator across the surface of the filler to achieve the correct contour and to level the surface. As soon as a contour that approximates to the correct one is achieved, stop working the paste – if you carry on too long the paste will become sticky and begin to 'pick-up' on the applicator. Continue to add thin layers of filler paste at twenty minute intervals until the level of the filler is just proud of the surrounding bodywork.

Once the filler has hardened, excess can be removed using a metal plane or file. From then on, progressively finer grades of abrasive paper should be used, starting with a 40 grade production paper and finishing with a 400 grade wet-and-dry paper. Always wrap the abrasive paper around a flat rubber, cork, or wooden block – otherwise the surface of the filler will not be completely flat. During the smoothing of the filler surface the wet-and-dry paper should be periodically rinsed in water. This will ensure that a very smooth finish is imparted to the filler at the final stage.

At this stage the 'dent' should be surrounded by a ring of bare metal, which in turn should be encircled by the finely 'feathered' edge of the good paintwork. Rinse the repair area with clean water, until all of the dust produced by the rubbing-down operation has gone.

Spray the whole area with a light coat of primer, either Holts Body + Plus Grey or Red Oxide Primer – this will show up any imperfections in the surface of the filler. Repair these imperfections with fresh filler paste or bodystopper, and once more smooth the surface with abrasive paper. If bodystopper is used, it can be mixed with cellulose thinners to form a really thin paste which is ideal for filling small holes. Repeat this spray and repair procedure until you are satisfied that the surface of the filler, and the feathered edge of the paintwork are perfect. Clean the repair area with clean water and allow to dry fully.

The repair area is now ready for final spraying. Paint spraying must be carried out in a warm, dry, windless and dust free atmosphere. This condition can be created artificially if you have access to a large indoor working area, but if you are forced to work in the open, you will have to pick your day very carefully. If you are working indoors, dousing the floor in the work area with water will help to settle the dust which would otherwise be in the atmosphere. If the repair area is confined to one body panel, mask off the surrounding panels; this will help to minimise the effects of a slight mis-match in paint colours. Bodywork fittings (eg chrome strips, door handles etc) will also need to be masked off. Use genuine masking tape and several thicknesses of newspaper for the masking operations.

Before commencing to spray, agitate the aerosol can thoroughly, then spray a test area (an old tin, or similar) until the technique is mastered. Cover the repair area with a thick coat of primer; the thickness should be built up using several thin layers of paint rather than one thick one. Using 400 grade wet-and-dry paper, rub down the surface of the primer until it is really smooth. While doing this, the work area should be thoroughly doused with water, and the wet-and-dry paper periodically rinsed in water. Allow to dry before spraying on more paint.

Spray on the top coat using Holts Dupli-color Autospray, again building up the thickness by using several thin layers of paint. Start spraying in the centre of the repair area and then, with a side-to-side motion, work outwards until the whole repair area and about 2 inches of the surrounding original paintwork is covered. Remove all masking material 10 to 15 minutes after spraying on the final coat of paint.

Allow the new paint at least two weeks to harden, then, using a paintwork renovator or a very fine cutting paste such as Turtle Wax New Color Back or Holts Body + Plus Rubbing Compound, blend the edges of the paint into the existing paintwork. Finally, apply wax polish.

Plastic components

With the use of more and more plastic body components by the vehicle manufacturers (eg bumpers. spoilers, and in some cases major body panels), rectification of more serious damage to such items has become a matter of either entrusting repair work to a specialist in this field, or renewing complete components. Repair of such damage by the DIY owner is not really feasible owing to the cost of the equipment and materials required for effecting such repairs. The basic technique involves making a groove along the line of the crack in the plastic using a rotary burr in a power drill. The damaged part is then welded back together by using a hot air gun to heat up and fuse a plastic filler rod into the groove. Any excess plastic is then removed and the area rubbed down to a smooth finish. It is important that a filler rod of the correct plastic is used, as body components can be made of a variety of different types (eg polycarbonate, ABS, polypropylene).

Damage of a less serious nature (abrasions, minor cracks etc) can be repaired by the DIY owner using a two-part epoxy filler repair material like Holts Body + Plus or Holts No Mix which can be used directly from the tube. Once mixed in equal proportions (or applied directly from the tube in the case of Holts No Mix), this is used in similar fashion to the

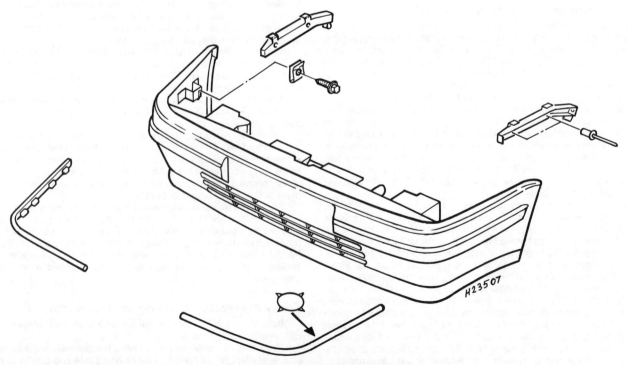

H23507

Fig. 11.1 Front bumper components (Sec 6)

bodywork filler used on metal panels. The filler is usually cured in twenty to thirty minutes, ready for sanding and painting.

If the owner is renewing a complete component himself, or if he has repaired it with epoxy filler, he will be left with the problem of finding a suitable paint for finishing which is compatible with the type of plastic used. At one time the use of a universal paint was not possible owing to the complex range of plastics encountered in body component applications. Standard paints, generally speaking, will not bond to plastic or rubber satisfactorily, but Holts Professional Spraymatch paints to match any plastic or rubber finish can be obtained from dealers. However, it is now possible to obtain a plastic body parts finishing kit which consists of a pre-primer treatment, a primer and coloured top coat. Full instructions are normally supplied with a kit, but basically the method of use is to first apply the pre-primer to the component concerned and allow it to dry for up to 30 minutes. Then the primer is applied and left to dry for about an hour before finally applying the special coloured top coat. The result is a correctly coloured component where the paint will flex with the plastic or rubber, a property that standard paint does not normally posses.

5 Major body damage – repair

Where serious damage has occurred, or large areas need renewal due to neglect, it means that complete new panels will need welding in, and this is best left to professionals. If the damage is due to impact, it will also be necessary to check completely the alignment of the bodyshell, and this can only be carried out accurately by a Renault dealer using special jigs. If the body is left misaligned, it is primarily dangerous as the car will not handle properly, and secondly, uneven stresses will be imposed on the steering, suspension and possibly the transmission, causing abnormal wear, or complete failure, particularly to such items as the tyres.

6 Front and rear bumpers – removal and refitting

Removal
Front bumper
1   Where applicable, remove the foglamp from the front bumper as described in Chapter 12.

Fig. 11.2 Front bumper mounting bolts located near the inner side of the headlights (Sec 6)

2   Apply the handbrake then jack up the front of the car and support it on axle stands.
3   With the bonnet open, unscrew the two front mounting bolts located near the inner side of the headlights.
4   Unscrew the four screws securing the sides of the bumper to the wheelarch mudguard. There are two on each side.
5   Unscrew the two bolts securing the bumper to the front subframe.
6   Unscrew the two side mounting bolts, then withdraw the bumper from the car.
7   If necessary unbolt and remove the mounting brackets, and where applicable unbolt the spoiler extension from the bottom of the bumper.

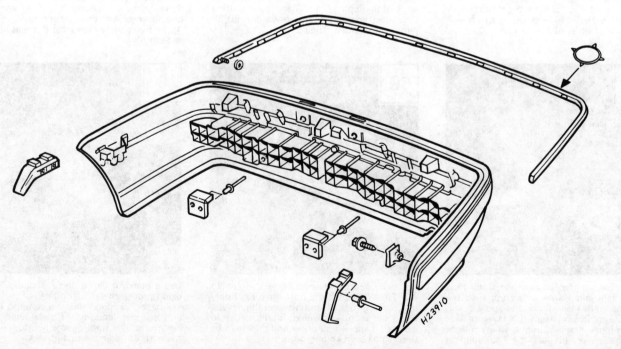

Fig. 11.3 Rear bumper components (Sec 6)

This photographic sequence shows the steps taken to repair the dent and paintwork damage shown above. In general, the procedure for repairing a hole will be similar; where there are substantial differences, the procedure is clearly described and shown in a separate photograph.

First remove any trim around the dent, then hammer out the dent where access is possible. This will minimise filling. Here, after the large dent has been hammered out, the damaged area is being made slightly concave.

Next, remove all paint from the damaged area by rubbing with coarse abrasive paper or using a power drill fitted with a wire brush or abrasive pad. 'Feather' the edge of the boundary with good paintwork using a finer grade of abrasive paper.

Where there are holes or other damage, the sheet metal should be cut away before proceeding further. The damaged area and any signs of rust should be treated with Turtle Wax Hi-Tech Rust Eater, which will also inhibit further rust formation.

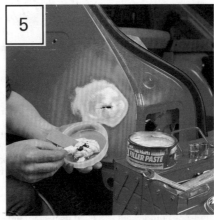

For a large dent or hole mix Holts Body Plus Resin and Hardener according to the manufacturer's instructions and apply around the edge of the repair. Press Glass Fibre Matting over the repair area and leave for 20-30 minutes to harden. Then ...

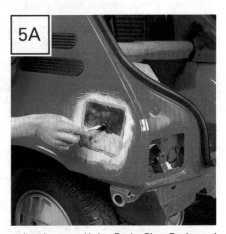

... brush more Holts Body Plus Resin and Hardener onto the matting and leave to harden. Repeat the sequence with two or three layers of matting, checking that the final layer is lower than the surrounding area. Apply Holts Body Plus Filler Paste as shown in Step 5B.

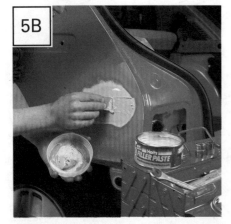

For a medium dent, mix Holts Body Plus Filler Paste and Hardener according to the manufacturer's instructions and apply it with a flexible applicator. Apply thin layers of filler at 20-minute intervals, until the filler surface is slightly proud of the surrounding bodywork.

For small dents and scratches use Holts No Mix Filler Paste straight from the tube. Apply it according to the instructions in thin layers, using the spatula provided. It will harden in minutes if applied outdoors and may then be used as its own knifing putty.

Use a plane or file for initial shaping. Then, using progressively finer grades of wet-and-dry paper, wrapped round a sanding block, and copious amounts of clean water, rub down the filler until glass smooth. 'Feather' the edges of adjoining paintwork.

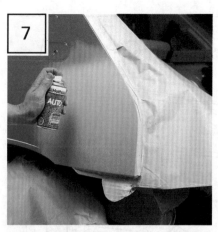

7 Protect adjoining areas before spraying the whole repair area and at least one inch of the surrounding sound paintwork with Holts Dupli-Color primer.

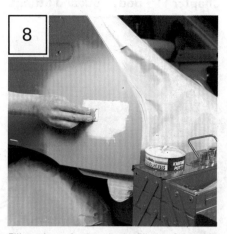

8 Fill any imperfections in the filler surface with a small amount of Holts Body Plus Knifing Putty. Using plenty of clean water, rub down the surface with a fine grade wet-and-dry paper – 400 grade is recommended – until it is really smooth.

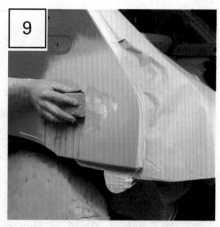

9 Carefully fill any remaining imperfections with knifing putty before applying the last coat of primer. Then rub down the surface with Holts Body Plus Rubbing Compound to ensure a really smooth surface.

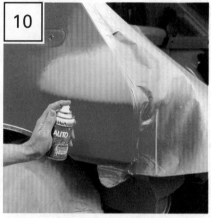

10 Protect surrounding areas from overspray before applying the topcoat in several thin layers. Agitate Holts Dupli-Color aerosol thoroughly. Start at the repair centre, spraying outwards with a side-to-side motion.

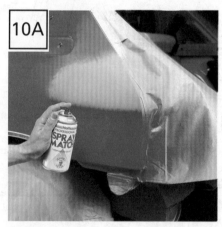

10A If the exact colour is not available off the shelf, local Holts Professional Spraymatch Centres will custom fill an aerosol to match perfectly.

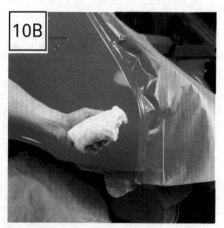

10B To identify whether a lacquer finish is required, rub a painted unrepaired part of the body with wax and a clean cloth.

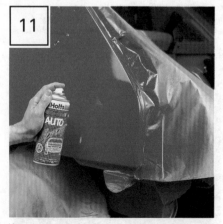

11 If *no* traces of paint appear on the cloth, spray Holts Dupli-Color clear lacquer over the repaired area to achieve the correct gloss level.

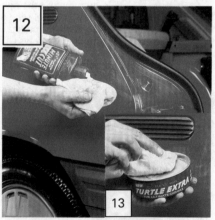

12 The paint will take about two weeks to harden fully. After this time it can be 'cut' with a mild cutting compound such as Turtle Wax Minute Cut prior to polishing with a final coating of Turtle Wax Extra.

13

14 When carrying out bodywork repairs, remember that the quality of the finished job is proportional to the time and effort expended.

6.11 Rear bumper to crossmember bolt

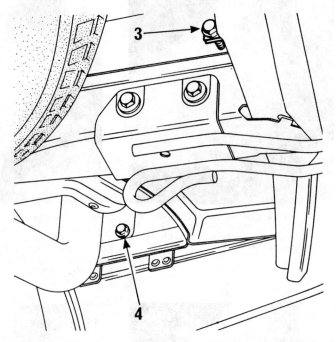

Fig. 11.5 Rear bumper crossmember bolts (3) and right-hand mounting bolt (4) (Sec 6)

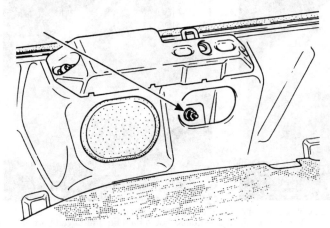

Fig. 11.4 Rear bumper centre retaining nut (Sec 6)

bumper to the crossmember (photo). Also unscrew the right-hand mounting bolt.

12   Unscrew the four screws securing the bumper to the rear wheelarches, then withdraw the bumper from the car.

Refitting

13   Refitting is a reversal of removal.

7   Bonnet – removal, refitting and adjustment

Removal

1   Open the bonnet and support it in the open position using the stay.
2   Disconnect the windscreen washer hose by prising out the rubber grommet on the right-hand corner, then pulling the T-connector from the access hole and disconnecting the right-hand hose (photos).
3   Mark the outline of the hinges with a soft pencil, then loosen the four mounting screws using a Torx key (photo).
4   With the help of an assistant, remove the stay, unscrew the four screws and lift the bonnet from the car (photo).

Rear bumper

8   Working inside the rear luggage compartment, remove the container carrier on the left-hand side for access to the side mounting bolt. Unscrew and remove the bolt.
9   Prise out the grommet from the centre of the rear luggage compartment panel, then unscrew and remove the centre retaining nut.
10   Chock the front wheels, then jack up the rear of the car and support it on axle stands.
11   Working beneath the car, unscrew the two bolts securing the

7.2A From the bonnet prise out the windscreen washer rubber grommet ...

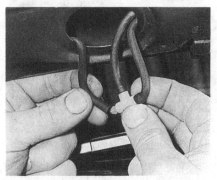

7.2B ... and disconnect the supply tube

7.3 Bonnet hinge mounting on the bonnet

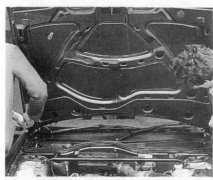

7.4 Removing the bonnet

7.5 Bonnet front corner support rubber buffer

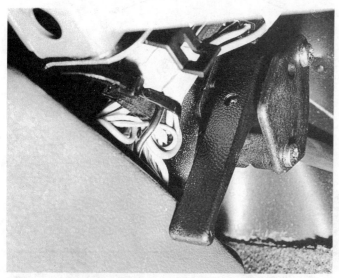

8.3 Bonnet release handle located under the left-hand side of the facia

the bonnet as necessary by repositioning it on the hinges. Adjust the front height if necessary by repositioning the lock with reference to Section 9, then turn the rubber buffers on the engine compartment front cross panel up or down to support the bonnet (photo).

8 Bonnet release cable – removal and refitting

Removal

1   With the bonnet open, disconnect the cable eye from the lever on the rear of the lock, then unclip the outer cable.
2   Working inside the car, remove the glovebox with reference to Section 30.
3   Unscrew and remove the two screws securing the release handle to the left-hand side panel under the facia (photo).
4   Release the outer cable from its clips and withdraw it through the bulkhead.

Refitting

5   Refitting is a reversal of removal.

Refitting

5   Refitting is a reversal of removal. Position the bonnet hinges within the outline marks made during removal, but alter its position as necessary to provide a uniform gap all round. Adjust the rear height of

9 Bonnet lock – removal and refitting

Removal

1   With the bonnet open, disconnect the cable eye from the lever on the rear of the lock (photo).
2   Unscrew the two retaining bolts and remove the lock from the car.

9.1 Bonnet lock assembly

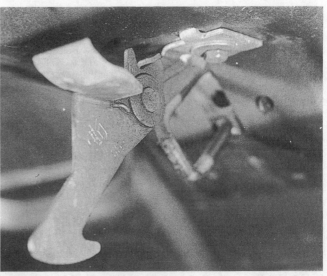

9.3 Bonnet striker and safety catch

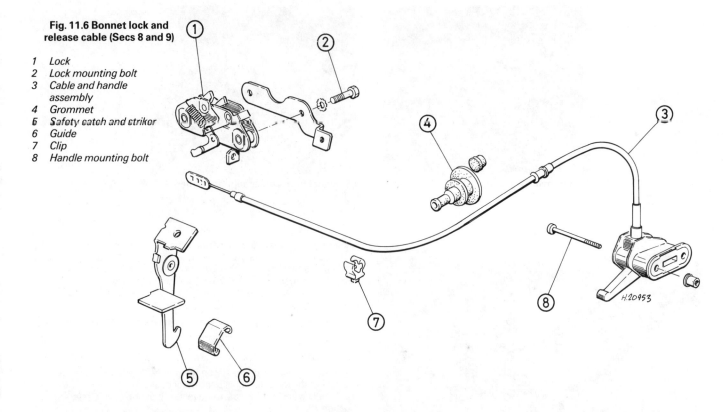

Fig. 11.6 Bonnet lock and release cable (Secs 8 and 9)

1   Lock
2   Lock mounting bolt
3   Cable and handle
    assembly
4   Grommet
5   Safety catch and striker
6   Guide
7   Clip
8   Handle mounting bolt

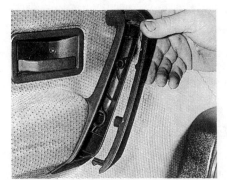

10.1 Removing the plastic insert from the door grip

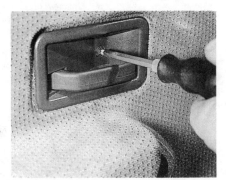

10.2A Remove the screw ...

10.2B ... and remove the interior door handle finger plate

Refitting

3   Refitting is a reversal of removal, but adjust the lock height so that the bonnet line is flush with the front wings and shuts securely without force. If necessary adjust the lock laterally so that the striker enters the lock recess correctly, however it may also be necessary to reposition the striker itself (photo).

10   Door inner trim panel – removal and refitting

Removal

Front door

1   Using a screwdriver, prise the plastic insert from the door grip. Unscrew the screws and remove the grip from the inner trim panel (photo).
2   Remove the screw from the interior door handle finger plate. Pull the plate out and disconnect it from the pull rod (photos).
3   Turn the loudspeaker cover anti-clockwise and remove it. Remove

the screws and withdraw the loudspeaker, then disconnect the wiring (photos).
4   Remove the screws and withdraw the loudspeaker holder and side pocket from the trim panel (photos).
5   Remove the screw, then remove the exterior mirror inner plastic cover taking care not to damage the plastic retaining posts (photo).
6   Where applicable, remove the window regulator handle, but first note its position with the window fully shut. If necessary, use a tool similar to that shown in Fig. 11.7 together with a piece of cloth.
7   The trim panel is clipped in place and sealed with mastic. If the mastic has hardened, it may be necessary to cut it free using a knife or small saw. Try prising the panel from the door carefully with a wide-bladed screwdriver before cutting the mastic. Prise the panel by inserting the screwdriver under the retaining clips to avoid tearing the inner surface of the panel.
8   Where applicable, disconnect the wiring from the power window switch.

Rear door

9   Using a screwdriver, prise the plastic insert from the door grip. Unscrew the screws and remove the grip from the inner trim panel.

10.3A Removing the loudspeaker cover ...

10.3B ... and loudspeaker

10.4A Remove the front mounting screws (arrowed) ...

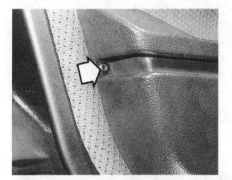

10.4B ... and rear mounting screws ...

10.4C ... and remove the loudspeaker holder and side pocket

10.5 Removing the exterior mirror inner plastic cover

10.11 Window regulator handle removal

10.12 Ashtray holder removal

10.14 Applying mastic to the inner door panel before fitting the trim panel

10   Remove the screw from the interior door handle finger plate. Pull the plate out and disconnect it from the pull rod.
11   Check that the window is fully shut, then note the position of the regulator handle. Pull the handle direct from the splines and remove the bezel – the handle is only a press fit on the splines (photo).
12   Remove the ashtray, then remove the screws and withdraw the ashtray holder from the trim panel (photo).
13   The trim panel is clipped in place and sealed with mastic. If the mastic has hardened, it may be necessary to cut it free using a knife or small saw. Try prising the panel from the door carefully with a wide-bladed screwdriver before cutting the mastic. Prise the panel by inserting the screwdriver under the retaining clips to avoid tearing the inner surface of the panel.

Refitting

14   Refitting is a reversal of removal, but apply suitable mastic to the inner door panel before fitting the trim panel (photo). Check the retaining clips for breakage and renew them if necessary.

11 Door window glass and regulator – removal and refitting

Removal

Front door window glass and regulator

1   Remove the inner trim panel as described in Section 10.
2   Remove the lower rubbing strip.
3   Disconnect the lifter from the bottom of the window glass by pulling the fastener sharply from the plate pin (photo). With the window free from the pin, lower the plate into the bottom of the door.
4   Release the pad on the rear edge of the window glass from its slide channel, then push the window forwards and lift it out from the outside.
5   Where applicable, reach inside the door and disconnect the wiring plug from the winder motor.
6   Unscrew the bolts and nuts securing the regulator assembly to the inner door panel (photo).

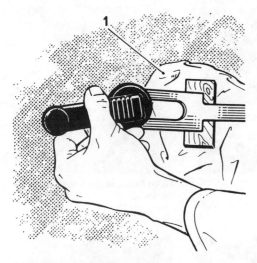

Fig. 11.7 Using a special tool to remove the window regulator handle (Sec 10)

1   *Protective cloth*

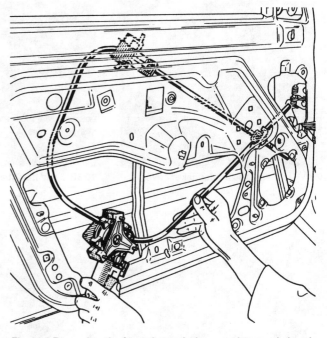

Fig. 11.8 Removing the front door window regulator and electric motor (Sec 11)

7   Tilt the assembly so that the motor/regulator is at the bottom, then withdraw the assembly through the aperture.

8   The electric window control cable may be renewed if necessary, however refer to Fig. 11.9 and, on four-door models, cut the cable to the required length before fitting it.

Rear door window regulator

9   Remove the door inner trim panel as described in Section 10.

10   Lower the window glass so that the lifter is visible, then unscrew the two screws securing the lifter to the bottom of the window (photo).

11.3 Front door window lifter (arrowed)

11.6 Front door window regulator mounting nuts

11.10 Rear door window lifter

11.11A Rear door window regulator front mounting bolts ...

11.11B ... rear upper mounting bolt ...

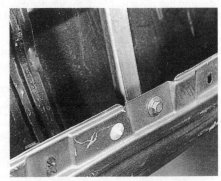

11.11C ... and rear lower mounting bolt

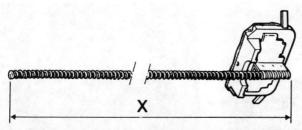

Fig. 11.9 Front door electric window control cable length for four-door models (Sec 11)

$X = 1013 \pm 5\,mm$

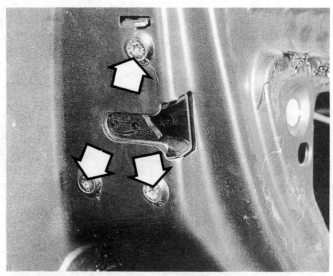

12.3 Door lock mounting screws (arrowed)

Fully raise the window and hold it in this position using a block of wood or alternatively by using wide adhesive tape.
11   Unscrew the bolts securing the regulator assembly to the inner door panel (photos).
12   Tilt the assembly, taking care not to catch it in the internal locking rod, then withdraw it through the aperture.

Rear door window glass

13   Remove the door inner trim panel as described in Section 10.
14   Remove the inner and outer rubbing strips.
15   Lower the window so that the lifter is visible, unscrew the lifter screws, then lower the window to the bottom of the door.
16   Unscrew the rear guide mounting bolts located at the top and bottom of the guide, then remove the guide.
17   Raise the window and remove it from the inside of the door.

Rear door fixed window

18   Remove the main window glass as described previously.
19   Pull the fixed window forwards and withdraw it from the door.
20   Remove the lower stop from inside the door.

Refitting

21   Refitting is a reversal of removal. When refitting the rear door window glass, before tightening the lifter screws have the window 25 to 50 mm open and press it firmly into the rear guide. This will align the window correctly. The lifter screws are accessed through the small hole in the inner door panel with the window in this position.

12   Door lock, lock cylinder and handles – removal and refitting

Removal
Door lock

1   Remove the door inner trim panel as described in Section 10.
2   Reach inside the door and disconnect the exterior handle control rod and the locking rod from the lock.
3   Unscrew the lock mounting screws from the rear edge of the door (photo).
4   Where applicable, disconnect the wiring from the central locking motor (photo).
5   Disconnect the interior handle operating rod, then withdraw the lock through the aperture in the door inner panel.
6   Where applicable, the motor may be removed from the lock by unscrewing the single retaining screw.

Lock cylinder

7   Remove the door inner trim panel as described in Section 10.
8   Reach inside the door and disconnect the operating rod.
9   Pull out the retaining clip, then withdraw the lock cylinder from the outside of the car.

Interior handle

10   Remove the door inner trim panel as described in Section 10.

12.4 Central locking motor for the front door lock (arrowed)

11   Remove the screw from inside the handle finger plate, withdraw the handle, and disconnect it from the operating rod.

Exterior handle

12   Remove the door inner trim panel as described in Section 10.
13   Disconnect the operating rods from the lock.
14   Insert a screwdriver through the hole in the inner door panel, unscrew the mounting screw, then withdraw the handle from inside the door.

Refitting

15   Refitting is a reversal of removal

13   Door – removal, refitting and adjustment

Removal

1   Disconnect the door check link by unscrewing the Torx screw on the door pillar. If necessary, the link may be unbolted from the door (photos).
2   Support the door on blocks of wood.

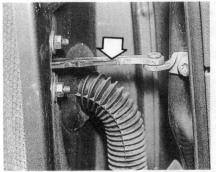

13.1A Front door check link (arrowed)

13.1B Front door check link from inside the door (arrowed)

13.6 Door striker

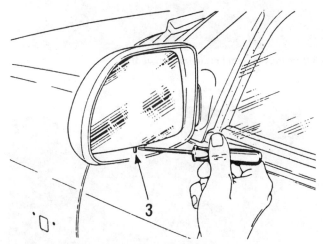

Fig. 11.10 Pushing the tab (3) outwards to remove the wire spring type exterior mirror (Sec 14)

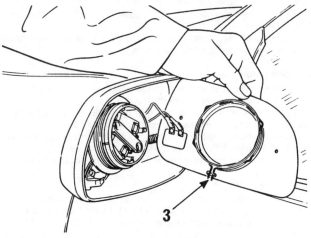

Fig. 11.11 Inside view of the tab (3) on the wire spring type exterior mirror (Sec 14)

3   Prise off the caps covering each hinge pin.
4   Using a cranked metal rod of suitable diameter as a drift, drive out the upper and lower hinge pins.
5   Lift the door from the hinges.

Refitting and adjustment

6   Refitting is a reversal of removal, but check that the door is correctly aligned with the surrounding bodywork with an equal clearance around its edge. Adjustment is made by loosening the Torx screws and moving the door within the elongated mounting holes. A shim is fitted between the hinge plates and door for vertical alignment with the rear pillar. Check that the striker enters the lock centrally when the door is closed, and if necessary loosen it with a Torx key, re-position and re-tighten it (photo).

14   Exterior mirror and glass – removal and refitting

Removal

Mirror glass

1   There are two types of mirror glass fitted – one is retained with a wire spring, and the other by plastic clips. The former type is identified by having a small tab located under the bottom edge of the mirror.
2   To remove the wire spring type, use a small screwdriver to push the tab outwards, then withdraw the mirror and disconnect the heater wiring from the rear of the mirror (where applicable).
3   To remove the plastic clip type, it is recommended that a suction

14.3 Removing the plastic clip type exterior mirror glass

14.5 Disconnecting the wiring plug for the exterior mirror

14.6 Removing the exterior mirror

15.1 Hinge mounting on the boot lid

15.5 Boot lid mounting on the body

pad is used to pull it out, together with a small screwdriver to release the clips (photo).

Mirror assembly
4   Remove the door inner trim panel as described in Section 10.
5   Where applicable, disconnect the wiring plug (photo).
6   Unscrew the three nuts and withdraw the mirror assembly from the door while feeding the wiring harness through the rubber grommet where applicable (photo).

Refitting

Mirror glass
7   Before refitting the wire spring type, refit the clip then press the mirror into position. To refit the plastic clip type, press the mirror inwards until the clips snap into place.

Mirror assembly
8   Refitting is a reversal of removal.

15   Boot lid – removal, refitting and adjustment

Removal
1   Open the boot lid and mark the position of the bolts on the hinges with a pencil (photo). Where applicable, disconnect the wiring for the central locking.
2   Place cloth rags beneath each corner of the boot lid to prevent damage to the paintwork.
3   Disconnect the strut by prising out the retainer with a small screwdriver and pulling the strut from the boot lid ball.
4   With the help of an assistant, unscrew the mounting bolts and lift the boot lid from the car.
5   If necessary, the boot lid hinges may be unbolted from the body (photo).

Refitting and adjustment
6   Refitting is a reversal of removal, but check that the boot lid is correctly aligned with the surrounding bodywork with an equal clearance around its edge. Adjustment is made by loosening the mounting bolts and moving the boot lid within the elongated mounting holes. Check that the lock enters the striker centrally when the boot lid is closed, and if necessary adjust the positions within the elongated holes.

16   Boot lid support strut – removal and refitting

Removal
1   Support the boot lid in its open position.
2   Disconnect each end of the support strut by prising out the retainers

16.2A Prising the retainer from the boot lid upper strut mounting

16.2B Boot lid lower strut mounting

17.2 Boot lid lock

17.3 Boot lid lock operating rod (arrowed)

17.5 Boot lid striker

18.2A Remove the screws and hooks ...

18.2B ... and unclip the trim panel from the tailgate

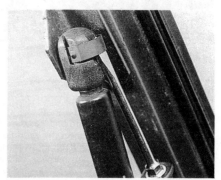

18.4 Disconnecting the strut from the tailgate

with a small screwdriver and pulling the strut from the ball mountings (photos).

Refitting

3   Refitting is a reversal of removal, but note that the piston end of the strut faces downwards.

17   Boot lid lock and lock cylinder – removal and refitting

Removal
Lock

1   Open the boot lid, then disconnect the operating rod from the lock by reaching through the aperture.
2   Using a Torx key, unscrew the lock mounting bolts and withdraw the lock from the boot lid (photo).

Lock cylinder

3   Open the boot lid, then disconnect the operating rods for the lock and central locking unit (where applicable) by reaching through the aperture (photo).
4   Using a pair of pliers, pull out the retaining clip, then withdraw the lock cylinder from the boot lid.

Refitting

5   Refitting is a reversal of removal. When refitting the lock, check that the striker enters the lock centrally when the boot lid is closed, and if necessary re-position the striker by loosening the mounting screws (photo).

18   Tailgate – removal, refitting and adjustment

Removal

1   Open the tailgate and support it in the open position.
2   Remove the screws and hooks, and unclip the trim panel from the tailgate, then disconnect the rear window washer tube (photos). Where applicable also disconnect the wiring for the central locking.
3   Unclip and remove the headlining rear cover strip.
4   Support the tailgate in the open position, then disconnect the struts by prising out the spring clip retainers (photo).
5   With the help of an assistant, unscrew the mounting nuts and lift the tailgate from the rear of the car.
6   If necessary, the hinge can be removed from the tailgate by driving out the pin with a suitable drift.

Refitting and adjustment

7   Refitting is a reversal of removal, but check that the tailgate is correctly aligned with the surrounding bodywork with an equal clearance around its edge. Adjustment is made by loosening the mounting bolts and moving the tailgate within the elongated mounting holes. Check that the striker enters the lock centrally when the tailgate is closed, and if necessary adjust the position of the striker within the elongated holes. The striker position also determines the rear height of the tailgate.

19   Tailgate support strut – removal and refitting

Removal

1   Support the tailgate in its open position.

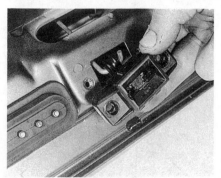

20.3A Removing the tailgate lock ...

20.3B ... and central locking unit (where fitted)

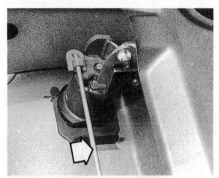

20.4A Central locking unit operating rod on the tailgate lock cylinder (arrowed)

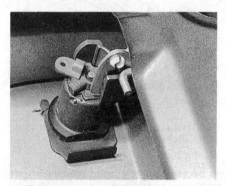

20.4B Disconnecting the lock operating rod from the tailgate lock cylinder

20.5 Removing the lock cylinder from the tailgate

20.6 Tailgate striker

2   Disconnect each end of the support strut by prising out the spring clip retainers with a small screwdriver and pulling the strut from the ball mountings.

Refitting

3   Refitting is a reversal of removal, but note that the piston end of the strut faces downwards.

20   Tailgate lock and lock cylinder – removal and refitting

Removal

Lock

1   Open the tailgate, then remove the two screws and hooks and unclip the inner trim panel.
2   Using a Torx key, unscrew and remove the lock mounting bolts.
3   Pull out the lock and at the same time turn it to release the operating rod from the cylinder assembly. If necessary, also remove the central locking unit (photos).

Lock cylinder

4   Open the tailgate, then disconnect the operating rods for the lock and central locking unit (where applicable) by reaching through the aperture (photos).
5   Using a pair of pliers, pull out the retaining clip, then withdraw the lock cylinder from the tailgate (photo).

Refitting

6   Refitting is a reversal of removal. When refitting the lock, check that the striker enters the lock centrally when the tailgate is closed, and if necessary re-position the striker by loosening the mounting screws (photo).

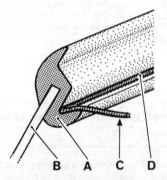

Fig. 11.12 Cross section of the rear side window (three-door hatchback) with cord inserted for refitting (Sec 21)

A   Weatherseal
B   Window glass
C   Refitting cord
D   Groove

21   Rear side window (three-door hatchback) – removal and refitting

Removal

1   On the appropriate side remove the rear side shelf, side panel trim, pillar upper trim and rear quarter panel trim.
2   Using a blunt ended instrument, push the inner lip of the weatherseal beneath the window frame starting at the top. Support the window on the outside during this operation.
3   With the weatherseal free, withdraw the window from the body.

Refitting

4   Clean the window and aperture in the body.
5   Fit the weatherseal on the window, then insert a cord in the

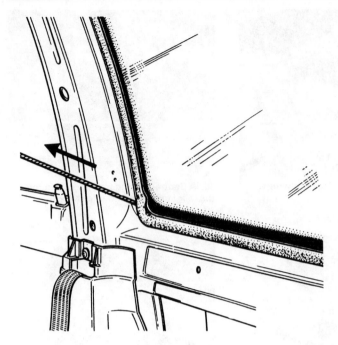

Fig. 11.13 Pull the cord to locate the lip of the weatherseal over the aperture (Sec 21)

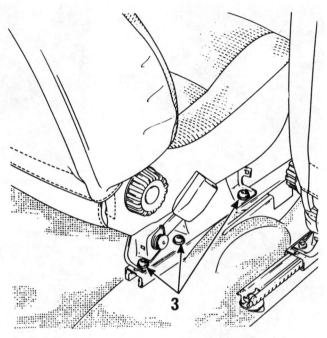

Fig. 11.14 Mounting bolts (3) located on the inner side of the seat (Sec 24)

weatherseal groove so that the ends project from the bottom of the window and are overlapped by approximately 200 mm.
6   Locate the window on the aperture in the body and pass the ends of the cord inside the car. Have an assistant hold the window in position.
7   Slowly pull one end of the cord so that the lip of the weatherseal goes over the aperture, and at the same time have the assistant press firmly on the outside of the window. When the cord reaches the middle top of the window, pull the remaining length of cord to position the other half of the weatherseal.
8   Refit the trim panels in reverse order.

22   Windscreen and rear window/tailgate glass – general information

The windscreen and rear window/tailgate glass are bonded in place with special mastic, and special tools are required to cut free the old units and fit replacements, together with cleaning solutions and primers. It is therefore recommended that this work is entrusted to a Renault dealer or windscreen replacement specialist.

23   Body exterior fittings/exterior trim panels – general information

The front wing side protection strip can be removed by partially removing the plastic wheelarch, then removing the clip or metal nut from inside the wing. Using a screwdriver lift the front of the strip to free the pin from the hole, then push the strip to the rear. The strip is refitted by pressing it until the clip engages.
The door protection strips can be removed by removing the mounting screws from inside the door then pushing the strip forwards. Align the clips when refitting the strips.
The sill protection strips can be removed by prising up their end covers and unscrewing the retaining screws, then pulling the strip forwards. The clips may be removed from the sill by turning them through 90° with a pair of pliers.

24   Seats – removal and refitting

Removal
Front seat
1   Push the seat fully forwards, then unscrew the mounting bolt from the outer rear of the slide. Remove the moulding by pulling it forwards.
2   From the side of the seat unscrew the two mounting bolts securing the seat to the slide.
3   On the inner side of the seat unscrew the three mounting bolts, then remove the seat from inside the car.
4   If necessary, the slides may be removed by unscrewing the nuts from under the car. Note the position of the spacers (photos).

Rear seat
5   Fold the rear seat backrest forwards, then raise the two levers on the hinges and remove the backrest from the car (photo).
6   To remove the seat cushion, tilt the cushion forwards then release the two brackets from the location holes and remove the cushion from the car.

Refitting
7   Refitting is a reversal of removal.

25   Interior trim panels – general information

1   The interior trim panels shown in Fig. 11.15 are retained with plastic clips which may easily break on removal. It is recommended that the clips are renewed after removal to ensure secure fitting.
2   To remove the centre pillar upper trim, first remove the coat hanger, seat belt mounting and height adjustment pushrod, then release the trim and seals and remove the sliding cover (photo).
3   To remove the side lower trim, first remove the centre pillar upper trim, then remove the screws and the lower belt mounting. Release the rear and front ends then remove the trim from the rear of the car (photo).
4   To remove the front pillar upper trim, first remove the centre pillar upper trim, then remove the screws and withdraw the trim downwards and rearwards.

24.4A Seat slide mounting bolt viewed from under the car

24.4B Removing the seat slide from inside the car. Note the spacer

24.5 Rear seat hinge pin

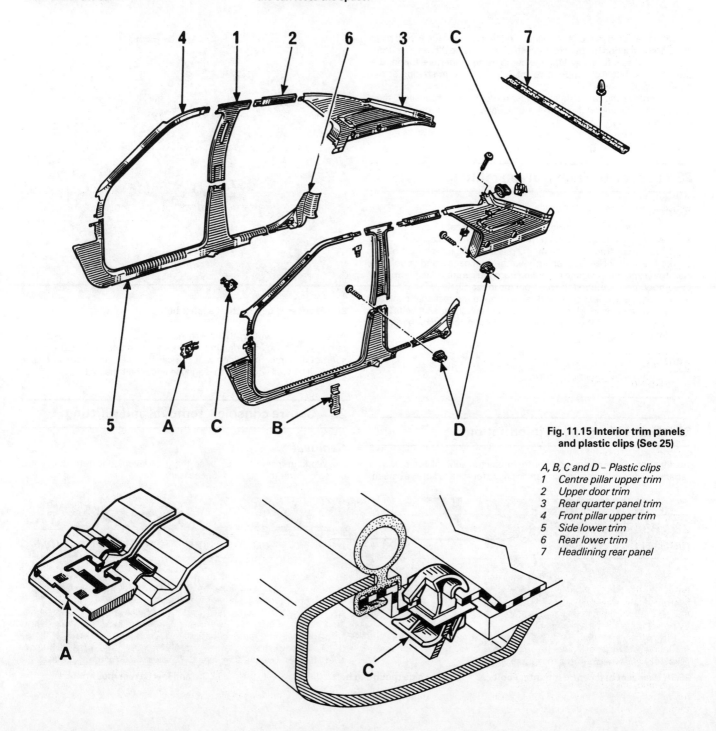

Fig. 11.15 Interior trim panels and plastic clips (Sec 25)

A, B, C and D – Plastic clips
1 *Centre pillar upper trim*
2 *Upper door trim*
3 *Rear quarter panel trim*
4 *Front pillar upper trim*
5 *Side lower trim*
6 *Rear lower trim*
7 *Headlining rear panel*

25.2 Removing the coat hanger

25.3 Side lower trim top mounting screw

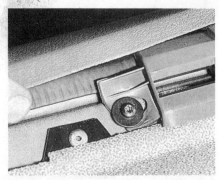

25.5 Rear quarter panel trim front mounting screw

5   To remove the rear quarter panel trim, first remove the centre pillar upper trim, rear door upper and lower trim, and the headlining rear trim. Remove the seal from the luggage compartment aperture frame, the side shelf, and the two upper screws. Release the trim starting at the door seal end (photo).

6   To remove the rear side shelf, first remove the centre shelf, then disconnect the wiring from the loudspeaker and remove the five mounting screws.

26   Seat belts – removal and refitting

Removal

1   To remove a front seat belt stalk, move the seat to the rear then unscrew the mounting bolt and remove the stalk from the seat.

2   To remove a front seat belt inertia reel and belt, unbolt the bottom anchor from the inner sill, then remove the trim panels and unbolt the inertia reel and upper sliding mounting from the centre pillar (photo). On three-door models, unbolt the rail from the inner sill.

3   To remove the rear seat belts, first remove the rear seat backrest and cushion then prise off the plastic caps and unbolt the seat belts from the body. To remove the inertia reel it will first be necessary to remove the trim panels (photos).

Refitting

4   Refitting is a reversal of removal.

27   Sunroof – general information

Most models are equipped with an electric sunroof fitted with a separate sliding sun visor which can be pulled forward to act as a screen.

26.2 Front seat belt bottom anchor bolt

At the time of writing there was no information available regarding removal, refitting and adjustment procedures. If a fault develops in the sunroof, it is recommended that the car be taken to a Renault dealer who will be well equipped to diagnose and repair the unit.

28   Centre console – removal and refitting

Removal

1   Working inside the car prise the gear lever boot from the centre console. Refer to Chapter 7 if necessary.

26.3A Rear seat belt centre mounting bolt ...

26.3B ... side mounting bolt ...

26.3C ... and inertia reel mounting

28.2 Wiring to the switches and cigar lighter on the rear of the centre console

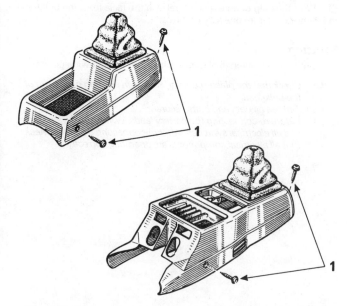

Fig. 11.16 Centre console types and retaining screws (1) (Sec 28)

2   Remove the mounting screws and lift the centre console from the car. Where applicable, disconnect the wiring from the switches (photo).

Refitting

3   Refitting is a reversal of removal.

29 Facia – removal and refitting

Removal

1   Disconnect the battery negative lead.
2   Remove the centre console with reference to Section 28.
3   Remove the front left-hand and right-hand pillar upper and lower trim with reference to Section 25.
4   Remove the steering wheel with reference to Chapter 10.
5   Remove the steering column upper and lower shrouds.
6   Remove the combination switch from the steering column with reference to Chapter 12.
7   Unscrew and remove the two screws securing the facia to the top of the steering column, then remove the moulding and disconnect the ignition switch.
8   On models with a non-adjustable steering column, unscrew and remove the steering column mounting bolts and lower the column away from the facia.
9   On models with an adjustable steering column, set the steering

wheel in its lowest position, then remove the adjusting locknut and control lever. The steering column mountings do not have to be removed.
10   Remove the screw securing the choke control knob to the facia, then disconnect the warning light wiring and push the knob back into the facia.
11   Disconnect the speedometer cable.
12   Remove the screws from the heater control panel and lower cover, disconnect the wiring and push the panel inside the facia (photos).
13   Remove the screws securing the heater unit to the facia, and the screws securing the moulding on the heater unit. Release the wiring harness for the centre console.
14   Disconnect the wiring connectors on the left and right-hand A-pillars.
15   Unscrew the earth cable mounting bolts.
16   Remove the courtesy light switches from the A-pillars. Disconnect the wiring plugs located in the pillars.
17   On the left-hand side of the engine compartment, remove the cover and disconnect the engine wiring harness.
18   Remove the plastic mudguard from the left-hand wheelarch, then unclip the engine wiring harness. Pass the harness inside the car.
19   Remove the scuttle grille from the right-hand side.
20   Disconnect the right-hand wiring harness from the windscreen wiper, the battery positive terminal and the heater matrix motor.
21   Using a screwdriver prise off the facia mounting covers from the left and right-hand lower corners. Unscrew and remove the two nuts.
22   Prise the two upper covers from the left and right-hand speakers on the facia, then remove the two nuts from the facia upper mountings.

29.12A Remove the screws ...

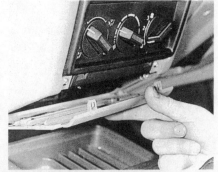

29.12B ... and remove the heater panel lower cover

29.12C Removing the heater control panel

23   With the help of an assistant, release the facia from the bulkhead and withdraw it from one side of the car.

Refitting

24   Refitting is a reversal of removal but note the following points:

    (a)   *Check that the plastic centring knob is in position on the top of the bulkhead*
    (b)   *Tighten all nuts and bolts securely*
    (c)   *Before re-connecting the battery leads, switch off the ignition and all electrical switches. After re-connecting the leads check that all electrical components are operating correctly*

30   Glovebox – removal and refitting

Removal

1   With the glovebox open, pull out the hinge pins and withdraw the glovebox from the facia.
2   If necessary the lock may be removed from the glovebox lid and the facia.

Refitting

3   Refitting is a reversal of removal.

Chapter 12 Electrical system

Contents

Specifications

System type .... 12 volt, negative earth

Battery
Type .... Low maintenance or maintenance-free
Capacity .... 35, 50 or 65 Ah

Alternator
Type .... Paris-Rhone or Ducellier
Output .... 60, 70 or 90 amps
Regulated voltage .... 13.5 to 14.8 volts

Starter motor
Type .... Pre-engaged
Commutator diameter:
   New .... 30 mm
   Minimum .... 28.9 mm
Armature endfloat.. 0.05 to 0.3 mm
Minimum brush length .... 7 mm

Fuses

Fuse	Rating (amps)	Circuit(s) protected
1	30	Left-hand window
2	30	Right-hand window
3	10	Left-hand side and rear lights
4	10	Right-hand side and rear lights, lights-on buzzer, switch lighting
5	10	Rear foglight
6	10	Flasher
7	30	Air conditioning
8	20	Engine electric cooling fan

Fuse	Rating (amps)	Circuit(s) protected
9	30	Air conditioning
10	–	Not used
11	–	Not used
12	5	Automatic transmission
13	15	Anti-lock brakes
14	20	Sunroof, trip computer, heated rear screen, defrosting rear view mirrors
15	5	Alarm
16	–	Not used
17	10	Clock, radio, trip computer, alarm
18	20	Heater blower
19	30	Headlamp washers
20	10	Windscreen wiper timer
21	30	Central door locking
22	20	Heated rear screen
23	15	Radio, interior lights, luggage compartment
24	30	Accessories cut-off (cuts off power to interior lights, clock etc. before the ignition)
25	15	Clock, trip computer, alarm, rear view mirrors
26	15	Windscreen wiper, windscreen washers
27	10	Heated seats
28	15	Rear screen wiper, cigar lighter, reversing lights
29	10	Stop lights

Bulbs

	Wattage
Headlamp:	
Standard	60/55
Halogen	55
Front sidelamp	5
Front foglamp	21
Front direction indicator	21
Front repeater	5
Rear sidelamp	5
Rear direction indicator	21
Reversing lamp	21
Stop lamp	21
Rear foglamp	21
Number plate lamp	5
Interior lamp	10
Instrument panel illumination	1.2 or 2

Torque wrench setting

	Nm	lbf ft
Battery retaining clamp bolt	10	7

1 General information and precautions

Warning: *Before carrying out any work on the electrical system, read through the precautions given in Safety first! at the beginning of this manual*

The electrical system is of 12 volt negative earth type, and consists of a battery, alternator, starter motor and related electrical accessories, components and wiring.

The battery, charged by the alternator (which is belt-driven from the crankshaft pulley), provides a steady amount of current for the ignition, starting, lighting and other electrical circuits.

The starter motor is of the pre-engaged type incorporating an integral solenoid. On starting, the solenoid moves the drive pinion into engagement with the flywheel ring gear before the starter motor is energised. Once the engine has started, a one-way clutch prevents the motor armature being driven by the engine until the pinion disengages from the flywheel.

It is necessary to take extra care when working on the electrical system to avoid damage to semi-conductor devices (diodes and transistors), and to avoid the risk of personal injury. In addition to the precautions given in Safety first! at the beginning of this manual, observe the following when working on the system.

Always remove rings, watches, etc before working on the electrical system. Even with the battery disconnected, capacitive discharge could occur if a component live terminal is earthed through a metal object. This could cause a shock or nasty burn.

Do not reverse the battery connections. Components such as the alternator, fuel and ignition control units, or any other unit having semi-conductor circuitry could be irreparably damaged.

If the engine is being started using jump leads and a slave battery, connect the batteries positive-to-positive and negative-to-negative – see 'Booster battery (jump) starting' at the beginning of this manual. This also applies when connecting a battery charger.

Never disconnect the battery terminals, any electrical wiring or any test instruments, when the engine is running.

Never use an ohmmeter of the type incorporating a hand-cranked generator for circuit or continuity testing.

Always ensure that the battery negative lead is disconnected when working on the electrical system.

2 Electrical fault finding – general information

1   A typical electrical circuit consists of an electrical component, any switches, relays, motors, fuses, fusible links or circuit breakers related to that component and the wiring and connectors that link the component to both the battery and the chassis. To help you pinpoint an electrical circuit problem, wiring diagrams are included at the end of this manual.

2   Before tackling any troublesome electrical circuit, first study the appropriate wiring diagram to get a complete understanding of what components are included in that individual circuit. Trouble spots, for instance, can be narrowed down by noting if other components related to the circuit are operating properly. If several components or circuits fail at one time, then the problem is probably in a fuse or earth connection, because several circuits are often routed through the same fuse and earth connections.

3   Electrical problems usually stem from simple causes, such as loose or corroded connections, a blown fuse, a melted fusible link or a faulty relay. Visually inspect the condition of all fuses, wires and connections in a problem circuit before testing the components. Use the diagrams to note which terminal connections will need to be checked in order to pinpoint the trouble spot.

4   The basic tools needed for electrical fault finding include a circuit tester or voltmeter (a 12-volt bulb with a set of test leads can also be used), a continuity tester, a battery and set of test leads, and a jumper wire, preferably with a circuit breaker incorporated, which can be used to bypass electrical components. Before attempting to locate a problem with test instruments, use the wiring diagram to decide where to make the connections.

Voltage checks

5   Voltage checks should be performed if a circuit is not functioning properly. Connect one lead of a circuit tester to either the negative battery terminal or a known good earth. Connect the other lead to a connector in the circuit being tested, preferably nearest to the battery or fuse. If the bulb of the tester lights, voltage is present, which means that the part of the circuit between the connector and the battery is problem free. Continue checking the rest of the circuit in the same fashion. When you reach a point at which no voltage is present, the problem lies between that point and the last test point with voltage. Most problems can be traced to a loose connection. **Note:** *Bear in mind that some circuits are only live when the ignition switch is switched to a particular position.*

Finding a short circuit

6   One method of finding a short circuit is to remove the fuse and connect a testlight or voltmeter to the fuse terminals with all the relevant electrical components switched off. There should be no voltage present in the circuit. Move the wiring from side to side while watching the test light. If the bulb lights up, there is a short to earth somewhere in that area, probably where the insulation has rubbed through. The same test can be performed on each component in the circuit, even a switch.

Earth check

7   Perform an earth test to check whether a component is properly earthed. Disconnect the battery and connect one lead of a self-powered test light, known as a continuity tester, to a known good earth point. Connect the other lead to the wire or earth connection being tested. If the bulb lights up, the earth is good. If the bulb does not light up, the earth is not good.

Continuity check

8   A continuity check is necessary to determine if there are any breaks in a circuit. With the circuit off (ie no power in the circuit), a self-powered continuity tester can be used to check the circuit. Connect the test leads to both ends of the circuit (or to the positive end and a good earth), and if the test light comes on, the circuit is passing current properly. If the light does not come on, there is a break somewhere in the circuit. The same procedure can be used to test a switch, by connecting the continuity tester to the switch terminals. With the switch turned on, the test light should come on.

Finding an open circuit

9   When checking for possible open circuits, it is often difficult to locate them by sight because oxidation or terminal misalignment are hidden by the connectors. Merely moving a connector on a sensor or in the wiring harness may correct the open circuit condition. Remember this when an open circuit is indicated when fault finding in a circuit. Intermittent problems may also be caused by oxidized or loose connections.

General

10   Electrical fault finding is simple if you keep in mind that all electrical circuits are basically electricity flowing from the battery, through the wires, switches, relays, fuses and fusible links to each electrical component (light bulb, motor, etc.) and to earth, from where it is passed back to the battery. Any electrical problem is an interruption in the flow of electricity from the battery.

3   Battery – testing and charging

1   Where a conventional battery is fitted, the electrolyte level of each cell should be checked and if necessary topped up with distilled or de-ionized water at the intervals given in Chapter 1. On some batteries the case is translucent, and incorporates minimum and maximum level marks. The check should be made more often if the car is operated in high ambient temperature conditions.

2   Where a low-maintenance battery is fitted, it is not usually possible to check the electrolyte level.

3   Periodically disconnect and clean the battery terminals and leads. After refitting them, smear the exposed metal with petroleum jelly.

4   When the battery is removed for whatever reason, it is worthwhile checking it for cracks and leakage.

5   If topping up becomes excessive, and this is not due to leakage from a fractured casing, the battery is being over-charged, and the voltage regulator will have to be checked.

6   If the car covers a very small annual mileage, it is worthwhile checking the specific gravity of the electrolyte every three months to determine the state of charge of the battery. Use a hydrometer to make the check, and compare the results with the following table.

	Normal climates	Tropics
Discharged	1.120	1.080
Half charged	1.200	1.160
Fully charged	1.280	1.230

7   If the battery condition is suspect, first check the specific gravity of electrolyte in each cell. A variation of 0.040 or more between any cells indicates loss of electrolyte or deterioration of the internal plates.

8   A further test can be made using a battery heavy discharge meter. The battery should be discharged for a maximum of 15 seconds at a load of three times the ampere-hour capacity (at the 20 hour discharge rate). Alternatively, connect a voltmeter across the battery terminals and operate the starter motor with the HT king lead from the ignition coil earthed with a suitable wire, and the headlamps, heated rear window and heater blower switched on. If the voltmeter reading remains above 9.6 volts, the battery condition is satisfactory. If the voltmeter reading drops below 9.6 volts, and the battery has already been charged, it is faulty.

9   In winter when heavy demand is placed on the battery (starting from cold and using more electrical equipment), it is a good idea to have the battery fully charged from an external source occasionally, at a rate of 10% of the battery capacity (ie 6.5 amps for a 65 Ah battery).

10   Both battery terminal leads must be disconnected before connecting the charger leads (disconnect the negative lead first). Continue to charge the battery until no further rise in specific gravity is noted over a four-hour period.

11   Alternatively, a trickle charger, charging at a rate of 1.5 amps can safely be used overnight.

4   Battery – removal and refitting

Removal

1   The battery is located beneath a plastic cover on the right-hand side of the bulkhead. First check that all electrical components are switched off in order to avoid a spark occurring as the negative lead is disconnected. Note also that if the radio has a security coding, it will be necessary to insert this code when the battery is re-connected.

2   Remove the plastic cover from over the battery. To do this first pull up the weatherseal, then remove the screws and lift the cover from over

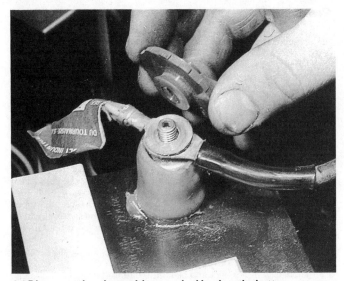

4.4 Disconnecting the positive terminal lead on the battery

4.5 Unscrewing the extended clamp bolt to remove the battery clamp

the battery. The cover may be stuck to the windscreen, however a sharp pull will release it.

3   Loosen the plastic nut on the negative terminal clamp, then lift the clamp and lead from the terminal and place it on the bulkhead. This is the terminal to disconnect before working on any electrical component on the car. If the terminal is tight, carefully ease it off by moving it from side to side.

4   Loosen the plastic nut on the positive terminal clamp (photo), then lift the clamp and lead from the terminal and place it on the bulkhead. If necessary, the nut can be removed completely and the lead disconnected from the clamp.

5   Unscrew the extended clamp bolt and remove the clamp from the front of the battery (photo).

6   Lift the battery from the tray keeping it upright and taking care not to touch clothing.

7   If necessary, remove the battery tray from the bulkhead.

8   Clean the battery terminal posts, clamps, tray and battery casing. If the bulkhead is rusted as a result of battery acid spilling onto it, clean it thoroughly and re-paint with reference to Chapter 1.

Refitting

9   Refitting is a reversal of removal, but always connect the positive terminal clamp first and the negative terminal clamp last.

5 Charging system – testing

1   If the ignition warning lamp fails to illuminate when the ignition is switched on, first check the wiring connections at the rear of the alternator for security. If satisfactory, check that the warning lamp bulb has not blown and is secure in its holder. If the lamp still fails to illuminate check the continuity of the warning lamp feed wire from the alternator to the bulbholder. If all is satisfactory, the alternator is at fault and should be renewed or taken to an automobile electrician for testing and repair.

2   If the ignition warning lamp illuminates when the engine is running, ensure that the drivebelt is correctly tensioned (see Chapter 1), and that the connections on the rear of the alternator are secure. If all is so far satisfactory, check the alternator brushes and commutator, as described in Section 7. If the fault still persists, the alternator should be renewed, or taken to an automobile electrician for testing and repair.

3   If the alternator output is suspect even though the warning lamp functions correctly, the regulated voltage may be checked as follows.

4   Connect a voltmeter across the battery terminals and then start the engine.

5   Increase the engine speed until the reading on the voltmeter remains steady. This should be between 13.5 and 14.8 volts.

6   Switch on as many electrical accessories as possible and check that

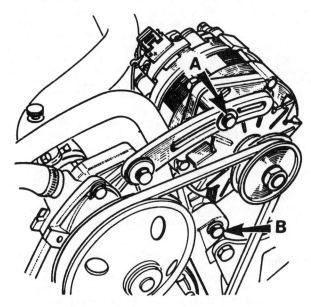

Fig. 12.1 Alternator adjustment bolt (A) and pivot bolt (B) on the 1397 cc (C1J) engine (Sec 6)

the alternator maintains the regulated voltage at between 13.5 and 14.8 volts.

7   If the regulated voltage is not as stated, the fault may be due to a faulty regulator, a faulty diode, a severed phase winding or worn brushes, springs or commutator. The brushes and commutator may be attended to, as described in Section 7, but if the fault still persists the alternator should be renewed, or taken to an automobile electrician for testing and repair.

6 Alternator – removal and refitting

Removal

1   Disconnect the battery negative terminal.

2   Apply the handbrake, then jack up the front right-hand side of the car and support it on axle stands. Remove the cover plate from inside the wheelarch.

6.3 Plastic protection cover on the alternator (arrowed) – 1390 cc (E6J) engine

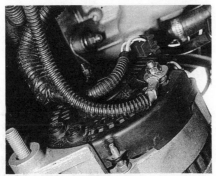

6.4 Electrical lead connections to the rear of the alternator – 1390 cc (E6J) engine

6.12 Engine supported on a wooden block with engine mounting removed – 1390 cc (E6J) engine

6.13A Removing the alternator pivot bolt (arrowed) – 1390 cc (E6J) engine

6.13B Alternator mounting bracket (arrowed) – 1390 cc (E6J) engine

6.19 Alternator pivot bolt (A), tensioner locknut (B), and tensioner bolt (C) on the 1721 cc (F2N) engine (arrowed)

1390 cc (E6J) engine

3 Remove the plastic protection cover from the alternator (photo).
4 Make a note of the electrical lead locations at the rear of the alternator and disconnect them (photo).
5 Loosen the adjustment bolt on the adjustment link, followed by the pivot bolt on the bottom of the alternator.
6 Swivel the alternator towards the engine, then slip the drivebelt off of the pulley.
7 Disconnect the right-hand steering track rod end from the stub axle carrier with reference to Chapter 10.
8 Using a parallel pin punch, drive out the double roll pin securing the right-hand inner driveshaft joint yoke to the differential sunwheel stub shaft. Drive out the small inner roll pin first, then drive out the outer roll pin.
9 Unscrew and remove the two bolts securing the right-hand stub axle carrier to the suspension strut. Note that the nuts are on the brake caliper side.
10 Pull the top of the stub axle carrier outwards until the inner end of the driveshaft is released from the sun wheel stub shaft. Support the driveshaft and stub axle carrier in this position.
11 Working under the car unscrew the nut from the bottom of the right-hand engine mounting.
12 Using a hoist attached to the engine or alternatively a trolley jack and wooden block beneath the engine sump, raise the engine approximately 150 mm. Unbolt the engine mounting from the cylinder block, then lower the engine onto a wooden block interposed between the cylinder block/sump flange and the engine subframe (photo).
13 Remove the alternator pivot and adjustment bolts and withdraw the alternator from the engine. If required, the alternator mounting bracket may be unbolted from the cylinder head at this stage (photos).

1397 cc (C1J) engine

14 Make a note of the electrical lead locations at the rear of the alternator and disconnect them.
15 Loosen the adjustment bolt on the adjustment link, followed by

the pivot bolt on the bottom of the alternator.
16 Swivel the alternator towards the engine, then slip the drivebelt off of the pulley.
17 Remove the alternator pivot and adjustment bolts and withdraw the alternator from the engine.

1721 cc (F2N) engine

18 Make a note of the electrical lead locations at the rear of the alternator and disconnect them.
19 Loosen the pivot bolt on the bottom of the alternator and the tensioner locknut on the adjustment bracket (photo).
20 Unscrew the tensioner bolt so that the drivebelt tension is fully released. Remove the drivebelt from the alternator pulley.
21 Remove the alternator pivot bolt and adjustment locknut, then withdraw the alternator from the engine.

Refitting

22 Refitting is a reversal of removal. Tension the drivebelt with reference to Chapter 1.

7 Alternator brushes and regulator – checking and renewal

1 Disconnect the battery negative terminal.
2 Note the locations of the wiring connectors and leads at the rear of the alternator and disconnect them. If preferred the alternator can be completely removed to provide easier working conditions, particularly in the case of the 1390 cc (E6J) engine.
3 Note the location of the lead on the B + terminal, then unscrew and remove the nuts and lead and remove the plastic rear cover (photo).
4 Unscrew the two small screws or nuts securing the regulator and

PARIS-RHONE

DUCELLIER

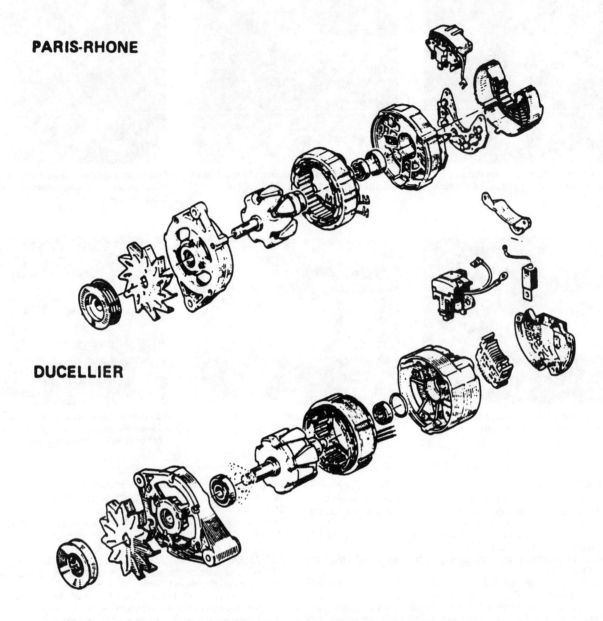

Fig. 12.2 Exploded views of the Paris-Rhone and Ducellier alternators (Sec 7)

7.3 Alternator brush and regulator lead to the B + terminal (arrowed)

7.4A Unscrew the two small screws (arrowed) ...

7.4B ... and remove the regulator and brushbox assembly

7.5 Measuring the length of the alternator brushes

7.6 Alternator slip rings (arrowed)

brushbox assembly to the rear of the alternator. Lift off the regulator and brushbox, disconnect the electrical lead(s), noting their locations, then remove the regulator and brushbox assembly from the alternator (photos).

5   Measure the length of each brush from the end of the holder to the top of the brush (photo). No dimension if given by Renault but as a rough guide 5 mm should be regarded as a minimum. If either brush is worn below this amount, obtain and fit a new brushbox. If the brushes are still serviceable, clean them with a petrol-moistened cloth. Check that the brush spring pressure is equal for both brushes and gives reasonable tension. If in doubt about the condition of the brushes and springs compare them with new parts at a Renault parts dealer. The regulator can be separated from the brushbox after removing the cover if necessary.

6   Clean the slip rings with a petrol-moistened cloth, then check for signs of scoring, burning or severe pitting (photo). If evident, the slip rings should be attended to by an automobile electrician.

7   Refitting is a reversal of removal.

8   Starting system – testing

1   If the starter motor fails to operate, first check the condition of the battery by switching on the headlamps. If they glow brightly then gradually dim after a few seconds, the battery is in an uncharged condition.

2   If the battery is satisfactory, check the starter motor main terminal and the engine earth cable for security. Check the terminal connections on the solenoid, located on the starter motor.

3   If the starter still fails to turn, use a voltmeter, or 12 volt test lamp and leads, to ensure that there is battery voltage at the solenoid main terminal (ie the cable from the battery positive terminal).

4   With the ignition switched on and the ignition key in position D check that voltage is reaching the solenoid terminal with the spade connector, and also the starter main terminal beneath the end cover.

5   If there is no voltage reaching the spade connector there is a wiring

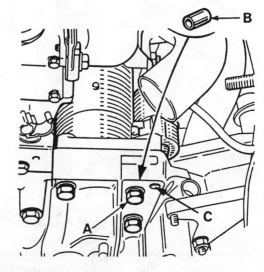

Fig. 12.3 Starter motor locating dowel positions (Sec 9)

A   Position for 1397 cc (C1J) engine
B   Locating dowel
C   Position for 1390 cc (E6J) and 1721 cc (F2N) engines

or ignition switch fault. If voltage is available, but the starter does not operate, then the starter or solenoid is likely to be at fault.

9   Starter motor – removal and refitting

Removal

1   Disconnect the battery negative terminal.

9.5 Starter motor terminals on the solenoid (arrowed)

9.6 Starter motor support bracket on the rear facing side of the cylinder block (arrowed)

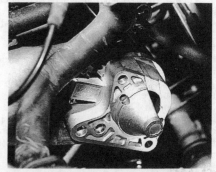

9.7 Withdrawing the starter motor

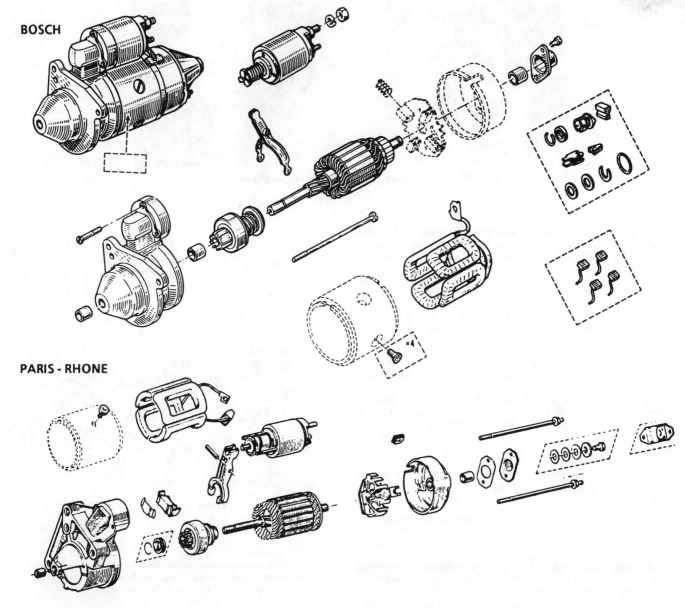

Fig. 12.4 Exploded views of the Bosch and Paris-Rhone starter motors (Sec 10)

2   Apply the handbrake, then jack up the front of the car and support it on axle stands.
3   For improved access, remove the air cleaner assembly as described in Chapter 4.
4   Where applicable, remove the exhaust heat screen.
5   Disconnect the battery supply cable and solenoid feed wire from the starter solenoid terminals (photo).
6   Unscrew the bolt securing the starter motor support bracket to the rear facing side of the cylinder block (photo).
7   Unscrew the three bolts securing the starter motor to the transmission bellhousing and withdraw the starter from the engine (photo). On the 1721 cc (F2N) engine, remove the starter motor from behind the right-hand front wheel. Note the position of the locating dowel in the upper rear bellhousing bolt hole and make sure that it is in the same place for refitting. There are two possible locations for this dowel as shown in Fig. 12.3.

Refitting

8   Refitting is a reversal of removal, but tighten the bellhousing bolts before the support bracket bolt.

10 Starter motor brushes – checking and renewal

1   Remove the starter motor from the car as described in Section 9.
2   Unscrew and remove the two through-bolts then remove the support bracket from the commutator end of the starter motor (photo).
3   Where fitted, remove the cap plate from the rear cover, and the bolt and washers between the rear cover and armature.
4   Unscrew the two screws and withdraw the end cover. As the cover is being removed, release it from the rubber grommet over the field cable (photo).
5   Disconnect the brushes from their holders by lifting the springs with a screwdriver, then remove the brush holder assembly (photo).
6   Measure the length of the brushes and compare with the minimum dimension given in the Specifications. If either brush is worn to or below this figure, renew all of the brushes. Note that new field brushes must be soldered to the existing leads.
7   Clean the brush holder assembly and wipe the commutator with a petrol-moistened cloth. If the commutator is dirty, it may be cleaned

10.2 Starter motor through-bolt (arrowed)

10.4 Removing the starter motor end cover

10.5 Starter motor brush and retaining spring

with fine glass paper, then wiped with the cloth.

8   Fit the new brushes using a reversal of the removal procedure, but make sure that they move freely in their holders.

11   Fuses and relays – general information

1   The fuses and relays are located below the passenger side glovebox. Access is gained by turning the two screws a quarter turn, then tilting open the lid. Symbols on the reverse of the lid indicate the circuits protected by the fuses, and four spare fuses are supplied together with plastic tweezers to remove and fit them. Further details

Fig. 12.5 Fuse location chart (Sec 11)

11.2 Removing a fuse with the tweezers

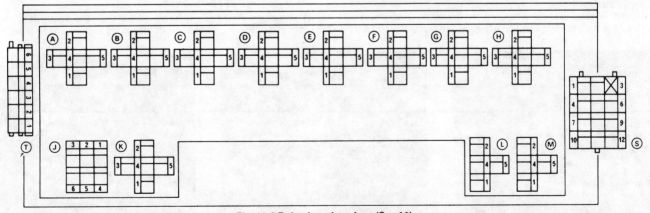

Fig. 12.6 Relay location chart (Sec 11)

A Front foglamp shunt	F Trip computer lighting
B Front foglamp shunt	rheostat relay
C Front foglamp relay	H Heated rear window relay

J Door locking timer	S Diagnostic plug
L Flasher unit	T Windscreen wiper timer
M Lights 'on' warning buzzer	

11.4 Relays located on the fusebox

on fuse ratings and circuits protected are given in the Specifications.

2   To remove a fuse, use the tweezers provided to pull it out of the holder (photo). Slide the fuse sideways from the tweezers. The wire within the fuse is clearly visible and it will be broken if the fuse is blown.

3   Always renew a fuse with one of an identical rating. Never renew a fuse more than once without tracing the source of the trouble. The fuse rating is stamped on top of the fuse.

4   The various relays can be removed from their respective locations by carefully pulling them from the sockets (photo).

5   If a system controlled by a relay becomes inoperative and the relay is suspect, operate the system and if the relay is functioning it should be possible to hear it click as it is energized. If the relay proves satisfactory, the fault lies with the components or wiring of the system. If the relay is not being energized, then it is not receiving a main supply voltage or a switching voltage, or the relay is faulty.

12   Switches – removal and refitting

Ignition switch

1   Disconnect the battery negative terminal lead.

2   Unscrew the cross-head screws and remove the steering column shrouds (photos). Where applicable, also remove the internal cover.

3   Note the wiring routing, then disconnect the two black and grey connectors.

4   Using an angled cross-head screwdriver, remove the small grub screw located on the top of the ignition switch.

5   Insert the ignition key and turn it to the garage position (position 3).

6   Depress the retaining lugs and withdraw the switch assembly.

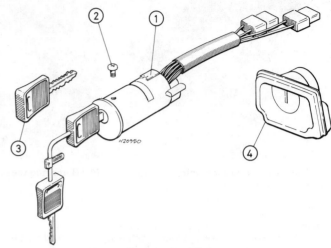

Fig. 12.7 Ignition switch (Sec 12)

1	Ignition switch	3	Key
2	Grub screw	4	Rubber grommet

7   Refitting is a reversal of removal.

Steering column multi-function switches

8   Disconnect the battery negative terminal lead.

9   Remove the steering wheel with reference to Chapter 10.

10   Unscrew the cross-head screws and remove the steering column shrouds. Where applicable, also remove the internal cover.

11   Unscrew the mounting screws, withdraw the switch from the steering column, and disconnect the wiring plug (photos).

12   Refitting is a reversal of removal.

Facia switches

13   Disconnect the battery negative terminal lead.

14   Prise the switch from the facia using a small screwdriver (photo).

15   Disconnect the wiring plug.

16   Refitting is a reversal of removal.

Door switches

17   Disconnect the battery negative terminal lead.

18   Prise the switch from the inner door panel using a small screwdriver (photo).

19   Disconnect the wiring plug (photo).

20   Refitting is a reversal of removal.

Courtesy lamp switches

21   With the door open, prise the switch from the door pillar using a small screwdriver (photo). Pull out the wiring slightly and tie a piece of

12.2A Remove the screws ...

12.2B ... and withdraw the steering column shrouds

12.11A Unscrewing the mounting screws for the steering column multi-function switch

12.11B Removing the windscreen wiper/washer switch

12.11C Disconnecting the wiring plug

12.14 Prising out a facia switch

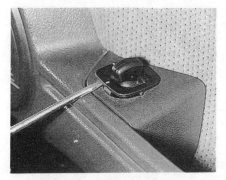

12.18 Prising out a door switch

12.19 Door switch and wiring plug

12.21 Removing a courtesy lamp switch

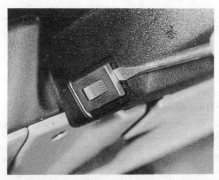

12.24 Prising out the instrument panel rheostat ...

12.25 ... and disconnecting the wiring plug

12.27 Make a slit in the carpet with a knife ...

12.28 ... and disconnect the wiring plug

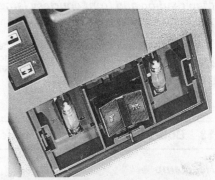

12.31 Map reading and front courtesy lamp switch with the lens and cover panel removed

12.32 Depress the tabs with a screwdriver to remove the switch

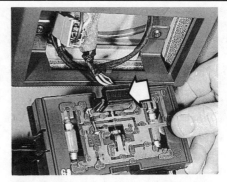

12.33 Wiring plug (arrowed) on the rear of the map reading and front courtesy lamp switch

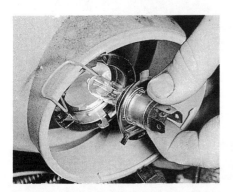

13.4 Removing the headlamp bulb

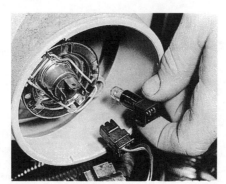

13.7 Removing the front sidelamp bulb

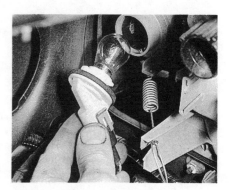

13.12 Removing the front direction indicator bulb

string to it to prevent it dropping into the door pillar.
22   Disconnect the wiring from the switch.
23   Refitting is a reversal of removal.

Instrument panel rheostat

24   Prise the rheostat from the steering column shroud using a small screwdriver (photo).
25   Disconnect the wiring plug (photo).
26   Refitting is a reversal of removal.

Handbrake warning lamp switch

27   Make a slit in the carpet just to the rear of the handbrake lever (photo).
28   Disconnect the wiring from the switch (photo).
29   Unscrew the mounting bolt and remove the switch.
30   Refitting is a reversal of removal.

Map reading and front courtesy lamp switch

31   Using a small screwdriver prise off the lens and cover panel (photo).
32   Release the switch assembly from the headlining by depressing the plastic tabs at each end of the switch (photo).
33   Disconnect the wiring and remove the switch (photo).
34   Refitting is a reversal of removal.

13   Bulbs (exterior lamps) – renewal

Headlamp

1   Turn the headlamp plastic rear cover through 90° to remove it.
2   Pull off the wiring connector.
3   Release the spring clip and pivot the clip clear.
4   Withdraw the bulb from its location in the headlamp (photo). Take

care not to touch the bulb glass with your fingers – if touched, clean the bulb with methylated spirit. Fit the new bulb using a reversal of the removal procedure, but make sure that the tabs on the bulb support are correctly located in the lens assembly.
5   Holts Amber Lamp is useful for temporarily changing the headlamp colour to conform with the normal use in Continental Europe.

Front sidelamp

6   Turn the headlamp plastic rear cover through 90° to remove it.
7   Disconnect the wiring plug and pull out the bulbholder (photo).
8   Remove the bulb from the bulbholder.
9   Fit the new bulb using a reversal of the removal procedure.

Front direction indicator (single headlamp models)

10   Unhook the retaining spring from the rear of the direction indicator unit.
11   Move the direction indicator unit forwards in order to release it.
12   Turn the bulbholder and release it from the rear of the direction indicator unit (photo).
13   Depress and twist the bulb to remove it from the bulbholder.
14   Fit the new bulb using a reversal of the removal procedure.

Front direction indicator (double headlamp models)

15   Push one side of the lens inwards, then insert a screwdriver behind the lens and lever it out. Release the base.
16   Depress and twist the bulb to remove it from the base.
17   Fit the new bulb using a reversal of the removal procedure.

Front direction indicator repeater

18   Carefully prise the lamp from the front wing, taking care not to damage the paintwork.
19   Pull out the bulbholder and wiring, then remove the capless bulb (photo).
20   Fit the new bulb using a reversal of the removal procedure.

13.19 Removing the front direction indicator repeater bulb

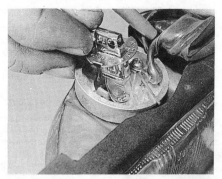
13.23 Removing the front foglamp bulb

13.26A Rear lamp cluster covers and plastic nuts

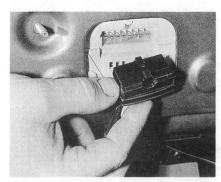
13.26B Disconnecting the rear lamp cluster wiring plug

13.27A Removing the rear lamp cluster bulbholder on the Hatchback ...

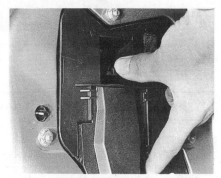
13.27B ... and on the Saloon

13.27C Rear lamp cluster bulbholder and bulbs on the Hatchback

13.28 Removing a bulb from the rear lamp cluster bulbholder

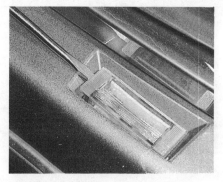
13.30 Prising out the number plate lamp

Front foglamp

21   Unscrew the two screws and pull the lens forward. Disconnect the two wires and remove the lens unit.
22   Pull off the rubber cover, or turn the bulbholder and remove it from the lens unit.
23   Depress and twist the bulb to remove it, or release the spring clip and lift out the bulb (photo).
24   Hold the new bulb in a piece of paper or cloth then fit it in the bulbholder.
25   Refit the bulbholder/cover using a reversal of the removal procedure.

Rear lamp cluster

26   Working in the rear luggage compartment, unscrew the two plastic nuts and remove the outer cover. Disconnect the wiring plug and

remove the inner cover (photos).
27   Squeeze together the two tabs and withdraw the bulbholder from the rear of the lamp cluster (photos).
28   Depress and twist the bulb to remove it (photo).
29   Fit the new bulb using a reversal of the removal procedure.

Number plate lamps

30   Prise the number plate lamp from the rear bumper using a small screwdriver (photo).
31   Disconnect the wiring plug from the lamp.
32   Remove the lens cover, then release the festoon type bulb from the spring contacts (photo).
33   Fit the new bulb using a reversal of the removal procedure, but check the tension of the spring contacts and if necessary bend them so that they firmly contact the bulb end caps.

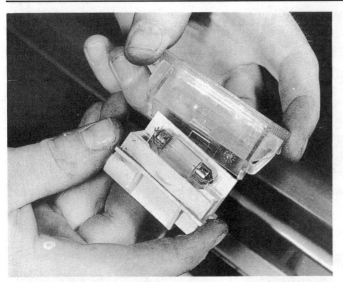

13.32 Removing the number plate lamp lens cover

---

14   Bulbs (interior lamps) – renewal

Courtesy lamps

1   Prise out the lamp using a small screwdriver (photo).
2   Release the festoon type bulb from the spring contacts.
3   Fit the new bulb using a reversal of the removal procedure, but check the tension of the spring contacts and if necessary bend them so that they firmly contact the bulb end caps.

Luggage compartment lamp

4   Prise out the lamp using a small screwdriver (photos).
5   Release the festoon type bulb from the spring contacts.
6   Fit the new bulb using a reversal of the removal procedure, but check the tension of the spring contacts and if necessary bend them so that they firmly contact the bulb end caps.

Instrument panel

7   Remove the instrument panel as described in Section 16.
8   Turn the bulbholder a quarter turn to align the shoulders with the slots, then to remove it and pull the capless bulb from the bulbholder (photo).
9   Fit the new bulb in reverse order.

Map reading and front courtesy lamp

10   Using a small screwdriver prise off the lens and cover panel (photo).
11   Release the appropriate festoon type bulb from the spring contacts.
12   Fit the new bulb using a reversal of the removal procedure, but check the tension of the spring contacts and if necessary bend them so that they firmly contact the bulb end caps.

Automatic transmission selector illumination

13   Prise out the lever surround, then pull the bulbholder from under the selector lever position indicator and remove the bulb.
14   Fit the new bulb in reverse order.

Glovebox lamp

15   Open the glovebox, then prise out the lamp using a small screwdriver (photo).
16   Release the festoon type bulb from the spring contacts.
17   Fit the new bulb using a reversal of the removal procedure, but check the tension of the spring contacts and if necessary bend them so that they firmly contact the bulb end caps.

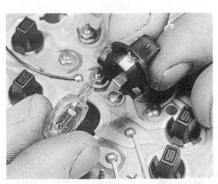

14.1 Removing a courtesy lamp

14.4A Removing a luggage compartment lamp on the Hatchback ...

14.4B ... and on the Saloon

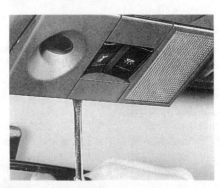

14.8 Removing an instrument panel bulb from its bulbholder

14.10 Prising off the lens and cover panel from the map reading and front courtesy lamp

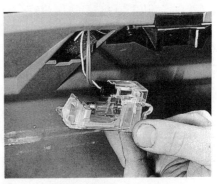

14.15 Glovebox lamp removed for removal of the bulb

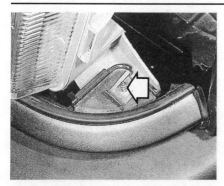

15.6 Headlamp retaining screw location (arrowed)

15.7 Removing the headlamp

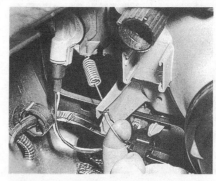

15.9 Unhooking the front direction indicator retaining spring

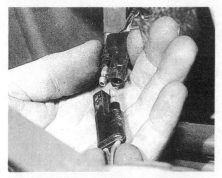

15.20 Disconnecting the front foglight wiring

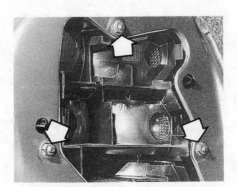

15.24 Rear lamp cluster mounting nuts on the Saloon (arrowed)

15.26 Disconnecting the number plate lamp wiring

15   Exterior lamp units – removal and refitting

Headlamp unit

1   Turn the headlamp plastic rear cover through 90° to remove it.
2   Pull off the wiring connectors.
3   Remove the direction indicator as described later in this Section.
4   Unscrew the four mounting nuts from the rear of the headlamp.
5   Unscrew the screws located on the inner side of the headlamp.
6   Withdraw the headlamp forwards and at the same time release the lug so that the hidden mounting screw can be removed (photo).
7   Remove the headlamp from its location (photo).
8   Refitting is a reversal of removal, but before tightening the front inner screw align the outer edge of the direction indicator in relation to the front wing. Finally adjust the headlamp aim as described in Chapter 1.

Front direction indicator (single headlamp models)

9   Unhook the retaining spring from the rear of the direction indicator unit (photo).
10   Move the direction indicator unit forwards in order to release it.
11   Turn the bulbholder and release it from the rear of the direction indicator unit.
12   Remove the direction indicator unit from the car.
13   Refitting is a reversal of removal.

Front direction indicator (double headlamp models)

14   Push one side of the lens inwards, then insert a screwdriver behind the lens and lever it out.
15   Release the base unit, then disconnect the wiring connector.
16   Refitting is a reversal of removal.

Front direction indicator repeater

17   Carefully prise the lamp from the front wing taking care not to

damage the paintwork.
18   Pull out the bulbholder and wiring, then remove the lamp.
19   Refitting is a reversal of removal.

Front foglights

20   Unscrew the two cross-head securing screws, withdraw the foglight unit from the bumper, and disconnect the two wires (photo).
21   Refitting is a reversal of removal, but if necessary adjust the foglight by turning the adjustment screw located on the upper corner of the foglight.

Rear lamp cluster

22   Working in the rear luggage compartment, unscrew the two plastic nuts and remove the outer cover. Disconnect the wiring plug and remove the inner cover.
23   Squeeze together the two tabs and withdraw the bulbholder from the rear of the lamp cluster.
24   Unscrew the mounting nuts and withdraw the rear lamp cluster from the rear of the car (photo).
25   Refitting is a reversal of removal.

Number plate lamps

26   Prise the number plate lamp from the rear bumper using a small screwdriver, then disconnect the wiring plug (photo).
27   Refitting is a reversal of removal.

16   Instrument panel – removal and refitting

Removal

1   Disconnect the battery negative terminal lead.
2   Remove the steering wheel with reference to Chapter 10.
3   Unscrew the cross-head screws and remove the steering column shrouds. Where applicable, also remove the internal cover.

16.5 Unscrew the top screws ...

16.6A ... bottom left screw ...

16.6B ... and bottom right screw ...

16.6C ... and remove the instrument panel visor

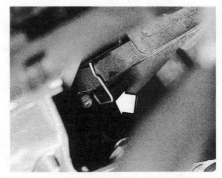

16.7 Speedometer cable retaining spring at the transmission end (arrowed)

4   Remove the steering column multi-function switches with reference to Section 12.

5   Unscrew and remove the screws securing the top of the instrument panel visor to the facia (photo).

6   Unscrew and remove the screws securing the bottom of the instrument panel visor to the facia and remove the visor. The screws are located on each side of the steering column (photos).

7   Working in the engine compartment, pull out the spring clip and disconnect the speedometer cable from the transmission (photo). Release the cable from the support clips in the engine compartment.

8   Unscrew the screws securing the top of the instrument panel to the facia, then pull out the panel until there is sufficient room to reach behind it and disconnect the speedometer cable (photos).

9   Note the location of all the wiring connectors then disconnect them from the rear of the instrument panel. Withdraw the instrument panel from the facia.

Refitting

10   Refitting is a reversal of removal. On completion check the function of all electrical components.

16.8A Remove the securing screws ...

16.8B ... and pull out the instrument panel

19.2 Removing the clock

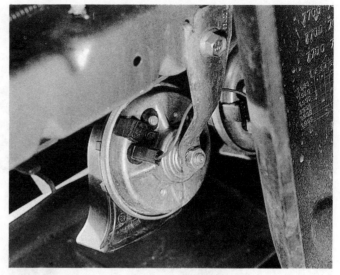

20.1 Horn location

17   Instrument panel components – removal and refitting

Removal

1   Remove the instrument panel as described in Section 16.
2   Prise the plastic hooks outwards and remove the front cover.
3   To remove the speedometer extract the two screws from the front and rear of the unit.
4   To remove the coolant temperature indicator extract the printed circuit nuts and the two retaining screws.
5   To remove the fuel gauge extract the printed circuit nuts and the two retaining screws.
6   To remove the tachometer extract the single rear screw and the two front screws.
7   To remove the oil level indicator, first remove the tachometer, then extract the printed circuit nuts and the two retaining screws.

Refitting

8   Refitting is a reversal of removal.

18   Cigar lighter – removal and refitting

Removal

1   Disconnect the battery negative terminal lead.
2   Pull out the ashtray.
3   Push the cigar lighter out of its location and disconnect the wiring.
4   To remove the fixed metal section of the cigar lighter, push from behind the main body while releasing the two tabs. Also remove the plastic cover.

Refitting

5   Refitting is a reversal of removal.

19   Clock – removal and refitting

Removal

1   Disconnect the battery negative terminal lead.
2   Carefully prise the clock from the facia and disconnect the wiring

Fig. 12.8 Correct position of the speedometer cable retaining clip in the rear engine mounting bracket (Sec 21)

plug (photo). The clock is retained by plastic clips which are pushed aside as the clock is removed.

Refitting

3   Refitting is a reversal of removal.

20   Horn – removal and refitting

Removal

1   The horns are located on the body front valance behind the front bumper (photo). To remove a horn, first apply the handbrake then jack up the front of the car and support it on axle stands.
2   Disconnect the battery negative terminal lead then reach up and disconnect the horn supply lead.
3   Unscrew the nut securing the horn to the mounting bracket and remove the horn from the car.

Refitting

4   Refitting is a reversal of removal.

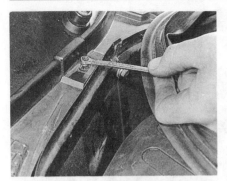

22.5 Unbolting the plastic cover from the plenum chamber

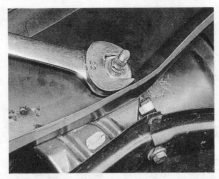

22.6 Unscrew the windscreen wiper spindle housing nuts ...

22.7 ... and mounting bolts (arrowed)...

22.8 ... then disconnect the wiring plug ...

22.9 ... and remove the wiper motor and linkage

22.10 Disconnecting the windscreen wiper linkage

21 Speedometer drive cable – removal and refitting

Removal

1   Refer to Section 16 and remove the instrument panel sufficiently to allow the speedometer cable to be disconnected.
2   Where a trip computer is fitted, disconnect the sender unit from the upper and lower cable sections.
3   Pull out the clip and disconnect the cable from the outside of the gearbox. Release the cable from any ties.
4   Withdraw the speedometer drive cable into the passenger compartment through the bulkhead.

Refitting

5   Refitting is a reversal of removal, but ensure that the transmission retaining clip is located as shown in Fig. 12.8.

22 Windscreen wiper motor and linkage – removal and refitting

Removal

1   Operate the wiper motor then switch it off so that it returns to its rest position.
2   Disconnect the battery negative terminal lead.
3   Remove the windscreen wiper arms with reference to Chapter 1.
4   Remove the battery as described in Section 4.
5   Unbolt and remove the plastic cover from the plenum chamber just in front of the windscreen (photo).

6   Unscrew the nuts from the spindle housings protruding through the windscreen valance (photo).
7   Unscrew and remove the mounting bolts (photo).
8   Disconnect the wiring plug (photo).
9   Withdraw the wiper motor and linkage assembly from the bulkhead (photo).
10   If necessary the linkage may be separated from the motor by removing the cranked arm and unbolting the linkage (photo).

Refitting

11   Refitting is a reversal of removal.

23 Tailgate wiper motor and linkage – removal and refitting

Removal

1   Operate the wiper then switch it off so that it returns to its rest position. Note that the wiper motor will only operate with the tailgate shut as the spring tensioned connector pins must be in contact with the contact plates.
2   Disconnect the battery negative terminal lead.
3   Remove the wiper arm with reference to Chapter 1.
4   Unscrew the nut from the spindle housing protruding through the tailgate (photo).
5   Remove the trim panel from inside the tailgate.
6   Disconnect the wiring plug, then unbolt and remove the wiper assembly from inside the tailgate (photos).
7   If necessary, the connector pin assembly and connector plate assembly may be removed and the wiring disconnected (photos).

Refitting

8   Refitting is a reversal of removal.

23.4 Unscrewing the rear wiper spindle housing nut

23.6A Disconnect the wiring plug ...

23.6B ... then unbolt and remove the tailgate wiper motor and linkage

23.6C Tailgate wiper motor and linkage

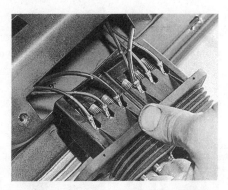

23.7A Removing the tailgate connector pin assembly ...

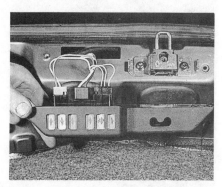

23.7B ... and tailgate connector plate assembly

24 Windscreen/tailgate/headlamp washer system components – removal and refitting

Removal

1   To remove the washer reservoir and pump, unscrew the mounting screw(s) and lift the reservoir from the front right-hand corner of the engine compartment. Where applicable, the front washer reservoir also supplies the rear tailgate wash by means of a tube running along the right-hand lower edge of the floor area and up the right-hand rear corner pillar.

2   Disconnect the wiring from the pump then disconnect the plastic tubing from the reservoir.

3   Empty the reservoir of any remaining fluid then pull the pump from the rubber grommet.

4   Disconnect the tubing from the pump and remove the grommet from the reservoir.

Refitting

5   Refitting is a reversal of removal.

25 Radio/cassette player – removal and refitting

Removal

1   Disconnect the battery negative terminal lead. If the radio has a security code, make sure this is known before disconnecting the battery.

2   In order to release the radio retaining clips, two U-shaped rods must be inserted into the special holes on each side of the radio (photo). If

25.2 Using the U-shaped rods to remove the radio/cassette player

possible, it is preferable to obtain purpose made rods from an audio specialist as these have cut-outs which snap firmly into the clips so that the radio can be pulled out.

3   Withdraw the radio sufficiently to disconnect the feed, earth, aerial and speaker leads (photo).

Refitting

4   Refitting is a reversal of removal.

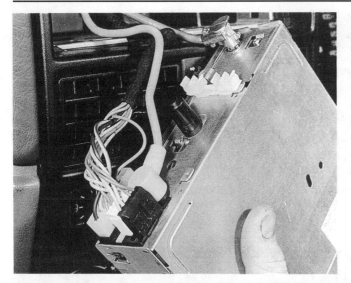

25.3 Aerial lead and wiring connections to the rear of the radio

26.2A Rear speaker on the Hatchback

26.2B Rear speaker on the Saloon

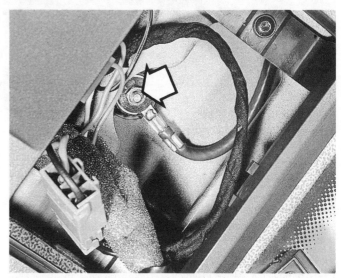

27.2 Aerial lead connection to the aerial (arrowed)

26 Speakers – removal and refitting

Removal

1   To remove a front speaker located on the top right or left-hand side of the facia panel, prise out the speaker grille then remove the screws and disconnect the wiring.

2   Access to the rear speakers is gained by opening the rear tailgate/bootlid. Disconnect the wiring then remove the screws and withdraw the speaker (photos).

3   To remove a door speaker, turn the speaker cover anti-clockwise and remove it. Remove the screws and withdraw the speaker, then disconnect the wiring.

Refitting

4   Refitting is a reversal of removal.

27 Radio aerial – removal and refitting

Removal

1   Remove the map reading and front courtesy lamp switch assembly with reference to Section 12.

2   Unscrew the nut from the bottom of the aerial, disconnect the lead, then remove the aerial from the outside of the car (photo).

Refitting

3   Refitting is a reversal of removal.

28 Engine oil level sensor indicator – general

1   On certain models, a gauge is provided on the instrument panel to inform the driver of the level of oil in the sump.

2   The gauge is controlled by an electronic circuit located in the instrument panel which receives information from a sensor located in the sump. The sensor contains a high resistance wire, and the thermal conductivity of this wire alters according to its depth of immersion in the oil.

3   If the engine develops a fault, the following test can be carried out to isolate the component concerned.

4   Remove the sensor from the sump by disconnecting the two wires and unscrewing the unit from its mounting.

5   Using an ohmmeter, check the resistance across the sensor terminals. A reading of between 5 and 30 ohms should be shown. If not, the sensor is faulty and should be renewed.

29.2A Remove the screw from the remote control door locking transmitter ...

29.2B ... and separate the covers

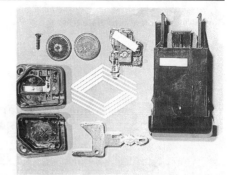

29.2C Internal components of the remote control door locking transmitter

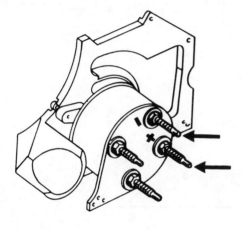

Fig. 12.9 Terminals (arrowed) on the rear of the engine oil level sensor gauge (Sec 28)

6 If the sensor is satisfactory, remove the instrument panel, as described in Section 16, and check for continuity from the sensor wiring connectors to the appropriate terminals in the instrument panel multi-plug. If there is no continuity, trace the wiring until the break or poor connection is found and make the necessary repair.

7 If the wiring is satisfactory, remove the gauge from the instrument panel and connect an ohmmeter across the positive and negative terminals. If there is no reading, the internal continuity of the gauge unit is broken and it should be renewed.

8 If the sensor and gauge are proved satisfactory, and all connecting wiring is in good condition, then the computer is faulty and should be renewed.

9 Refit any removed components using a reversal of the removal procedure.

29 Ignition key/remote control door locking transmitter – general

1 The ignition key incorporates an infra-red remote control door locking transmitter. The transmitter signal is decoded by a receiver mounted on the roof console and this activates the electro-mechanical system to lock or unlock the doors.

2 The transmitter is powered by two 1.5 volt alkaline type batteries which have a life of approximately 12 months. The batteries can be renewed after unscrewing the transmitter case screw and opening the case to gain access (photos).

3 In the event of a fault occurring in the system it is recommended that you seek the advice of a Renault dealer as specialist knowledge and equipment are necessary for accurate fault diagnosis.

30 Wiring diagrams – explanatory notes

The wiring diagrams included overleaf are of the conventional and the current flow type, where each wire is shown in the simplest line form without crossing over other wires.

Symbols used on wiring diagrams

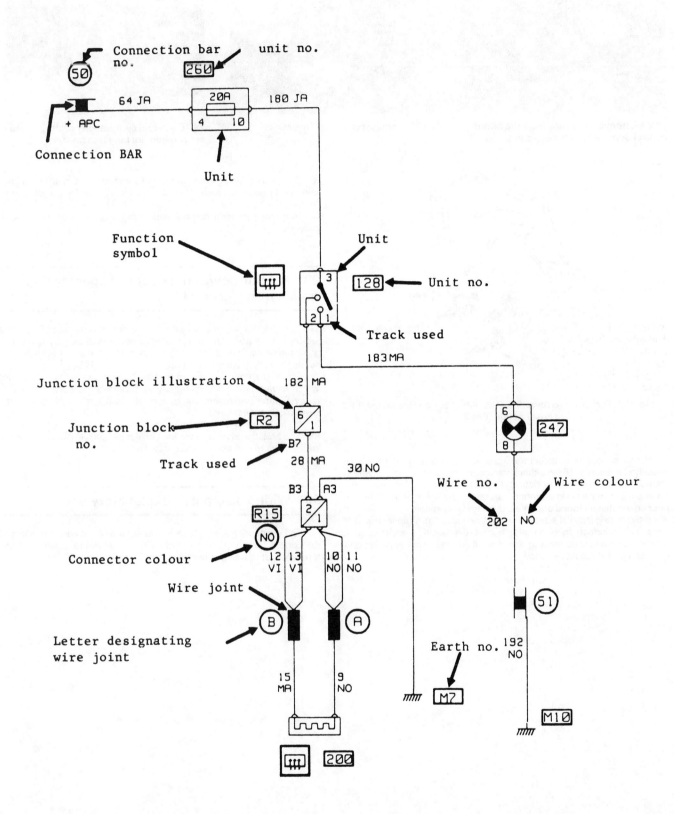

Wiring diagram colour key

BA	White	NO	Black
BE	Blue	OR	Orange
BJ	Light brown	RG	Red
CY	Transparent	SA	Pink
GR	Grey	VE	Green
JA	Yellow	VI	Mauve
MA	Brown		

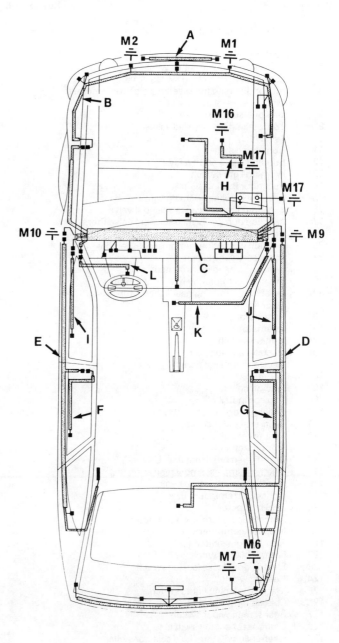

Notes:

The boxed numbers with an R prefix and circled letters indicate junction blocks and connections into the main harness, and should be ignored.

Earthing points are represented by boxed numbers with an M prefix – these correspond with the accompanying illustration (note that a left-hand drive vehicle is shown). A fuller list of earthing points is given at the end of the main key.

M1	Front right-hand earth
M2	Front left-hand earth
M6	Rear right-hand lamp earth
M7	Rear left-hand lamp earth
M9	Front right-hand door pillar earth
M10	Front left-hand door pillar earth
M16	Engine/body earth
M17	Body/engine earth
A	Front foglamp harness
B	Front face harness
C	Dashboard harness
D	Rear side right-hand harness
E	Rear side left-hand harness
F	Left-hand rear door harness
G	Right-hand rear door harness
H	Engine earth harness
I	Left-hand front door harness
J	Right-hand front door harness
K	Courtesy light harness
L	Pedal harness

Key to wiring diagrams

1	Driving-school unit		151	Rear left-hand wheel sensor
2	Battery cut-out		152	Front right-hand wheel sensor
3	Tachograph		153	Front left-hand wheel sensor
4	Right-hand door locking switch		154	Luggage compartment switch
5	Left-hand door locking switch		155	Reversing lights switch
6	Air conditioning fan assembly electronic module		156	Handbrake switch
7	Module-control resistor unit		157	Brake pedal switch
8	Line pressure sensor (AT)		158	Full-load switch
9	Torque-limiting solenoid valve		159	'No-load' switch
10	1st switch		160	Stop-lights switch
11	Dog clutch switch		161	Glovebox switch
12	Running lights earth relay		162	Flow meter
13	Warning light switch		163	Starter
14	Rear door locking switch		164	Cold air blower
15	Rear door locking warning light		165	Luggage compartment light
16	Injection pump advance solenoid valve		166	Right-hand number plate light
17	Injection pump advance solenoid valve thermal switch		167	Left-hand number plate light
35	Vehicle position sensor		168	Glovebox light
36	Position correction compressor assembly		169	Fuel vapour rebreathing solenoid valve
37	Accessory central unit		170	Power-assisted steering solenoid valve
38	Retracting headlights computer		171	Air conditioning clutch
39	Right-hand retracting headlight motor		172	Right-hand rear light
40	Left-hand retracting headlight motor		173	Left-hand rear light
101	Cigar lighter		174	Rear right-hand foglight
102	Distributor		175	Rear left-hand foglight
103	Alternator		176	Front right-hand foglight
104	Ignition switch		177	Front left-hand foglight
105	Electromagnetic horn		178	Rear right-hand door pillar switch
106	Electropneumatic horn		179	Rear left-hand door pillar switch
107	Battery		180	Driver's door pillar switch
108	Ignition coil		181	Passenger door pillar switch
109	Trip computer		182	Right-hand reversing light
110	Braking pressure assembly unit		183	Left-hand reversing light
111	Ignition assistance unit		184	Right-hand sidelight
112	Rear timer unit		185	Left-hand sidelight
113	Front timer unit		186	Power-assisted steering electric pump assembly
114	Dim-dipped headlight unit (UK models only)		187	Heater fan
115	Electric pump assembly regulating unit		188	Cooling fan motor assembly
116	Headlight washer timer unit		189	Speaker
117	Lights 'on' reminder buzzer		190	Rear left-hand speaker
118	ABS computer		191	Speaker in front right-hand door
119	Automatic transmission computer		192	Speaker in front left-hand door
120	Injection computer		193	Injector no 1
121	Rear foglight switch		194	Injector no 2
122	Front foglight switch		195	Injector no 3
123	Electric door locks locking switch		198	Injector no 6
124	Heater switch		199	Fuel tank sender unit
125	'Hazard' warning lights switch		196	Injector no 4
126	Cold air blower switch		197	Injector no 5
127	Rear screen wiper switch		200	Heated rear screen
128	Heated rear screen switch		201	Rear right-hand window winder
129	Gear-changing threshold selector switch		202	Rear left-hand window winder
130	Right-hand rear electric window switch		203	Driver's door window winder
131	Left-hand rear electric window switch		204	Passenger door window winder
132	Driver's side electric window switch		205	Pressure switch
133	Passenger side electric window switch		206	Air conditioning three-purpose pressure switch
134	Electric rear view mirror switch		207	Low coolant
135	Rear electric window over-ride switch		208	Integral electronic ignition module
136	Choke flap switch		209	Combined lighting/direction indicators switch stalk and horn push
137	Flasher unit		210	Clock
138	Rear right-hand electric door locking switch		211	Rear screen wiper motor
139	Rear left-hand electric door locking switch		212	Windscreen wiper motor
140	Driver's door electric locking switch		213	Front interior light
141	Passenger door electric locking switch		214	Rear right-hand interior light
142	Luggage compartment lid electric locking switch		215	Rear left-hand interior light
143	Low windscreen washer fluid level sensor		216	Front right-hand brake pad
144	Low coolant level sensor		217	Front left-hand brake pad
145	Windscreen wash/wipe combined switch		218	Fuel pump
146	Pinking sensor		219	Headlight washer pump
147	Atmospheric pressure sensor		220	Rear screen washer pump
148	Oil pressure sensor		222	Throttle butterfly potentiometer
149	TDC sensor		223	Idling potentiometer
150	Rear right-hand wheel sensor			

Key to wiring diagrams (continued)

224	Power-assisted steering pressostat
225	Diagnostic plug
226	Right-hand headlight
227	Left-hand headlight
228	Idling speed regulator
229	Horn relay
230	Rear foglight relay
231	Front foglight relay
232	Starter relay
233	Cold air blower relay
234	Fan motor assembly relay
235	Heated rear screen relay
236	Fuel pump relay
238	Injection locking relay
239	Driver's side electric rear view mirror relay
240	Passenger side electric rear view mirror relay
241	Lighting rheostat or shunt
242	Lambda sensor
243	Oil level sensor
244	Coolant temperature sensor
245	External temperature sensor
246	Electric diesel fuel cut-off
247	Instrument panel
248	Fan motor assembly thermal switch
249	Infra-red transmitter
250	Speed sensor
251	Coolant dual-function thermal switch
253	Front right-hand speaker
254	Front left-hand speaker
255	Right-hand direction indicator
256	Left-hand direction indicator
257	Pre-heater unit
258	Heater plugs
259	Thermal switch
260	Fusebox
261	Radio
262	Air conditioning cooling fan assembly
263	Rear screen wash/wipe switch
264	Electric door locks timer unit
265	Map-reading light switch panel
266	'No-load/Full-load' switch
267	Right-hand side repeater light
269	Idle cut-out
270	8x thermal switch
271	Thermistor
272	Air temperature sensor
273	Speed threshold sensor
274	Air conditioning solenoid valve
275	Auxiliary fuel pump timer
276	'One-touch' window winder switch unit
277	Filament failure unit
279	Anti-percolation relay
280	Integral electronic ignition cut-off relay
281	Dipped beam headlight relay
282	Fuel filler flap electric lock
283	Auxiliary fuel pump
284	Right-hand headlight wiper motor
285	Left-hand headlight wiper motor
286	Rear screen washer switch
287	Ballast coil relay
288	Running light main relay
289	Running light side and rear lights relay
290	Running light dipped beam relay
291	Carburettor solenoid valve
292	Lighting rheostat relay
293	General power supply
294	Heated rear screen timer-unit
295	Tell-tale and warning lights unit
296	Foglight shunt relay
297	Front foglight shunt
298	Heater device
299	Accessories plate
300	Rear crossmember interior light
301	ABS electric pump assembly relay
303	Automatic transmission selector lever lighting
304	Sunroof
305	Advance correction solenoid valve
306	Advance correction thermal switch
307	Accessories plate earth shunt
309	Multi-function switch buzzer
301	Injection power module
311	Interior light timer
312	Fuel consumption cut-off relay
313	Rev counter relay
314	Headlight wiper relay
315	Windscreen wiper 2nd speed relay
316	Ignition 4x relay
317	Sunroof switch
318	Carburettor base resistor
319	Air conditioning control panel
320	Basic/air conditioning fan motor assembly
321	Air conditioning fan assembly resistor
322	Power-assisted steering/air conditioning solenoid valve diode
324	Excess-speed relay
325	Radio satellite control
326	Excess speed warning
327	Fuel tank sender unit electronic unit
328	Front left-hand interior light
329	Front right-hand interior light
330	Rear cigar lighter
331	Cruise control switch
332	Window winder 'one-touch' switch
333	Safety belt switch
334	Thermal cut-out
335	Fan motor assembly 1st speed relay
336	Fan motor assembly 2nd speed relay
337	Fan motor assembly 3rd speed relay
338	Turbo pressostat regulator
339	Cold start injector
340	Timed thermal switch
341	Idling speed regulating valve
342	Turbo safety pressostat
343	Oil temperature sensor
344	Regulator pneumatic pump
345	Regulator safety solenoid valve
346	Regulator pump solenoid valve
347	Car radio feed
348	'One-touch' window winder switch upper plate
349	Ignition distributor
350	Rear left-hand brake pad
351	Rear right-hand brake pad
352	Front left-hand seatback motor 1
353	Front left-hand seatback motor 2
354	Front left-hand seat raising motor
355	Front left-hand seat motor
356	Front right-hand seatback motor 1
357	Front right-hand seatback motor 2
358	Front right-hand seat raising motor
359	Front right-hand seat motor
360	Voice synthesizer control
361	ABS hydraulic assembly
362	Plates with battery + terminals
363	Voice synthesizer unit
364	Voice synthesizer speaker
365	Right-hand tweeter speaker
366	Left-hand tweeter speaker
367	Bonnet right-hand switch
368	Bonnet left-hand switch
369	Turbo bearing cooling pump
370	Dim-dipped headlight resistor (UK models only)
371	Fuel vapour absorber
372	Luggage compartment opening/closing unit
373	Cruise control unit
374	Front left-hand seatback adjusting switch
375	Front right-hand seatback adjusting switch

Key to wiring diagrams (continued)

376	Front left-hand seat adjusting switch
377	Front right-hand seat adjusting switch
378	Front left-hand seat raising device regulating switch
379	Fast idling relay
380	Trip computer unit
381	Carburettor
382	Inlet manifold relay
383	Inlet manifold thermal switch
384	Manifold heater
385	Heated driver's seat
386	Heated passenger seat
387	2 bar oil pressure sensor
388	4-wheel drive warning light switch
389	Central speaker
390	Foglight shunt
391	Rear timer unit
392	Trip computer run-through switch
393	Air conditioning/power-assisted steering solenoid valve
394	Electric aerial
395	Automatic transmission stop lights switch
396	'Full-load' switch
397	Anti-percolation fan motor assembly
398	Exhaust gas recirculation solenoid valve
399	Anti-pollution relay
400	Anti-pollution system diode
401	Anti-pollution system solenoid valve
402	Oil thermal switch
403	Injector
404	Injection pump advance solenoid valve
405	Load leaver switch
406	Pre-heating thermal switch
407	Air recirculation flap control
408	Evaporator sensor
409	Power-assisted steering electric pump assembly relay
410	Idling cut-off relay
411	Air conditioning pressostat
412	Fast idling solenoid valve
414	'Water in diesel fuel' warning light
415	Headlight wipers solenoid valve
416	Idling cut-off capacitor
417	Air conditioning recirculation relay
418	Passenger compartment temperature sensor ventilator
419	Air conditioning control unit
420	Mixer flap
421	Clutch pedal switch
422	Cruise control on steering column switch no. 1
423	Cruise control on steering column switch no. 2
424	Cruise control excess speed relay
425	ABS plate
426	Solenoid valve controlling opening of boost pressure phase
427	Alarm unit
428	Bosch ABS main relay
429	Bosch ABS auxiliary relay
430	Bosch ABS diode unit
431	Trip computer resetting switch
432	ABS main solenoid valve
433	Alarm sensing unit
434	ABS cut-off pressostat
435	ABS solenoid valve unit
436	Turbo regulation switch
437	Throttle butterfly casing heater
438	Bonnet switch
439	ABS computer relay
440	Heated seat control
441	Automatic transmission
442	Self-fed alarm siren
443	Automatic transmission electric control valve
444	Map-reading light
445	Fuel pump ballast resistor
446	Headlight adjusting switch lighting
447	Rear foglight switch relay
448	After-ignition junction plate

449	Diesel fuel heater resistor
450	Diesel fuel heater relay
451	Diesel fuel heater thermal switch
452	Perimeter sensing unit
453	Volumetric sensing unit
454	Volumetric sender/receiver
455	Anti-pollution solenoid valve diode
456	Fuel pump ballast relay
457	1st notch switch
458	Rear foglight and reversing light
459	Rear screen wiper timer
460	Rear axle switch
461	ABS excess voltage protection relay
462	Tailgate number plate lighting
463	Rear quarter lighting
464	Interior light switch
465	Turbo bearing cooling pump timer
466	Shunt unit
467	Dipped beam headlight/side and rear light relay
468	Driving school car dipped beam headlights diode
469	Driving school car monitor control unit
470	Driving school car windscreen wiper fast speed relay
471	Electric window switch relay
472	Radio cut-off relay
473	Voice synthesizer test switch
474	Air conditioning compressor switch relay
475	Recirculation motor
476	Integral transmission unit
477	1st switch
478	Heating accelerator pump
479	Heating accelerator thermal switch
480	Injector no 5
481	Injector no 6
482	Dog clutch solenoid valve
483	Acceleration sensor
484	4x4 transmission solenoid valve
485	Multi-purpose switch
486	Passenger belt switch
487	Enrichener solenoid valve
488	Enrichener thermal switch
489	Rear left-hand 1st notch switch
490	Front right-hand 1st notch switch
491	Front left-hand 1st notch switch
492	Telephone radio
493	Rear left-hand seat
494	Rear right-hand seat
495	Front right-hand seat
496	Front left-hand seat
497	4x4 ABS accelerometer
498	Vertical accelerometer
499	Longitudinal accelerometer
500	Transverse accelerometer
501	Seat and rear view mirror memory unit
502	Variable steering computer
503	Decoder computer
504	Rear right-hand map-reading light
505	Rear left-hand map-reading light
506	Accessories take-off
507	Front and rear foglight and 'hazard' warning light switch
508	Right-hand luggage compartment light
509	Left-hand luggage compartment light
510	Memory seat sensors
511	Interior lights central switch
512	Map-reading light switch
513	Ergonomic seat inflation switch
514	Ergonomic seat inflation pump
515	Seat memory unit
516	Seat memorising unit
517	Seat memory and control keyboard
518	Pulse generator
519	Front left-hand door/field light
520	Front right-hand door/field light
521	Rear right-hand door/field light

Key to wiring diagrams (continued)

522	Rear left-hand door/field light
523	Driver's door lighting
524	Passenger door lighting
525	Rear right-hand door lighting
526	Rear left-hand door lighting
527	Rear left-hand window driver's switch
528	Rear right-hand window driver's switch
529	Central interior light
530	Cruise control stop switch
531	Cruise control clutch switch
532	Passenger window driver's switch
533	Vehicle position correction switch
534	Controlled suspension switch
535	Gearchange selection warning light
536	Headphone jack socket
537	Left-hand headlight corrector motor
538	Right-hand headlight corrector motor
539	Engine compartment lighting switch
540	Variable power steering motor
541	Illuminating courtesy mirror
543	Variable movement shock absorber computer
547	Rear left-hand shock absorber solenoid valve
548	Rear right-hand shock absorber solenoid valve
549	Front left-hand shock absorber solenoid valve
550	Front right-hand shock absorber solenoid valve
551	Front right-hand vehicle level sensor
552	Front left-hand vehicle level sensor
553	Rear right-hand vehicle level sensor
554	Rear left-hand vehicle level sensor
556	Tailgate position switch
557	Tailgate closure assistance motor
558	Tailgate closure on/off switch
559	Tailgate closure assistance unit
560	Tailgate opening switch
563	Air-to-oil intercooler cooling fan assembly
564	Air-to-oil intercooler cooling fan assembly relay
565	Anti-percolation timer thermal switch
610	ABS fault-finding switch
643	Anti-percolation resistor

Not all items fitted to all models

Earth points

M1	Front right-hand earth
M2	Front left-hand earth
M3	Bodywork earth
M4	Gearbox earth
M5	Tailgate earth
M6	Right-hand rear light earth
M7	Left-hand rear light earth
M8	Injection system earth
M9	Front right-hand pillar earth
M10	Front left-hand pillar earth
M11	Dashboard earth
M12	Steering mounting earth
M13	Centre console earth
M14	Horn mounting earth
M15	Heater bulkhead earth
M16	Engine/body earth
M17	Body/engine earth
M18	ABS earth
M19	ABS electronic earth
M20	Heated rear screen earth
M21	Alternator earth
MX	Radio telephone earth

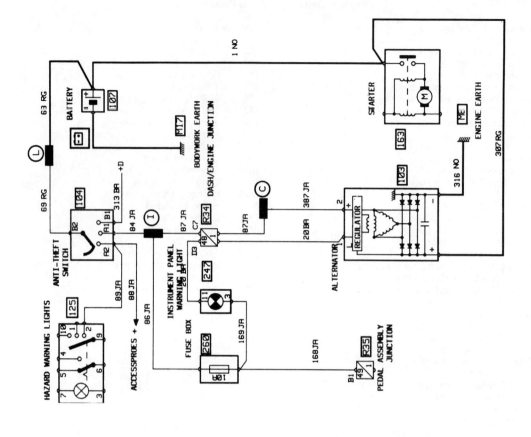

12.11 General feed wiring diagram – except 1721 cc (F2N)
See page 268 for key

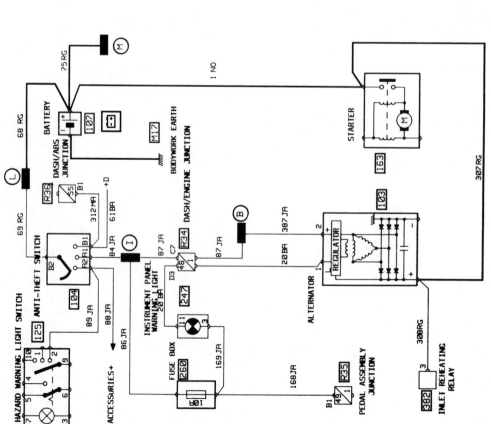

12.10 General feed wiring diagram – 1721 cc (F2N)
See page 268 for key

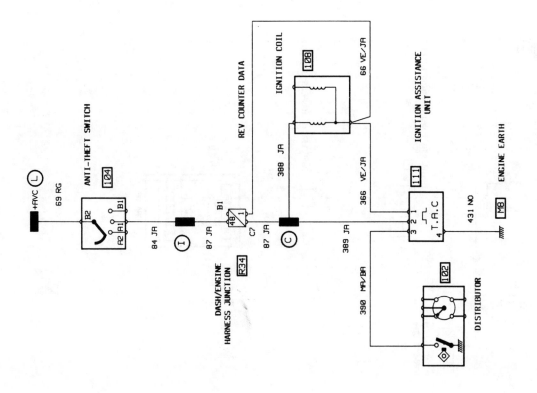

12.13 Ignition system wiring diagram – 1397 cc (C1J)
See page 268 for key

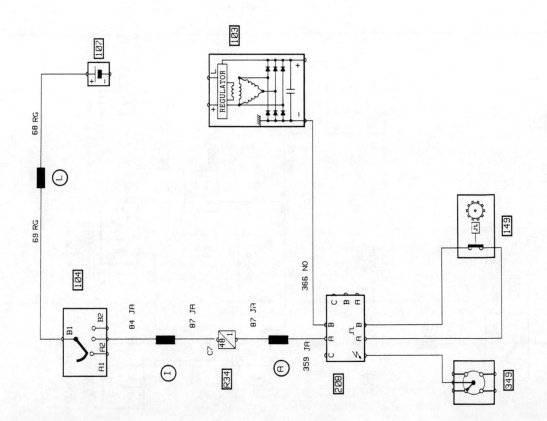

12.12 Ignition system wiring diagram – 1390 cc (E6J)
See page 268 for key

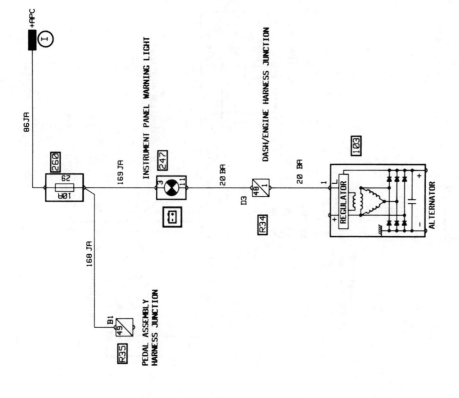

12.15 Charging system warning light wiring diagram
See page 268 for key

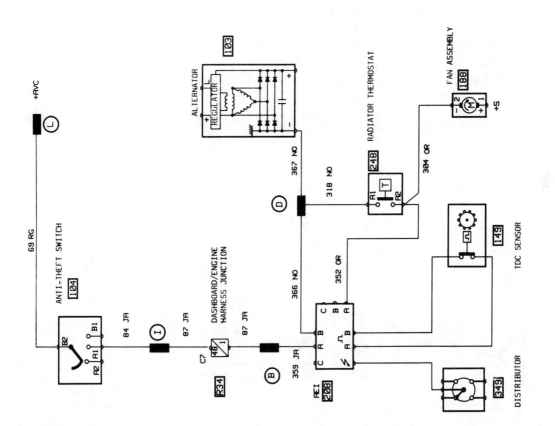

12.14 Ignition and charging wiring diagram – 1721 cc (F2N)
See page 268 for key

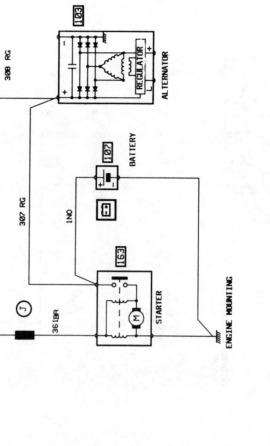

12.17 Starter motor wiring diagram – 1721 cc (F2N)
See page 268 for key

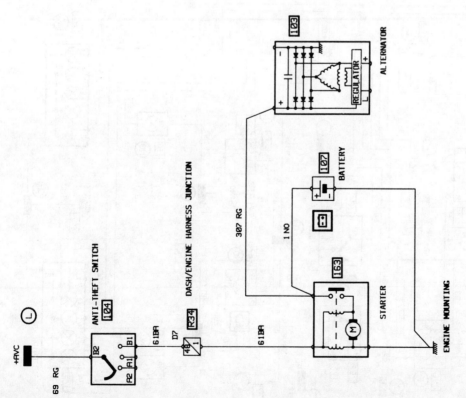

12.16 Starter motor wiring diagram – 1390 cc (E6J) and 1397 cc (C1J)
See page 268 for key

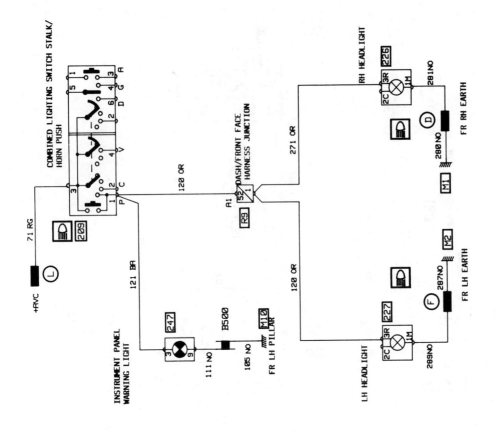

12.19 Single headlamp wiring diagram
See page 268 for key

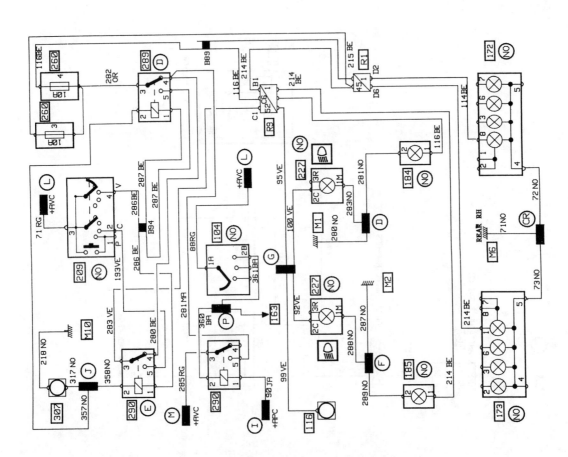

12.18 Lighting wiring diagram
See page 268 for key

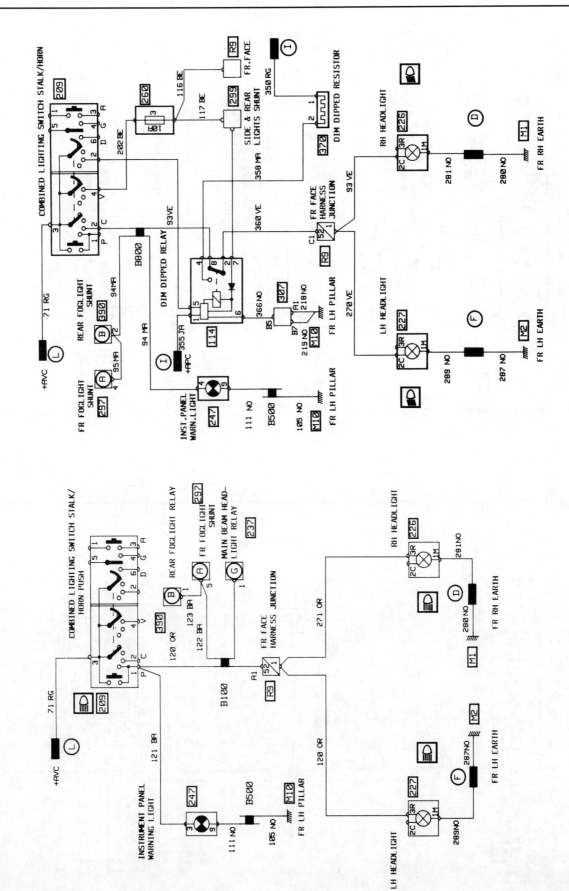

12.21 Dim/dip headlamp wiring diagram
See page 268 for key

12.20 Main headlamp wiring diagram
See page 268 for key

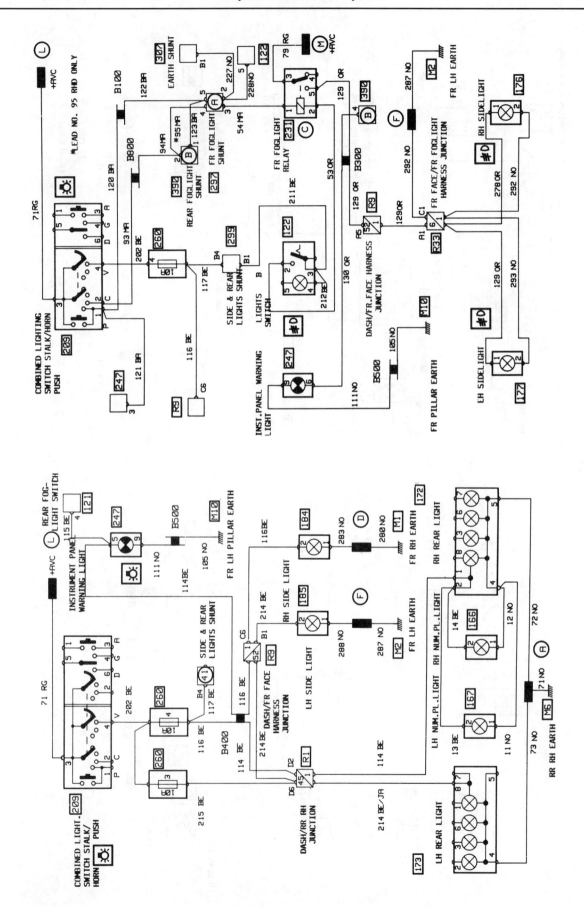

12.23 Front foglamp wiring diagram
See page 268 for key

12.22 Sidelamp wiring diagram
See page 268 for key

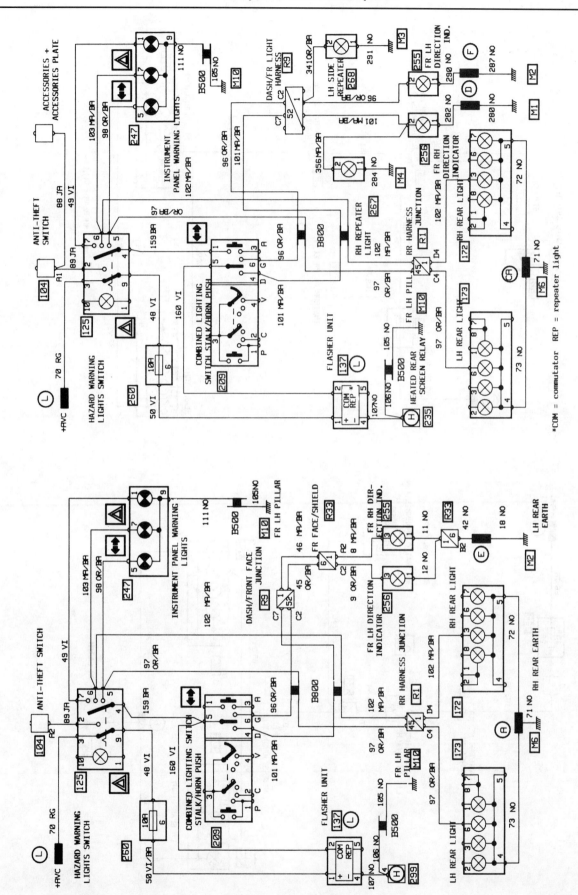

12.25 Direction indicators and repeater wiring diagram
See page 268 for key

*COM = commutator REP = repeater light

12.24 Direction indicators and hazard wiring diagram
See page 268 for key

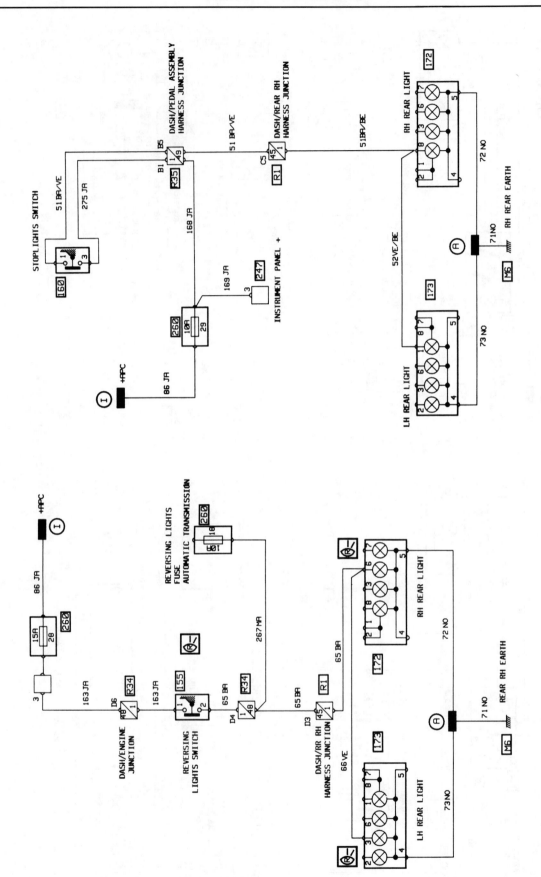

12.27 Stoplamp wiring diagram
See page 268 for key

12.26 Reversing light wiring diagram
See page 268 for key

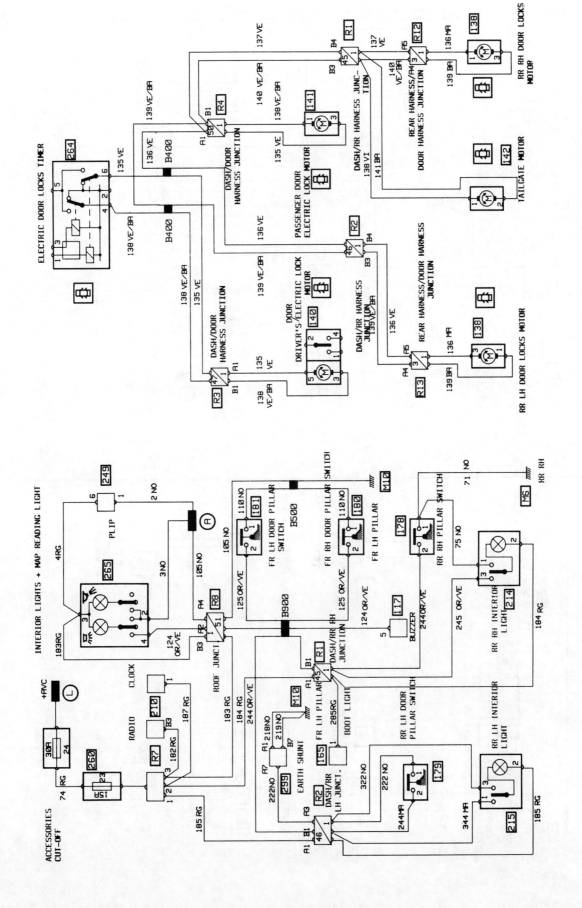

12.29 Central locking wiring diagram
See page 268 for key

12.28 Interior light wiring diagram
See page 268 for key

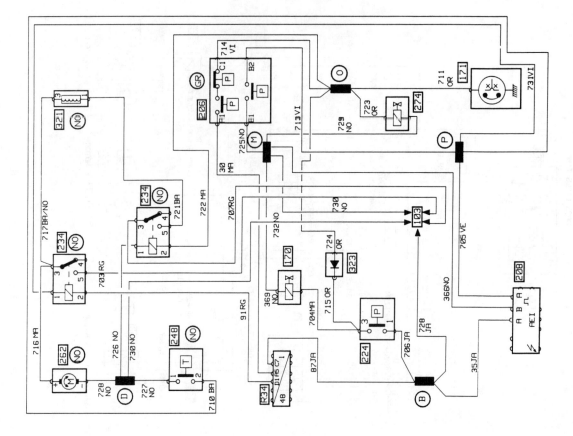

12.31 Air conditioning wiring diagram – engine area
See page 268 for key

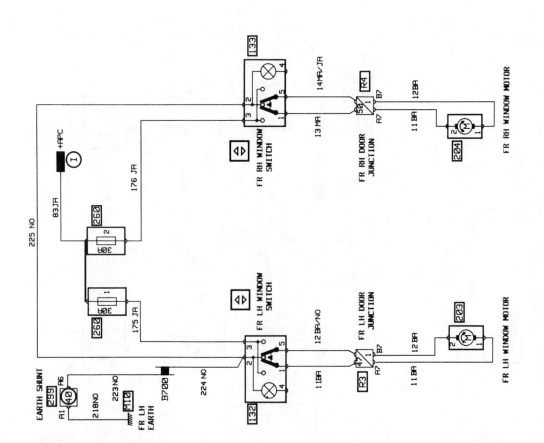

12.30 Electric windows wiring diagram
See page 268 for key

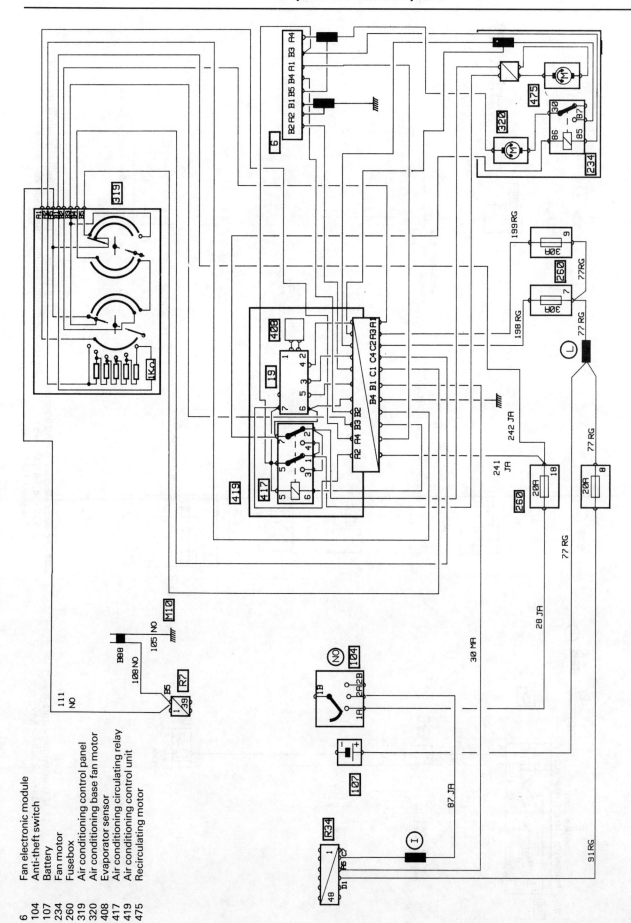

12.32 Air conditioning wiring diagram – in-car area
See page 268 for key

6   Fan electronic module
104 Anti-theft switch
107 Battery
234 Fan motor
260 Fusebox
319 Air conditioning control panel
320 Air conditioning base fan motor
408 Evaporator sensor
417 Air conditioning circulating relay
419 Air conditioning control unit
475 Recirculating motor

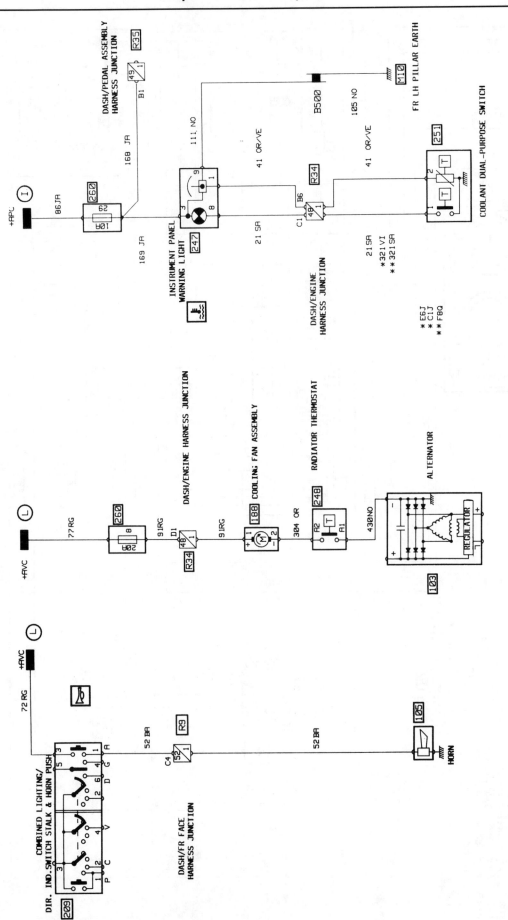

12.35 Coolant temperature gauge wiring diagram
See page 268 for key

12.34 Engine cooling fan wiring diagram –
1390 cc (E6J) shown
See page 268 for key

12.33 Horn wiring diagram
See page 268 for key

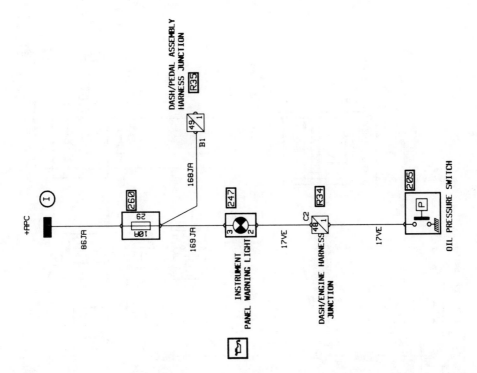

12.37 Oil pressure warning light wiring diagram
See page 268 for key

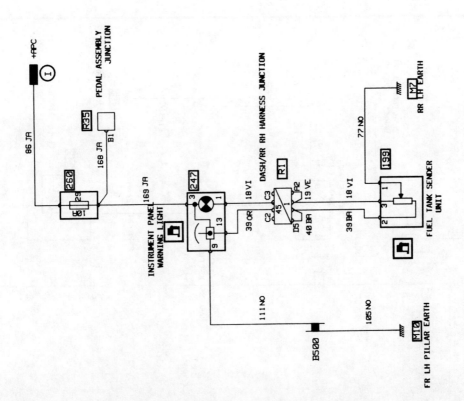

12.36 Fuel tank sender unit
See page 268 for key

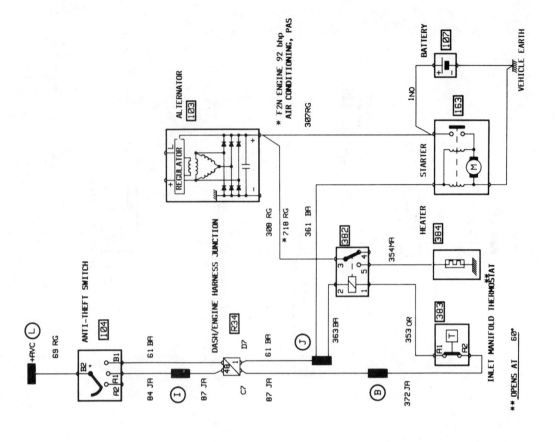

12.39 Inlet manifold pre-heater wiring diagram – 1721 cc (F2N)
See page 268 for key

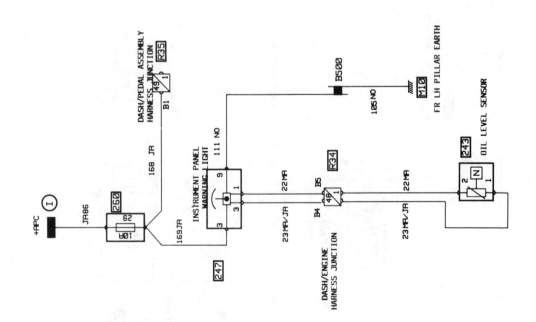

12.38 Oil level sensor wiring diagram
See page 268 for key

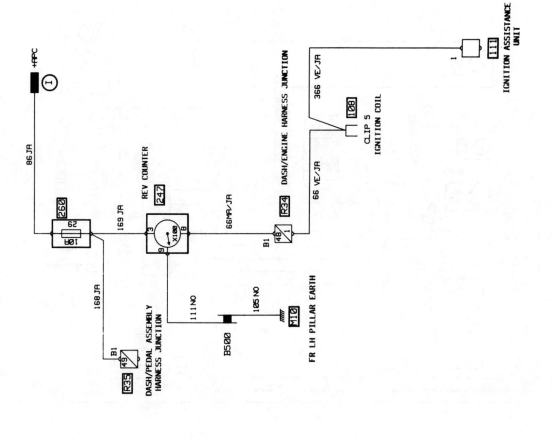

12.41 Tachometer wiring diagram – 1397 cc (C1J)
See page 268 for key

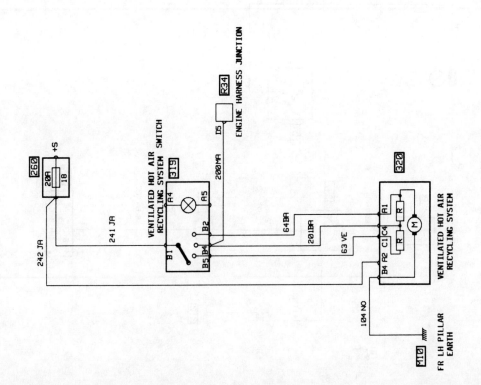

12.40 Heating system wiring diagram
See page 268 for key

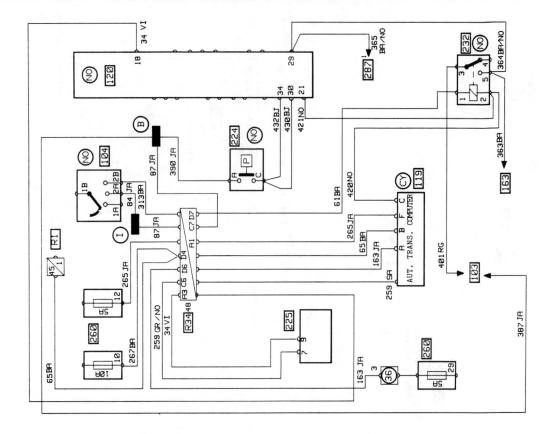

12.43 Automatic transmission wiring diagram
See page 268 for key

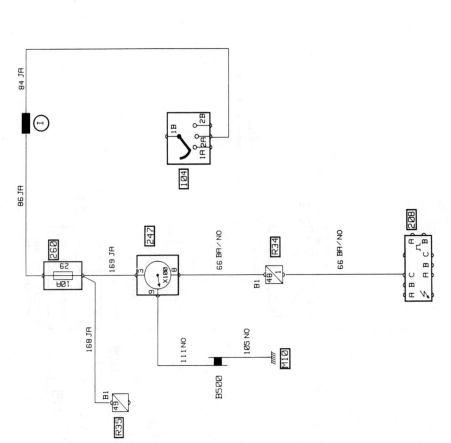

12.42 Tachometer wiring diagram – 1390 cc (E6J) and 1721 cc (F2N)
See page 268 for key

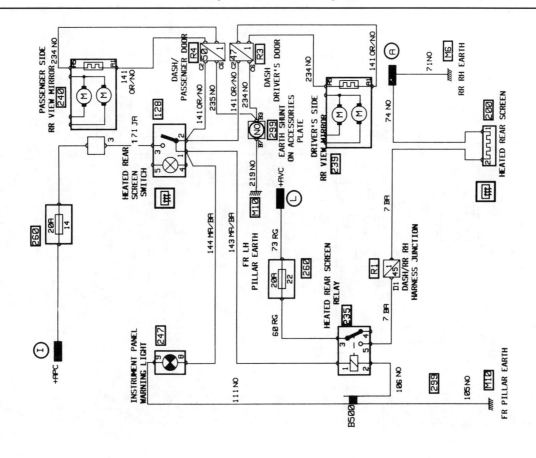

12.45 Heated rear screen and rear view mirrors
See page 268 for key

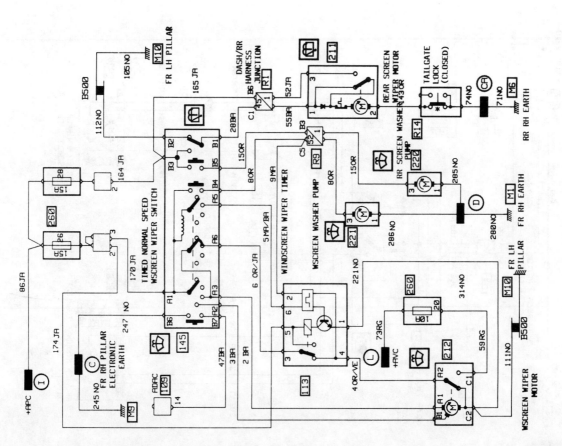

12.44 Windscreen/rear screen wiper wiring diagram
See page 268 for key

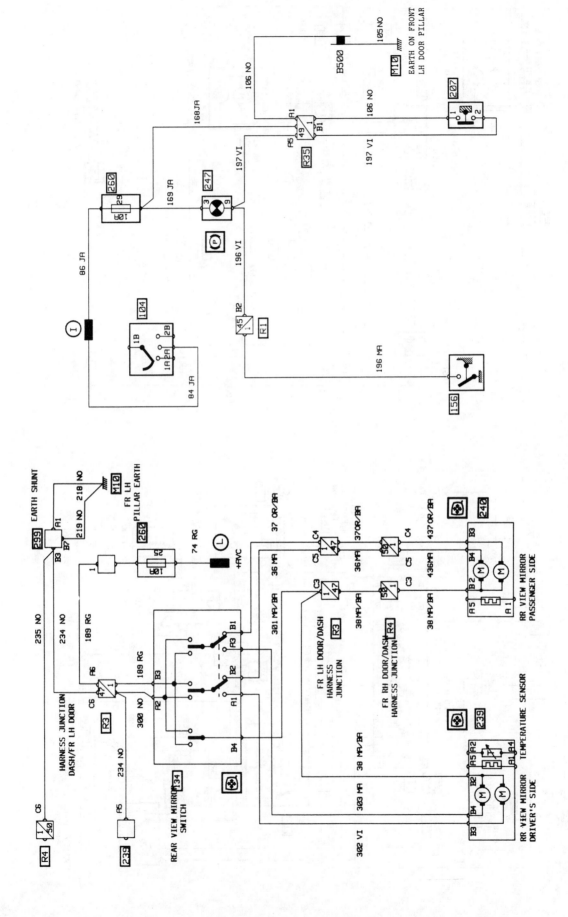

12.47 Handbrake and fluid warning wiring diagram
See page 268 for key

12.46 Electric rear view mirrors wiring diagram
See page 268 for key

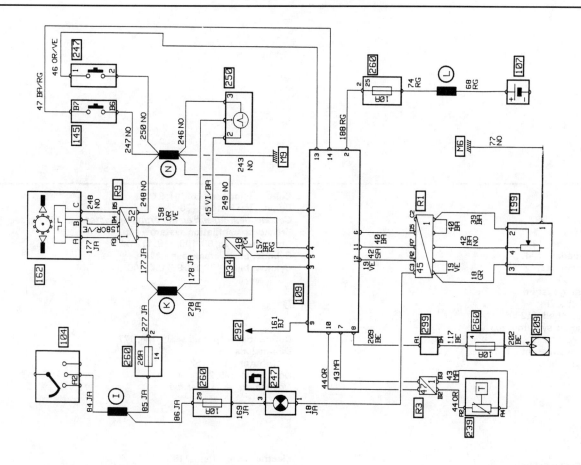

12.49 Trip computer wiring diagram
See page 268 for key

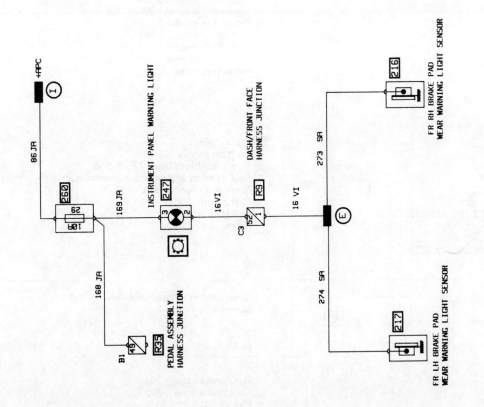

12.48 Brake pad wear warning wiring diagram
See page 268 for key

Index

W